Amitai Etzioni, former Chairman and Professor of Sociology at Columbia University, is the first University Professor of George Washington University. He founded the Center for Policy Research in 1968 and has been its Director since that time. From 1979 to 1980 he served as Senior Advisor in the White House. A 1982 study ranked Dr. Etzioni as the first of a group of thirty who made "major contributions to public policy analysis" in the last decade.

An Immodest Agenda

REBUILDING AMERICA BEFORE THE TWENTY-FIRST CENTURY

Also by Amitai Etzioni:

Social Problems
Genetic Fix: The Next Technological Revolution
The Active Society: A Theory of Societal and Political Processes
Political Unification: A Comparative Study of Leaders and Forces
Modern Organizations
Winning Without War
A Comparative Analysis of Complex Organizations

An Immodest Agenda

REBUILDING AMERICA BEFORE THE TWENTY-FIRST CENTURY

Amitai Etzioni

New Press

McGRAW-HILL BOOK COMPANY

New York   St Louis   San Francisco
Hamburg   Mexico   Toronto

1 2 3 4 5 6 7 8 9 0   D O D O   8 7 6 5 4 3

ISBN 0-07-019723-7

LIBRARY OF CONGRESS CATALOGING IN PUBLICATION DATA

Etzioni, Amitai.
  An immodest agenda.

  1. United States—Economic policy—1981–
I. Title.
HC106.8.E89   338.0973   82-7136
ISBN 0-07-019723-7   AACR2

Book Design: Judy Allan (The Designing Woman)

For Ethan, Oren, Mike, Dari, and Benji,
My sons,
For your future
            Abba

Contents

Acknowledgments

This is the first book I have written at my new home, The George Washington University, after serving for twenty years at Columbia University. I am deeply indebted to George Washington University President Lloyd H. Elliott, Provost and Vice President for Academic Affairs Harold F. Bright, and especially to Dean Henry Solomon, for creating the position of University Professor at George Washington University, and appointing me as the first one. The position allowed me to work in a highly productive, congenial, and stimulating environment. Vice President for Policy Studies and Special Projects Louis H. Mayo provided me with additional facilities for this volume, above and beyond the call of duty. Joe Slater made possible two Augusts of writing at his Aspen Institute, a non-stop intellectual feast.

My first memoranda about reindustrialization were written while I was guest scholar at The Brookings Institution, for which I am indebted to Bruce MacLaury. Joe Pechman's Friday Fellow lunches constituted the finest intellectual football I ever witnessed or participated in. Several memos I composed while serving at the White House in 1979–80 are incorporated into Part II of this volume.

I discussed my ideas on economic policy with a large variety of colleagues and people in the world of business and labor, too numerous to list. I am particularly indebted to Don Patinkin for his introducing me to economics; to Rudy Penner, Herbert Stein, and Michael Boskin—for thoughtful differing views; to George Eads, Fred Kahn, Felix Rohatyn, Van Doorn Ooms, and Al Sommers for equally thoughtful—but somewhat less divergent—perspectives. Barber Conable, Alexander Trowbridge, and George Soros greatly enhanced whatever sense of reality the book reflects.

Dialoguing with Noel Epstein did more than anything else to keep this book going. William H. Becker graciously agreed to review my forays into economic history.

Mary Pockman stayed with the book from its first draft to be the most accomplished editor I have worked with in twenty years. She made numerous suggestions which enhanced the clarity and coherence of the book; whatever uncouth sentences remain are here over her protest. Susan Luipersbeck, Ann MacDonald, and late in the book, Paul Jargowsky, served as indefatigable, diligent, and incisive research assistants. Debi Lapham typed several drafts, and deserves a special recognition for unbounded patience.

Without the support of the Center for Policy Research this book would not have been written.

Introduction

High among the curses that haunt us is the quest for simple, quick cures. "We must get the government off our backs" is a catch phrase that captures the social philosophy currently dominant in the United States. There is less wrong with what this view encompasses—than with what it leaves uncovered. Merely cutting back government will not set America on a course of recovery *unless* these efforts are coupled with a period of reconstruction of community—of family, schools, neighborhoods, and nation—and, above all, individual renewal.

We entered the 1980s in a state of multiple deterioration, evident in the economic, social, political, and ethical spheres. Fortunately, this deterioration has not advanced far; there are still large areas of strength in all these realms. However, all demand our attention and endeavors, as a community and as individuals. As our predicament is many-sided, so must be our response.

The President of the United States, the majority of the public leadership and of the public itself, have embraced a half-truth as the basis of our dominant social philosophy and public policy. The half that is true is that at the root of our deteriorating state lies excessive governmental intervention in private lives. The half that is amiss is the assumption that merely slashing the government will restore America's economic, social, political, and ethical vigor.

Two key considerations are overlooked in our quest for simple solutions. One concerns individuals. They are said to be the sources of private initiative, entrepreneurship, and good common sense. They are to take off, like so many released stallions, once the government shackles are removed.

But what state are they in? Are they really raring to go? Or have years of being hamstrung weakened these sources of a free and energetic America? Have decades of me-ism turned them into cut-off individuals, isolated from others, and even from self? Are the majority of Americans quite unready to fend on their own, and will they be quick to call again for government help? In short, are not weakened individuals the other side of excessive government? Most important, if the answer to all these questions is in the affirmative, *what must be done to rehabilitate America's individuals* as government is cut?

Second, the notion that less-government-and-more-reliance-on-individuals is our salvation overlooks the importance of a third realm, the community. What community encompasses, what is amiss in this realm, and how it may be rebuilt are central concerns of the first part of this volume. Suffice it to say here that individual renewal and community rebuilding sustain each other, and that without both we shall soon turn again to push excessive government and excessive individualism.

To telescope what I am trying to say: The Moral Majority has a point; we must concern ourselves more with the family, school, neighborhood, nation, and character. That they wish to *impose* their cures, and that their cures will do precious little to alleviate our problems, if not exacerbate them, should not lead us to concede these issues to such wrong-headed people. Reconstruction of community is a pressing task for America in the coming years.

If the people I part ways with are new Whigs, this does not make me a new Tory. To argue for community is not necessarily to argue for the status quo, or for authority per se, although both have been frequently linked with the call for community. My concern with community is not with its existing structure, but with the human bonds it nurtures and the civility it requires.

If there is an area in which the half-truth of the slash-the-government blessing is dominant, it is in matters economic. Part II of this volume asks what else must be done if the economy is to be viable again. Special attention is focused on how we restore the foundations—the productive sectors (infrastructure, capital goods) and the motivation to save, invest, and work.

Most books about the future either try to predict what will happen, a tough task at best, or list what the author wishes the future to be like, a noble but often quite an unrealistic undertaking. My endeavor is to understand our present predicament, and to ascertain where we might be headed and what might be done to alter our course. At issue is not what I believe in or find commendable. The list of all the things one values rolls off all too easily. However, we have all discovered over the last years one certainty: We cannot do all that is of merit, serve all that is just, attend to all that is needed. We have rediscovered scarcity. Whether we like it or not, we are forced to decide where to focus our efforts, what to accord first priority, what will have to be deferred.

The title of the book is anything but accidental. Each term in the title is a code word. I called the book an *agenda* because at best I can help outline some of the key issues about which we must reason with each other, in order to agree what is to be done, and push forward. There are deep reasons that I, like many before me, cannot prescribe detailed effective programs. One is that the proper response to many of the problems that plague us is not a wise decision the president can make once we can whisper into his ear, or a "good" set of bills Congress can pass, which we can help draft. At issue is the extent to which we all are willing to tighten our belts for a transition period to provide the resources for reconstruction; the extent to which we are willing to examine whether our retreat from institutions (such as the family and even the nation) has reached a point that we must recommit more of our personal energies to shared concerns and endeavors—in short, the extent to which we are ready to be less preoccupied with self and more with "us."

One can indicate the reasons such a change of perspective is required, the directions such a change of heart might lead, but not the future in detail. The details can be worked out only by renewed Americans working with one another, in their myriad social circles and nationwide.

I called the book *immodest* because merely setting an agenda turned out to entail a rather awesome list of matters that command attention, even as I left out many worthy concerns. At issue is not merely the tax policy, the size of the government deficit, or any other item of economic policy, or even all of them together. Equally at issue is the human factor, the role to be played in the next years by the millions of Americans who make up the American society and who ultimately provide for all the policies and actions to be undertaken, in social, political, ethical, and economic matters. Where the title reads "immodest," "complex" could also have been written.

This book focuses on the next years, the balance of the century, because I believe the longer run is even more difficult to foresee, and because what we do next lays the groundwork—or fails to prepare—for all that is to follow. Predictions about the year 2000 and beyond are easy. It is more useful—and frankly, in my judgment, more responsible—to deal with the 1980s and early '90s.

The agenda under discussion is not mainly one for the government to follow. Indeed, Part I of the book deals largely with matters our families, schools, social circles, and political action groups—and above all, each of us as an individual—must attend to. It concerns our relationship to our fellow persons, our commitments to the community and its institutions, our response to the power wielders, and, more than these, our relations to our selves. Part II deals with economic policies, drawing on my work on reindustrialization, which has already gained some following. In the end these two parts must of course be joined; there is but one America, one future, one we must all fashion together in the next years.

Amitai Etzioni
Washington, DC 1982

PART ONE
REBUILDING OF COMMUNITY

CHAPTER ONE
Excessive Individualism

THE HOLLOWING OF AMERICA

"We must get the government off our backs" quickly captures a social philosophy which has recently become dominant in America. Scores of public opinion polls could be cited, all attesting to the prevalence of this view. Typically, seven out of every ten Americans agree with the statement "the government has become far too involved in areas of people's lives."[1] But what if decades of shouldering the load have weakened our backbone and shortened our ligaments? Then sorry will be the day the nation's recovery agenda is limited to reducing the government; rehabilitation of the private realm is equally necessary.

It is my thesis that millions of individual Americans, the pillars of a free society and a vigorous economy, have been cut off from one another and have lost their effectiveness. Many Americans, at least as the species is currently encountered in the vast lands between Mexico and Canada, are no longer willing or able to take care of themselves, and each other. Indeed, the rise of ego-centered individuals has paralleled the rise of big government. *Both* constitute a retreat from community, from family, schools, and neighborhoods, and from a viable and effective self.

To put it differently, we have experienced a hollowing of America, in which community was whittled down. Greater reliance on government has been accompanied by promotion of a particular brand of individualism best labeled egotism, sometimes referred to as "me-ism"

3

or hedonism, and, we shall see, built into antisocial interpretations of the psychology of self-actualization.[2] Thus, the decline of the family was accompanied both by a growing demand for government to take care of sick older persons (in publicly financed nursing homes) and by a lessened sense of children's duty toward their elders. Similarly, the growing demand for the government to provide daycare centers for children was accompanied by parents' lessened ability, and sometimes lessened willingness, to care for their children. The demand for more police was accompanied by less neighborly vigilance, and the demand for more government imposition of ethical standards, by less ethically committed individuals.

Conservatives will argue that the rise of government has diminished individuals. Liberals may argue that weakened individuals required more reliance on the state. Actually, the two forces feed into each other: More government lessens the individual, and diminished individuals foster more government.

While these forces feed into each other, they are not linked in a simple fashion so that cutting back one automatically secures healthy growth of the other. Reducing the government does not by itself secure reconstruction of individuals. And without such reconstruction a vacuum will be created, leaving a viable community and a strong economy unprovided for. This in turn will soon lead either to a backlash demand for bigger government, or to a further increase in alienation, which ultimately cannot but bring about economic, social, and national catastrophe.

THE REAGANITE AGENDA

The Reagan administration, whose coming to power was widely regarded as launching a new direction for America, made the economy its first, overriding concern upon entering office. Indeed, other issues, from moral/social questions to foreign policy, were deliberately downplayed in 1981, to keep all eyes on the cure to be administered to the economy. Public opinion polls show that most Americans concurred: 66 percent of a national sample of adult Americans cited an economic issue as the most important problem facing the country, while only 18 percent named a foreign policy issue, and the remainder cited energy or other problems.[3]

The 1981 correctives suggested by the administration for our economic ills were first, second, and above all: less government. The theme that underlies and that provides philosophical direction to the Reagan administration and the large conservative groups that support it in Congress and the nation is reducing the role of government in society. Cutting government's expenditures, reducing its income (by tax cuts), reducing its intervention in private decision-making (by hundreds of administrative acts and deregulation), and capping the civil service are the four legs of the Reagan 1981 economic recovery program. In a lighter vein, Murray Weidenbaum, President Reagan's chief economic adviser, gave as the administration's motto, "Don't stand there, *undo* something."[4]

While by the beginning of 1982 much attention was being paid to some possible tax increases, they must be seen in the context of very large tax reductions already introduced. A tax reduction of roughly $750 billion (over five to six years), followed by a tax increase of even $150 billion, still amounts to a very hefty tax cut. Similarly, it is true that individuals may have lost much of what they gained from the 1981 tax cut (25 percent over three years) because inflation moved them into higher tax brackets (Harvard economist Martin Feldstein estimated a net tax cut of only 3 percent.)[5] But this is nevertheless a reduction to be contrasted with years of continued tax increases, and the corporations fared substantially better.

Some say that government has only been transferred from the federal to the state and local level. But by most measures, whatever increases in state and local government have accompanied the post-1980 reductions of the federal government, they have not matched the federal cutbacks.

Most important, these objections do not take into account the considerable change in direction achieved by reversing or cutting back thousands of government regulations and guidelines. From airbags to auto emissions, from drug testing to bone content in ground meat, from requirements that colleges spend equal amounts on male and female athletes to rules concerning approval for building hospitals—just as once all was embraced by regulation, so, since 1980, the less-government cure has been applied across the board.

Equally important has been a change in climate. Business executives and financiers, instead of being concerned and hobbled by fear of actual or potential government intervention or restraint, have come to feel they have much freer rein, if not active allies in Washington, both in the White House and in Congress. Several Reagan acts are significant not only in their economic consequences but also in their message, in the signal they broadcast. In the Reagan economic recovery budget, as food stamps, school lunches, educational and health programs were cut back, the windfall profits tax on "new" oil was reduced from 30 percent to 15 percent over a period of four years, the maximum capital gains tax rate was lowered from 28 percent to 20 percent, and small business was accorded several special breaks. (In all it was estimated that business would benefit from more than $179 billion in reduced corporate taxes over a period of six years.)[6] Only a blind and deaf corporate head, board member, or investor would miss the point.

An obvious question about this approach has been raised, from David Stockman to the liberals. Is it fair? Are the burdens this approach imposes on the truly needy, the cutbacks in social programs, really necessary for economic recovery or are they mainly a "transfer payment" to the corporations and the rich? It is a subject that needs to be explored—as it is daily—elsewhere. I will assume, whatever one's conclusions about the social consequences and merits of this approach, that all agree that government, in general, has grown excessive, needs cutting in one way or another. Even those who wish to draw more on it again in the future agree that government as correctly constituted has grown too bureaucratic, over-regulating, and alienating.

My main thesis is that much more needs to be done. We Americans tend to search for prime causes and simple correctives. Cut government, and the economy will be rejuvenated, and we all will live happily ever after. This is a typical, simplistic perception and prescription. The fact is that major societal building stones other than the economy have deteriorated: the family, the schools, the community, and the members of society themselves, the individuals. Hence, the "recovery" must encompass these institutions and persons.

THE NEW WHIGS

The preoccupation with lessening the government and with the economic realm has deeper roots than public clamor and a clever set of tactics. (Social-ethical issues are said to have been downgraded because the Reagan camp itself has been deeply divided on these matters and what is to be done about them, while there was a much higher level of consensus on economic policy.) At the root lie deep differences between two world-outlooks, social philosophies, systems of beliefs, differences hidden by the label both share—conservatives. One camp stresses individuals as the ultimate source of rights, principles and power, as the effective actors. The other, we shall see, sees more value in community and authority.

While the ideas of the first camp are typically presented in terms of the economic realm, the same notions are applied to the political realm—all rights are rights of individuals, although for some purposes, especially shared safety, they may surrender some of their rights and powers to the state—and the social/moral realm—individuals should not be coerced to go to school with people of another race, to wear seat belts, to refrain from smoking, because each individual is sovereign. Similarly, while the notion of an invisible hand that guides individuals, each pursuing his own good, toward a blessed shared condition is most often presented in matters economic, it is applied by some across the board. For instance, educational vouchers are promoted, to allow parents to send their kids to either private or public schools. This position attracts advocates for a variety of reasons, including those who wish to appeal to Catholic voters or to the more affluent parents who already send their children to private schools. But it also has a philosophical justification: Parents, not the government, know what is best for their children, and thus they should be free to choose the school. The resulting competition between private and public schools will improve education for all.

I need to fix a label to this position before I contrast it with the other branch of conservative thought and social philosophy. *Laissez-faire* conservatism might do, but it is a longish label and we are all tired of "isms." "Libertarian conservatism" might serve, because it reminds us of the link between the conservative position before us and the one recently championed by the libertarians. However, it is a label without evocative power, and without history. I'll use the term "New Whigs." Those familiar with the Whigs of history will find numerous differences between their general position and the specific policies they advocated,[7] and those of the contemporary Whigs. The main theme that ties the two together is the basic principle of their position, the key assumption that the individual has ultimate value, and that all else is derivative. The individual is the center of creation, the sun around which the planets arrange themselves.

How up-to-date this seventeenth-century Whig core theme is today, is quickly captured in a few statements about the early Whigs. They are reported to have subscribed to Locke's notion that all "men were naturally equal, in the sense that none had special rights of jurisdiction [such as government] over others; and all had rights of life, liberty, and property, which the state existed solely to protect. Thus against the positive Tory conception of the state, the Whigs visualized a negative function, to make possible the free play of individual and corporate energies in religion, politics, and trade."[8] Moreover, to the Whigs, society was "mainly an aggregation of individuals."[9] There is very little here that a Friedmanite or Reaganite could not comfortably endorse, indeed champion, in the 1980s.

Milton Friedman is the philosopher-king of the contemporary new Whigs. His collaborators and followers in intellectual and media circles number in the thousands and in the community his legions are countless. Friedman, like other prolific writers, cannot be neatly summarized in a few sentences. But since the essence of his position is familiar, a brief rerun, focusing on what is essential for the point at hand, should do.

Friedman argues that there are two ways people make decisions and relate to one another: through the market and through the government. The first way is based on individual dignity and freedom, the second on coercion. The market, he writes in *Capitalism and Freedom,* "permits unanimity without conformity; . . . it is a system of effectively proportional representation. On the other hand, the characteristic feature of action through explicitly political channels is that it tends to require or to enforce substantial conformity. The typical issue must be decided 'yes' or 'no'; . . . the number of separate groups that can in fact be represented is narrowly limited, enormously so by comparison with the proportional representation of the market."[10] Hence, the coercive nature of the government versus the freedom of the market.

Irving Kristol has already pointed out that to the extent Friedman deals at all with genuine consensus, with the coming together of a community on value-issues, which is essential for action in unison, his treatment is a rather odd one, to wit, "the mere aggregation of selfish aims" in a "blind and accidental arithmetic, [whose] legitimacy is infinitely questionable."[11]

One is tempted to argue with Friedman on *his* ground. Is the market a representative system? Of what? Does it not act in response to the number of dollars one has, a far cry from one person, one vote? And is the number of dollars a person commands, dollars that drive the system, truly a reflection of that person's virtue, industriousness, and entrepreneurship? Or does it not also reflect that person's social privileges, parental connections, ability to corner the market? Do we not need to rely on the government at least to correct those great injustices the market wreaks? And did Friedman never hear that a central function of government is making budgets, in which numerous groups are accommodated on a proportional—not "yes" or "no"—basis? Friedman's answers vary from a limited recognition of the need for such correctives (which hence requires no modification in his basic position) to a suggestion that the cure by government intervention is worse than the market imperfections it tries to compensate for.

Whatever counter-arguments one might bring to bear in favor of a role for government, the main point I need to make lies elsewhere, in the realm lost in the simple opposition of the goversment to the market: the community. People do not relate to one another only as participants in economic transactions or as subjects of a government. They relate as parents and children, as brothers and sisters, as neighbors and friends, as co-workers and members of the same ethnic groups and national community. The nature of these relationships is captured by such terms as affection and mutual respect, sense of duty and concern, involvement in the community. These relationships point to the existence and significance of a third realm between government and market, the realm of community.

Not all the old Whigs emulated by the new ones lived in long-past centuries. Friedrich von Hayek (author of *The Road to Serfdom* and *The Constitution of Liberty*) has written widely and cast his influence deeply over the last two generations. He introduces himself as "simply an unrepentant old Whig."[12] His main point relevant to the issue at hand is his strong defense of political freedom *cum* individualism versus notions of social and economic bases of freedom.

Hayek is of course a *laissez-faire* conservative and a champion of the free market in all matters concerning economic policy. But he reaches beyond that. He sees any government action that reduces the differences among people—in the name of equality, or equity, or as a way to secure the socio-economic prerequisite of freedom—as diabolical. The individual as-he-or-she-is is sacred. Adamant opposition to any government intervention to reduce these differences is the essence of his position. A progressive income tax, for instance, is thus a hideous thing precisely because it puts a supra-individual notion above the sanctity of individuality.

Harvard philosopher Robert Nozick elaborates this point. In a recent statement in the press he summarized his own position:

> Society isn't a race organized to give prizes. It's not that there's one contest we're all engaged in, so it's unfair if some people have a better start than others. What we have are a lot of disparate relationships of friendships, marriages— and people in all of these relationships are choosing whom to interact with and on what basis.[13]

He hence is basically opposed to government action to equalize people.

Nozick's opposition to government acts, his belief in individual choice, and his opposition to the imposition of public shared goods carry him to encompass national security.

> I would say that those members of the American Communist Party who do not think that the United States is facing any external threat, and don't want there to be that sort of national defense, and don't view themselves as getting anything good by it, should not be forced to contribute to national defense.[14]

A more individualistic position is difficult to imagine. In a private communication, Nozick clarifies this statement:

> I *do* accept taxation for the "public good" (in the economists' sense) of national security. But that justifies taxing only those for whom national defense *is* a good. So, in principle, we wouldn't tax members of the Communist Party for it, but we would tax me and you!

In his major book *Anarchy, State, and Utopia*, he puts it in more technical terms:

> Individuals have rights, and there are things no person
> or group may do to them (without violating their rights).
> . . . The fundamental question of political philosophy . . .
> is whether there should be any state at all.[15]

The Libertarian Party captured only about 1 percent of the 1980
vote, but libertarian philosophy has a wider following. Its tenets further illustrate the point. Libertarians are so preoccupied with fending
off the government dragons—and celebrating the individual—that
nothing in between meets their eyes. Thus, the 1980 platform of
the Libertarian Party opens with the statement that the members of
the party "challenge the cult of the omnipotent state and defend
the rights of the individual" and "hold that all individuals have the
right to exercise sole dominion over their own lives."[16] The platform
then discusses a variety of subjects, from crime to mental health,
from education to pollution, without ever recognizing any way of
existence but the duality of the state versus the individual. Typically,
it urges that the Social Security system be repealed without even a
passing suggestion that voluntary associations, charities, and members
of the community may in the process consider taking on some of
the burdens—not as a matter of coercive requirement but as an appeal
to individual conscience.

A good part of the recent public dialogue in the wide area of risk-
taking further illustrates the New Whig position. Aside from bemoan-
ing the costs, inefficiencies, and inequities that government protection
of consumers, workers, and the environment imposes, critics make
a philosophical case for individuals' right to make these decisions
on their own. The familiar position is well represented by Herbert
E. Markley, Chairman of the Board of the National Association of
Manufacturers, under the banner "It's Your Freedom They're After!
The Power-mad Bureaucrats":

> We've got good sense. We know a good cereal from a
> bad cereal. We don't need always more bureaus and commis-
> sions to protect us from ourselves.[17]

Time pundit Hugh Sidey takes the next step by reminding us,
approvingly, of John Stuart Mill's position that every person should
be given "all possible liberty . . . even if some people insist on using

that liberty to hurt or diminish themselves."[18] The effects on others (from loved ones to innocent bystanders) and the desire of people to rely on institutions they created in stronger moments to help them in weaker moments are not acknowledged.

This libertarian notion is further applied to a very wide range of human behavior, from the right to smoke to the right to commit suicide, to the use of seatbelts and motorcycle helmets. James J. Kilpatrick is distressed that the state regulates drugs—prohibits, for instance, the use of Laetrile despite the fact that it has not been proven a poison, merely ineffectual in fighting cancer.[19] He does not dismiss the problems raised by the "freedom" of hucksters to manipulate dying, emotionally distraught cancer victims, nor the consequences for them and their children and spouses of deferring proper treatment—he simply does not deal with them. Fully competent individuals and a threatening state are the only actors in his scene.

The same notion is applied even to the draft, or conscription, as libertarians prefer to call it. Thus, for instance, Reagan's Secretary of Defense, Casper Weinberger, prefers voluntary service to the draft on "philosophical" grounds. This position disregards the fact that under economic pressures in, say, a government-engineered recession "to wring out inflation," many of the poor, especially the black poor—particularly under reductions in unemployment benefits and other social programs—must enlist or starve. Freedom to choose here is clearly a right reserved for the privileged members of society. A conservative may argue that "successful" members of society deserve this "extra" benefit; but they should not hide the desire to add to their privileges under a Whig equality-of-freedom-to-all argument.

In health care the libertarian position appears in blaming the victim for accidents and ill health, rather than blaming the manufacturers of dangerously designed autos, appliances, and toys, and hazardous chemical pollutants; or blaming nature, or the limitations of medical and other health services. If *you* just live right, eat right, drink right, you'll be healthy. Thus Aaron Wildavsky, a leading conservative political scientist, simply pronounces that "most accidents occur at home and most industrial accidents are traceable to individual negligence," without reference to data or sources of evidence, although he writes in the *American Scientist.*[20] He then takes off in the familiar damn-government-regulation direction. There is evidence that our lifestyles do affect our health, but not as strongly as the ideological position implies. Moreover, one's lifestyle is not freely shaped by oneself; it is affected by the community one lives in. I may drive as carefully as the ideal graduate of a driver education class, but my life may be shortened by a community that tolerates drunken driving and refuses to pay for highway dividers. And I may do five "relaxation response" exercises a day and think only positively, and still be stressed sick by a harsh work environment.

It would be unfair to say that New Whigs always ignore the realm of community and the social bonds among individuals. However, when they do treat community ties, the New Whigs tend to depict them as market-like relations. One may refer to the New Whigs' perspective as "economic imperialism," because it portrays the whole social world as dominated by the market, or the society itself as a market of sorts. A key book presenting this approach, within the academic context rather than the more extensive intellectual and related media world, is that of Gary S. Becker, a University of Chicago economist, appropriately titled *The Economic Approach to Human Behavior.*[21] One reviewer has already preceded me in calling Becker's position a "brand of economic imperialism."[22] The usual connotation of imperialism is that one country extends its domain to include the territory of others. For Becker, the discipline of economics extends its domain over all human behavior.

Others have viewed the Adam Smith mentality, in both its economic and societal applications, as the domination of the rationality or utilitarian principle. It amounts to the same thing. In one case, a slice of the world in which rational-utilitarian principles are relatively applicable is viewed as the model for the whole array of human relations to follow; in the other, the same limited and limiting principles are applied to the whole human spectrum. In either case the resulting picture is highly misleading and the implied prescription is deeply dehumanizing.

In academic works that feed into this world-view, marriage, crime, and even altruism are studied and explained as "utility maximization" behaviors, and the only utility served is ego's. Thus, marriage is said to be transacted (my word) if the expected benefits exceed the costs (in the sense of opportunities forgone). Divorce is nothing more than a change in the balance sheet. And "love and other emotional attachments, such as sexual activity or frequent close contact with a particular person, can be considered particular nonmarketable household commodities."[23] Law is not viewed as worthy of adherence for its own sake, but as a set of costs (probability of detection times size of punishment) and benefits (size of the loot).

In sociology a school of thought called "exchange theory" has gained vogue in recent years.[24] Markets are, of course, places of exchange, but in this approach people are assumed to be preoccupied, in general, with their self-interest, to be cool and calculating, not emotionally tied to each other or committed to shared values and bonds. Since altruistic acts embarrass the theory, long essays are written and theorems advanced to show why these acts, in one way or another, "ultimately," are self-serving.

How does an "exchange" sociologist see courtship, involvement, and, ultimately, love? No tender feelings, pangs of the heart, loss of some of self into a new "we" here, but a two-legged prestige calculator. That is, people are said to date and even hitch up for life because they use their mates to raise their status. People are said to pick and drop potential partners until they find those most likely to jack up their social ranking.[25] Similarly, acts of kindness, gifts, and solicitude are depicted as calculated to elicit the desired countergifts and support.

There is surely an element of truth in all that; even a loving person may think about the effect a mate's beauty, ancestry, wealth (or whatever sells in the prestige market) will have on his "standing." However, anyone who believes this to be the essence of love lives in a much depleted world, quite like one who thinks that a botanical classification captures the essence of a flower. And while the giver of gifts may well think about a return, there is enough more to gift giving, from the joy of giving to the strengthening of affective bonds with the receiver, to make a market-like analysis of these relationships a poor caricature of the interpersonal realm. Worst, these notions feed into a culture that leans in this ego-centered way to begin with.

THE NEW TORIES

Within the position so often referred to these days simply as conservative there is a second, quite different, camp, which stresses the importance of community and, within it, authority. Family, schools, local community, and nationhood have the centrality the market has in the eyes of the New Whigs. The key concern of this position is the decline of the prerogatives of the body-community. The community and its authorities are seen as standing above the individual and are assumed to take priority over him. The community is not like a government, ultimately created by individuals and elected to represent individuals. Instead, it is perceived as the body into which individual cells are incorporated. It is not possible, within this context, to think of free-standing and self-guided individuals, any more than a human body can be seen as a bunch of molecules that have decided that it is to their advantage to work together in a given pattern. The term "organic" is often employed to emphasize the unavoidable and natural link of the parts to the whole—and the unquestioned moral status and prerogatives of the whole.

The deeper reason community and authority are accorded top billing is that individuals are assumed to be born with an unsavory moral nature. Without norms imposed by authority they would savage each other. Hence, while the New Whigs wish individuals to heed their own choices, the New Tories do not particularly welcome free choice. "Everyone is free to do what they want—as long as they do what they are told," a wit put it. Seriously, freedom is accepted, but only within set values and norms determined by authorities.

While New Whigs contend that the least government is the best government, New Tories are willing to use the government to impose what they consider morally right, although they would prefer that some other community authority, say a church, be able to do so. They are not troubled by the undemocratic nature of their position, because they firmly believe in the absolute values the authority imposes. The Moral Majority's strenuous efforts to outlaw abortion are a case in point. Laws requiring the teaching of creationism are another. No free individual choice here.

Historically, Tories, like Whigs, have taken many different positions, and there have been quite different Tories over the centuries. However, the essence of their position and the point most relevant to the contemporary New Tories is the emphasis on community and authority. Thus, whatever else they said, "in any event, the Tory would find reason to justify unity and authority."[26] The Tories saw in community what medieval theorists saw in the unity of Christendom: "The whole was greater than its parts . . . and each individual had an appointed place" and responsibility.[27]

The New Tories we hear about most are the Moral Majority. They are primarily concerned with social-ethical matters; there is not an economist-leader among them. Their specific agenda runs to prayer in schools, fighting crime in the streets, prohibiting abortion, securing women's nonrights, and a revival of patriotism. True to Tory tradition, they wish to impose minority normative positions on these issues on the total community.

Less frequently noted is that aside from being authoritarian, they are so blinded by their intolerant beliefs that they are socially incompetent. What they seek, if some tyrant granted it all, would do very little good, and possibly considerable harm, on the matters *they* are after. Thus, even if all the school children of America recited a prayer twice each morning, right before they pledged allegiance to the flag, this would not add to their moral fiber any more than swearing by the flag makes them true patriots. Even if the last abortion were outlawed, this would do nothing to preserve family, and might well contribute to its demise. And the imposition of the death penalty would at best have a very small marginal effect on criminality. Moral authoritarianism is not only undemocratic and intolerant, but also quite unproductive.

Within the group often called neoconservatives there is an important element of New Tories, albeit significantly more sophisticated and moderate in their position than the Moral Majority. It includes such key academic figures as Samuel P. Huntington, Edward C. Banfield, and Ernest Van den Haag. And, in his recent work, Robert Nisbet shows a touch of the new blue. (Other, more popular neoconservatives, such as Irving Kristol, Daniel Bell, James Q. Wilson, and Nathan Glazer, do not qualify.) A visit with a few of these New Tories will do.

Harvard political scientist Samuel P. Huntington burst upon the academic scene in 1957 with his book *The Soldier and the State.*[28] In it he portrayed a military academy, West Point, as the epitome or model of an orderly community:

> There is ordered serenity. The parts do not exist on their own, but accept their subordination to the whole. Beauty and utility are merged in gray stone. Neat lawns surround compact, trim homes, each identified by the name and rank of its occupant. The buildings stand in fixed relation to each other, part of an over-all plan, their character and station symbolizing their contributions, stone and brick for

the senior officers, wood for the lower ranks. The post is suffused with the rhythm and harmony which comes when collective will supplants individual whim. West Point is a community of structured purpose, one in which the behavior of men is governed by a code, the product of generations. There is little room for presumption and individualism. The unity of the community incites no man to be more than he is. In order is found peace; in discipline, fulfillment; in community, security.[29]

His final stanzas counsel not only admiration but emulation:

West Point is a gray island in a many colored sea, a bit of Sparta in the midst of Babylon. Yet is it possible to deny that the military values—loyalty, duty, restraint, dedication—are the ones America most needs today? That the disciplined order of West Point has more to offer than the garish individualism of Main Street?[30]

In his bicentennial contribution to *The Public Interest*, entitled "The Democratic Distemper," Huntington diagnosed America's sociopolitical ailments as stemming from "an excess of democracy," adding, "Al Smith once remarked, 'The only cure for the evils of democracy is more democracy.' Our analysis suggests that applying that cure at the present time could well be adding fuel to the fire."[31]

By 1981 Huntington's position had moderated, but in his newest book his concern with authority still dominates.[32] He sees the sixties and seventies ("the S&S Years") as years of explosive passion and ideology, years in which protest, moralism, and democratic ill-temper had the upper hand. They left in their wake washed-out authority structures up and down the American society, which we need to restore.

Vigorous and responsible national leadership requires a network of petty tyrants. The protests, exposure, reforms and realignment of the S&S Years substantially shredded that network.[33]

More deeply, in Huntington's view, America suffers from a deficient state. The American political culture favors adversary relations among groups, pluralism in contrast to well-ordered states such as Japan and the nations of Europe. American statehood, such as it is, suffers from anemic authority, and hence the absence of means to pull all together into a coherent whole.

New Whigs, liberals, and people dedicated to democracy share one notion New Tories most deeply challenge: that as all individuals are created equal, no one has the right to impose his or her values on all the others. To the New Whigs *et al.* the polity is procedural—a way to sort out the will of the majority. New Tories who believe in absolute values see little merit in such an open procedural approach.

Political philosopher Leo Strauss of the University of Chicago argued for the place of absolute values in several books: *Natural Right and History* (1953), *What Is Political Philosophy* (1959), and *Liberalism Ancient and Modern* (1968), the last being his most important book. In it he traces the development of liberal political philosophy and argues that it has lost touch with its classical foundations. By teaching "the equality of literally all desires," liberalism has lost the basis for directing society in positive directions. Liberal tolerance thus leads to a spurious freedom in a decaying society. He calls this "the crisis of liberal democracy," which leads inexorably to a "victory of the gutter." By refusing to make moral judgments, liberalism is "fiddling while Rome burns." *True* liberalism must assert that some values are intrinsically better than others and must be recognized.[34]

This tendency toward tolerance, Strauss believes, "is pushed to the extreme where tolerance becomes perverted into the abandonment of all standards and hence of all discipline." Standards are both right and just, and are rooted in the nature of man. Political philosophy can discern these standards, and can evaluate them. Thus,

> true liberals today have no more pressing duty than to counteract the perverted liberalism which contends "that just to live, securely and happily, and protected but otherwise unregulated, is man's simple but supreme goal," and which forgets quality, excellence or virtue.[35]

Strauss illustrates that the route from subscribing to absolute values to a "regulated" life is an extremely short one.

Sociologist Robert Nisbet's earlier and widely studied book *The Quest for Community*,[36] published in 1953, would not qualify him as a New Tory. Its main concern is with community per se. Nisbet was and continues to be more concerned with binding individuals into informal structures, groups, and associations than with joining them in a single community. He agrees with John Dewey that "individuals who are not bound together in associations . . . are monstrosities."[37] Nor is his well-placed concern about excessive individualism Tory in itself. In his view, both Protestantism and modern capitalism emphasize the individual, rather than the group, as the central social unit: "In both spheres there is a manifest decline of custom and tradition and a general disengagement of purpose from the contexts of community."[38] Both, Nisbet writes critically, draw on "the supposition that society's well-being is best served by allowing the individual the largest possible area of moral and social autonomy."[39]

In his later years, though, responding with growing emotion to the disruptions of the sixties, Nisbet rose for authority in terms that, while they do not come close to those of Huntington, indicate a moderate New Tory element. In *Twilight of Authority,* published in 1975, he argues with great power for the social bond and authority, against excessive government and individualism, and observes,

> Despite the American creed of individualism, which locates motivation and achievement in the recesses of the individual mind and character, human accomplishment in almost any form is the product of association, usually in small and informal structures whose essence is a high degree of autonomy.[40]

While he strictly opposes investment of more power in the state, Nisbet sees the social foundation in multiple powerful local communities, voluntary associations, and other such social bodies. However, when he turns to the internal structure of these social bodies, his fear of excessive preoccupation with egalitarian values drives him to favor strongly constituted authorities within each. "Our gravest problem at the present time, in many respects, is the disrepute into which this word, this unavoidable necessity, has fallen as the consequence of the generalized philosophy of equalitarianism."[41] What word? *Hierarchy.* He agrees with an earlier conservative, Edmund Burke, on the virtues of elites ("Woe to the country which would madly and impiously reject the service of the talents and virtues, civil, military, or religious, that are given to grace and to serve it") and on the merit of "title to command."[42] "Hierarchy in some degree," Nisbet says, is

> an ineradicable element of the social bond, and, with all respect for equality before the law—which is, of course, utterly vital to free society—it is important that rank, class, and estate in all spheres become once again honored rather than, as is now the case, despised or feared by intellectuals.[43]

In short, the New Tories are as aware of community as the New Whigs are neglectful of it. And the New Tories are as willing to incorporate the individual into a community, fashioned by its authorities, as the New Whigs are willing to build on free-standing individuals, aggregated somehow.

THE OPEN COMMUNITY

I find it essential to recognize a realm of community between that of the state and that of the individual, for both heuristic and normative purposes. Many have preceded me in drawing the lines in this particular way.[44] While the three realms tend to penetrate one another, each has its own dominant logic of relations. Thus, although one can find representative touches in the market, it is basically not a representative system, but an allocative one. And people in love may calculate a bit, especially before they get involved in a relationship and as it recedes. Most people who care for each other, though, are not primarily calculating, but involved with each other emotionally, and committed to each other morally.

Moreover, as I see it, a wholesome relationship between community and member-individuals is based on a creative tension and a continuous search for balance, not domination of one by the other. If we view the community as merely an aggregation of individuals temporarily joined for their convenience, we leave out the need for commitment to serve shared needs and for involvement in the community that attends to these needs. If we see the community as *the* source of authority and legitimacy, and seek, in the name of duty to it, to impose behavioral standards on individuals, this leaves insufficient basis for individual rights. It also prevents the community from being creative and responsive to a changing world, by removing the opportunity for the evolution of differing positions, which could in time replace the community's dominant norms.

There are two main schools of interpretation of Jean Jacques Rousseau. One makes him the ideologue of collectivism, the "total surrender" of individual rights to society, and thus an extreme Tory, if not a father of totalitarianism.[45] However, according to the "best interpretations" of Rousseau, as philosopher Robert Derathé put it, Rousseau saw in liberty the most precious of possessions; individuals "can no more be deprived of it rightfully than they can be deprived of life itself."[46]

Rousseau was drawn to various modes of intellectual mischief, because he sought to obliterate the duality and tension between individual rights and shared needs, on which community rights are based. They become quite superfluous once one embraces the tension, which maintains a balance between individual and societal rights, rather than fights it. My Rousseau is certainly the one who balances reason with sentiment, individual liberty with societal survival, and the will-of-all with the general will.

I use the term "open community" to try to capture the need to provide full moral status both for individuals and for their shared union. An open community is much more integrated than an aggregate of self-maximizing individuals; however, it is much less hierarchical and domineering than an authoritarian community.

To put it differently, I suggest that we need to transcend both the Hobbesian and the Lockeian ideas of our civics textbooks and common cultural heritage: We need to reject the Hobbesian notion that we must subordinate our individual rights as a prerequisite of security. The challenge to the union is not so great that we all have to yield for the Leviathan to shield us. Nor can we do with the Lockeian notion that all rights are invested in individuals, who may or may not wish to delegate some of these rights, on the basis of their deliberations, to a community. *Both individuals and community are completely essential, and hence have the same basic status.*[47]

There results an unavoidable, even useful tension between the two human elements. Individuals may pull to diminish community; the community may pull excessively to incorporate individuals. But if neither element gains ascendancy, and if the excesses of one are corrected by protecting the other, a balanced, open community may be sustained.[48]

IN HISTORICAL PERSPECTIVE

In order to formulate a responsible position on which to base an agenda for the future, one must add to the preceding analysis of the essential elements the additional insights historical perspective provides. Irving Kristol effectively reminds us how swiftly this perspective turns about:

> Back in the 1950s, everyone was worried about the tyranny of "Mom" and its supposedly deleterious psychological consequences. Well, "Mom" is gone, replaced by "Mrs. Robinson," flailing away on the tennis court at the frustration of all her impossible dreams.[49]

The historical perspective deeply affects not only our view as to the relative status of the twin essential elements at any given point in history, but also in what direction a society has been tilting and hence in what *opposite* direction it must be coaxed if the open community balance is to be sustained. This is the deeper reason intellectuals, not beholden to any one regime, tend to be critical: They argue for the side other than the one that dominates. There is no shortage of defenders of the element that has gained the upper hand. But these are to true intellectuals what the court prophets were to the true ones in the Old Testament. True prophets are not out to win the king's pleasure; they seek to countervail his authority and thus balance the scales of legitimation.

To put it differently, if one lived in a highly authoritarian environment—as the early Whigs did in seventeenth-century Britain, before its monarchy became quite constitutional, and when one church dominated and fought dissenters—one might well emphasize individual rights against excessive community. But it would not be because one did not recognize the essentiality of both elements, but because one element was all too well attended to, while the other languished. For the same reason, in the contemporary U.S.S.R. the intellectuals' responsibility and ethical position is clearly to promote individual rights. On the other hand, at the core of one of our metropolitan centers, where a mass society unloads its cut-off individuals in high-rise buildings, with few social ties in the neighborhood or at work, where prople are not involved with one another or their shared existence—here the cause of community must be explained again no matter how often it has been done before.

The founding fathers of the American polity had good reason to enshrine the individual. Their America was created by individuals escaping excessive community and authoritarian powers that spoke for a deity or political entity. The very process of emigration required taking leave of community bonds. Once the immigrants arrived on these shores, the sparsely settled land, the open frontier, the lack of an established civil order all favored the individual as the center of the polity, economy, and social philosophy.

But obviously the America of the 1980s is light years away from the very small, farming, horse-and-buggy society of the founding fathers, or even that of the early entrepreneurs who launched the industrial age in the 1820s. The American condition has become *less* appropriate for a high degree of individualism.

Changes in objective conditions have increased the need to curb individual excesses in order to protect each individual's rights. The facts in support of this thesis are, in themselves, well known. They are briefly recited here because their ramifications are too often ignored in contemporary discussions about the proper place of individualism in late-twentieth-century America. The elementary facts are these: a sparsely settled land has become a crowded territory. The obsolescent image of individuals in America is sustained by a television series such as *The Waltons,* which depicts in romantic glow a self-supporting farmer, his farm surrounded by vast unsettled land, remote from any and all other settlers. The urban and suburban centers in which most Americans now live prescribe much closer quarters. A fire started in the Waltons' house could rarely touch another, but in the places most of us now live fires can jump quickly from one individual house to another. Sewage dumped from one house in a vast territory may foul that family's land; the individual is free to choose whether or not to build a septic tank. Sewage dumped in a city street will plague thousands. A stranger wandering onto the Waltons' turf will stand out. Anonymity in a city crowd is a major opportunity for crime and requires a shared approach to curbing violence.

The same holds for economic interdependence. In farming America, a community was fairly self-sufficient; even if the roads washed out, if no new supplies arrived for months and the markets were inaccessible, the family and the local community could make do. In contemporary America, a prolonged rail or truck strike will severely disrupt the whole economy. And as everybody knows, but few champions of individualism note, a bunch of Arab sheiks in the Middle East can hold up all Americans for ransom by stopping oil supplies, as they did in 1973. And there is precious little individual Americans can do, acting *individually*, to stop interruption of vital supplies to a modern, complex economy.

The international security of the United States affords a similar lesson. For centuries America was protected by the oceans and by a weapons technology that respected distances. But as long-range missiles shrank distances and expansionist super-powers rose, individuals' ability to defend themselves with muskets—still a favorite patriotic theme—all but vanished. Our security now rests on *shared* defense. It in turn defines the extent to which the country needs to tax and draft individuals.

Do all these changes in the historical circumstances Americans now face spell a need for more government, for fewer individual rights and freedom? Not at all. They indicate the need for more shared concerns and greater commitment to the community. Government is neither the sole nor the best custodian of these concerns. Thus if urban neighborhoods can reduce anonymity (through block associations) and activate their own councils and anticrime patrols, there is less need for police (and for the taxes to pay for them). If the citizens of a town will drive their garbage to the dump, rather than dump it in the street or put it out for collection, there is less need for government to provide garbage collection and exact the taxes to pay for it. Even the draft can be avoided if enough people volunteer to serve their country.

Where do the New Whigs, the New Tories, and those concerned about an open community fit into this historical perspective? The New Whigs correctly sense the excesses of government, but to overcome them they have celebrated individuals as if they were self-sufficient units, able, while seeking to serve self, to provide not only for economic well-being but also for well-being in the social and moral realms. The New Whigs share the "credit" for excessive celebration of the individual through their espousal of highly popular psychological theories that are either outright hedonism or the antisocial strands of self-actualization. There is a strong affinity between the pleasure-maximization of ego and the notion that each individual knows what is best for him or her and need not be concerned with shared or transcending matters.

Here lies the critical error of the age: Maximization of individualism will serve neither the economy nor the community. Nor will it serve individual well-being. The New Tories have seen the need to restore community. But in their zeal, in their inability to adapt their concern for community to an open relationship, they promote a community that seeks to impose its moral tenets on individuals, even if this violates their basic rights.

The quest for an open community requires a more balanced approach than that of either Whigs or Tories. However, when this is put in historical context, it becomes evident that the immediate concern is to protect the community from excesses of individualism, rather than vice versa.

WHAT KIND OF INDIVIDUAL?

As a first approximation, we have stuck to the traditional reference to individuals and to the community as two clearly distinct entities. In this terminology it makes sense to talk about assemblages of individuals deciding to form a polity, and to speak of aggregates of individuals without community—as in the notion of "the greatest happiness of the greatest number." However, a basic conclusion of social science, spelled out in the next chapter, is that this concept of an individual is an optical illusion. The individual and the community make each other and require each other.

It is possible to think abstractly about individuals apart from a community, but, we shall see, if individuals are actually without community, they have very few of the attributes we commonly associate with the notion of an individual person. Certainly such cut-off, isolated individuals have little in common with those integrated into a well-balanced open community, sustaining it and being nourished by it. The irony of the political, social, and psychological philosophies that celebrate the individual to the neglect of the community is that the individual they promote, and in a deep sense assume, is not to be found without a viable community.

CHAPTER TWO

Renewed Americans: The Need for Mutuality

MUTUALITY INTRODUCED

For everything there is a season. Let this be the season for renewal—renewal of persons as whole selves and as members of a community. The term "renewal" carries both religious and secular meanings, all appropriate. In the Judaeo-Christian tradition it may refer, at the extreme, to a single conversion from being self-centered to becoming God-centered. Most of the time, though, both the Old and New Testaments recognize that there is a continuous tug of war between forces that debase, pull us down to our selfish animal origins, and forces that propel us to nobler, higher reaches. After periods in which we retreat toward the elementary self, it's time to renew the whole self and the self-involvement in the commonweal.

In the secular vein no one has flagged the need better than John Gardner. Particularly in *Self-Renewal,* he identifies the need for revitalizing the person within the community. Individuals need to be free of both complete self-preoccupation and complete dependence on others, Gardner says; we need mutually fruitful relationships with others. To achieve this renewal, "we need not surrender our individuality. But we must place it in the voluntary service of larger objectives. If something prevents this outcome, individual autonomy will sour into alienation or egocentrism."[1]

The attribute we Americans need most for the next generation is an enhanced commitment to others and to shared concerns. I say "enhanced" because the commitment has not vanished but waned, and because a larger measure is required if Americans are to do with less government and yet sustain themselves as a community. The commitment required is not for ego to sacrifice itself to other, or to a higher cause, but for both ego and other to attend to each other and to their shared world. I hence refer to it as "mutuality."

The question may well be raised, do not all people at all times require mutuality? They undoubtedly do. The special historical situation of Americans is that we have neglected this universal requirement in recent decades; indeed, millions have embraced social philosophies that challenge this need.

A dominant American theme, strongly advanced in the 1970s, has been hot pursuit of a status that exists nowhere and is not attainable, a life of individuals dedicated to their own needs, to their self-fulfillment, free from duties to others and the commonweal. This is a mentality quite compatible with the age of abundance, of unprecedented and encompassing affluence. However, by the time "letting go" and each doing his or her own thing had been established, the economic, international, and societal underpinning of such a self- and world-view had already been substantially eroded. The need to rebuild the economy, national security, and the community calls for a social philosophy and an individual orientation that are much less ego-centered.

We thus enter a period in which we require more mutuality than before—while we command less.

The changed conditions do *not* require that we reinstate worn-out authoritarian father-figures, yesterday's dictates and structures— learning by rote, women subject to men, unquestioning submission to authority ("because I say so")—or a renewed quest for an American century, *i.e*, a U.S.-dominated world. What is called for is the next step of a dialectic progression that started with traditionalism, moved through a period of retreat from society, and now is ripe for a third stage, that of reconstruction of individuals and community. Indeed, much of this chapter is a dialogue (argument, if you insist) with the "second stage," retreatist social philosophies. As I see it, just as traditionalism subjugated the individual, so the retreatist orientation pushed individuals toward excessive focus on ego. The next stage calls for what initially cannot be depicted more clearly than as a "better" ego-other balance. This chapter seeks to spell out this balance and justify the need to seek it.

HUMAN NATURE: THE NEED FOR MUTUALITY

For many reasons contemporary Americans tend to disregard the importance of the bonds that tie individuals. To begin with, individuals are the visible units. Individuals are invested in bodies and associated with them, which makes them three-dimensional figures, easy to delineate and recognize. As sociologist Robert N. Bellah has observed, radical secular individualism builds on the assumption that "the biological individual is the only human truth."[2] Mutual bonds, commonweal needs, and duty to others are abstractions, ethical or social science characterizations, invisible states of mind and feelings—not two-legged living beings.

Second, the social philosophy of the founding fathers, as influenced by John Locke and Adam Smith, among others, and passed on from generation to generation of Americans, perpetuates the notion that individuals "preceded" society and polity, which they then contracted to be. That this popular story was made up for heuristic purposes—to make it easier to explain social bonds and our shared existence to the less educated—is commonly ignored.

The fact is that individuals are born into an existing community, which historically precedes them. Never mind who started the human race "first," Adam and Eve, or God. This was, after all, a very long time ago. Certainly ever since that original day, individuals have been born into the human race. Moreover, they are born without any of the individual attributes we associate with the term. As anyone knows who has raised children, or is familiar with the accounts of infants left to grow up on their own in attics or adopted by animals, they are born unable to walk erect or communicate by the use of symbols, an essential basis of language and culture. More important, they will not learn to do either on their own. To put it more succinctly but not at all too sharply, newborns are animals and will remain so, will crawl on all fours and bark, unless and until the community and its agents laboriously teach them to walk erect and talk, and introduce to them a set of values. Ergo, whatever happened when civilization first dawned, all the individuals we ever encounter are created by their community. Individuals may all have been made in God's image, but God delegated creation to the community of parents, educators, and neighbors.

The Effects of Isolation

Empirical studies and psychological analysis strongly suggest that individuals are not able to function effectively without deep links to others. Without deep, continuous, and meaningful bonds, individuals risk losing their humanity.

An examination of what scientists call a "limit" situation, an extreme one, is often used to highlight the effects of a factor. By studying the effect of, say, extremely cold temperatures on a metal, we learn about what more moderate degrees of cold will do, although these effects will only become visible after prolonged exposure. Following this tradition, let us examine the effect of extreme isolation to highlight the effect of being cut off in general.

As Bernard Berelson and Gary Steiner note in their overview of more than one thousand social science studies, *Human Behavior,*

> Total isolation is virtually always an intolerable situation for the human adult—even when physical needs are provided for.[3]

Informal accounts of people placed in isolated situations support this conclusion.

> In 1821, in Auburn Prison, eighty men were sentenced to solitary confinement; a year later five were dead, one had thrown himself from the gallery, another was mad, and the rest were melancholy.[4]

Sometimes prisoners befriend rats, showing, "with their tragi-comical devotion, the intensity of this social hunger."[5]

The experience of American POWs during the Korean War is often cited in reports on the effects of isolation. Thirty-eight out of fifty-nine Air Force men in the POW camps "confessed" to nonexistent U.S. bacteriological attacks on Korea,[6] and many of the Army men collaborated with their communist captors. To extract confessions from the Air Force prisoners, "isolation and extreme psychological pressures were the techniques used. A prisoner was kept by himself, often in the most confined and uncomfortable surroundings."[7]

Not all the men complied with their captors; one notable exception was a captain who refused to cooperate even after fourteen months in solitary confinement.[8] On the whole, though, the American prisoners were more susceptible to communist techniques than were prisoners from some other countries. The Turkish prisoners, for instance, withstood the pressure of isolation almost 100 percent.[9] According to military investigators, the Turks "stuck together as a group and resisted as a group."

> When a Turk got sick, the rest nursed him back to health. If a sick Turk was ordered to the hospital, two well Turks went along. They ministered to him hand and foot while he was there, and when he was discharged, brought him back to the compound in their arms. They shared their clothing and their food equally.[10]

By contrast, many Americans thought of themselves "not as a group bound by common ties and loyalties, but as isolated individuals."[11]

In a study of widows and widowers, the researchers expected to find high death rates following loss of a spouse, as earlier studies had recorded. They found instead that in the first months after bereavement, the loss of a spouse had no significant effect on mortality rates for either sex. In the longer run, however, the mortality rate was 26 percent higher for widowers than for a matched group of married men. Among women there continued to be no significant difference between the widowed and the married.

The investigators suggest that the higher mortality among widowers than among married men is due not to the stress of the loss itself, but to the stressful life situation, including separation from close social support, that follows. This interpretation receives additional support from their findings that widowers who did not remarry had significantly higher death rates than those who did, and that for both widows and widowers, living alone was associated with significantly higher mortality than living with someone. Why loss of a spouse had so much less effect on death rates among women is unknown, but the investigators hypothesize that women have greater adaptability, including a higher capacity to deal with the isolation of widowhood.[12]

The preceding accounts concern involuntary solitude. Voluntary isolation may not have the same devastating effects, but it too is often reported to produce harsh consequences. Accounts of arctic explorers and solitary voyagers tend to support the notion that prolonged isolation is psychologically harmful.[13]

In laboratory experiments, even those of short duration, isolation produces psychological stress. For instance, in one experiment:

> Each volunteer was confined to his seat, got no word from the outside, heard only the steady hum of machinery and had to pay constant attention to a TV screen. Every person in the . . . experiments saw hallucinations. Their idea of time and space and even their own bodies became distorted.[14]

In short, as one review work summarizes:

> Reports from both [experimental and real-life] settings contained descriptions of illusions and hallucinations, disorganization of goal-directed thinking, impaired time perception, distortion of body image, increased preoccupation with body sensations and inner thought processes.[15]

Humans, at least most of us, cannot remain psychologically "sound" without some solid contacts with others.

The underlying reason for our need for bonds with others is that human attributes grafted upon our biological base are difficult to sustain. Even without full isolation, they require continuous reinforcement or they will erode. Mothers and fathers attend to their kids not because of some biological instinct, but because that is what is expected of them, what they are appreciated for. If nobody cares whether they do or not, parenting will slacken. What holds for parenting holds with more force for less sacred, socially sanctioned relations, such as friendships and neighborly sensitivity. In short, we *are* all each other's keepers. Children "validate" their parents; workers, each other and their supervisors; and so it goes.

For the same basic reason, mutuality is not an altruistic affair. There is an expected reciprocity of affection and respect. Individuals are so composed that they need to receive affection and respect regularly, just as batteries need recharging. True, some people have larger psychic batteries, and hence can go longer without being recharged. This makes them somewhat less dependent on others than those who need more frequent recharging. However, in the long run (defined in weeks, not months or years) all people require some recharging. Similarly, some people are more energized by affection, some are fueled better by respect, but none can do without either, and both are granted by meaningful others. In short, individuals need others for their continued existence as persons.

These two bases of individual existence, the way people are created and the way they are maintained, are closely linked. The deepest reason individuals depend on continuous support from others is that others made them. Dependence here is not that of the welfare literature, where the term refers to *over*dependence, inability or reluctance to function autonomously, but dependence as in an arch of bricks, in which each brick supports all the others, and together they make the arch.

The Need for Affection and Respect

Support by others works most effectively when it is mutual: Ego provides for another person's need for affection and that person provides for ego's. When ego gives and the other does not reciprocate—the widow and her rebelling teenager—ego will find affection elsewhere (*e.g.* from friends) or will tend to show psychological damage (depression, psychosomatic illnesses).

Which others? First and foremost, *close* others—one's spouse, children, friends, neighbors—with whom intimate, secure, continuous bonds can be forged, the source of deep affection.

Affection can be generated in a large variety of social relationships, from fraternities to bowling teams, but it is typically in small, intimate groups. Hence, the yearning for small-town America and the neighbor's fence in mass-society America, and the quintessential quest for closeness in the communes of hippies and other cultists.

Respect can be more readily commanded in larger social circles; it is less intimate. Priests and doctors used to command respect throughout the community and to some extent still do. This respect is extended to them by most people they encounter, even those who do not know them well.

Respect is intimately tied to shared concerns and to community values. The respect an army officer commands has been quite different in peacetime, during World War II, and in the Vietnam era. And, studies show, people who engage in activities of which the community disapproves—prostitutes, for instance—are not respected and are hurting as a result.

In short, individuals require both affection, generated in small groups, and respect, gained by activities that are consonant with community values and that respond to shared concerns.

Social scientists might point to additional complexities resulting from the fact that an individual is often looped into more than one circle of intimacy or respect; for example, a man's affection for his mother and for his wife are not always easy to reconcile, and his son and his country club may not respect the same activities. We need not follow this course here except to note that the more complex the society, the more difficult it is to work out a well-entrenched pattern of affection and respect. But however simple or complex the society, the main point stands: Individuals are not viable unless integrated into a web of mutual affection and respect. They must maintain human bonds—or be deformed.

The emphasis here is on the *individual's* needs. That society will self-destruct if each individual is indifferent or hostile or exploitive to all others, that it will falter if shared concerns and future are ignored, is self-evident.

To refer to this basic need for interpersonal bonds, and to the conduct and disposition that reinforce rather than erode them (and in the process sustain the social world), I use the term *mutuality*. It is not a need usually found on the map of ego psychology. Indeed the conventions of the language are helpful here: They resist reference to *one* person's mutuality, or description of someone as "very mutual." This resistance serves to remind us that individuals' mutuality is created among them. It is not something each person creates on his or her own, which each brings to a relationship; it is constructed by individuals working with one another, mutually.

THE DECLINE OF MUTUALITY

Mutuality was never as high in American society as it was in what sociologists like to call "traditional societies," long-established, rural societies. A high degree of mobility and urbanization account for America's lower level of mutuality. In recent decades, two other factors, a rise in the proportion of people who live alone and a change of mentality, further cut into mutuality, just as we need it more than before. This deserves some elaboration.

Mobility and Shallow Relations

Americans move around more than most people, and hence find it more difficult to sustain intensive friendships and bonds among neighbors, even kinship. In an average year, some 40 million Americans move. Put another way, every ten years, between 40 and 60 percent of an average American town's population leaves.[16]

To some extent such data overstate the case. For instance, one study found that 85 percent of recent moves were within the same metropolitan area, 60 percent were within five miles, and 25 percent were within the same neighborhood.[17] And there are some indications that the U.S. mobility rate may be decreasing somewhat; a Census Bureau study measuring mobility revealed that 17.7 percent of the population moved between March 1975 and March 1976, a drop from the levels of the previous twenty years, when each year about 20 percent of the population moved.[18] On the other hand, the average worker kept his job for shorter periods: 3.6 years in 1978 as compared to 4.6 in 1963.[19] This shortens the life of job-connected social relations.

Still, Americans have been and are moving more frequently than people in most other industrialized countries. One analysis, based on data for the 1960s, found that while the average American moves about fourteen times in his lifetime, the average Briton moves about eight times, and the average Japanese only about five times.[20] A population expert in France estimates that addresses change in his country at about half the U.S. rate.[21] Other countries founded by immigrants, notably Canada and Australia, have mobility rates similar to that of the United States.[22]

Since the United States has long been a highly mobile society, a national character has emerged that provides compensatory adaptations for the relative dearth of stable, lasting relationships. It fosters the quick formation of new relationships. At its extreme, this character shows up in services such as Care-Ring, which for a dollar a day brings people cut off from close ties regular calls from a "telephone companion."[23] Quickly formed relationships, however, are seldom as secure and deep as relationships that have been reinforced over years. And while the mails and phone can connect friends, notes one observer,

> technology . . . is unable to completely vanquish distance. And distance undoes the ties formed by frequent contact— the thing that makes friends friends. People do indeed lose each other, and the pain of that loss, renewed every two or three years, makes people withdraw from further contact.[24]

Urbanism Revisited

While the American rate of mobility seems not to have changed much over the years, mobility may have become more isolating because of the way we move. Vance Packard suggests that in frontier times,

> people typically traveled in wagon trains where they developed a deep sense of shared experience and companionship. At the end of their journey they usually located in villages small enough in scale so that they soon knew everyone. And they depended on one another for protection from Indians, outlaws, and marauding wolves or mountain lions. Today's mobility is likely to be a more solitary act that ends by putting the mover among a mass of disoriented neighbors.[25]

Therefore, Packard believes, in present-day American society,

> rootlessness seems clearly to be associated with a decline in companionship, a decline in satisfying group activities, a decline in mutual trust, and a decline in psychological security. It encourages a shallowness in personal relationships and a relative indifference to community problems.[26]

The sociological literature about the isolation associated with the rise of urbanism will easily fill a library shelf. That city life is isolating—"People do not know their next-door neighbor, after they have lived in the same building for years"—has become a widely known truism. Indeed it has already generated its own revisionism, to wit, to show that there are some village-like pockets in cities. This is true enough, but all it does is modify and moderate the generalization about the effect of urbanism, not change the basic finding. Urbanism, which by now encompasses most Americans—even many farmers commute from a nearby city or lead a city-like life—diminishes mutuality.

Isolated Living and Orientation

On top of these longstanding factors, there has been a rise in the number of single persons (due to divorce and deferral of marriage), and of old people living on their own (due to the unequal life expectancies of men and women). During the 1970s, the number of males living alone nearly doubled; that of females increased by almost 50 percent.[27] In 1980, 23 percent of all households—nearly one out of every four—consisted of one person living alone.

Also, single people who have had a series of scarring experiences often develop a fear of being involved in close, meaningful relations. Various mechanisms to avoid involvement have been long known, but seem to be more widely adopted today. This is reflected in the rise of ersatz relations and situations that provide quick substitutes for the genuine items—from singles bars to one-night stands. The great interest in various therapeutic groups, cults, and communes also reflects the yearning for mutuality that often is not available in "normal" urban existence.

Stanford psychologist Philip G. Zimbardo writes of "a mysterious kind of 'legionnaire's disease' of which the chief symptoms are isolation and a loss of naturalness in our relations with other people." Among people whose separateness from others is marked, he distinguishes two main groups—the shy, who want contact with others but avoid affective relations, and those who are indifferent to others. He likens the indifferent to Mr. Spock in *Star Trek*, a person whose "executive-command programming" lacks feeling or affection.[28]

The popular press is never far behind the social scientist these days.[29] Thus, the *Washingtonian*, after telling its readers that about one third of us are chronically lonely, and that studies show that loneliness is bad for your body and soul, counsels the use of TV sets, cats, even fish, and dressing up for dinner—with self—as ways to cope.[30] Somehow these prescriptions simply reflect the problem more than they offer a cure.

Even technological developments seem to be isolating. Television has for decades reduced opportunities for interaction, dialogue, and plain talk. In recent years millions of youngsters have turned to play with computerized games, both in arcades and at home, instead of with each other (although some of the games—actually surprisingly few—involve more than one player). The symbol of the age may become a teenager with his ears plugged with earphones, eyes riveted to a Pac-Man, fingers manipulating a joy-stick.

The Role of Mentality

Particular attention should be paid to a change in mentality that promotes excessive individualism, both because this factor has been accentuated relatively recently, and because it is more readily reversible than most. I use the term *mentality* to refer to the psychic, cultural, and social beliefs, sentiments, and opinions that together define the way people think about themselves, others, and the world they live in, as well as their orientation in time. The term suggests that the way people view these matters is organized in patterns rather than accidentally or *ad hoc.* The term *mind-set* is sometimes used for the same basic notion.

Most people, most times, are not aware that they have a mentality. They tend to believe that they, others, and the world "are" the way they see them. In turn, they base their conduct and aspirations in part on what their mentality tells them about human nature. One acts quite differently if one believes man is wolf to man, everyone is out for himself, clawing his way in a jungle, than if one believes people are beholden to each other and are one another's keepers.

The term "secular religion" was introduced by sociologist Robert Bellah to refer to contemporary mentality. Once God played the key role; the Lord's teaching explained the world and one's place and course within it. As the American society started to congeal, especially after the Civil War, and secularization gradually set in, various humanist "secular religions" spread, until they became for most Americans the prevalent source of explanations of what makes people what they are, how they relate to each other and behave. Since then, only for a minority do notions of temptation by the devil, God's will, and sins-committed-by-fathers-visited-upon-their-sons still explain why Joe is poor, Jane a juvenile delinquent, or John an alcoholic.

The American secular religions often draw on a potpourri of individual-based psychological explanations that have been widely accepted as accounting for individual conduct, social circumstance, and life patterns. Other cultures are more concerned with concepts such as "class," which most Americans reject as irrelevant to democratic America, because they associate the term with either the rigid class structure of traditional Europe or with the Marxist critique of the West. Similarly, most Americans see power theories as more applicable to elite-dominated societies of the right or left, and view America as democratic in government and society. In line with their highly individualistic tradition and view of society, Americans find psychological explanations more compatible.

Some social scientists argue that what people believe, whether it is religious or secular, psychological or political, is not all that consequential. Indeed, they say, beliefs often reflect other conditions, especially economic and technological factors. Thus, they would argue, as millions of women joined the labor force, they became economically independent of their husbands, and hence more able to initiate or accept divorce. This in turn spurred a more tolerant view of divorce. Similarly, the child development theories of Piaget, widely understood to call for letting children develop on their own rather than guiding them closely, gained popularity when parents spent more time at work and less at home.

The majority of social scientists (including this one) respond that there is a large grain of truth in the notion that factors other than mentality also guide how people behave, and, as well, affect the content of the dominant religions and mentalities. But this does not mean that the latter do not play a significant role. Indeed, people in the same economic circumstances behave differently according to what they believe in, and how they see themselves, others, the world around them and their relations to it.

The Role of Pop Psychology

At the core of the mentality that prevailed in the sixties and much of the seventies are highly popularized versions of several brands of psychology, especially one referred to as "humanistic." Before I outline the relevant concepts and their mutuality-diminishing effect, I must stress that humanistic psychology is not one integrated body of scientific knowledge; it encompasses a large variety of ideas, concepts, insights, not all of them compatible. And other psychological "schools" and other sources of humanistic concepts, from educators to followers of Zen Buddhism, also fed into the new mentality. The net result is a vague, far from consistent, but, we shall see, highly popular new view of self, others, and the world.

At issue is not what various psychologists have written as scholars, but those of their ideas that have found their way into the mentality of millions, including many who never heard the term humanistic psychology. Within the intellectual realm, what Abraham Maslow, Carl Rogers, or Erik Erikson has actually written is all-important; from the viewpoint of American society, what popular psychology holds is much more consequential.

The effect of such popular psychological notions is illustrated in the behavior of parents. They used to feed their infants on a precise four-hour schedule even if the babies cried themselves blue in between (or at least made the transgressing mother, who fed her child off-schedule, feel quite guilty). In more recent years, pop psychology has told parents to let an infant dictate the schedule, commanding nourishment, change of diapers, or cuddling whenever the child so much as whimpers (at least until the parents are blue with exhaustion and feel guilty when they skip a response). Let no one say pop psychology's effects are trivial.

The Promotion of Ego

It is not my purpose to study the many aspects of the prevalent pop psychology; some I find quite enriching, others highly questionable. Here my concern is only with their effect on mutuality. The net effect of pop psychology in recent decades has been to undermine mutuality and promote an ego-centered mentality. I use the term *ego-centered* advisedly. The term more often used is *self-centered.* However, as I maintain that self thrives best when deeply related to others and community, at the same time maintaining its autonomy, I need a different term to refer to a mentality that overlooks the vital bonds between ego and others, or tries to promote ego at the cost of others or without regard to others. "Ego-centered" brings to mind not concern with self, but consuming preoccupation with self. What concerns me here is not that being ego-centered is unethical by some set of values I adhere to, which it is, but that it violates what is known about human and social nature and that hence it is ultimately self-defeating and socially destructive. (Humanistic psychologists will properly cry out here in anger, if not horror: "We—promote egotism?" Most don't, most of the time. But the popular understanding of some of their ideas, we shall see, does.)

How widespread is adherence to the ego-centered mentality? Daniel Yankelovich's studies lead him to estimate that 17 percent of Americans are deeply committed to a philosophy of self-fulfillment, and another 63 percent embrace it in varying degrees. (Twenty percent are traditionalists.) [31] Yankelovich describes this philosophy as one of *duty* to self, a preoccupation with ego, and a sense that ego-*needs* both are pivotal and take priority over others' needs, especially over work and commitment to spouse, and, at the extreme, even over one's children.[32] Duty to self is expressed in insensitivity and disregard for others and community. Among the indications Yankelovich used were that these people said they "spend a great deal of time thinking about myself"; that "satisfactions come from shaping oneself rather than from home and family life"; that they express a strong need for "new experiences" and for more excitement and sensation. They also tend to feel free to look, live, and act however they want, even if this violates others' concepts of what is proper.[33]

Some critics have questioned Yankelovich's assessment, either by raising general questions about the reliability of public opinion poll data or by pointing to the fact that 63 percent of Americans subscribe both to the new and the old mentalities, in rank confusion. I have followed Yankelovich's work closely and I have found him to be one of the most reliable and thoughtful students of American public opinion. True, such data have inherent problems, but this does not invalidate a particular finding a critic does not care for. As to the ambivalent majority, the 63 percent, they do embrace—in varying degrees—a new mentality. That they also hold on to old beliefs is important but does not belie the fact that a total of 80 percent of Americans have been affected by the new mentality. As far as my thesis is concerned, even if Yankelovich's estimates are off by 20 to 30 percent, which is hard to believe, it would still follow that millions of Americans embrace, to some extent, the new view of their world, others, and themselves.

A major study conducted by the Institute for Social Research at the University of Michigan comes to a similar conclusion. The study is based on two national surveys, one carried out in 1957, the second in 1976. A major finding is that people have shifted "inside," from preoccupation with the outer world (the world of both material goods and social relations) to preoccupation with inner psychological and relational problems.[34] The authors report the same phenomenon as Yankelovich, a refocusing on the self. They also report a rise in ego-segregation, with 76 percent of the 1976 respondents reporting they feel at least in one way "different from most other people," compared to 69 percent in 1957 (already within the era of declining mutuality).[35] Asked to describe their good side, in 1957 people stressed social virtues, being good parents or spouses, while in 1976 greater stress was put on "inner," personal qualities.[36]

A 1981 survey, conducted by Doyle Dane Bernbach, Inc., adds a bit more evidence. The survey focuses on the effects of recent dire economic conditions. It found a small drop (4 percent) in those who "agree strongly" that "happy family life is more important than anything else"—within one year. The proportion who feel they may have to provide less for their families so they can obtain important things for themselves rose from 20 percent to 26 percent, within the same period of a growing sense of economic squeeze. There was a parallel drop in those willing to make a personal sacrifice for their country (from 73 percent to 68 percent). All in all, the report concluded, "there's been a rise in the desire for individualism and activities that contribute to physical and emotional well-being. It's as if someone proclaimed, 'You really can't help the country, you might as well help yourself.' "[37] Even the people the Peace Corps draws are now reported not to be out to serve but out for personal satisfaction or adventure.[38]

Yankelovich points out that a concern with self-fulfillment is not necessarily destructive to self or community. For instance, it leaves room for the quest for work that is socially approved and useful, and self-actualizing to boot.[39] However, when self-fulfillment is pushed to the point that a narrow view of self disrupts ego's organic ties to others, destructiveness does set in. Thus, if a frantic quest for ever more self-fulfilling relationships makes one continually question and frequently drop existing ones, then the pursuit of an idealized relationship, which may exist nowhere, leaves one with insufficient, anemic, or troubled relationships—a diminished mutuality, if not isolation.

Similarly, if one quits job after job in the quest for one that has no routine, drudgery, or submission to authority, one may end up having to do work that is particularly unfilfilling, as one's record agitates against choice employment. And those who seek more sexual partners, and more variety of sexual "experience," "excitement," and "sensations," often find that whatever short-lived pleasures they gain are more than outweighed by losses in affection-providing, relatively anxiety-free, mutual relationships. These rest on at least a measure of continuity and stability and are more encompassing than multiple sexual contacts.

To put it more generally: The question is not whether one seeks self-fulfillment, but whether one seeks it in avenues that are constructive for self, mutuality, and community—or in ways that disregard or undermine all these.

Abraham Maslow is probably mentioned most often in the pop psychology of self-actualization. Maslow is remembered as having posited a hierarchy of human needs "that has become part of the conventional wisdom of our time." [40] A person's lower needs include the need for food and shelter, "creature comforts"; once these are satisfied, it's time to lift one's preoccupation with them and move on to higher needs, those for affection and self-esteem, and the pinnacle, self-actualization.

Maslow, however, has said little on the rather vital question, at what level are lower needs satisfied so that it is time to move up in the hierarchy of needs? Does one first attend to minimum comfort—a starving person does not worry much about other matters—or does one *sate* these base needs before other concerns are activated? And what is the relationship between affection and self-esteem—and self-actualization?

The full recognition of these two needs makes a crucial difference for the issue at hand. The need for affection is a vital element of our concept of human bonds; it is a major source of the need for mutuality. The need for affection refers to the need to have a deep, positive, emotional involvement with another person, usually on a reciprocal and basically egalitarian basis. Love and friendship are the prime examples, but "caring and being cared for" [41] and "belonging" also express this need. Unrequited love, without mutuality, does not meet a person's need for affection. And while there is affection up and down the status structure (as in a relationship between father and son), even in these hierarchical relationships, the affection *element* is relatively egalitarian. *To assume people have a basic need for affection is to assume that they require a strong, reciprocal— i.e., mutual—interpersonal bond.*

The need for self-respect is less obviously tied to a positive involvement of ego in interpersonal relationships or a group. If self-generation and self-validation were possible, they would provide a sustainable psychic foundation for an egotist orientation. But nothing is further from the social reality. Self-respect rests on validation by others, others who matter, often close others—that is, on respect. As the terms suggest, self-respect is ego's appreciation of ego; respect is the standing ego is accorded by others. While the two never correlate perfectly, in "normal" people they are closely associated on most fronts, most of the time. Ego can tell himself that he is an outstanding runner, provider, or parent; but if the referee declares him last to cross the finish line, the court declares him bankrupt, and his kids run away from home, he will adjust his self-respect downward—or he is at least partially psychologically maladjusted.

Nor can self-respect usually be anchored in pursuits in conflict with the values of the community. (Revolutionaries are an exception.) Studies show that while thieves and prostitutes may find some respect in their subcultures, they are aware that their activities are not validated by the prevailing value systems.[42] (Of course, when there are no such value systems, people have varying degrees of difficulty in anchoring their self-respect, but this is not an indication that self-respect can be dissociated from the community and the respect of others when these systems are intact.)

In contrast to this emphasis on affection and self-respect, as vital and society-building steps preceding and mitigating self-actualization, pop psychology plays up self-actualization per se. As a result it tends to encourage ego-separation and egotist orientations because (a) it focuses on individual needs; (b) it makes self-actualization the *pinnacle* of these needs; that is, it sees affection and self-respect as "lower" needs than self-actualization; (c) it does not *explicitly* call for duly attending to affection and self-respect before and as the highest need is sought; (d) it does not face the needed balance between self-actualization on the one hand, and affection and self-respect, the personal bases of mutuality, on the other.

The guidance offered by an author, a conception, or a therapist may encourage followers to seek self-actualization that is compatible with attending to these "lower" needs, or to attempt a balance of efforts to sate both "lower" and "higher" needs. On the other hand, it may foster a quest for self-actualization that ignores or even denies the need for affection and self-respect. Which way such guidance leads is the test of its effects on the issues that concern us here.

Often the tipoff as to where a writer, intellectual, or acquaintance stands is found in terms such as "individual needs," which of course exist and should not be neglected. They become injurious to ego-other balance, to mutuality, though, when they are elevated to be the pivotal bases of one's view of self, others, and the world. Another term is "human nature," which implies, if it does not say so explicitly, that because x, y, or z is in my nature, I cannot and should not resist it, but on the contrary, should act on it.

Pushed to an extreme and popularized, such notions result, for example, in *How to Be Your Own Best Friend,* a book that became popular in the early 1970s. Psychologists Mildred Newman and Bernard Berkowitz assert: "We are accountable only to ourselves for what happens to us in our lives." [43] They advise people how to change the way they relate to their parents:

> In a very ruthless, primitive way, you have to choose yourself over them. If you go on subordinating your needs and impulses and wishes to theirs, you will never come into your own.[44]

A much-postered quote of Frederick Perls, father of Gestalt therapy, promotes ego-segregation if not isolation:

> I do my thing and you do your thing. . . . I am not in this world to live up to your expectations, and you are not in this world to live up to mine. You are you and I am I; if by chance we find each other, it's beautiful. If not, it can't be helped.[45]

Many critics have questioned this focus on the self. Peter Marin, for example, asks,

> If we are each totally responsible for our fate, then all the others in the world are responsible for *their* fate, and, if that is so, why should we worry about them? [46]

Yankelovich sees the "self" psychologies as self-defeating:

> You do not get in touch with the essence of self solely
> by looking inward. There is no "real" me—a tiny homuncu-
> lus hidden beneath layers of frozen feelings. You are not
> the sum of your desires. You do not consist of an aggregate
> of needs, and your inner growth is not a matter of fulfilling
> all your potentials. By concentrating day and night on your
> feelings, potentials, needs, wants and desires, and by learn-
> ing to assert them more freely, you do not become a freer,
> more spontaneous, more creative self; you become a nar-
> rower, more self-centered, more isolated one. You do not
> grow, you shrink.[47]

Robert Bellah writes that the contemporary American mentality
urges upon us the vision "that we are alone, that we are here to
pursue our own interests, that neither anyone nor anything can save
us except ourselves. It tells us that we must mistrust every noble
impulse we feel because it must be only a form of our own self-
seeking." [48] The result is, as philosopher Donald Heinz put it: "There
is no *humanum*, only the individual. I am I, and you are you. There
is no 'we.' " [49]

Psychologist and philosopher Walter Tubbs, answering Perls, puts
it well:

> If I just do my thing and you do yours, we stand in
> danger of losing each other and ourselves. . . . We are fully
> ourselves only in relation to each other; the I detached
> from a Thou disintegrates. I do not find you by chance; I
> find you by an active life of reaching out. . . . I must begin
> with myself, true; but I must not end with myself: the
> truth begins with two.[50]

Maurice Friedman calls attention to the danger of relating to others
only for instrumental purposes—that is, to serve ego.

> Once we make ourselves the goal—even if we do so in
> the hope of becoming more of a person and thereby being
> able to help other people more effectively—we embark on

a path that is not likely to lead us beyond ourselves to genuine dialogue with others. Instead, we are more and more apt to view our relations with others in terms of our own progress toward becoming whatever we feel we should become.[51]

He points to danger in using others not merely for our material enrichment, but also as means for our psychic advancement:

> If I follow Fromm and other psychologists who tell me that it is important to have good relationships with other people so that I may be a mature and productive person, then the relationships are merely functional. . . . It is, of course, possible for a relationship that starts out as merely functional to end up being organic. . . . But this depends upon forgetting our original motivation and getting caught up in the relationship as something of reality and value in itself.[52]

From another perspective, group and family therapists make a similar point. The dominant modes of therapy, individual psychotherapy and psychoanalysis, tend to focus on ego, treating it as the sun of the human galaxy, which it is not. Instead, they should see the group or family as "more than the individual psychodynamics of its members," as Salvador Minuchin puts it,[53] should focus not only on ego, but also on relationships. According to Peggy Papp of the Ackerman Institute, a leading family therapy center, "We believe the ailment is not in the person, but between persons, and it is the 'between' that we treat." [54]

The Effect of Past Injustices

Ego-segregation may well have therapeutic merit when ego is entangled in "sick" or socially oppressive relations and structures. But then it must be viewed as a transitional phase, moving toward a new, reconstructed, "healthier" or more just world. To let ego stand as a lasting bastion ignores the data and psychological analysis on the need for deep interpersonal bonds.

One reason an observer, analyst, or activist can fail to see the need for reconstruction is a preoccupation with socially embedded injustice and a focus on tearing it out. Self-actualization is popularly understood to mean that a person fulfills him- or herself, overcoming external restraints and internal "hangups." Some advocates of self-actualization concentrate on the external restraints that stand in the way of self-fulfillment. According to a textbook summary of the position of Abraham Maslow and Carl Rogers, for example:

> Man seeks to fulfill and express his potentials and talents but is often thwarted by social forces of approval and rejection that force him to deny aspects of himself and thus prevent the development of his real self.[55]

This emphasis leads to the demand that society adjust to self, that society be reorganized so that self can be actualized.

A position taken by some feminists illustrates how such a preoccupation with correcting past injustice may create at least a transitional imbalance between seeking self-fulfillment and sustaining the bases of mutuality. As these feminists see it, a woman's spouse and children prevent her from "finding herself" and "expressing herself," because the prevalent mentality strongly demands, for instance, that she have children she doesn't want to have, that she stay at home rather than be gainfully employed elsewhere, or that she be subservient to her husband. To get out from under demands they find oppressive, some feminists have found it necessary to drop their families in the quest for self-fulfillment.

A woman writer, for example, explains her decision to remain childless:

> Writing is my religion. . . . I love writing of others' real worlds which are my fantasies. But to do this I must be apart; I must be free enough and alone enough to remain true to the child I once was, that I am still. Because I do not mock it, because I do not forget or replace it with another, the child in me remains alive and strong. It is the source of all my creativity.[56]

Betty Rollin, in an article entitled "Motherhood—Who Needs It?" writes:

> Women are now beginning to think and do more about development of self, of their individual resources. . . . It is not a question of whether or not children are sweet and

marvelous to have and rear; the question is, even if that's so, whether or not one wants to pay the price for it. It doesn't make sense any more to pretend that women need babies, when what they really need is themselves.[57]

A divorced woman who shares custody of her children with their father, who lives in another state, says, "It was the most painful thing I've ever done in my life, but in the last 5 years, I've had 20 years of growth I wouldn't have been able to achieve otherwise."[58]

Lillian B. Rubin's book *Women of a Certain Age* is of special interest in this context.[59] A rather late book in the feminist tradition, it draws on many that preceded it, and the tone of the author, who is trained in social science, is moderate, not shrill.

Rubin writes of her life as a wife and mother. "I awoke each day wondering how to fill the time, wondering how I'd ever gotten into this fix, wondering how I'd ever get out." Although she loved her husband and daughter dearly, they weren't enough. She also worked as a volunteer, but found it "almost disrespectful to myself to work without pay."[60]

Rubin's experiences and those of the women she interviewed reflect well the injustices women were subject to over centuries in all spheres of life, from the workplace to the bedroom. As one reads her book, it is understandable, maybe even necessary in a psychodynamic sense, that in rebelling against these historical impositions, women may wish or need to go beyond existing rules, to withdraw from them and break them, even to retreat to ego. What is missing from Rubin's book, though, is the next phase, the understanding that *new* mutualities are needed—that in learning to overcome the excessive demands of husbands, children, and "sexist" society, women will find no satisfactory solutions unless they acquire new mutuality-based relationships.

To argue that men are ego-centered too does not make ego-centering a sound basis for women's interpersonal relations or mutuality, but rather emphasizes that both men and women must evolve new kinds of bonds and community. This theme is advanced and championed by Betty Friedan in her 1981 book, *The Second Stage*.[61] It makes her one of the few leaders of any social movement to effectively make the transition from the first "anti-" phase to the second, reconstructive one.

The Present Context

In the historical context of oppressive duties, Paul Zweig relishes the liberties taken, for example, when individualism confronted the authority of the early Christian church, and celebrates their virtue.[62] But we must return to the current historical situation, to deal with the ever-present question of the balance between individualism and community. I suggest that, on balance, the American majority has gone quite far enough in dismantling past structures and patterns, although the degree and the details are open to debate. (Breaking away from old rules never takes place evenly on all fronts; specific groups, such as homosexuals in many parts of the country, still have a considerable way to go.) The pendulum is swinging toward the need for greater attention to the reconstruction of mutuality, the basis of a sound self and community; toward new or renewed patterns to fill the growing social void.

The critical point that must be stressed now in discussions of the relations among ego, others, and community is that just as others and community can oppress, repress, and enslave ego, they can also be the source of authentic, lasting satisfaction. The world beyond ego, the world that transcends it, is not necessarily repressive (as Freud argued in *Civilization and Its Discontents*), nor a dungeon without an exit (as Sartre has it). Nor is it inevitably a communion of I and Thou (Martin Buber). It can either restrict and restrain, or it can extend and enrich; but there is no escaping the social world. Ego cannot form a satisfying experience on its own, not merely for instrumental reasons (we need others for production, division of labor), but first and foremost for elementary psychic well-being, and, we shall see, the advancement of shared needs.

The sharp rise in government in the last decades may have been caused by the decline of mutuality and involvement in shared concerns, with the government stepping in as a kind of substitute-mutuality and community-of-last-resort. Or the expansion of government may have undermined mutuality and community, feeding into a retreat from community already under way for other historical reasons. Most likely *both* processes took place, with the government stepping in to help replace what the community was neglecting, to fill a vacuum, and at the same time overstepping, pushing back, further undermining the community. In either case, if government is now rolled back, without individual renewal, reconstruction of mutuality, and commitment to shared concerns, there will be an ever harsher void for ego and, soon, growing pressure to reinstate government.

DICTATES, INVOLVEMENTS, ASOCIAL GRATIFICATIONS, AND DUTIES

So far I have reviewed the reasons people need mutuality, what it is, the reason it has declined, and the historical context. Before I can advance the discussion of where we need to go from here I must deal with the question: What are the basic forms individual–society relations take? What suggestions do they imply for our future?

At issue are two divergent sources of human motivation: what is satisfying, and what is legitimate. Satisfaction is typically generated when response to a need, genuinely felt, is deferred and then provided: food to the hungry, libation to the thirsty, expression of affection to a loved one, returning home from work or a journey. Legitimate conduct is carried out in response to an inner sense that the step to be taken is *properly* required, for instance, heeding a sign not to speed through a school zone as children rush to it in the morning. As sociologist Peter L. Berger puts it, when people genuinely believe in the "rightness" of certain social arrangements, those arrangements are experienced as proper and worthy of support—that is, as legitimate.[63]

What is considered satisfying or legitimate is ultimately up to the individual. Propaganda, education, peer pressure, and commercials may tell a person that he should desire a deodorant, a black (or white) neighbor, to brush his teeth, or to pay taxes. But if the person involved does not find the deodorant satisfying or the demand to render taxes legitimate, they are not so for that person.

What is legitimate, of course, may well not be satisfying, and vice versa. A person may well *enjoy* speeding but realize it is not legitimate. And paying taxes may well be deemed legitimate but rarely gratifying. In effect, what we see here are two deeply divergent, though not necessarily incompatible, bases of personal conduct, one what is considered right, correct, proper, and the other, what is pleasurable, satisfying, rewarding.

When both dimensions are viewed together, as they must be in judging single acts, they result in four combinations:

1. Acts that are neither pleasurable nor legitimate, which I refer to as *dictates;* they stand over the individual as something the person

is coerced to do, at the point of a gun, under economic pressure, or because of powerful psychic threats. Dictates are particularly undermining to mutuality.

2. Acts that are both satisfying and legitimate (such as helping out a close friend) are *involvements*, which are particularly constructive for mutuality.

3. Acts that are legitimate but not satisfying, often perceived as *duties*, are taxing, but alienating only if pervasive.

4. Acts that are satisfying but not legitimate tend to promote ego-segregation and ego-centering, and are destructive to mutuality. I refer to these as *asocial gratifications*.

All this requires some elaboration before we can tie it back to where we are and where we are headed.

Dictates

The use of dictates is common in prisons, forced labor camps, and mental hospitals. However, they are not unknown in relations between bosses and employees—when their relations are basically hostile; between teachers and students in many schools; and between authoritarian parents and their teenagers, though of course in all these cases dictates are rarely as prevalent in the total fabric of the relationship as they are, say, in prisons. Dictates are particularly common in totalitarian regimes.

Dictates are a poor way of relating people and society. Individuals mobilized by dictates will withdraw their energies as much as possible, and seek a way to escape the situation or modify the structure, thus making social management at best costly and inefficient, if not outright unstable and untenable. Dictators do not sleep well at night; at least they ought not if they sense the latent reaction to their regimes. And the economies of prisons, or societies run basically like prisons, tend toward crude, low-quality, ineffectual, wasteful production.

The obvious question is why use dictates at all? The answer is that they are drawn upon when for one reason or another the society, or an institution, has evolved a pattern that conflicts with basic human needs, and hence is unable to use the other forms. People imprisoned find that they are deprived of most of their liberties and satisfactions. Whatever compelling reasons the judges had in punishing them in that way, the prisoners tend not to appreciate the confinement. Hence, prison authorities must dictate most of their policies and enforce them. Schools unable to convince students of the merit of the subjects taught and the ways they are taught, whatever good reason they may have for the way they proceed, will find themselves drawing heavily on dictates.

Involvements

Conduct that is basically both satisfying and legitimate produces a particularly effective bond among individuals, others, and their community. For the persons involved it generates a positive sense of belonging and of dedication. For the institution or community that can build on involvement, it makes for little need for close supervision, for high-quality work, and often for high productivity and low costs. Scientists and artists who pursue their own leads, executives turned on by their tasks, are cases in point. It is not that people thus involved know no drudgery, doubt, or hostile feelings. But their main, prevalent sense is that of double-positive involvement, making for effective participation.

Involvement-rich institutions are found only in free societies, in which the basic societal pattern is responsive rather than alien to basic human needs. Involvement may be particularly high in intensive situations such as social movements (say, among Peace Corps volunteers), but it is quite abundant in the best schools, colleges, and places of employment.

Why not rely only on involvement? Some societal needs are not ready-made to be satisfying. For instance, Americans tend to delegate to immigrants many jobs, from picking vegetables to textile work, that they are not willing to do at any price the economy can bear. Other work often has a sizable element of routine and drudgery that is difficult to eliminate (though often it can be further reduced). That is, the work is not and often cannot be made sufficiently satisfying to be involving. These are, so to speak, reasons inherent in the tasks.

Duties

Duties, conduct deemed legitimate but not gratifying, are a "must" if tasks that are menial, routine, or otherwise unappealing to most people are to be attended to. They may be reduced, especially if resources are plentiful and the frustrations the duties generate are relatively low. On the other hand, duties tend to expand when scarcity is severe. In neither case can the world of mutuality do without the imposition of some duties, which is what pop psychology tends to overlook.

Instead, it has promoted what one writer refers to as "a deification of the isolated self," a world view that seriously undermines a sense of duty to things beyond the self.

> What disappears in this view of things is the ground of community, the felt sense of collective responsibility for the fate of each separate other. What takes its place is a moral vacuum in which others are trapped forever in a "private" destiny, doomed to whatever befalls them.[64]

Related to this orientation is another characteristic of pop psychology: a tendency to describe community as something that is easily attained and requires no self-denial. As educator Parker Palmer complains, "For the affluent, community has become another consumer item: you can buy it in weekend chunks at human potential centers."[65] Moreover, he continues,

> another myth tells us that community equals utopia, that in easy access to one another and the comfortably supportive relationships which will result, we will quickly find ourselves brothers and sisters again.[66]

Yet as this critic and others like him point out, community and mutuality are not easily attained. While beneficial to the individual, they also require something of him.

A college president elaborates:

> The release from obligations which has been so enthusiastically sought is probably self-defeating. . . . No matter how we twist and turn and hide, we cannot ultimately avoid a recognition that there are requirements upon us that we owe to ourselves and to others, and the stability and serenity which we seek is not to be found in escape, but on the contrary in developing the highest degree of discipline of which we are capable.[67]

Asocial Gratifications

At first blush asocial gratifications may seem to be the category of human behavior least in need of explanation. People follow their heart's desire, take what they can get, without concern for others or the future of a relationship. However, the issue is colored by the fact that we do not normally face our "nature" directly, unaffected by our upbringing and culture. Thus, what we want for ourselves is highly edited. Asocial gratifications arise mainly when education and culture break down, when people become dislodged from their social moorings.

In recent years, as part of the "anti-" movements, as part of the criticism of America as it is and the efforts to evolve alternative cultures, emphasis has been put on returning to the primitive, to unedited urges, to listening to one's body. However, no mutuality or community can be sustained unless asocial gratifications remain only a small segment of human motivation and satisfaction. The social sources of gratification can be changed, but not the need to tie gratification to some socially approved and legitimate sources.

In Historical Perspective

It would be grossly oversimplified to suggest that Americans moved from the traditional era of dictates, against which they have rebelled in recent years, to an era of asocial gratifications, and are now ready to respond to the resulting vacuum with an era of new affirmation of commitments. Societies do not turn about like a marching band to a new tune. They are complex entities, which change gradually and incompletely. Millions may embrace a new mentality; others combine two perspectives in various mixtures.

Thus, while it is true that in traditional America duties ranked higher, there were always some who sought asocial gratifications, and others who were truly involved in what the society required. It was only as withdrawal (and, to a much lesser extent, rebellion) spread that duties came to be perceived as dictates. The role of women again provides one example: In traditional America, all but a few women accepted with little question their "duty" as mothers and wives. It was only with the rise of the women's movement and consciousness that many came to see in the prevailing division of labor, authority, and sexual freedoms and pleasures, not a God-given or natural pattern, but one men made and people could remake. Traditional women may not have enjoyed the prevalent men's notion of their being passive, quick sexual encounters, or their being expected to work at home, but by and large they did not see these demands as illegitimate. Only when legitimacy was withdrawn from these duties, and they became more and more widely perceived as dictates, was the time ripe for retreat to ego.

In the same vein, in the era of withdrawal from society only a minority of Americans really made the asocial pattern their predominant one, while another minority remained more or less traditional. What tipped the societal scale was the majority who were affected to one extent or another by the retreat to ego. Thus, traditionalism was followed by an uneven withdrawal into asocial gratifications, surely not unknown at the height of the traditional era, but not as prevalent.

Most relevant, the resulting vacuum creates a demand for new or renewed affirmation in the form of a higher level of commitment, or involvement or duty, without any expectation that commitment will become dominant in short order or encompass everybody.

CHAPTER THREE
Civility: In the Service of Shared Concerns

ESSENTIAL SHARED CONCERNS

Beyond reconstruction of mutuality, less government compels another individual attribute: a commitment to shared concerns, to matters that affect all but are not necessarily any one person's business.

One can reduce police patrols, but if neighbors do not watch one another's houses more attentively, the neighborhood will become more vulnerable. One can reduce government expenditure for environmental protection, but if individuals and corporations do not restrain their dumping, lakes and rivers will become unavailable for recreation, fish production, and for drinking water. It may well be that most individuals know better than the government what is best for them, and should be free to choose their course, but such freedom entails responsibilities and sensibilities. It is incompatible with each individual's trying to maximize his or her take, disregarding all others. And, while there are occasions on which unbridled pursuit of individual profit will result in larger production for all—that is, *shared* wealth will rise as that of *individuals* does—there are numerous other situations in which the *paradox of the commons* cannot be avoided. These are the situations in which ego pursuit of more for ego, freely chosen and rational, will destroy the shared (or common or public) goods.

Garrett Hardin argues persuasively that in relation to these shared goods, the *laissez-faire* notion of individualism is indefensible. It leads to what he calls "the tragedy of the commons," using tragedy in the sense of the remorseless, inevitable working of events. Hardin's metaphor is that of herdsmen grazing their cattle on a pasture open to all. Each herdsman, as a rational being seeking to maximize his own gain, asks: "What is the utility *to me* of adding one more animal to my herd?" The sensible course, he finds, is to add another animal, and another, and yet another.

> This is the conclusion reached by each and every rational herdsman sharing a commons. Therein is the tragedy. Each man is *locked in* to a system that compels him to increase his herd without limit—in a world that is limited. Ruin is the destination toward which all men rush, each pursuing his own best interest in a society that believes in the freedom of the commons. *Freedom in a commons brings ruin to all.*[1]

Hardin maintains that the logic of the commons has not been widely enough appreciated, citing such instances as the persistent problems of overgrazing (and thus erosion and weeds) on public lands in the American West and the common belief that the resources of the oceans are inexhaustible.[2] Sanitary landfills and crowded highways are mentioned by economist Thomas C. Schelling in his analysis of "the commons" as "a paradigm for situations in which people so impinge on each other in pursuing their own interests that collectively they might be better off if they could be restrained, but no one gains individually by self-restraint."[3]

Similarly, it may "make sense" for each individual to fell some trees for firewood and not to plant any, though this choice made by every individual may denude hillsides and valleys; and when the forest is finally replanted, it will take years to grow. Responding to rising inflation, it may "make sense" for each individual to spend more and save less, though this choice made by every individual may well drive inflation faster, which will hurt all.

In past decades, a frequently followed way to accommodate individual choices to the commons of shared concerns has been to rely on the government to achieve the reconciliation, often by limiting the individual's choices. But the government has turned out to be a poor custodian of shared needs, often providing ineffective and inefficient service; it frequently worked in ways that have alienated many individuals, and extended itself into more areas than were perceived as truly shared concerns.

Like the shepherd who cried "wolf" at every passing shadow, various groups have invoked shared concerns so often, for so many purposes, that the call has lost its credibility. In the early sixties, some black leaders argued that unless full social justice was implemented then and there, the nation would be destroyed in a racial conflict, its cities burned down, "no stone left standing on top of another." Similarly, in the early seventies, some environmentalists maintained that we would all choke or starve, whichever came first, unless "small-earth" resources were husbanded at the rate and in the ways they favored. At the same time, some energy specialists foresaw the end of the West unless we erected hundreds of nuclear reactors, while their opponents argued that these very same reactors would undo us if nothing else did. Little wonder Americans, not inclined to be preoccupied with shared concerns to begin with, in an era "drunk on the rhetoric of individualism,"[4] turned an increasingly deaf ear to this tune, rejecting "more" government.

But there are *essential* shared concerns, which *must* be provided for or a community cannot be. Other shared concerns may be important, desirable, of uppermost value to some or even many, but they are not as unavoidable as the essential ones. As my purpose here is to make the case for renewed individual commitment to shared concerns, I focus on these essential concerns. Once this commitment is re-established, each group of members of the community can decide what additional purposes they wish to promote to the level of shared concerns that all members of the community are to be expected to serve.

THREE DIMENSIONS

There are three dimensions to the individual's commitment to shared concerns, whatever their content: to play by the rules, to commit resources (including psychic energy and time) to the public realm, and to attend to some specific commonweal matters. These are next briefly introduced; the balance of the chapter is dedicated to explication of these three facets, a review of their current diminished status, and the ways they may be restored.

To play by the rules is one meaning of law and order, the basis of a civil society. In any sport, a game turns into a brawl unless there are rules that are understood and widely heeded by the players. Just so, a civil society turns into a jungle unless the laws provide a set of rules by which—within the limitations they set—differences among the members of society are worked out. In addition to the rules enacted into law, each community has a set of rules of ethical conduct (mores). They are not subject to court procedures and jail sentences, but they nevertheless play an integral part in reconciling individual choices and shared needs.

The term "law and order" in our society has acquired additional meaning. For both liberals and conservatives, it has come to stand for a *particular* set of rules. For many liberals, the rules seem unduly punitive, especially tight on minorities; for many conservatives, they offer a much-needed antidote to undue permissiveness. What concerns me here is not how tight the rules are, or which specific set is to be heeded, but the need for *some* shared rules and psychic investment in them. The individual basis of a civil order is a commitment, by most individuals most of the time, to abide by the rules—even when such compliance violates their self-interest.

A second requirement of a civil society is support for shared concerns, to countervail the centrifugal forces of interest groups. For the individual, this means a *commitment to the public realm*, to public action, to political involvement. Otherwise the public interest is short of energy, while those who seek to subvert it have a free rein.

A third requirement is support for essential shared concerns—first and foremost, national security. This support cannot be divided up among individuals. Hence, each individual must have some *involvement in commonweal matters*, aside from his or her concern for personal and subcommunity goals and goods. "The commonweal" is a useful term for the issues the community shares, rather than the community itself. Involvement in the community means participation in its social fabric and institutions, while commitment to the commonweal means individual involvement in shared concerns, from keeping the drinking water resources from running out to providing for public safety. It is akin to concern with the public interest; that is, I assume that the commonweal entails *some* concerns that are not necessarily the same as individual and subgroup interests, nor automatically reconciled with them.

I refer to these three attributes in combination—playing by the rules, participating in public life, and shouldering some specific shared concerns—as *civility*. This old usage of civility, meaning "deference or allegiance to the social order befitting a citizen,"[5]* is not wholly lost. For instance, it appeared often in news coverage of the riots in Britain in 1981. A *Washington Post* editorial referred to Britain's belief that "a special tradition of civility" made it "immune to the shocks caused elsewhere by social change and economic distress."[6] Columnist David Broder characterized Great Britain as the source of "both the rules of parliamentary democracy and the customs of civility that make it possible for such a system to work."[7] In focusing on this meaning of civility, we may seem to ignore its more recent common usage to mean good manners or sensitivity to the rules of proper social behavior, but this lighter meaning points the same way: In being courteous to one another we attend to the common good and restrain ego. Manners, though, are not as important as laws and mores. Civility is the individual psychic foundation of all shared rules, the public realm, and service of the commonweal.

COMMITMENT TO SHARED RULES

Need for Rules

Evolution, adjustment, and enforcement of *shared* rules, to which individuals feel committed, is an essential shared concern. At issue is not the preservation of any specific set of rules, but of *some* mutually agreed, acceptable, legitimate set of rules. These rules set limits on what one may do in pursuit of one's goal. One may not gun down a competitor, market untested drugs, pull a face mask in football.

New Whigs tend to argue that there is no need for any special institution to foster such limits; the situation itself will do so. If the commons are disregarded, they will be destroyed; their absence will teach the individual to heed them in the future. Moreover, since people are "not dumb," they will *anticipate* the intolerable effects of the destruction of the commons and, to the extent that such a

---

* By permission. From *Webster's Third International Dictionary,* © 1981 by G. & C. Merriam Company, publishers of the Merriam-Webster® Dictionaries.

loss is truly injurious, they will refrain from acting in ways that will undermine the commons. That is, they will never actually have to put up with dangerous drugs, a contaminated lake, catch-as-catch-can football.

Immanuel Kant advanced this notion eloquently in discussing the "illogic" of lying: *A* knows if he lies, so will *B,* and soon no one will trust anyone, making all commerce and human intercourse impossible. Hence, enlightened self-interest teaches us that the gains of lying are fleeting, self-contradictory, and not truly in our interest. The same has been said about stealing and murder. Those who indulge undermine property and life, and will not be safe themselves.

New Whigs like to cite Adam Smith's well-known notion that someone who "intends only his own gain" is "led by an invisible hand to promote . . . the public interest."[8] The "invisible hand" is the free market, and it is credited with all kinds of powers by those who champion it. Economists Milton and Rose Friedman, for instance, write:

> Adam Smith's flash of genius was his recognition that the prices that emerged from voluntary transactions between buyers and sellers—for short, in a free market—could coordinate the activity of millions of people, each seeking his own interest, in such a way as to make everyone better off. It was a startling idea then, and it remains one today, that economic order can emerge as the *unintended* consequence of the actions of many people, *each seeking his own interest.* (Italics added)[9]

New Whigs see the market as doing more than providing efficient self-regulation: It enables people to learn from experience. Yale political scientist Robert E. Lane explains:

> The market, for all its impersonality, is a great teacher, not wholly as the pinball machine instructs the descending ball, but rather as it structures rewards, punishes delinquencies, informs us in subtle ways about the vermicular pathways to success. It teaches, thus, as Skinner would have us taught—through contingency reinforcement; and we are apt pupils, for the stakes are high.[10]

Unfortunately, the world does not work the way Kant and other followers of this argument have it. The argument is pure logic, but people's behavior is not. All too many individuals discover that substantial gains can be had by violating rules precisely because most other individuals continue to heed them, at least for quite a while. Moreover, once the commons are undermined, as more and more individuals disregard them, it is often very costly, in economic and human terms, to reconstruct them. It takes years of considerable effort and sacrifice to reforest a denuded mountain, to restore a lake, to overcome institutionalized inflation. Anticipation of destruction of the commons and enlightened self-interest turn out in practice to provide an insufficient base for the protection of essential shared concerns. *It follows that to maintain rules, communities must deal with violators of a shared interest long before a breach of civility becomes common.*

Sustaining the rules requires (1) *preventive* mechanisms that seek to inoculate individuals with the need to abide by the rules before the commons are destroyed, and as a *matter of faith,* not calculation; (2) *policing* mechanisms that are activated when preventive inoculation fails; and (3) mechanisms to *modify* the shared rules as community needs, values, and perceptions change.

Containment, Subculture, and Dominance

A technical aside is needed here. As such discussions are usually conducted in qualitative rather than quantitative terms, an important gradation is overlooked. The precise issue is not to secure compliance with shared rules rather than violation, but to secure compliance at a *sustaining* level. Full compliance (100 percent) is practically unknown in all but the simplest, small, primitive societies. Full compliance in a complex society will usually turn out to be very costly to attain and to maintain. It suffices to keep violations rare enough (usually below the 2 percent level) to secure a sense of rules effectively backed. At this level, transgressions will be "marginal deviance," denounced by most and "unthinkable" by all who wish to be respected or to function freely within the community. In such communities, studies show, prostitutes are aware that they are grossly violating the rules of the society in which they practice, whatever brave face they put on their deviant behavior.[11] Studies of thieves illustrate the same point. Edwin Sutherland's 1937 study of a professional thief concluded simply: "The professional thief in America feels that he is a social outcast."[12] Thieves who are most aware that they are violating society's ethics are those who operate in cultures without criminal subcultures they can identify with. As Sutherland notes:

> Among the criminal tribes of India the individual was immersed almost completely in a consistent culture and felt no distress in attacking an outsider because this did not make him an enemy in any group which had significance for him. Nowhere in America, probably, is a criminal so completely immersed in a group that he does not feel his position as an enemy of the larger society.[13]

This was in the thirties. In contemporary America, it is common for numbers runners, bookies, and marijuana dealers to feel that there is little wrong with what they are doing, because such conduct is well above the 2 percent level, and whole subcultures have been formed that approve of such behavior.

One may argue about the historical accuracy of these comparisons. There may have been as many deviant subcultures in earlier America as there are now (although they seem to have grown in scope since the 1950s). My point is the difference between isolated incidents of violation, which do not threaten civility (indeed, the horrified response may serve to keep the antidotes exercised and strong), and massive or congealed subcultures of violation, which do undercut the legal and ethical bases of community.

Once marginal deviance breaks out of this confined level and rises, it tends to break into a much higher level, rising to a 30 percent or higher incidence of the behavior at issue, and to become dominant in some subcultures or sectors (e.g., violent crime in poor neighborhoods, fraud and abuse of patients in nursing homes). At this stage, more and more of those individuals who still play by the rules (in, say, a sport, in which the rules are backed by referees and sanctions, but not by the government) and more and more law-abiding citizens (in matters in which the rules are backed by the state) feel that civility is violated and threatened, and that they are fools or worse for obeying the rules.

Polls conducted in the sixties and seventies indicate that such a sense of increased violation of rules and diminished civility had taken hold in the United States. A 1976 Gallup survey, for instance, found that 66 percent of Americans thought that in that period people did not lead "as honest and moral lives as people did in the past." (In 1965, 52 percent of the people surveyed felt that way; in 1952, only 47 percent thought morality was declining, while 46 percent said it was not).[14] Other Gallup polls during this same period indicated that many people, especially in cities, thought crime was increasing.[15]

As the belief that lawlessness is increasing has spread, so too has the sense that it is not necessary to follow the rules, especially among the young. A 1976 survey of college students found widespread cheating on campus; 47 percent—nearly half—of the students polled believed that many successful students make it by "beating the system."[16]

Once transgressions break from the level of containment (below about 2 percent) to the subculture or sectoral level, (a) an effective drive to restore civility and reduce violations to the contained state may materialize, or (b) a demand for *new* rules/laws may rise, or (c) violations will rise still further, becoming the prevalent mode of behavior. In this stage, rules exist largely on the books, like paying in full taxes one owes in Italy or heeding the 55-mile-per-hour speed limit in certain western states.

The recent American condition, in many areas, has been far worse than contained deviance, with violation rising toward the 30 percent level and dominance in some subcultures and sectors. Currently, most criminals go unpunished. FBI statistics for 1,847 cities, for instance, show that in 1977, someone was arrested and charged in only 37.6 percent of the known cases of violent crime. A conviction, even on a lesser charge, resulted in only 14.4 percent. The statistics for property crimes, which are far more frequent, draw a similar picture. An arrest and charge resulted in 16.8 percent of the known cases, a conviction in only 6.0 percent.[17]

In more and more of the country, fear of crime is pervasive, and civil order is perceived either not to exist or not to be effectively sustained. In many cities, police tell people to walk at night in the middle of the street rather than on the sidewalk, because the light there is brighter; to travel in groups rather than walk alone, to buy locks and alarms, and otherwise turn their homes into bastions; and not to resist muggers. (A police film advises old people to lie down lest muggers throw them down and break their bones as well as rob them.) The net effect of all this advice is a sense that there is no source of effective protection. This, in turn, feeds into a tendency for citizens to rely on themselves for elementary safety. This is reflected in the mass purchases of firearms and chemical sprays.

Similarly, voluntary tax compliance is endangered as violations increase. The Commissioner of the IRS reported in 1981 that the IRS faced 3.6 million delinquent tax accounts. Additionally, the agency estimated it was losing roughly $23 billion to the "underground economy" of people who collect cash for their services or goods and pay virtually no taxes.[18] The size of the underground economy, the number of tax violations, and the amount of revenue lost because of noncompliance all appear to have increased during the 1970s. According to IRS estimates, underpayment of income taxes cost the government almost three times as much in 1981 as in 1973, $87 billion compared to $29 billion. The tax compliance rate for small proprietors (those with adjusted gross income of less than $10,000) dropped from 79.2 percent in 1965 to 43.2 percent in 1976; for medium-sized proprietors (adjusted gross income of $10,000 to $30,000) it fell from 91.4 percent in 1965 to 86.0 percent in 1976.[19] Similarly, the Census Bureau reports indirect evidence of an increase in the number of violations by individuals. Each year, the Current Population Survey asks sample households to list their sources of income. In 1972, 10.2 percent of those questioned did not respond to this question; by 1978, the proportion had risen to 18.3 percent.[20] The rising nonresponse rate is believed to indicate that more families have income they are trying to hide.

Moreover, the rationalizations people use to excuse tax evasion tend to fuel even more evasion or other sorts of dishonesty. As journalist Irwin Ross noted in a *Fortune* article:

> Far more consequential [than the economic aspects] are the pervasive cynicism and the erosion of civic morale that are produced by widespread tax evasion. While the motive for tax evasion is invariably financial, the rationalizations that accompany it are enveloped in an antigovernment animus. People who cheat on taxes are more predisposed than most to perceive the government as corrupt—which is taken as additional grounds for cheating.[21]

There is a widely perceived need to restore compliance to a much higher level, and to increase public commitment to civility, in the sense the term is used here. A prime example is the frequent call for stricter enforcement of the laws against criminals—above all for a higher probability that violators will be caught, arrested, convicted, and punished. This demand is paralleled by calls to abandon some rules and institute new ones that would command more commitment. Such calls are illustrated by those who would "decriminalize" prostitution, gambling, and the use of marijuana, either because they believe that these should not be matters for public rules or because they feel that, since these rules are so frequently violated, it would be better if there were fewer rules to observe and enforce, however morally desirable their observance may be. The new rules need not necessarily be more lax, only more legitimate. In schools, for instance, high expectations of self-discipline could replace demands for close adherence to an imposed code.

While violations of laws are easier to describe than transgressions of other rules and ethical mores, and data on them are more readily available, the ethical situation seems to parallel the legal part of civility. A sizable portion of the population, not just "professional crooks," engages in cheating or fraud at one time or another. For example, in a 1964 study, based on a sample of 1,219 teachers at 380 schools, "widespread" cheating on tests was reported in 22.1 percent of the schools.[22]

The Defense Department studied the Reserve Officer Training Corps (ROTC), which annually awards four-year scholarships to about 19,000 students. Upon graduation, these students are obligated to serve in the armed services for four years, but the legal obligation to serve is not incurred until the junior year. It was found that about half of the recipients were dropping out of the program by the end of their sophomore year. Such students benefit from up to two years of full scholarship without having to enter the armed services; many continue in school, paying for the remaining two years themselves.[23]

Scores of other pieces of evidence could be cited. However, it is not my purpose here to provide a statistical overview of the situation, but to illustrate the breakout of violation of laws and mores from the contained level to sub-area and sectoral levels, and the threatening impact on the civil order in general. The daily press is sure to provide additional accounts, if not in tomorrow's editions, sometime this week—whatever week it is.

Historical and Present Causes

The threatened condition of American rules reflects both historical forces and recent developments. Americans have traditionally been dubious about shared rules, because they were imposed and were considered, often for good reason, not legitimate. In a very elementary sense the United States was born out of a rebellion against such a set of dictates imposed by the British monarchy. And, true to our expectation that once a set of shared rules is destroyed, the road to new ones is long and arduous, it took many decades for intra-American shared rules to evolve and take.

The attitude captured in Western folktales, novels, and films is instructive. Individual cowboys, rangers, and settlers sought to maintain their own armories and impose their own justice by posses—often opposing the local sheriff. For not only was the sheriff weak, but he was often corrupt, either after personal gain or in cahoots with some families or merchants against the others. That is, the rules he imposed were heavily tilted and hence quite uncompelling. The engaging symbolism of the sheriff in *High Noon* is that he is evenhanded, a new kind of sheriff.

Over the decades there has been a very substantial increase in justice based on evenhanded rules, fairly imposed, and much less reliance on justice meted out by individual citizens and private use of arms, the ultimate destruction of shared rules. The process, though, is still incomplete. The majority of Americans are still distrustful of authorities to the point that they refuse to rely heavily on their justice. On the right, distrust of authorities—from fear that they will be taken over by the extreme left, to fear that they have already been captured by liberals—leads millions of Americans to demand the right to keep themselves armed. As one observer has noted, "The gun lobby's basic ammunition . . . is based on the contention that those who favor gun controls want to disarm the American people and leave them prey to armed marauders."[24]

An NRA hardliner put it a little more bluntly: "Take the guns away from the American citizen, this country will go Communist, just like Russia or any of your others. It's been a proven fact through history."[25] This same fear of a leftist takeover leads a smaller group to try to enforce their own mores, say by burning crosses on the front lawns of people they wish to chase out of their community.

On the left-liberal side, the fear of tilted authorities is at the root of opposition to national ID cards, central data banks, and a national police force, despite the fact that these might substantially help in fighting various forms of criminality. There is constant fear that a new McCarthy would use this central information and power to pursue, fire, jail all left-leaning people, Jews, intellectuals. If there were a more compelling sense that the tools of national rulemaking and enforcement would be used only for the purpose of imposing even-handed rules, they might be allowed more room.

There are other indications that Americans have not completely outgrown the Wild West, suspect-the-sheriff mentality. "Cops" and "robbers" are often implicitly viewed rather like two football teams that ought to be fairly matched; neglected are the facts that the police represent the community, the shared concerns, and the robbers' abusive individualism must be curbed. Thus, as the seventies ended, a number of congressmen began calling for a "taxpayers' bill of rights," because tax violators and the IRS were not fairly matched. Formal legislation promoting such rights, introduced by Texas Republican Jim Collins in 1979, had acquired seventy-four cosponsors by 1981.[26] As Collins explained:

> Any taxpayer that's filling out his return right now will tell you there isn't any equity; there's no balance about this thing. Here we have in the IRS the very best, the most capable people in the government. . . . And on the other side, we have this poor taxpayer who really doesn't understand it. I'll tell you what it's like. It would be like taking a first-grade football team . . . against the Cowboys. . . . [The IRS has] the best quarterbacks, and they know all the signals; and what we're trying to do is to establish a balance—an equity.[27]

Similarly, many Americans feel that traffic police should not be allowed to use radar to catch speeders. "It gives the police an unfair edge." Why unfair? Are cops and speeders two groups of runners to be given an even start at the gate?

The opposition to effective enforcement reflects the position that the rule is not necessarily legitimate in the first place. In San Francisco, a building inspector, charged with ensuring that no building add floors without a permit, used a helicopter to work more efficiently; he was soon grounded by a wail of complaints about this unfair advantage. Americans have often re-elected convicted mayors and congressmen, even while they were in jail, because all-politicians-are-crooks-anyhow and the individuals in question were "good otherwise," a clear sign of disrespect for the importance of being law-abiding. School children were asked to complete the following story: "One day the President was driving his car to a meeting. Because he was late he was driving very fast. The police stop the car." Two out of five children—42 percent—finished the story by letting the President get away with speeding, showing that, like their elders, they do not recognize that the law is above all citizens, including the President.[28] In the spring of 1973, as Watergate dominated the news, revealing corruption in the Nixon administration, a sizable part of the public—nearly half—did not consider it a serious matter; on the contrary, they saw Watergate as "just politics."[29]

In the same unconcern for commitment to shared rules, Congress enacts scores of laws imposed on all Americans *except* congressmen. For instance, members of Congress exempted themselves from the 1964 Civil Rights Act and the 1972 Equal Employment Opportunity Act, both of which protect employees from discrimination, and from the 1963 Equal Pay Act, which secures equal pay for men and women holding the same jobs. The same congressional exemption applies to the laws covering job discrimination, and even to the Fair Labor Standards Act, which sets minimum wage levels. (The people who are affected by all these exemptions, of course, are not members of Congress themselves but the people they employ, their staffs.) Similarly, while the rest of the country is struggling with the costs and technical difficulties involved in abiding by the Occupational Safety and Health Act, which regulates the work environment, Senate and House members need not be concerned with such matters; their staff members are not covered by the law. In December 1981 Congress passed itself a special tax benefit not available to other Americans (an automatic deduction for expenses *without* need to substantiate them), and added a special protection for its members against IRS audits.[30] In a society more dedicated to playing by the rules, fear of the fury such conduct would unleash would render it unthinkable.

On top of this tradition of distrust of rules, in recent years there has been a vast increase in the number, scope, and complexity of governmental rules, resulting in great difficulties in complying with them.[31]

A major corrective is built into the current agenda of less government in the form of deregulation (*i.e.*, removing many of the existing rules), accompanied by a systematic effort to make few new rules and to rely increasingly on freed individual choices. This approach is necessary, *but not sufficient.* Protecting commitment to the rules, an essential component of civility, also requires that individuals be committed to accept playing by the rules as a matter of faith. (How such a commitment may be instilled is discussed in Chapters 4, 5, and 6.) Such a commitment must be a product not only or even mainly of classes taught in schools or of adult education, but of the comprehensive development of a mentality that, instead of stressing winning above all, evolves and reinforces a commitment to playing by the rules. Such a mentality would see in serious rule violations not a "sporting matter" but a threat to civility and, ultimately, to community.

Take a rather trivial but familiar example. Each football season, millions watching TV regularly see football players, legally tackled, place the ball a foot or so forward from where it was grounded. The referee routinely disregards this infraction but acknowledges that he is aware it occurred by placing the ball back where it belongs. A more educational, rule-supporting course would be, after appropriate warning, to include such cheating in the acts covered by penalties.

A common political game must be stopped: It keeps the laws or mores to please one part of the community, the "do-gooders" or moralists or traditionalists, and allows easy violation to please the other part, those who wish to gamble, smoke marijuana, resort to prostitutes, and so on. In the same vein, rules in general, from speeding and double parking to paying taxes, should be either dropped or more widely enforced. Contemporary American conditions do not reflect an understanding of the completely self-evident fact that every violation disregarded hurts not merely the other side or the victim, but the shared rules themselves, by undermining the commitment to civility that is their ultimate foundation.

THE POLITY: COMMITMENT TO THE PUBLIC REALM

The revolution of entitlements and the rise of single-issue groups, two powerful trends of the seventies, point to the need for an individual who is less ego-centered and at least somewhat more committed to the public realm.

The revolution of entitlements is a concept evolved by the neoconservatives. With the rise of various social groups—especially minorities and women, but also children's advocates, handicapped people, older citizens, and so on—more and more factions came to demand a higher share than the market allotted them, in billions of dollars and in choice jobs—as a matter of right, of entitlement. The market-based allotment was perceived as unjust because past injustices make it impossible for these groups to compete fairly in the marketplace. Thus, if blacks have been disadvantaged for centuries and hence command less education, less skill, and less capital, to offer them equality of opportunity, it was widely argued, will not do, because they cannot compete as equals. Equality of *results* was emphasized, to be attained not in the marketplace but via the political process.

Affirmative Action programs have been a case in point: they measured whether universities, for instance, had equal numbers of men and women, in all departments and in all ranks, without seeking to prove that a less-qualified man was promoted over a more- or equally qualified woman. A surplus of men in any rank or department was considered a sufficient base for demanding redistribution toward equality of results—not opportunity—measured by equal distribution.

The trouble with such a process, neoconservatives pointed out, is not only that instead of rewarding initiative, hard work, and success, it is based on inherent qualities (such as sex and race), but that it is destructive of the economy. When the market allots, it takes from A to give to B; it cannot allot more than the total available. When the polity allots, it often dishes out more allotments than the economy yields, leading to depletion of the underlying, producing assets and to explosive inflation. As Harvard sociologist Daniel Bell observed in the mid-1970s:

> In the past, the claims of different groups could be dealt with by "the market," which meant that the responsibility for any outcome was dispersed. But when the government is the arbiter of claims, the conflicts become explicit and focused. . . . And when the basic allocative power is political rather than economic, there arises a question about restraints. The economic constraint on private wants is the amount of money that a man has, or the credit he is able

to establish. But what are the constraints on political demands?[32]

Another case in point is votes to increase Social Security payouts *without* increasing pay-ins, votes that in accumulation helped push the system to the verge of bankruptcy by the beginning of the eighties. In 1960, for instance, Congress voted to extend disability payments to people under age fifty; in 1965, it voted to extend hospital insurance coverage to all those who turned sixty-five—even if they did not qualify for monthly Social Security benefits.[33] In general, "social security benefit increases became a means by which politicians gratified constituents and sought to elicit their votes."[34]

While the main issue the neoconservatives point to is the use of the polity for allocations, they tend to focus attention on heretofore weak, excluded, disadvantaged groups, which had suffered in the marketplace and sought remedy through political action—minorities, women, the handicapped, senior citizens. However, the same explosive effects are generated by the rise in power of all interest groups, and by the decline of political parties and other mediating structures, such as voluntary associations and neighborhoods.

Single-issue groups are but the latest version of interest groups. Like other interest groups, they have little commitment to shared concerns, but serve to promote the causes or interests of their members. Single-issue groups differ from the age-old interest groups in that they are particularly narrowly focused and particularly adamant and hence difficult to negotiate with in order to create broad-based, community-building compromises. Community-building works best when constituent groups have a variety of interests and shared values on which one can draw in working out a compromise and a shared policy.

A rare, candid "insider's" view of the single-issue groups at work was provided by Oklahoma Congressman Michael L. Synar. Synar told of an amendment, offered for a bill on juvenile justice, that would make it easier to send juvenile offenders to adult jail—without a hearing. To his utter surprise, it passed by an overwhelming majority. When he asked why, he was told the vote would be used in the congressional report card of Christian Voice, a very active conservative religious group. Synar said that "special interests" have become a "dominant force in politics, financially and information-wise," "a petrifying force" with a powerful, intimidating presence in the Capitol. Many of these groups, he said, have an unyielding desire for retribution if he crosses them on the few highly selective issues they care about. For his active support of a fair housing bill, for instance, the real estate lobby marked him as a top target for defeat and flooded his district with anti-Synar mail.[35]

Joseph Califano, who served in two administrations, put it this way:

> Single-issue groups subvert the ability of the political system to compromise, regroup and move forward. If interest groups face off against each other on only one issue, they need not worry about their adversaries tomorrow on another. They tend to see only the horns protruding from their opponents' heads and the halos floating above their own. For leaders and followers of single-interest groups, the past embitters the future; it rarely, if ever, becomes prologue for constructive change.[36]

While the rise of entitlements and of single-issue groups has often been decried, their relevance to the issue at hand needs flagging. The new trouble, caused by the rise of these various kinds of interest groups, is due to the very development that makes their rise so pernicious for community-building: the decline of broad-based political entities, above all the political parties. As long as political parties commanded a substantial following, they served as a vehicle for many segments of the community, with varying perspectives and interests, to work out their differences—within the framework of shared conceptions of the common good. While traditionally the Democrats and Republicans had differing views of what America needed, both were genuinely concerned about the nation, as well as about their members. And once each party had its members in line to support a general policy direction, between them the two parties could work out national policies either in bipartisan coalitions—as they did in support of NATO, for example—or in the give-and-take engendered when one party dominated Congress, the other the White House (*e.g.,* during the Nixon and Ford administrations). While there were often considerable inter-party tensions, in the end national policies were usually worked out.

However, as all institutions and authorities weakened in the sixties and seventies, so did the political parties. Their eroding legitimacy has been reflected in a rising proportion of independent voters, low voter turnout, and an ever more critical attitude toward them. Polls conducted by the University of Michigan's Survey Research Center have charted this trend. In 1960, for instance, 46 percent of the registered voters identified themselves as Democrats; by 1980, the proportion had dropped to 41 percent. In the same two decades, the proportion of registered voters identifying themselves as Republicans decreased from 27 percent to 23 percent. The proportion of registered voters considering themselves independents increased, however, from 23 percent in 1960 to 34 percent in 1980.[37]

Voter participation has steadily decreased since 1960, when 63 percent of the voting-age population voted in a presidential election. In 1964, this participation rate decreased to 62 percent; in 1968, to 61 percent; in 1972, to 56 percent; in 1976, to 54 percent; and in 1980, to 52 percent.[38] From 1960 to 1980 the "party" of non-voters got more votes than either presidential candidate. In 1980, 47.5 percent did not vote, versus 26.8 percent for the GOP and 21.6 percent for the Democrats.[39]

The growing retreat from the party system is reflected in changed attitudes toward the parties and the way elections are conducted. Political scientist Everett Carll Ladd observes:

> The political parties, never especially strong institutions in the U.S., had been weakened further during the 1960s and 1970s. With more formal education and access to more sources of information, voters appeared increasingly to believe that they really didn't need the help of parties as active intermediaries between themselves and individual candidates for office.[40]

The increased use of television advertising by candidates and the growth of primaries and caucuses, often removed from party control, further decreased the parties' importance in elections. This in turn affected the kind of candidates who run, according to Brookings Institution scholar James Sundquist:

> Because these new candidates did not rise through disciplined organizations . . . they are individualists from the

beginning of their political careers. As candidates, they were self-selected, self-organized, self-propelled, self-reliant.[41]

The increased use of television has had a corresponding effect on the voters. As Walter Dean Burnham observes, voters are "no longer bound to party through the time-honored links of patronage and the machine," so politics has become "an indoor sport involving a host of discrete players rather than the teams of old."[42]

This retreat from political identification, participation, and involvement opened the way for interest groups, the undigested, uncontained, raw stuff of politics. The weakened political parties have often been unable to either "process" or countervail these groups.

A vivid example of the role interest groups play occurred in mid-1981 as President Reagan was pushing his economic recovery program through the House of Representatives. The media, which love a good fight, portrayed the issue as a struggle between Reagan and the Republican program on one side, and, on the other, the Democrats, headed by Speaker Tip O'Neill, Budget Committee Chairman Jim Jones, and Ways and Means Committee Chairman Dan Rostenkowski. Reagan was declared the winner when his tax bill passed by 238–195 in the House and 89–11 in the Senate. In the headlines, this was more than just a legislative victory: "Reagan's revolution rolls on" (*The Economist*), "Reagan Caps His Revolution with the Country's Largest Tax Cut" (*Time*) and "Reagan Sees 'New Renaissance' in Tax Bill" (*Washington Post*). By early fall 1981, columnists Rowland Evans and Robert Novak had released a book called *The Reagan Revolution.*[43]

Actually, both sides lost to the interest groups. The positions both Republicans and Democrats started with were modified not so much in response to each other's positions as to please interest groups, which in turn were represented by one or a few congressmen (for whose votes both sides were fighting). Nobody had a better vantage point to describe this situation than David Stockman. "The tax lobbyists . . . mobilized the business community, the influential economic sectors from oil to real estate. In a matter of days they created the political environment in which they flourish best—a bidding war between the two parties."[44] Thus, Congress wrote into the tax bill concessions to sugar farmers, savings and loan institutions, and oil companies, to name a few.

The total of concessions to the interest groups exceeded any difference that existed between the Republican and the original Democratic bills. For instance, at a critical juncture, Democrats favored a 15 percent tax cut in personal income tax over two years while Republicans favored 25 percent over three years, an estimated difference in revenues of $86 billion through 1986.[45] But the concession to oil producers alone was $11.6 billion.[46] Changes in leasing provisions that made it possible for firms to sell unused tax breaks were estimated to cost about $27 billion by 1986. Farmers and small businessmen sought and won changes in the estate and gift taxes which cost $15.3 billion. AT&T got an extra that could be worth $14 billion in the next decade.[47] All in all, concessions to various groups and congressional voting blocs added $177 billion dollars to the cost of the president's tax bill.[48] Indeed, soon after the Reagan "revolutionary victory," the bond market slumped; the Reagan administration was forced to change its course (*e.g.*, agree to water down its commitments to defense spending and against new taxes) because the tax cut that the interest groups had rung up, as well as loss of tax revenue and rising social costs due to the recession, resulted in a deficit much higher than the financial markets could tolerate or than the Reagan administration had planned.

In short, the revolution of entitlements, the rise of single-issue groups, and the further intensification of interest groups, combined with the decline of the political parties, created a growing political imbalance. In each polity, there are centripetal forces that work to preserve the community and the public interest and centrifugal forces that work to undo them. In the United States, the balance of these forces has been tilting away from community, reflecting in the polity a growing measure of the retreat from society we have already studied in the realm of beliefs and feelings, of mentality.

RECONSTRUCTION

A balance can be restored by higher mobilization of individuals into the public realm, political parties, and public interest groups, and the building of coalitions by these groups. While this sounds quite elementary, behind this statement is a whole theory of political action. As commonly understood and frequently taught, democratic theory rests on the notion that since each citizen has a vote, citizens who are dissatisfied with the way the government is run can vote out those who do not heed their wishes and elect those who do. Indeed, during the sixties, when many young Americans complained about U.S. involvement in Vietnam and other acts they did not care for, the frequent answer was "Don't take to the streets, take to the ballot boxes."

In practice democracies do not work that simply. The single most important reason is that thousands of decisions are made between elections, decisions that deeply shape the life of the country. Merely casting one vote once every two or four years does not suffice to keep the public interest at the fore between elections. Most decisions between elections are made by what has been called the "unholy alliance" of federal agencies in charge of a specific area (such as health or agriculture or energy), the relevant congressional subcommittees, and the interest groups. For these decisions not to ignore the public interest—or, to put it more mildly, for those few elected representatives who are involved to be supported in their representation of the public interest and to be discouraged from bending in the direction of the ever-present interest groups—the public needs to be mobilized.

How is this achieved? By political parties and public action groups countervailing the interest groups. When the Civil Rights Act of 1964 was advanced in Congress, the Americans for Democratic Action organized a coalition of thirty-four liberal groups, white and black, labor unions and students, to promote the act. When laws concerning drug testing are drafted, consumer groups must actively participate if the legislation is not to reflect first and foremost the viewpoints of the drug manufacturers. Similarly, environmentalists need to balance the oil companies, steelmakers, and copper producers.

The public action groups in turn gain their political energy from the contributions, voluntary work, and support of thousands of citizens who donate some portion of their time, resources, and psychic energy to one or more "substantive areas of concern." They must give more than an occasional vote for public interest to prevail.

Take, for instance, gun control. At issue here is not what policy is correct, but an illustration of how the American polity works and might work. As early as 1938, reports Gallup, the majority of Americans polled favored stricter handgun control.[49] A 1974 Gallup survey reported that 72 percent of those polled favored stricter laws requiring registration of firearms, while 28 percent opposed them; in 1975 it was 67 percent to 27 percent.[50] But the gun lobby, led by the National Rifle Association, has blocked all such measures even after the shootings of the Kennedys, King, Reagan, and the Pope. Several factors have been at work, but they come down to the fact that NRA members have been willing to generate much more political energy (in monies, votes, letter-writing) to block gun control than those who favored it have been in working for its passage.

One may say this cannot be helped; those who favor gun control simply do not "feel" as strongly about it as those who oppose it. In social science terms, for them gun control is not as salient and mobilizing an issue. But it *need* not be equally salient for those who favor gun control to prevail, as there are almost three Americans in favor for every one opposed. If the three were each committed to gun control only a third as strongly as those opposed to it are committed to stopping it, the majority would prevail. If those who favor gun control realize they need only increase *somewhat* their commitment to the public realm, they will find it easier to mobilize themselves and each other than if they feel they need to match "those fanatics."

The same holds for other issues. Inflation has greatly troubled Americans in recent years. In 1979, for example, over half of Americans said they were willing to cut back their standard of living and quality of life to fight inflation.[51] Indeed, for quite a few years, inflation ranked as the number one domestic issue. At the same time, interest groups have been pushing the price of sugar, milk, beef, steel way above their market levels. Americans' concern to reduce inflation was not effectively mobilized to countervail these groups, which had a field day until 1981, when their sway was lessened a bit.

A graphic example is the sugar producers' efforts to raise domestic sugar prices above free-market levels. The approximately twelve thousand sugar beet and two thousand sugarcane growers in the United States comprise only about 1 percent of the nation's farmers, yet their political influence has been disproportionately large.[52] During the 1981 bargaining for votes to support the Reagan administration's budget cuts, the sugar growers again won administration support for sugar price supports, a program its opponents—initially including the administration—said would add an additional $2 billion to consumers' sugar bills in 1982, and an estimated $5 billion by 1985.[53]

The 1981 victory for the sugar lobby was only the latest in a long series of support measures the industry has gained since the 1930s.

Both the Jones-Costigan Sugar Act of 1934 and the Sugar Act of 1948, which superseded it, protected domestic growers through import quotas. In 1974, after this legislation expired without being replaced, sugar prices fell as imports rose. The sugar growers wasted no time in pressuring Congress for new legislation protecting domestic sugar— and raising prices.

Moreover, the sugar growers gain their cut in the form most suited to their taste. The growers rejected the Carter administration's proposals for fewer import restrictions coupled with direct subsidies to the farmers. Instead, they won a complicated "price-support loan program," which gave the appearance of supporting free enterprise more than an outright subsidy program would have. Under this program, the federal government agreed to grant the growers loans and accept their sugar crop as collateral while farmers waited for the price of sugar to rise to an agreed-upon level. If sugar reached this price, the farmers could reclaim their crop, sell it, and repay the loan; if not, they could forfeit their crop and keep the loan monies. The "loan" was therefore not a loan in the commonly understood sense, but a guaranteed price to the growers. In 1978, the first year of the program, the federal government made sugar price-support loans totaling almost half a billion dollars. In addition, the federal government covered the costs of storing all that sugar, which it was unable to sell and much of which went bad, since it is not suitable for long-term storage.[54]

Consumers also paid for the loan guarantees, since the price level was set substantially higher than the free-market price; although the difference per pound was only a matter of pennies, it was estimated that in 1979, each one-cent increase in the price of a pound of raw sugar raised the nation's annual sugar bill by $224 million.[55] By the time the sugar provisions of the 1981 tax bill were being debated, this estimate was $300 million.[56]

Similar gains have been exacted by other interest groups at the expense of consumers. The dairy lobby, which Common Cause has identified as one of the most generous contributors to congressional campaigns, has worked to sustain a thirty-year-old price support system for dairy farmers similar to that for sugar growers. Under its provisions, the federal government establishes a price-support level for milk products in April and October of each year. The price support in fact acts as a floor for milk prices, because any farmer who thinks market prices are too low can sell to the government at the price-support level. The system encourages excess milk production; in 1980, for instance, milk production was at an all-time high, even though consumption had decreased.[57] Although the dairy lobby ran into some opposition in 1981, when the Reagan administration and Congress acted to reduce support prices, excess production was still expected to force the government to buy approximately 10 percent of all milk products in the United States in 1981. It has been estimated that dairy price supports cost the government $250,000 an hour.[58]

Many other examples of interest groups'winning sizable, highly inflationary concessions from the federal government could be listed in industries other than food producers. In 1978, for instance, the federal government established trigger prices for foreign steel—minimum prices for imports to provide a measure of protection for domestic steel producers. Although there is some disagreement about the economic effect of particular mechanisms, the cumulative impact of such policies is clear. As Brookings economist Robert Crandall notes,

> Steel import protection is only one example of an unfortunate trend. Textiles, shoes, television sets, meat, and even nails are protected in a similar manner. The sum of the price effects from all such policies could well have accounted for a large part of the recent acceleration in the inflation rate.[59]

In short, I maintain that inflation is not caused merely by the government's printing too much money, but also by interest groups' pushing up many prices *by political means.* And large proportions of the money the government prints go not merely to welfare, Medicaid, and other social programs, but into the pockets of these special-interest groups.

If the public must take on all these groups, from gun lobbies to milk, from steel to the bank lobby, when will citizens have time to do anything else? The answer lies in part in rotating the focus of the public's power, in part in building up credibility and hence a deterrent power. The public need not be at all times on its toes, watching all lobbies. The sugar program comes up at most a few times a year; so do subsidies (by whatever name) for the makers of shoes, steel, autos, and the rest. Moreover, the public could support general provisions against subsidies, against limiting imports ("for free trade"), against corporate bailouts. True, the interest groups will seek new ways to get their hands into the public till, but these take time to evolve and promote. Then the public—prodded by the press and public action groups—will need, on occasion, to act again.

Above all, once it becomes clear that the public will not brook such gross violation of the commons, elected representatives will be less inclined to bend, and interest groups more ready to relent, than they are now. We might even see a revival of the political parties, which would look after generalized issues, including the integrity of Congress and limitations on interest groups, and thus free the voters in part from the need to be constantly on guard.

However, all said and done, citizens will have to become less private, more public, more actively committed and involved in the shared concerns of the community, or there will not be sufficient public energy to contain, roll back, and deter the interest groups. True, this would require some diminution of private pursuits, but plenty of room would be left for those. And, it cannot be stressed enough, public action is not sheer labor; it too generates satisfaction.

John W. Gardner provided a keen analysis of both the problem and the solution in a major address at Brown University. The reality of stalemated government, he said, belies the old notion that a plurality of interest groups would work itself into a balanced system, without any effort, by "something like Adam Smith's 'invisible hand' [to] ensure a good result in the free market of competing interests." He painted a vivid picture of the work of interest groups:

> Imagine a checkerplayer confronted by a bystander who puts a thumb on one checker and says "Go ahead and play, just don't touch this one," and then another bystander puts a thumb on another checker with the same warning, and then another bystander and another. The owners of the thumbs—the interest groups—don't want to make the game unwinnable. They just don't want you to touch their particular checker.[60]

Transferring decision-making to the local level helps little, Gardner added, because there we encounter the same interest groups merely playing out their role on a different stage.

Most important, Gardner called attention to the role the American people must play in the solution. "No community or nation can survive without some willingness on the part of subgroups to see their self-interest and their future as indissolubly linked to that of the larger group."[61] It is necessary to keep one eye on the shared condition, future, and fate while the other is looking out for one's own gain. I would add that in addition to the proper perspective, citizens must provide energy, the political equivalent of muscle power.

In the public arena, policies evolve and advance or are blocked according to a vectorgram of power. Power is reflected in ability to mobilize votes, funds, volunteers, and ability to capture the public's imagination and mind. The rise of interest groups and the decline of political parties have made it easier not only to block policies than to advance them, but also to heed special concerns and neglect shared ones. The question is where the balancing power, the vector favoring shared concerns, is going to come from. One answer lies in an unspoken agreement (or changed perspective) among the interest groups to play with one hand tied behind their backs, not to go for all they can, in order to maintain and preserve the shared concerns. This occurs, for instance, when labor unions are asked to act with restraint in order to avoid runaway inflation, and they, in return, expect business groups not to lavish dividends on stockholders, and "options" and other perks on executives.

A second answer lies in revitalization of the political parties, together with other American institutions. David Cohen, a former president of Common Cause, suggests several reforms for that purpose. First, he recommends that party agendas "identify specific priorities and commitments, rather than serve as a collection of interest-group wish lists," and that officeholders and party officials be held accountable for supporting the party's agenda. Second, he suggests that some of the campaign-financing reforms instituted in the early 1970s be changed to enable the parties to fund their own activities and to have a larger role in funding their chosen presidential candidates. Third, Cohen recommends that political parties provide more services to their supporters, such as publishing officeholders' voting records, which would, among other things, "help to counterbalance the myriad of narrower voting records published by a variety of interest groups." Fourth, he proposes that at least four times a year, political parties be provided with free air time on radio and television to present their views on issues. Fifth, to discourage crossover voting, he advocates allowing only party registrants to vote in presidential primaries.[62]

These changes would probably work best if they were combined with others. For instance, Congress could be made much more resistant to interest groups if representatives ran for election every four years instead of every two, if elections were publicly financed, and if candidates were prohibited from accepting funds from any private sources, including campaign contributions and lecture fees, now allowed.

But above all, there is great power in the large number of "disinterested" individuals—the public. If they would both somewhat increase their attention to public matters and act on these concerns, there would be sufficient power to curb the interest groups and to support those who act in behalf of shared concerns.

There are scores of avenues to this enhanced citizenship. It begins with following more news, attending somewhat more public meetings, making somewhat higher contributions to public action groups and political parties, voting more regularly. For many, it might be best also to follow one or two policy areas closely, whether education or energy or health policy (not merely a specific issue, such as prayers in schools or a solar bank). This allows greater command of the issues one acts on, and in addition it is often the best way to learn how public affairs work in general and how to be effective.

Active (not activist) citizens would soon have a deterrent effect on interest groups and on elected representatives, who would be forced to stop the most flagrant violations of public interest. This effect in turn would allow public attention to focus on additional, less pivotal, matters.

At the same time, the public must develop an eye to separate major and secondary issues from trivia. We tend to move from disregarding public life to seeing a scandal every time a public servant uses his official car to drive to the supermarket. When Joseph Califano was Secretary of HEW, with a budget of roughly $147 billion,[63] more fuss was made, for instance, about his hiring a chef to cook his meals at HEW than over the fact that having promised to cut out $6.5 billion his own inspector general had reported lost to fraud and abuse,[64] Califano in effect cut very little and instead eased out the inspector.

The danger of preoccupation with trivia is double: (1) it deflects public power from where it could accomplish much more, and (2) it soon exhausts itself, as there are very few who never transgress in minor matters.

There is no easy way to define where major and secondary issues end and trivia start (especially as a purist can see ethical significance in items of both categories). One guideline that might help is to treat as of lesser importance all matters that are readily recognized as not important *in themselves* but made important by attributing symbolic significance to them. To start with the Califano example, the chef is not important in himself; people are concerned about what he stands for, symbolizes. In contrast, a saving of $6.5 billion is important in itself, apart from whatever symbolism may be attached to it.

Americans are keenly aware of public images and symbols, played up by the media; often they find it easier to deal with symbols than with substance. The sociological fact nevertheless is that often the preoccupation with looking right comes not on top of acting right and being right, but *instead* of acting right. Hence, for the public to look behind symbolism to what is actually achieved (or neglected) is an antidote to excessive PR and will go a long way to focus attention on substantive issues.

In short, if individuals somewhat increase their commitment to the public realm; if increased mobilization is accomplished, with some issue specialization; if it is focused on major and secondary matters rather than entangled with trivia, it will not be long before the shared concerns will be energized.

INVOLVEMENT IN COMMONWEAL ISSUES

We are all prisoners of the language we speak and think in. A contrast we constantly use is that of "private sector" and "public sector." Two social scientists, Joseph Bensman and Robert Lilienfeld, observed recently: "We usually tend to think of the 'public' versus the 'private' in economic terms, as in public or private ownership. In political terms, 'public' means the government, and 'private' means the individual."[65] If indeed this were the limit of our options, private (market or individual) versus public (government), those shared needs that cannot rely on aggregation of private actions would indeed compel a large government sector. Fortunately the world is not a simple dichotomy; there is a large sector that is public but not governmental: public service by individuals, institutions, and corporations. It is hence possible to reduce the government sector without neglecting shared concerns so long as the nongovernmental public realm is appropriately expanded.

What are these shared concerns? And what is this public nongovernmental realm? The argument against *laissez-faire* conservatism usually starts with national security. "Everyone" can see it is a matter not to be left in private hands. No serious person objects to the idea that as long as security requires nuclear armaments, these should not be in private hands.

Once granted that for some shared concerns the government is the best agent, the typical pro-public argument proceeds like the often-told tale of Bernard Shaw's encounter with a beautiful woman. He asked if she would spend the night with him for a million pounds, a thought she was willing to entertain. When he then asked if she'd consent for a five-pound note, she answered, clearly miffed: "What do you think I am?" Shaw is said to have retorted: "We've already answered *that* question; now we're just haggling about the price."

Once granted that there is a need for a public sector, in violation of the purist *laissez-faire* position, advocates of the public sector are quick to produce a much longer list of tasks the government is best suited for or "must" attend to. These include:

1. The monetary system, issuance of currency and its control. A modern economy, it is said, can barely function if every bank is free to issue its own currency and free to disregard the commitment to maintain its value. The United States tried that in the mid-nineteenth century, and the demand for government controls was overwhelming.

2. Free-market competition, it has been argued many times, needs protection from foreign and domestic monopolies. That is, even if one fully recognizes the virtues of free competition, it seems unable to protect itself from the use of power concentrations to maintain an unfair, disproportional, even dominant market position, undermining the free market. Thus, the free market is said ultimately to rest on the protection of the government.

3. Freedom of choice, advocates of the government remind us, is based on informed individuals. But the information needed for rational choice is often not provided by industry; hence the need for the government to secure it. A case in point is the content of

foods. Unless the government requires listing of additives, from sugar to colors, the consumer is unable to choose the foods desired. After all, not every shopper can drive to the supermarket with a van full of mice and start food testing before buying ice cream (for toxic dyes), bread (for excessive iron), cheese (for additives), and so on.

4. There are areas, such as basic research, in which the profit is remote and elusive. Still, a strong economy, health, and science are said to require investment in them. Hence, it is said, government must undertake responsibility for funding basic research. Explains Senator Harrison Schmitt, chairman of the Subcommittee on Science, Technology, and Space:

> Government must fund those costly research and develop-   '
> ment programs, such as in nuclear fusion, space, defense,
> and global environment, which are obviously necessary but
> far beyond the risk-taking potential of the private sector
> under any foreseeable economic and regulatory conditions.[66]

While the editors of *Business Week* believe external factors have discouraged the private sector from funding basic research, they admit that private funding of such research has been a pittance:

> Inflation, shortsighted management, and government reg-
> ulation have conspired to spur companies to put their money
> into short-term applied research projects rather than explor-
> ing basic science, which could open up new possibilities.
> Between 1960 and 1974, industry cut its share of basic re-
> search funding in half, to 4 percent from 8 percent of its
> R&D spending, where it has remained since.[67]

5. Private firms and individuals, in their pursuit of gain, disregard "externalities," as the environmentalists have stressed in recent years. Externalities are

> the effects of a firm's actions, or an agency's or a person's,
> that are beyond and outside—"external to"—the firm's ac-
> counting or the agency's perview or the person's interests
> and concerns, but within the accounting, the purview, or
> the interest of somebody else.[68]

Diseases caused or aggravated by air pollution are an example of externalities, which the environmentalists say private firms do not take into account sufficiently in making production decisions.

The only way to force private firms to mitigate these externalities is government intervention, say its advocates. According to Peter Drucker:

> What was an "externality" for which the general public paid becomes business cost. It therefore becomes a competitive disadvantage unless everybody in the industry accepts the same rule. And this, in most cases, can be done only by regulation—that means by some form of public action.[69]

6. Equity, social justice, attention to the vulnerable members of society, culture, art are all social "goods" that, it is often said, require government support, as the marketplace will not provide for them on its own.

Other lists have been drawn up, but the point is the same: the marketplace, the uncoordinated, catch-as-catch-can individualism built into private decision-making and market "coordination," is said not to be a reliable basis for ministering to these shared concerns. So goes the age-old debate on free enterprise and individualism versus government supplements and antidotes.

As this debate intensified in recent years, it evolved the following features:

1. The government list of shared concerns was extended, enlarged, and elaborated beyond all those listed above to encompass practically all personal habits, from smoking to dieting, from attitudes toward gays to interracial relations. Scores of other common goals were added, from beautification of highways to teaching children how to brush their teeth. This confused the issue, because critics of the government role easily found marks of excessive penetration and intervention, which they used to condemn the role of government *in general.*

2. Many of these additions were nowhere near so firmly based on an evolving consensus as the government's security role. Large

groups of Americans opposed these expanded government roles. Busing for the purpose of racial integration is one example. A Gallup poll in 1974 found that a clear majority of those questioned—65 percent—were opposed to the busing of schoolchildren.[70] In general, the proportion of Americans who feel the government is too powerful rose from 44 percent in 1964 to 69 percent in 1976.[71] Big government replaced big business and big labor as the number one public enemy. And the proportion of Americans who thought they could trust the federal government to do what is right "always" or "most of the time" declined continuously from 76 percent in 1964 to 32 percent by 1974.[72]

3. Once the government had taken on numerous additional missions, some highly complicated, it became apparent that many were particularly unsuited for government action. Often because of insufficient resources, the government failure rate was very high, further undermining its general credibility. As Everett Carll Ladd, Jr., director of the Social Science Data Center at the University of Connecticut, summed up in 1978:

> Not since the days of the Great Depression have Americans been so complaining or skeptical about the quality and character of their country's public performance. . . . Confidence that government can accomplish those things the people want done has declined over the past fifteen years to a point lower than at any time in the modern era.[73]

4. Methods and tools of accountability lagged, leaving a wide trail of abuse and corruption, which further eroded tolerance for the role of government as an agent of shared concerns.

All these combined to generate a societal tidal wave of reaction against "the public sector," sweeping all in its path, rather than focusing on excessive governmental goals, less consequential programs, and wasteful or corrupt ways of doing business. Most important from our viewpoint, this reaction, in summarily upholding the private approach instead of the public, not only overlooked the question of the proper division of labor between the private sector and the government (few really expect to close government down), but disregarded the nongovernmental public sector—the public role of individuals, corporations, and institutions. As this reaction swept the country in the late seventies and early eighties, no systematic answer was given to the question: If the government is to be rolled back from area after area, what will take its place?

True, part of the answer is—nobody. Thus, the government has on occasion supported third-rate cultural festivals, either because some bureaucrats could not tell quality from trash, or because interest groups, working through congressional committees, influenced the allocation of funds. If government support for such projects is eliminated, they do not have to be supported by someone, somehow.

Moreover, quite a few "good" government-financed activities may be deemed too costly once they are considered not in terms of desirable versus undesirable, but in terms of costs versus benefits, or the costs of this goal versus others. To take an extreme example, the Occupational Safety and Health Administration (OSHA) has tried to limit workers' exposure to benzene, a common industrial chemical that may cause leukemia. Richard Wilson, a Harvard physicist, has estimated that a full ban on benzene would prevent one leukemia death every two or three years—at a cost of $500 million annually.[74]

But what about the "rest"? A closer look suggests that many items on the government agenda can be turned over to individuals, institutions, and corporations, but only if *a change of attitude and ways of doing business* makes them somewhat less private, somewhat more involved with the commonweal and less inclined to act on the notion that whatever is good for the individual or the private institution is good for America.

I focus here on the change in orientation individuals have to undergo. The role of institutions and corporations is discussed separately in later chapters. Changes in institutions and corporate management are taken into account here only to the extent that modified individual orientation has to build directly on such changes.

To make clear the required modification in personal orientation, I briefly suggest several examples, not to explore any of them in their own right, but to illustrate the general point. For example, if we are to rely less on government-financed nursing homes, mental hospitals, programs for the handicapped, and student loans, family members will more often have to take care of one another. This requires both greater family-based mutuality and greater financial commitments to such purposes.

One might say that it is all very well to expect the rich to help their kin who are in need; they can always hire a nurse or a tutor, or have one spouse stay home. The poor, however, can ill afford such additional commitments. Granted, the level of affluence definitely affects the ease with which people can help each other, and in this sense less government is particularly hard on the poor. But the fact is that in the past, minorities, which tend to be much less well off than the white majority, have much more often taken care of "their own" than have the more affluent. Blacks and Hispanic Americans, for example, are much less likely to commit their elders to nursing homes than white folks are. And generations of immigrants, typically less well off than those already settled, more often helped their kin with loans and solace.

The issue becomes clearest when one focuses not on the poorest or the richest, but on the mass of people in between. They all have a measure of choice as to how they commit their resources: replace a car earlier, buy more fashionable clothes, take a trip to Europe— or spend more money, time, and energy on their kin.

One must further note that the investment is rarely simply a net loss for ego. If grandparents are integrated in the home, they often ease the problems of child care. And, as has often been pointed out, grandchildren and grandparents tend to be psychologically beneficial for each other. Similarly, loans to, say, a sister, an uncle, or a child at college are often implicitly associated with a return of support when one is in need oneself.

What a person does is in part a question of means; the more one commands, the easier it is to take care of the more vulnerable family members. But it is also in part a question of orientation, which is what concerns me here. People who are quite affluent but do not see themselves as having to shoulder these "social" duties will not do so; and those less well off but appropriately committed will do much more with love and whatever resources they have.

To make this general case, for the association between less government and the need for more social services by individuals, is not to question that some persons require care in public institutions. *E.g.* there are disturbed persons who are violent and who need to be restrained. But study upon study has shown that they are but a fraction of the persons in state run institutions. Many are there because their families have learned to rely on the government for care rather than make a personal or financial sacrifice. Similarly, it's easier to turn to a bank loan, at government-subsidized rates, to pay a student's college fees, than for the family to pool its resources or expect the student later to "repay" his parents, by supporting them in their old age or paying the college costs of a sibling. But this attitude contributes to both the swelling of the government and the decline of the family.

Some might object that while doing social services via the government reallocates wealth among classes and races, attending to these matters within the family, neighborhood, or voluntary association does not serve such reallocation. However, it is this reallocative thrust that has generated a good part of the backlash against the government. In other words, the suggestion that the family and other social groupings attend to more social needs is not a *cause* of less willingness to support government reallocation but a *result* of its loss in legitimation.

The needed change in individual orientation is in part a matter of mentality, of what is considered legitimate and satisfying behavior, but it is also affected by institutional and corporate arrangements. As the majority of both men and women now work outside the home, there is less time and psychic energy for children, elders, the mentally disturbed, or the handicapped. Part of the answer lies in more flexible work patterns, allowing employed family members more leeway— flexi-time, part-time positions, and shared jobs. All are aimed at freeing some time and energy for the home without requiring family members to give up gainful work, which most cannot afford and many do not wish to do. While it is true that these arrangements are occasionally subsidized by corporations, this is neither typical nor necessary. On the contrary, in many situations these patterns repay corporations with a more satisfied and productive labor force. Although some studies show that more satisfied people do not necessarily work harder, there are also data indicating that they are more punctual and less often absent, characteristics that also contribute to productive capacity.

Although the examples of greater individual involvement in commonweal issues discussed so far are focused on the closest circle of mutuality, the family, and on the so-called human services, the same point applies to other circles and other issues. Take public safety. At first blush, if there is a justified government mission it is police work. But here, too, government excesses, waste, and corruption abound, and there is room for some government rollback—if individuals are more involved in the commonweal. Already the need for police is reduced by the hundreds of thousands of private guards hired by neighborhoods and housing developments. In addition, many neighborhoods have formed voluntary neighborhood patrols, which do quite well to reduce the police load, as long as they stick to their policing mission and do not turn into vigilantes or morals squads.

If people are willing to invest more time, energy, and money in becoming informed, the need for government to regulate consumer products will decline. Thus, instead of the government's requiring more and more information on every label, the public could obtain this information, at somewhat greater effort, from central posting points in the shop (showing, for example, ingredients), or from looseleaf books (available in drugstores to replace package inserts). More tests by privately funded organizations (such as Consumers Union, with a recent subscription price of fourteen dollars a year) could substitute for some of the tests now conducted by federal agencies.

Well, the pro-government argument goes, but this assumes government-*required* release of information by the corporations. Yes and no. Even those who favor less government may agree that there is room for some such requirement. At the same time there are many less onerous and costly ways to make information available. Consumers Union already tests products on its own—whether their producers like it or not. Thus, for example, if each auto buyer interested in information would pay Consumers Union, say, fifty dollars, it could crash-test quite a few autos, and the information would become available without any government requirement.

In short, both sides to the debate of government versus unbridled individuals have missed a vital point. The position that the government is the best custodian of shared concerns has been vastly oversold and overextended, and it has backfired. The *laissez-faire* notion that individualism can replace it all overlooks the need for individual commitment to shared concerns. This commitment has three facets: individual commitment to play by the rules (existing or modified); a willingness to dedicate some of self to the public arena, without which the public interest will be left without the necessary political energy; and a commitment to a measure of service to one another, without which essential human needs will not be served, soon promoting again the quest for more government. Together, the three-faceted commitment makes for civility. A review of the contemporary American condition suggests that the individual foundations of civility have deteriorated, which in turn, we have seen, points to the ways and direction reconstruction is to proceed.

CHAPTER FOUR
The Triple Role of Institutions

THE INSTITUTIONAL MISSIONS

Social institutions—the family, the school, neighborhoods, voluntary associations—serve to countervail excessive individualism, to sustain mutuality and civility in three ways:

1. They stand between the individual and the government, protecting each from the other.
2. They set patterns and make arrangements that discharge at least some of the tasks that otherwise are loaded on the government or overwhelm individuals.
3. They "educate" individuals. They introduce and reinforce a mentality that sustains individuals' mutual and civil commitments.

By "social institutions" I mean the significant, persistent elements in the life of a society or culture that center on a fundamental human need, activity, or value. They may be local (such as a block association or a local community) or nationwide (such as many voluntary associations). This meaning of "institution" is broader than another frequently used, when a particular prison or college is called "an institution." My use emphasizes that an institution is not simply a set of buildings or even a group of people; it is part of the encompassing structure of the community.

THE DETERIORATED STATE OF
THE INSTITUTIONS

Over the last decades the foundations of all American institutions have eroded, and the institutions have, in varying degrees, deteriorated and become hollow (although certainly they have not collapsed). Hence, their ability to fulfill their roles has been diminished.

Some may cheer this development as preparing the ground for radical societal change that will lead from destruction of the existing society to a brave new world. They must recognize that in America, institutional deterioration has not led to collapse, and newly created alternative institutions, from communes to free clinics and alternative schools, have fared much worse than the old, tattered ones. While people may disagree as to how well these alternative institutions (and those who build and rely upon them) function, there can be no disagreement that they tend to come and go at such a rapid pace, and serve such a tiny portion of the population, that at least so far they have provided precious little "alternative" to the prevailing community structure. Those who argue that these are but forerunners and testing grounds for bigger and better alternative structures to come must note that, so far as statistics are available, alternative institutions, far from catching on, are on the decline. And, as sociologist S. M. Lipset has pointed out, they tend to thrive in highly atypical circumstances, for instance at the margin of university campuses such as Berkeley or the University of Chicago, or in neighborhoods such as Greenwich Village in New York City.[1] Hence, in the American situation, the prospect is not radical change but reconstruction in both senses: returning to old structures, and rebuilding, modifying, and changing them in the process.

However one views the alternative structures, by the early eighties erosion was the prevalent state of the family as traditionally understood. Numerous schools are not working at all, while many others function rather poorly.[2] The typical institutions of the urban neighborhood used to be the church, the labor union, and the political party. Church attendance has declined gradually but almost continuously since 1955.[3] The influence that people report religion has on their lives has fallen much more sharply.[4] While interest in religion is still keen, even reviving a bit most recently, much of it is invested in charismatic movements, not churches, although some of the revival spills back into them. Labor unions are on the decline. The proportion of the nonagricultural labor force belonging to unions decreased from one third in the late 1950s to one fifth by the end of the 1970s. In early 1982, according to a *Washington Post*/ABC News poll, 57 percent of those interviewed agreed that "labor union leaders are out of touch with the workers they represent."[5]

Despite increased efforts and expenditures to enlist new members, as the eighties began unions were winning only about 45 percent of the representation elections conducted by the National Labor Relations Board, compared to 60 percent in 1965.[6] Instead of gaining more and more benefits for their members, labor unions find themselves negotiating "givebacks" in the form of reduced benefits or even wage cuts, to protect jobs in industry (Chrysler), newspapers (the *Philadelphia Bulletin*), and local government (New York City). With increasing frequency, labor unions find that the political candidates they endorse, their members pass by, further undermining the unions' political power. We have already seen the deteriorated state of the political parties.

A significant body of data collected by public opinion studies is relevant here. The Louis Harris polling organization has periodically asked a random sample of Americans how much they trust the leadership of various American institutions. By implication, the answers indicate the legitimacy of the institutions themselves. (You can hardly have great confidence in an institution headed by people you do not trust.) While the questions have varied somewhat, since 1966 each survey has included nine major institutions: TV news, medicine, the military, the press, organized religion, major companies, Congress, the Executive Branch, and organized labor. In 1966, 43 percent of Americans expressed a great deal of confidence, on the average, in the leadership of these institutions. In the following years the proportion indicating great confidence dropped, reaching a low of 20 percent in 1976 and remaining below 30 percent until the end of the decade. It was 23 percent in 1979.[7] (Typical of the ambivalence of the public's feelings the proportion reporting "no confidence" rose only slightly, from 12 percent in 1966 to 19 percent in 1975 and 1976; the important change was the increase in those who had "some confidence" instead of "a great deal."[8])

Other evidence corroborating the fall in legitimation of American institutions draws on a completely different set of public-opinion questions. It finds a quite similar rise in the level of alienation or lack of legitimation. Surveys have repeatedly asked people the same questions concerning their feelings about being in America. For example, whether or not they feel "left out of things"; or that what they think "doesn't count very much anymore"; or that "the rich get richer and the poor get poorer." According to an index based on these questions, the proportion who feel alienated rose from 29 percent in 1966 to 59 percent in 1974, and since then has remained quite high, reaching 62 percent in 1980.[9]

Institutions that are seen as neither legitimate nor effective do not and cannot discharge their triple role. I hold that because in the longer run these missions must be carried out if mutuality and civility are to be sustained, a period of institutional reconstruction is now needed. While the following discussion of these three roles of social institutions is necessarily somewhat abstract, as I deal with cross-institutional concepts, it will lead directly to a more concrete examination of the family, schools, and corporations.

THE MEDIATING ROLE

The mediating role of institutions is typically discussed as a matter for totalitarian societies to worry about, one pluralistic societies such as ours avoid by their very nature. However, it is my thesis that America recently came to experience a *mild* case of decline in this role of institutions, and the attending consequences.

The mediating role of institutions, like most social business, is best seen in historical and comparative perspective. Historically, the nation-state arose in Europe as a countervailing and liberating force, releasing individuals from the bondage of serfdom on feudal estates dominated by local lords. The nation-state penetrated these local communities and introduced the notion of the legal equality of all individuals (or "citizens"), where previously lords and a minority of free people had not only practical but also legal superiority over the serf majority. Thus, the representatives of the rising state voided old standards, such as the medieval notion that killing a free person was a much more serious crime than killing a serf, which was regarded as akin to property damage. Legally, all persons were to be treated equally.

What is less often emphasized is that in the process of building the nation-state, where there had been only scattered local lordships, the state undermined the power of the local communities and their lords and established its own power and jurisdiction. Historically, this reduction of local autonomy, this accumulation of central power, which in the contemporary context sounds antilibertarian, was the foundation on which liberties and equality before the law were built. Without some diminution of local power, there was no national power, no shared community, no nationwide legality. That is, in the context of the late Middle Ages and the original nation-building, a *measure* of statism, enlarging the power of the central government, was compatible with building up the individual and his autonomy within the local community.

However, as the state's power rose and the decline of local power accelerated, intellectuals, typically leaning into the historical winds of their times, raised the fear that the state's amassment of power would advance beyond what was needed to shore up individuals and would *level* rather than balance local power. Instead of adding another circle of mutuality on top of the local community, the state would seek to monopolize it. This would leave individuals to depend on the state as they had on the local lord, or more so, as the means of domination also grew.

Alexis de Tocqueville is typically cited as the intellectual who argued most cogently for the need to protect the local communities, and more generally social institutions, as the bases of *individual* strength. While Tocqueville wrote about mass democracy (whose rising tyrannical leaders he feared), especially in the United States, his thesis was actually borne out by the totalitarian regimes of Communist Russia and Nazi Germany. These governments destroyed or gained control of local communities and social institutions, in the process penetrating deeper into them than feudal governments ever did. They weakened or controlled schools and churches, labor unions and voluntary associations—and all other bases that could provide individuals with circles of mutuality and bases for action not derived from the central state.

America's institutional decline, a key part of the retreat from society, differs so vastly in degree from that in totalitarian societies that one may well say our malaise is no closer to theirs than the common cold is to pneumonia. The trends, though, are similar: the growth of government in size, scope, missions, and control of private decision-making is paralleled by a decline of institutions. These two trends, intensified by an ego-centered mentality, have resulted in cut-off in-dividuals, deficient in mutuality and civility. The great difference between the American and the totalitarian development is that in the United States, the buildup of government has been mild in-deed compared to that in totalitarian states, and so has the parallel institutional deterioration and the denuding of individuals. Still, in either society, when the question arises which way one must now lean, the answer is indisputable: toward institutional reconstruction to correct for both excessive government and excessive individual-ism.

This issue has been addressed by two social scientists, Peter L. Berger and Richard John Neuhaus, in a volume whose title yields too much to the governing mentality: *To Empower People.* Their actual subject is divulged by the subtitle: *The Role of Mediating Structures in Public Policy.* That role, the authors write, is to correct for the ten-dency to seek "a unitary national community rather than a national community composed of thousands of communities."[10] That is, the ultimate protection of individual liberties is not a strong state, but a state balanced by viable social institutions. Local communities are but one form institutions take. Voluntary associations are another. For example, they can rise to defend a person they believe has been falsely accused, as Arthur Miller and a circle of friends did for Peter Reilly, who had been convicted of murdering his mother. They can mobilize group action to protect civil rights, as the Urban League, the NAACP, and NOW do. And these circles of mutuality and volun-tary associations can carry a good part of the required service to shared needs, and thus make the individual much less dependent on—and hence much less vulnerable to—the state. Thus, for example, if kin, friends, and neighbors help each other, individuals cannot so readily be manipulated by the fear that an official will cut off their loans, welfare checks, or food stamps unless they toe the line.

Parker Palmer sums up this assessment well:

> In mass society the person stands alone without a network of associations to protect personal meaning, to enlarge per-sonal power, or to learn the habits of democracy. The loneli-ness of men and women in such a society is a measure of their political impotence; and it is a small step from mass society to a totalitarian one.[11]

On the other hand:

> Political scientists have long known that community in all
> its forms can play a key role in the distribution of power.
> Families, neighborhoods, work teams, church and other vol-
> untary associations mediate between the lone individual
> and the power of the state. They provide the person with
> a human buffer zone so that he or she does not stand alone
> against the state's demands. They amplify the individual's
> small voice so that it can be heard by a state which can
> turn deaf when it does not want to listen.[12]

Berger and Neuhaus make it clear that they do not favor, any more
than Tocqueville would, a return to institutional domination—that
is, to a situation in which, for example, a local community can prohibit
individuals from reading pornographic books or from cohabitating
across racial lines, or from being gay or radical. But writing within
the contemporary American context, they, and I, see the erosion of
institutions as a greater nationwide danger at this time than the opposite, domination. While there are clearly some local communities
that are too intrusive, on average the data support the concern that
social institutions (of which local communities are but one prime
case) are currently weak in their capacity to fulfill their mediating
role, to prevent individuals from turning often to the state, overload-
ing it, and becoming dependent on and vulnerable to it.

PATTERN SETTING AND SERVICE PROVISION

The second role of institutions is to set patterns for specific services,
from education to health care, and help provide them. The point is
elementary: The more human needs can be served by institutions,
which are neither governmental nor, of course, "individual," the fewer
missions must be discharged through government bureaucracies or
shouldered by each individual. Very few would still hold that those
in need of a loan in a crisis, a supportive voice, or a warm embrace,
should turn *first* to a government bank, HHS-hired counsel, or a
state-provided social worker; that they would not often be better
served by kin, neighbor, community, or other sources of mutuality,
a credit union, voluntary nursing service, block association, carpool,
or self-help group.

One tends to overlook in this context an instrumental service institutions render by providing preset patterns. Individuals find it difficult to invent mutuality patterns *ad hoc*, as the need arises, and to create their own expressions of civility. Attending to shared concerns is much more effective when individuals can activate or join in existing preset patterns, as long as they can be modified according to individual preferences and changing circumstances. Thus, it is much easier to join a babysitting co-op, in which parents trade babysitting, than to form one. It is much easier to join and work with a local United Appeal, YMCA, or block association than to launch one. And it is much easier to form a new organization if one is thoroughly familiar with the rules and arrangements of existing similar ones than if one must start from scratch. Only those who have experienced the difficulties and frustrations that face the uninitiated, as they try to form patterns of mutuality new to them and formulate new channels for civility, fully realize the many ways these efforts can and do fail, and the benefits of drawing on available but adaptable institutional patterns.

Indeed, one of the great difficulties of our era is the lack of established patterns and mores in a multitude of new situations—parents' living to a much older age; kids' returning to their parents' home after college or divorce; relations with ex-spouses; the rise of stepparents. Moreover, old patterns need adjusting to a new world. When both spouses are gainfully employed, for example, many a woman feels that her husband's income is "ours," her own "mine"; couples who have lived together without marrying find few rules to follow when they break up.

The problem has been intensified by the recent mentality that has not only celebrated the individual but, in the name of spontaneity and the virtue of acting on impulse, has opposed all institutional patterns—not merely obsolescent ones—as unnecessary at best, restrictive and oppressive at worst. In contrast, it is my position that preset patterns are the social equivalent of prefabricated houses: They are a major source of human economy, saving much cost in friction, time, energy, even when they are not as elegant and do not fit as perfectly as custom-built patterns. The latter tend to serve few, at high costs, and they evolve so slowly that in most matters most individuals are either left on their own or turn to the state.

In addition to setting patterns, institutions command resources they can allocate to specific services. We frequently talk as if monies are either the taxpayers' or the government's ("Uncle Sam is everyone's partner" is an often-repeated line). Historically this may well be true; if we traced to their origin all funds that hospitals, schools, parks, and so on command, we might well find they had either been given by individuals or allotted from tax revenues (or, if you wish, all funds are "originally" those of individuals, including those the government taxes away and then "gives" to whomever it fancies). The practical point, though, is that at any particular time, institutions command sizable assets. These resources are often used to support the patterns the institution favors. Thus if an institution holds that a child-care center is an important new service, it will not only provide the patterns (who is entitled to use it, who will supervise, how many children per professional, what kind of insurance, whether employees can drop by during work hours or breaks) but also finance the service in part or in full. Pattern-setting, the first task, and service-provision, the second, often, but not necessarily, go together.

Whenever the social forces that promote less reliance on government are at the helm, the question arises to what extent the private sector and voluntary efforts can attend to the needs that government is ceasing to serve—and that are believed to require service. (This is quite properly a question of degree; providing service through the community does not mean ceasing to provide service through the government, but changing the balance between the two.) This question is raised not only about the needy but also about art, science, public parks, and so on. Attention usually focuses, as it should, on the number one question, the size of resources available. Thus, corporations typically argue that they cannot be expected to put up, as contributions, millions upon millions of dollars on top of what they already offer, to fill the gaps the government rollback creates. And voluntary agencies seek various indirect ways to enhance their capacity to serve that are nevertheless chargeable to the government, *e.g.*, changing the income tax laws to allow more Americans to deduct charitable contributions.

The point the preceding analysis adds to all this is that, aside from what is obviously the first question, who will give how much for what causes, another matter deserves attention. That is the matter of pattern-setting. If people are helped to work out forms for mutual help, their ability to assist one another increases and their need to rely on the government, on corporations, or on voluntary agencies diminishes, especially in matters that are not economic in nature, such as emotional or psychic support. This is not to suggest that the needy be fed social arrangements instead of meals, but that meals and a pal may be secured not only through appropriations but through new definitions of proper conduct—less selfish ones.

THE EDUCATIONAL-EXPERIENCE DIMENSION OF INSTITUTIONS

"Education" brings to most minds a vision of schools and youth. In contrast, social scientists have long stressed that education is a lifelong process that starts in the family, intensifies in schools, and continues at work, even in retirement. This view sees all institutions as having an educational dimension, although some, of course, are much more dedicated to education than others. Thus, the military is an educational institution, often more effective than many public schools. Similarly, many young workers learn more through on-the-job training conducted by corporations than in vocational education classrooms.

In the same vein, social sciences tend to see education as much more encompassing than schooling. Beyond the transmission of knowledge and development of skills, education embraces character formation, the evolution of one's values and mentality. And, it cannot be stressed enough in view of the preoccupation with curriculum and methods of teaching, the experiences generated by the various institutions are as important to education as cognitive inputs. For example, the data strongly suggest that whether teachers (and parents) smoke or not affects their pupils' (offspring's) smoking more than lectures, preaching, slides, and brochures on the subject.

Education, carried on by all leaders and other persons in positions of authority, provides role models that are a source of emulation, *i.e.*, of nonrational learning. But much more is at work than that. The *total setup*—leaders, peers, the structure of the situation—is educational. It provides educational experiences, experiences that affect character, values, and mentality, apart from skills and knowledge, for better or for worse. Thus, a youngster who in his first job works under a fair-minded foreman with dedicated coworkers, and is fairly evaluated and reasonably paid has quite a different *educational* experience from the one whose boss is arbitrary, coworkers alienated, evaluation haphazard or biased, and pay low and unrelated to effort. I say "the first job" only because it tends to be more consequential than subsequent ones; each job has an educational-experience content.

One more sign that contemporary American institutions have deteriorated and reflect a retreat from society is that they are conducted as if those who run and staff them are unaware of, or have deliberately decided to ignore, the educational-experience–producing dimension of their institutions. The reasons seem to vary from managerial overload (such as preoccupation with financial survival and power struggles) to "trained incapability" (people who are trained as MBAs, accountants, or engineers may be blinded to the educational dimension by their special perspectives).

The issue has often been raised in one specific context: public works and training for them. Conservative rhetoric calls for taking people off welfare and putting them to work, and training them if they are not "employable." This approach tends to ignore that most people on welfare are children, others are disabled, and still others are mothers of several young children. For those able to work, moreover, often no jobs are available. But let us focus on those who can be put to work. If they are to be trained properly, they need work that has the proper educational-experience content and structure. Raking leaves, the example commonly given as "something they could do if all other jobs are closed, just get them to work," disregards the educational dimension. If the purpose is indeed to prepare people to be self-propelled, motivated to seek work and keep a job, the last thing they need is a job which is completely uninvolving, which pays poorly, in which output is meaningless for those employed, which neither commands respect nor leads to future advancement in pay or status. Even if one looks at public jobs and training programs only from the viewpoint of "getting people off welfare," lasting solutions lie in programs that meet rather than violate the educational-experience requirement.

Reports abound of similar encounters in other institutions. The experience of university students is frequently that professors are absent from the classroom while they earn consulting fees elsewhere; that professors rush into class poorly prepared; that graduate students substitute for luminaries. This is part of the education for which the students and their families have paid dearly. People whose credit is investigated are often mystified by their low ratings and frustrated in trying to correct them. Various groups such as women, minorities, senior citizens, immigrants, handicapped, youth—together the overwhelming majority of Americans—each have their own accounts of insulting experiences.

People who check into hospitals frequently find physicians disinclined to explain in detail the procedure to which the patient is to submit. From numerous accounts of such encounters published over the last decade, two stand out. One is by Cornelius Ryan, the popular historian, who kept a journal of the treatment of his cancer; his wife published it, in conjunction with her own notes, after his death.[13] Ryan reports that when he continued to have some discharge following a prostate inflammation, the specialist his internist sent him to see told him bluntly that it might be benign or "neoplastic," the first indication Ryan had that it could be cancerous. The next moment the doctor was on the phone arranging his admittance to a hospital.

> "Look," I recall saying, "you're moving too fast for me to even understand what's to happen. I haven't agreed to any of this. I'd like to talk with Dr. Neligan [his internist] before any further decisions are made."
> "I already have. While you were dressing. He agrees we should go ahead."[14]

Once the biopsy showed cancer, the following exchange took place:

> "Please tell me exactly what you have found," I said.
> "I think, Mr. Ryan, much of the findings are too technical to go into. I would prefer to explain this in my own way." . . .
> "Doctor," I began, "the technical findings concern me and my future. I'd very much appreciate your telling me what they are."
> He did not unbend.
> "You are a difficult man, Mr. Ryan, in your persistence in groping for details you could not possibly understand."[15]

When Ryan was told that the radical treatment the doctor prescribed as the only reasonable treatment (although later Ryan found that three other specialists completely disagreed) involved excision of the testicles, and Ryan was pondering the matter, the specialist, to top it all:

> "Why not now?" he asked. "You are illogical. If you were a black man and I told you I intended to perform a radical prostatectomy, I could cope with your attitude. In my experience I've found that a black will do anything to keep his sexual organs intact—even die from the disease although the cure is there. But you're an educated man. I'm sure you can adjust to the trauma of the sex part of this. After all, you and your wife are surely not expecting any more children."[16]

Martha Weinman Lear, in *Heartsounds,* provides a similar account of the treatment of her husband after a heart attack.[17]

The point is not that all doctors conduct themselves this way or that all hospital treatments are impersonal. However, the frequency of such reports suggests, aside from growing awareness of the problem, the searing negative impact of this kind of experience. That is what is at issue here.

The net effect of coping daily with the social institutions in America appears to be, for many, "learning" to feel unrespected, unloved, limited in rights, as if one were engaged in non-legitimated activities. Otherwise, two thirds of all Americans would hardly feel alienated.

Institutional reconstruction requires, first of all, self-analysis by each institution as to what kind of educational experience it imparts, and why. If the educational experience is found to diverge from what is sought, one should resist the tendency to engage in some form of public-relations campaign, to divert attention from the issue by focusing on other great achievements ("We are the hospital that made a breakthrough in . . .") or assure the public that all is well by playing up some instance of compassionate behavior ("We flew a boy in from Tibet and repaired his heart free of charge").

Turning to public relations is tempting because once an educational deficiency in an institution is recognized, the costs of reconstruction (in funds and human adjustment) are usually substantial. A public-relations campaign costs much less and does not require the institution to change its way of being. The trouble with this approach is that it is impossible to paper over alienating experiences. Public-relations efforts aimed at legitimating an institution's misdirected endeavors are most unlikely to succeed.

To effect change, the institution's priorities must be reordered in a way that is widely accepted by its staff. Thus, if physicians are to spend more time communicating with patients, the hospital must downgrade other activities, research for instance, unless it has a sudden windfall of new funds to increase its staff. If universities are to demand that professors be more faithful in attendance and forego part of their extra-institutional work, the universities may have to raise the faculty's salaries. And so on. Even if all that is required is a change of attitude, developing it and sustaining it still competes with other priorities.

IN SUMMARY

It is my thesis that the deterioration of American institutions has advanced to a point that reconstruction is overdue if the institutions are to continue to fulfill effectively their mediating, pattern-setting, and educational roles. This reconstruction is necessary for both individual renewal and community-rebuilding. Viable institutions, we shall see, help foster mutuality and civility, two key individual attitudes. And revitalized institutions, discharging effectively their triple roles, are the foundation of a reconstructed community. The following chapters examine the condition of specific key institutions and the opportunities for their reconstruction.

CHAPTER FIVE

The Essential Family: Education for Mutuality and Civility

THE FAMILY AS THE "FIRST" EDUCATIONAL INSTITUTION

The family is widely considered the "first" institution, the elementary cell of social life. It is here that mutuality is first experienced and civility is first taught. In other words, the family is the first *educational* institution. All other institutions build on the family's educational achievements—or must remedy its failures—in evolving the personal foundation of relating to others (mutuality) and to community (civility).

The family is also the most elementary mediating structure; its members are the "others" most likely to rally to one's defense against the state. (Totalitarian governments, from Nazi Germany to post-revolutionary Russia, have tried to diminish the family or to control it.) Moreover, the family, by setting patterns and providing services for its members, reduces the demands on the state—so long as it is functioning well itself.

Family: Dead or Alive?

Before one can ask whether most American families are able to educate, mediate, or provide patterns and services effectively, a prior question claims attention: Is the family an "endangered species"? Is its very existence threatened? The answer is far from simple. Different social scientists and social commentators focus on different historical and sociological features of the family. According to which characteristics are used, it can be argued that the traditional family is long dead and buried—or that it is alive and well in contemporary America. Thus, Janet Norwood, commissioner of the Bureau of Labor Statistics, told a House subcommittee that in 1980 just 6 percent of all U.S. families fit the traditional model.[1] Ruth Messinger, a New York City Council member, putting the same figure somewhat more vividly, told a meeting of single parents that the "mythical nuclear family today describes only one in 17 American families."[2] These statements define as traditional families only those that comprise a father who is the sole wage earner, a mother who is a full-time homemaker, and *exactly two children.* Similarly, another popular estimate, that 17 percent of all households conform to the traditional pattern, has been cited by Betty Friedan.[3] "Households" is a more inclusive category than "families," and this estimate includes households with one or more children, not just those with precisely two.

On the other hand, Sar A. Levitan looks at the bright side of the statistics—almost 70 percent of all children live with their natural parents, for instance; although divorce rates are high, the majority of divorced persons remarry—and concludes that "there is no reason to place the family on the endangered-species list."[4] Others, to show that all is well, point out that an estimated 92 percent of all Americans will marry at one point or another in their lives.[5] But marriages last a shorter time than they used to, second marriages end in divorce even more often than first ones, and people live longer. The result is that people spend a much smaller part of their lives married— and it is time in marriage, not participation in marriage ceremonies, that matters, both for the availability of the most stable first circle of mutuality and for the rearing of children. Also, data that combine first and subsequent marriages ignore the effects of remarriage on stepchildren.

In answering this question I use a traditional criterion: survival of the *nuclear* family (neither extended nor single parent) characterized by two spouses, whether they work at home or outside it, have no children or quite a few. By this standard, the American family is neither dead nor well but declining. For half a generation (from 1965 to 1980), the proportion of married couples in the population has dropped steadily and the proportion of households headed by a single person has increased at an accelerating pace.

In August 1975, the U.S. Census Bureau published a series of four quite different projections about the future of the family, some more pessimistic than others.[6] According to the *most pessimistic* of the four, by 1990 the number of American husband-and-wife families would be 59.0 million, accounting for 61 percent of all households. Even this projection was too optimistic, judging by what has already happened. It called for 51.0 million families in 1979 (65 percent of all households), but the actual number was 47.7 million (62 percent).[7]

More specifically, from 1965 to 1970, the proportion of married couples in the population decreased each year by an average of 0.4 percent; this decline accelerated over the next five years to an average of 0.9 percent, and for 1975 to 1979 to an average of 1.05 percent.[8] According to my calculations, if the nuclear family continued to be dismembered at the same accelerating rate, by the year 2008 there would not be a single American family left. I do not believe this will actually occur; I expect some major social force to change the present course of the American nuclear family, if only because no complex society has ever survived without a nuclear family. But one cannot ignore the fact that the present trend is over fifteen years old and has been accelerating.

By the mid-1970s, the divorce rate had increased to the point that there was one divorce for every two marriages in the United States. Significantly, more of these divorces involved children; twice as many parents divorced in 1975 as had a decade earlier.[9]

These demographic changes have been paralleled by a shift in attitudes. Divorce continues to be destigmatized. In 1960, when asked whether divorce in this country should be easier or more difficult to obtain, 10 percent of those polled said easier, 61 percent said more difficult. By 1978, after divorce *had* been made easier, more people than in 1960 said it should be easier to obtain (28 percent), and fewer said more difficult (44 percent).[10] Also, this period has seen remaining single in a more positive light. While in earlier ages remaining single was frowned upon, the new attitude is captured by books such as *Living Alone & Liking It,*[11] which promised to show readers "how to make living alone a time of personal fulfillment, unlimited freedom, and exciting new experiences."[12]

The Essential Family Introduced

While the traditional nuclear family has been declining, other units called "families" have grown more common. When one asks whether new social formations, or social formations that have recently become more popular, qualify as families or not, the underlying issue is, qualify for what?

Soviet or Chinese writers often depict the family as a revolutionary marching band, a couple pulling together for a bright Red future, careful not to allow their personal needs to intrude. Indeed, in quite a few Soviet novels, the classic triangle, with its conflicts and jealousies, is not husband, wife, and lover, but husband, wife, and tractor. The conflict is resolved when the couple ends up happily plowing the land together. In contrast, many American commercials depict a family composed of people whose care and affection are expressed and measured by removing the ring around the collar, and intergenerational respect by producing spotless glasses to serve the in-laws. Obviously the essential features of a marching family are quite different from those of one preoccupied with consumption.

In an Age of Reconstruction

The family Americans require for an era of reconstruction is one that *at least* attends to its educational mission and provides patterns of mutuality for all its members. Education, particularly character formation, is the essential family task, for the obvious reason that children are first formed by families, and undereducation there tends to have a "domino" effect in all the institutions that follow. If the family does not lay the needed psychic foundation, schools become overloaded and less able to do their job, and they in turn overload the institutions of work and public safety.

We have already seen that if the government is to be relied upon less for social services, other social units will have to pick up some of those services. The family was historically a main source of such services, patterned on mutuality, and it can become so again. But while providing patterns of mutuality is an essential feature of the family America now needs, it is second in importance to the education of children. Adults can find mutuality elsewhere, but there is no adequate substitute for the family in forming the basic character of the young. A society in which all marriages ended when children reached eighteen would have a much better chance of functioning well than one in which, say, only half of the families broke up during the formative years of young children, and the other half lasted until the death of one of the spouses.

The mediating mission of social institutions is not less important, but a family that is effectively held together for purposes of education and social service will most likely fulfill its mediating role. Moreover, other institutions, especially local communities and voluntary associations, are as good or better at this mission than the family, because they are much more powerful a match for the state.

In advancing this analysis, then, I focus on what might be termed *the essential family*, the family able, at the least, to educate its young and to provide at least some mutuality for its members. When the traditional family is being dismembered, it is vital to distinguish from other elements, those that must be maintained if the family is to fulfill its vital roles. Only thus can reconstruction focus on essentials, and not be confounded by preoccupation with historically unique features or vain attempts to recapture them.

For example, in the early United States, lifelong monogamy was a family ideal most Americans seem to have subscribed to, and many practiced, in some instances even frowning on remarriage by widows. Note that in those days life expectancy was considerably shorter. Far more women died in childbirth, and infectious diseases took their toll of adults as well as children. In Massachusetts in 1850, for instance, the average person could expect to live to about age forty,[13] rather than to age seventy-three, as in America today.[14] Hence, lifelong monogamy in early America seldom meant forty or fifty years together, as it well might today.

When one now explores the future reconstruction of the family as an institution, one must ask whether lifelong monogamy is an *essential* feature, or whether it would suffice if marriages lasted at least as long as the formative years of the children and were continuous enough to provide for mutuality—both needs that, say, two marriages each lasting twenty years could serve quite effectively. My purpose here is not to answer the question whether lifelong monogamy is essential, but to illustrate the difference between essential and other features.

TWO ESSENTIALS FOR EDUCATION

The historical features of the nuclear family include two parents married to each other, one at home full time. Are these historical features essential to the educational mission of the family, or can education of the young be carried out effectively by parents who both work away from home, or by parents who are not married to each other, or, above all, by single parents? The question has two sources. The first is the general societal forces that buffet the traditional nuclear family. These include strong economic forces, especially the very considerable increase in the proportion of married women gainfully employed outside the home, and therefore much less dependent on their husbands. As divorce has thus become economically more feasible, legal changes have made it much easier to obtain. The general withdrawal from institutions also affects the traditional family. So has a general rise in ego-centered mentality, reflected in this area by the growing number of people who find singlehood preferable, not marrying and often living alone, and by the growing number who choose to have fewer children or none. As the family has become less sustainable, more people come to wonder—could we do without it?

Second, the forces that erode the traditional nuclear family are egged on by a specific mentality that directly challenges the need for the nuclear family, and celebrates new, or newly popular, social formations such as living together and single parenthood. This mentality deserves special attention because it accelerates processes that may need moderating, and because it is the most readily reversible factor of the anti-family lot.

A key element of this anti-family mentality is its positive view of the rising divorce rate. Thus, for instance, it is argued that second marriages are better than first ones. In an article entitled "Second-Time Winners," Leslie Aldridge Westoff, a Princeton demographer, writes about "blended" or "reconstituted" families rather than second marriages.[15] (The labels are important; "blended" or "reconstituted" is more approving than "second time around.") She reports that for the couples she interviewed, the first marriage was a dry run; in the second marriage they applied the lessons learned, did not repeat the same mistakes, and chose mates more wisely. "In retrospect many of the couples saw their first marriage as a kind of training school. . . . Divorce was their diploma. All agreed that the second marriage was the real thing at last. With both partners older, more mature, somewhat expert at marriage, everything moves more smoothly, more meaningfully."[16]

While Westoff may feel she is just reporting the results of some interviews with some couples, the implication to the reader, the music

her writing—and that of many others—intones, is that the first marriage is to the second what premarital sex is to marital sex: Evidence
shows it improves it. And indeed *if* there were sufficient data to
support a view of the first marriage as a dry run, there would be
less reason for concern. But Westoff herself laments the lack of systematic research on second marriages; her notions are based on a few
interviews. She also concedes that second marriages are even less lasting than first ones, noting the findings of demographer Paul Glick
that 59 percent of second marriages may end in divorce, compared
to 37 percent of first marriages.[17] Nationwide behavioral data, people
"voting" with their lives, are more conclusive than what a few couples
told an interviewer, and the national vote is that second marriages
are less tolerable, on average, than first ones. The ideological nature
of Westoff's and other such writing stands out when they continue
to extol the virtues of divorce on the basis of such impressionistic
data against much systematic data to the contrary.

Nor does Westoff show that remarriages, even those that last, have
no major detrimental effect on the children. There is no reason to
believe that children also consider their parents a dry run and their
stepparents an improvement.

If we are to rely on a detailed, intimate study of a small number
of relationships, Westoff's work must be contrasted with that of the
Grant study of second marriages. It found that by 1973, fourteen
out of seventeen men who had obtained a divorce before 1967 had
remarried. Of those fourteen second marriages, eight had ended in
a second divorce, and four were classified by the researchers as weak;
only two remarriages, "both of short duration at that time," appeared
unambiguously happy.[18]

Despite the frequency of divorce and the millions of children involved, studies of the effects of divorce and remarriage on children
are far from conclusive. A recent overview of the state of this knowledge typically focuses on the numerous factors involved (after all,
there are many different kinds of divorces, stepchildren and so on),
rather than on drawing conclusions.[19] Nevertheless, the fragmentary
findings that exist suggest that at least for significant numbers of
the children of divorced parents, considerable and lasting psychic
damage is caused.

Psychiatrist James M. Herzog, of the Children's Hospital Medical
Center in Boston, has studied the effects of the absence of an active

father figure on young children referred to him through clinic or school. His findings imply that the father's absence may have specific and long-range consequences for the way young children deal with aggressive drives. Among the 72 children of divorce that he studied, absence of the father was especially disruptive for the children, almost all of them boys, aged 1½ to 5. The very youngest typically had nightmares about monsters; those 3 to 5 years old were apt to be highly macho, hyperaggressive, much occupied with ideas of stern male discipline. In children 5 to 7, both boys and girls, depression—aggression turned inward—was the more common result. Herzog suggests that parents monitor and absorb a variety of feelings and conflicts for one another, and that this interaction creates a "protective shield" that allows both to be caring, effective parents. When the father leaves, this shield may break down, leaving the children vulnerable.[20]

A study of more than eighteen-thousand children in elementary and secondary schools in fourteen states, one of the largest focused on one-parent families, finds much trouble. These children are reported to achieve less in school, to be absent more often, and—most indicative—to cause more disciplinary problems than children of married couples.[21]

Jessie Bernard reviewed several studies of stepchildren.[22] She found a more varied and complex picture than the other studies cited above, but she did not find the evidence compelling. Economic background factors often confound the picture.[23] However, to the extent that conclusions can be drawn, they suggest that stepchildren do suffer in comparison with other children.

Beyond celebrating divorce, the anti-nuclear-family mentality disregards the differences between essential and nonessential features. Historically, in the United States most families (though certainly not all) had a husband gainfully employed, a wife at home full time, children, and a marriage that lasted. When it is argued now that "the family" is down and out and, by implication, that it is too late to salvage the family and that on the face of it, the family is not necessary (if we have survived without it, who needs it?)—the argument mixes essential with nonessential features. A wife at home is *not* an essential feature, we shall see. Hence the decline of this feature is not indicative of the state or need of the family. On the other hand, for the educational mission of the family, it *is* essential to have active and involved parenthood, accorded sufficient time, psychic energy, and commitment, at least for the formative years of the children, especially from birth until age six but preferably until the end of adolescence.

I call this essential feature *basic parenting.* If the family does not provide basic parenting, the youngsters it delivers to the doorstep of the school are underdeveloped persons. This makes it impossible for the school to function effectively and to develop the youngsters' personalities for the next set of institutions, those of adult life, of work and of community. Aside from delivering underdeveloped persons, such a family will not be able to collaborate with the schools, collaboration that is needed for their educational work. Such a family also will, on average, be less likely to provide a model for stable, continuous mutual relations.

Basic parenting does *not* require a mother at home. It can be provided, for example, by both parents' sharing the basic parenting duties, so that one or the other is at home while children are in infancy and when they return from child-care centers, kindergarten, or primary school. This in turn can be achieved through paternity leaves, flexitime, shared jobs, and other arrangements.

What the child requires above all is someone who cares and educates, adults who have a commitment to parenting and the energy to back it up, and a relationship to emulate. Hence, parents who are overworked, habitually drunk or drugged, or consumed by their own personal problems are unable to provide basic parenting effectively. It can be given by fathers as well as by mothers, nor does a parent have to be a person not gainfully employed. At the same time, basic parenting *does* tend to conflict with both parents' working full-time outside the home, especially at jobs that are physically or psychologically exhausting.

In any other industry, if you remove a million employees without reducing the job requirements very much, nobody would deny that the industry is woefully shorthanded. If we take a million women out of a million households to work outside the home, and replace them with precious little in child-care services, few babysitters, and little more grandparenting, then the parenting "industry" is woefully shorthanded (and television sets and the streets are overworked). This is not an argument for women to stay home to do the parenting, but for *someone* to do more of it.

The second feature essential for a family to carry out its educational mission is a *mutually supportive educational coalition.* The educational agents must be mutually supportive primarily because the specific educational tasks are in part contradictory. One task is to promote achievement, the other to provide secure emotional support. In studies of small groups, Harvard sociologist Robert F. Bales found that groups that functioned effectively had two mutually supportive leaders, an instrumental leader who pushed the group to greater productivity and an expressive leader who provided emotional security and support.[24] Morris Zelditch's studies of the family as a small group suggest that parents tend to specialize in a similar way, one giving children deep emotional support, the other, pressure to grow.[25]

These studies do not provide conclusive evidence—Bales himself has expressed some reservations about his findings—but they are highly suggestive as to the functioning of the family as a group. It seems that in their education, children need two kinds of parenting, the expressive and the instrumental. Given only emotional security, the child will tend to underachieve; given only pressure to grow, the child will tend to grow up obsessively driven.

Most parents or other educators are at best good at carrying out one of these educational tasks, not both, because the two tasks rely on conflicting personality types—the promotion of achievement is more a Type A, driven behavior, and giving emotional support is more a Type B, relationship-oriented task. Again, historically, in the white American middle class, men were more often Type A and thus pressed for achievement, while women tended more to be Type B and thus the main source of emotional support (although exceptions abounded). But this does not mean that the future family must divide the two tasks this way; the requirement is only that both be covered.

Disregarding the question of who carries out what task, the two educational partners must support each other to achieve the essential combined effect, one in which emotional security lets the child dare to grow and the pressures of growing are relieved by emotional support.

Continuity—not necessarily lifelong, though the longer the better—is a prerequisite for a successful educational coalition; character formation is hardly a short-term undertaking. John Bowlby, a leading British psychologist whose central concern has been the personality development of children, makes this point:

> All the evidence is that children prosper if they have a
> couple of parents with whom they live and the home is a
> stable, predictable one. . . . I think the crucial thing is

that the parents provide stable continuity, and on top of that one can build variety. But the variety is not a substitute for the continuity.[26]

The sequence of divorce followed by a succession of boy- or girl-friends, second marriages, and frequently another divorce and another turnover of partners, means a repeatedly disrupted educational coalition, with each change in participants involving a change of educational inputs for the child. It is not as though each new partner can sign up for the previous one's educational post and policies; the educational input each provides is deeply affected by his or her total personality and upbringing. In effect, any change of parenting partners means deep disruption, though of course having many disruptions cuts deeper into the effectiveness of the educational coalition than having just one or two.

SINGLE, SURROGATE, LIVE-INS, AND EXTENDED

In the traditional nuclear family, the two essentials of basic parenting—that there be an educational team with two partners, and that the team be mutually supportive and continuous—were the joint task of husband and wife. With the decline of that traditional family, new social formations need to be examined to see how well they can provide these essentials.

Surrogate parents (grandparents, nannies) can provide some basic parenting if they have the same features required of parents: sustained commitment and the physical and psychic ability to back it up. Mere "custodial" care—the kind many cleaning women are expected to provide on the side, or that of grandparents who drop in to watch TV and babysit—is obviously insufficient. It does not provide affection, respect, encouragement to achieve. "Latchkey" children—children who are on their own when they come home from school, sometimes identifiable by the keys on strings around their necks—are of course deprived, at least in part, of basic parenting, especially if they are young or have no adult supervision for prolonged periods.

This is no small matter. The percentage of married women who are employed has risen dramatically, from 23.8 percent in 1950[27] to 49.4 percent in 1979.[28] Moreover, according to a recent report by the Population Reference Bureau, the most striking increase has taken place among mothers of young children; in 1950, only 12 percent of married women with children under age six were employed, but in 1980, 45 percent were working.[29] The problem, to reiterate, is not that *women* left the home to work, but that both parents work away from home. If for every woman who decided to work outside the home, a husband stayed home, or both took three-quarter-time jobs, or flexitime ones—the homes would not be so empty.

Another relevant statistic is the rise of the number of children who live with one parent. In 1979, 18.5 percent of children under eighteen, nearly one of every five, lived with only one parent, compared to 11.9 percent in 1968.[30] It is now estimated that almost half of the children born in any year will live with only one parent at some time before they are eighteen.[31] Among single-parent families, a growing number are headed by unwed mothers. The number of children born to unmarried women in 1978 was 543,900, or one of every six U.S. births, compared to 398,700, or one of every nine births, in 1970.[32] In 1979 the percentage of children under eighteen who were living with a never-married mother was more than three times as high as it had been a decade earlier.[33] For these children the issue is not how much they will see their father and mother, but, typically, how much they will see their mother.

Most single parents are employed—in 1979, 64 percent of separated and divorced women with children under eighteen[34]—and at a time when neither economic conditions nor the political climate favors taxpayer-subsidized assistance for any but the neediest, many single parents have little choice. It is estimated that more than 4.5 million children aged six to thirteen spend a lengthy period each workday unsupervised.[35] According to one study, in 1980, 65 percent of working parents with children at home had no child-care arrangements other than care by the parents themselves.[36]

As part of the ideology that tries to legitimate absent parenting it has been argued that "quality" counts; that if you cannot spend much time with your child, you can make up for it by making the minutes you do provide "count."

Pop psychologists who promote this notion do not cite any data to show that one can make minutes into quality time on order. Indeed, it is more plausible that quality time occurs when you have longer stretches of "quantity" time, at moments that are neither predictable nor controllable. Most important, there is no evidence that quality time can make up for long stretches of no time, of parental absence.

There is no definitive evidence that single parents cannot carry out the task of basic parenting effectively, but there are some signs that many cannot. There are good data to show that married couples who are in deep conflict with each other do not provide the needed parenting. The proper question hence is not whether parents are married or single, but whether they are able to provide energy and continuity for education, and a role model for mutuality. The small group data of Bales suggest that only about 10 percent of the individuals in the groups studied were equipped to juggle differing kinds of social behavior and switch back and forth between the two kinds of leadership, expressive and instrumental; the rest were well able either to give emotional support or to push for achievement, but not both.[37]

Need the parents be a husband-wife team? Not necessarily. A mother and grandparents or a father and sister in one household; two unmarried persons who live together for many years and have a sound, continuous mutuality; one parent and a nanny who is part of the family—these or some other combination can provide basic parenting as well as a married couple, and better than a married couple that is overworked or uncommitted to parenting or in deep conflict.

Grandparents who live at the other side of the city and drop in, or who have kids over occasionally, can fulfill many *other* roles— but not basic parenting. Frequently changing *au pair* girls or cleaning women will not do, nor will a rapid succession of live-in boyfriends or girlfriends. What seems essential is that both kinds of partners, expressive and instrumental, be present and available, and that they work together effectively over an extended period.

Continuity, we have suggested, is an essential basis for the educational coalition. It *may* work if the two partners keep working together; it cannot work if they keep changing. This holds equally for a coalition of husband and wife, spouse and live-in, and other partners. It is one reason a nanny who for a child's formative year is integrated into the family, and especially into the family's educational "policy," is often a highly effective surrogate parent, while a succession of babysitters as a rule are not.

In short, basic parenting is served best if the relationship between partners is both mutually supportive and sustained. It is more difficult to provide successful basic parenting for either single parents with rapidly changing partners, or for two parents whose soured marriage has damaged or destroyed their mutuality, especially as it concerns the educational coalition.

Marriage obviously differs from living together, first and foremost in the additional commitment entailed; and second in that on the average, the partnership lasts longer and may be somewhat more likely to work out joint educational "policies." Note that I refer here to people who have children. Those who live together as a trial-marriage of sorts, or senior citizens anxious not to lose their separate Social Security benefits, are not at issue. That those who live together often marry when a child is expected attests to a considerable awareness that under these circumstances the additional commitment marriage entails is useful. This awareness is also reflected in the fact that marriage remains the most accepted and legitimate parenting structure. A poll in 1978 found that 68 percent of Americans considered morally wrong "deciding to have children even though not legally married and don't intend to be," although in 1977 only 46 percent thought it was morally wrong for couples to live together unmarried.[38]

It follows that from the viewpoint of the issue explored here, that of the essential family, the arguments in favor of living together versus "getting married" are misfocused when they fail to specify whether the living-together status is to continue once children are expected. Many of the arguments in favor of living together have merit so long as children are not involved, and many of the arguments for marriage apply when they are.

The question then arises: In what institutional pattern is basic parenting most likely to be successfully provided? This is a statistical question, not an ethical one. Statistically, married people are more likely than single parents to provide basic parenting. Marriages are relatively more stable, on average, than couples living together or other partnerships; marriage is more legitimate and socially accepted when children are involved. Above all—all other things being equal—marriage provides more "availability" of parents (hours on the "job," psychic energy) than single parenthood. This is not to say that married couples are morally superior to single parents, or that all or most married couples are "good" parents, or that all or most single parents are "bad" ones. It suggests, however, that to the extent public policy and leadership affect these matters, they should encourage rather than undermine the institutional structure most likely, on average, to provide the required pattern: marriage.

Some writers are quick to point to the success of communal upbringing of infants in kibbutzim, the Israeli commune settlements. They fail to take into account that parents in kibbutzim are married and divorce is frowned upon; that parents maintain a close affective tie to their children (indeed, they take them to their living quarters or to recreational areas daily after work); and that parents maintain close ties with the infant-care nannies, both directly and via the close-knit community. Despite all this, the pressure in kibbutzim is toward dismantling the communal infant care and returning the children to their families. Indeed, full-time institutional communal care is now available in less than half the kibbutzim. Needless to say, in the United States in an age of less government, full-time communal care of infants, by qualified nannies responsive to the parents, is as likely to be introduced as six Sundays in a row. Substitutes for the nuclear family do not come easily.

THE FAMILY AS THE FIRST CIRCLE OF MUTUALITY

Providing mutuality, a vital individual need, is the family's second mission, second only to the education of the young. While mutuality can be and is generated among friends, neighbors, and co-workers, on the average these circles tend to be less stable, encompassing, and available than the nuclear family. Statistically speaking, the most effective first line of mutuality is that between husband and wife. Obviously single parenthood cannot provide a circle of mutuality for the adult members of the family as long as there is but one, and the mutuality of living together is less stable than that of marriage.

A brief examination of the anti-marriage literature, popular in the sixties and seventies, shows a fair measure of insensitivity to the need for mutuality. The literature draws on the same basic ego-centered themes that we sketched in discussing pop psychology in general. Michael Novak characterizes the resulting view of marriage:

> The central idea of our foggy way of life, however, seems unambiguous enough. It is that life is solitary and brief, and that its aim is self-fulfillment. Next come beliefs in establishing the imperium of the self. Total mastery over one's surroundings, control over the disposition of one's time—these are necessary conditions for self-fulfillment.

. . . In such a vision of the self, marriage is merely an alliance.[39]

Sometimes a main theme of a mentality is captured in a few lines, such as these from *Newsweek:* "Stuck marriages often break up—or worse, don't. Many go on to become what Dr. William B. Phillips, an Atlanta family counselor, calls 'The American Gold Watch Marriage'—short on excitement and fulfillment but long on security."[40] The implied value judgment is stark: It simply puts excitement and fulfillment above security and the continuity and stability it implies. It is not that no one is entitled to make such a choice, but need we assume it is automatically, across the board, the better one of the two options? Many married people, not imbued with the pop psychology, seem to feel otherwise, as their continued "stuck" behavior indicates.

The pop anti-family literature favors living together (or open marriage) over traditional marriage chiefly because it views the old bond not as enriching those it unites, but as a set of dictates that stands above the individual, constricting him or her.

In their book advocating open marriage, Nena and George O'Neill contend that "the traditional, closed marriage is a form of bondage, for both husband and wife."[41] They list six "psychological commitments" involved in a traditional marriage: "Possession or ownership of the mate . . . Denial of the self . . . Maintenance of the couple-front . . . Rigid role behavior . . . Absolute fidelity . . . Total exclusivity."[42] And they warn:

> Subtly, insidiously, often without your even knowing it,
> the clauses of the closed marriage contract begin to foreclose
> upon your freedom and your individuality, making you a
> slave of your marriage.[43]

Going a step further, other writers perceive remaining single and free from deep, involving relationships of any kind as maximizing freedom (heeding only those restrictions ego favors); they fail to deal with the consequences for mutuality. For instance, someone identified only as "Joan M., 31, college instructor" explains:

> Well, today I think I'll stay single forever. It's a hell of
> a lot more freedom than it would be either in a marriage

or an exclusive relationship. . . . This affords the opportunity of getting to know well and be friends with a lot of different people. No restrictions except the restrictions that I happen to choose.[44]

This avoidance of commitment is also one reason for living together instead of marrying:

> Between marrieds and non-marrieds alike, the emotional entanglement may be virtually identical, but that "tied down" feeling that afflicts so many marriages is greatly reduced when you're not legally joined.[45]

The same writer sees in the extended mutuality married people face with their kinfolks and friends only a source of demands, not of satisfactions:

> Marriage automatically carries with it another pressure—the ever-widening circle of involvement with family, in-laws, friends, society. And they all expect something of you. . . . When you live together, outside pressures are noticeably absent.[46]

The advocates of contractual marriage see two individuals, fully mature and independent, knowing what they need and want, working out a marital pattern:

> Both partners together decide what is right for them, and in a very real sense, they determine the dimensions, structures, and function of their new marriage. . . . There is recognition that the New Marriage is a flexible framework which may lead to other structures of togetherness.[47]

What advocates of contractual marriage disregard is the essence of a mutual relationship. Émile Durkheim observed long ago, in discussing business contracts, that contracts rest on *pre*contractual relations; on the assumption that most partners most of the time will be trustworthy and "decent" with each other, not try to exploit inevitable changes in the situation or exact the last possible ounce of flesh. The parties to contracts must realize that in the longer run they need each other, and hence that they ought to let each other get away with some asymmetrical, extracontractual gains—to sustain and nourish the longer-run relationship. Explicit constraints spelled out in the contract help to clarify relations, but most times, once they are activated—say, enforcement is sought in court—the underlying relationship is gravely undermined.

The same point holds, but with much greater force, in close interpersonal relations. Between spouses there is some room for negotiated agreements, on such matters as community property, who will take out the garbage and who will do the dishes, and so on. But the essence of the relationship must be affection and trust based on emotional involvement and faith, not calculations or excitement. No marital contract could explicate, for instance, the care one party "owes" the other in case of serious illness and what "return" the other will provide. Any attempt at a statement à la Blue Cross—"In case of 20 percent disability, I'll take care of you for up to thirty days, but if more, your coverage will run out"—would undermine the very nature of mutual relationships. These must be based on open-ended commitments. No contract could specify the limits of solace for a spouse who is a cancer patient or the victim of a stroke. Once the situation actually occurs, a spouse may be overwhelmed by the asymmetry of the demands to the point he or she will quit the marriage (though in fact this rarely happens). However, no secure, continuous relationship can be formed if limits to mutuality are established beforehand.

True, the old marriage "until death do us part" did not guarantee future "returns" or "fair" tradeoffs. There have been, for instance, scores of husbands who let their wives work while they studied medicine, only to break off the marriage when their own training started to pay off. The legal notion that under these circumstances the wife is entitled to some recovery (or better, a share of the earnings) is a constructive appendix to the marriage commitment. But the old concept of marriage, legitimizing a mutual commitment, including a duty to persevere—even if ultimately overwhelmed—provides a more effective basis of mutuality than marriage by contract.

While the notion of contractual marriage is an abstract concept of an ego-centered age, practiced by very few, the high favor accorded living together compared to marriage is more consequential. The ego-centered view of living together (as a standing arrangement, as distinct from a transitional phase) is well captured by a "30 year old medical technician":

> By living together, we avoid the problems and suffocating bondage of marriage. The piece of legal paper doesn't mean you're married. It just means you have to go through a lot of legal red tape to get a divorce if it doesn't work out. Living together avoids that mess. You can split any time you want.[48]

What is typically overlooked in such statements is the effect on the other person involved in the relationship. If the two sides are equally uninvolved, they can part like two chess players who decide not to play with each other anymore. But because intimate relations tend to be involved, and the partners' objective as well as subjective states are seldom symmetrical, dissolution is rarely without considerable human costs—*and* the fear of dissolution by one affects the other, while they are still in the relationship. This problem exists of course in marriage, but it is accentuated in less-committed, easier-to-break living together.

> The woman is usually aware, on some level, that she is taking the greater risk. For example, if a couple start living together in their 30s and then split up in their 40s, the man is in a better position to find a new partner. He is still considered extremely eligible, a bachelor with the added attraction of not paying alimony or child support. A woman in her 40s, unfair as it may be, has her choice narrowed by custom and prejudice.[49]

Marriage is more effective than living together in composing a new social unit, a new "we," a stronger basis of mutuality—as even proponents of living together recognize.

> Living together means doing what's right for you as an individual. Marriage carries with it traditional standards and norms. The emphasis is off the individual and the pressure is on "now we are one" partnership.[50]

A "recently divorced man of 28" concurs:

> We were together for four years before we decided to
> get married. . . . In the months after the wedding there
> was a definite change. Suddenly we were "planning for the
> future" and talking more and more about "responsibility."
> . . . We both need our independence, and somehow the
> act of getting married didn't allow us that anymore.[51]

Both these individuals correctly perceive the transformation, the
union built into a marriage, the addition of a "we" to the previous
two egos and the mutual commitment it involves. Community and
nation entail a similar transformation. The trouble is not so much
with the commitment a union requires from the egos, but with egos
that cannot find such union a source of gratification. True, every
relationship has some strains and sets some limits on ego, but on
balance, we have seen, individuals thrive best if they maintain a self
and at the same time are linked into unions, rather than break their
unions and remain cut off.

On the whole these writings show, as the few examples above illustrate, that the anti-marriage literature both draws on the ego-centered
mentality and feeds into it. In contrast, mutuality, which entails some
commitment to a shared world, sensitivity to and involvement with
others, and preference for continuity, is a foundation of marriage—
and is sustained by it. Transient relationships or relationships limited
by contract are compatible not with mutuality but with ego-centered
conduct. Little wonder the age of retreat from society and hollowing
of institutions finds its parallel in retreat from marriage and from
the family.

RECONSTRUCTION

If reconstruction of the essential family is to take place, the first
step might well be to face up to the anti-family themes, to reduce
the legitimation they provide to dismembering the family. This has
to proceed on several fronts. To begin, data may be brought to bear
on such misstatements as that marriage is basically doing well and
hence there is little to be concerned about, that divorce has no serious
ill effects on children, and so on. The American public dialogue is
particularly attentive to arguments backed up with data. As the field

has been dominated by interpretations that challenge the nuclear family, a correcting and balancing interpretation, on the side of the nuclear family, might be useful.

Second, an examination of the self-defeating nature of an unbounded quest for ego fulfillment, explored earlier in a general context, needs to be applied to family life. It is particularly damaging that the pro-family argument has been largely monopolized by groups such as the Moral Majority and the pro-life extremists. These groups seek to impose their values on the rest of society rather than take the trouble of making a compelling case for the nuclear family. They confuse the need for reconstruction of the family with a return to authoritarian, traditionalistic forms, and see the banning of abortion as the core issue, which it is not. The American family could be reconstructed even if abortions were strictly a matter of choice for the woman involved, in consultation with her physician (although for reasons spelled out elsewhere, I would urge that a married woman be expected to inform her husband before the fact).[52] Conversely, if every state in the union ratified a constitutional amendment prohibiting abortion, it would do precious little good and considerable damage to the future of the family. Clearly, the argument favoring the family must be endorsed by the mainstream of American thought, by "secular humanists," so that its sociological merits can be clearly separated from the New Tories, who with few exceptions, have been its key advocates so far.

Beyond a change of mentality and climate, there is a need for institutional changes. Here the concept of the *essential* family must be kept clearly in mind, so as not to overload the weakened family with nonvital demands.

Specifically, divorce, which has been made easier to the point that it can be obtained by mail order or by filling out some pre-packaged forms, should be made more of an opportunity for reconciliation, for instance by reinstating a thirty-day "cooling off" period, and using this period for counseling by professionals or clergy.

Changes in work patterns could go a long way to sustain the relationships of working couples. Frequent relocation of employees, often not really necessary but part of corporate tradition, could be curbed. Despite tales of commuting couples who maintain their marriages over thousands of miles, and about husbands who accept less-attractive jobs to accommodate moves required by their wives' careers, and vice versa, frequent relocations and geographic distance strain mutuality.

Scores of other steps have been suggested, from changing the Social Security rules that lead older persons (role models for the young) to live together rather than to marry, to adding classes in school on how people may better communicate and relate to each other, a subject at least as important as home economics.[53] (Churches have successfully developed such courses,[54] but their benefits should not be lost for those who are not connected to a place of worship.) What is at issue here is not the details but the orientation: including the essential family in the reconstruction of community.

WIDER CIRCLE: PATTERN-SETTING AND SOCIAL SERVICES

The family is a major social unit that will have to be reoriented and re-enabled if it is to pick up some of the social services the government is dropping. But while the family can play a role in setting patterns for—and actually providing—social services, this role is not as central as the educational one. Whatever the arrangements of Eskimos, pharaohs, or kibbutzim members, certainly in the America of today and the near future, for the character formation of children and as backup to schools, there is no substitute for the family. It is irreplaceable when it comes to first basic education. In contrast, social services *can* be provided by neighborhoods, voluntary agencies, even the government. Hence, even though drawing on the family for this purpose may seem desirable, it should not be allowed to take precedence over or conflict with the essential educational mission.

Education is first and foremost an endeavor of the *nuclear* family; in most American families, members of the extended family—to the extent that it exists at all—are able to play only a small educational role. Grandparents, uncles, cousins are often far away or preoccupied with their own nuclear families. (Important exceptions are to be found among minorities and among recent immigrants such as Hispanic Americans, and in small towns and villages.) Social services, on the other hand, can be and are more readily provided by a wider circle than the nuclear family. Grandfather may live in Florida but still can participate in securing a college loan for his Cambridge-bound grandson. Upon the death of a family member, brothers and sisters, dispersed across the nation, may converge to ease the strain on the family. Put it differently: Kin-based social services are a main basis for expanding the nuclear family's circle of mutuality to the extended family.

The complex relationship between pattern-setting and the provision of social services is evident in both the nuclear and the extended family. For example, say the government provides less support for college students and for the elderly, and parents must provide more, from nest eggs originally saved for retirement, for their offspring's college education. Under these circumstances it would help if the expectation of a return of support in old age were set, *not* via a contract but via new or renewed mores.

Family members are effectively moved by what they consider "proper" reciprocity. True, it is easier to make it work in frequent and relatively small occasions for give-and-take, like Christmas and birthdays, than in large, infrequent, more strung out "exchanges," like children's "repaying" their parents. The more frequent exchanges allow backing up the mores of "good conduct" with adjustments of the reciprocating gift. Thus, if another person does not return an "appropriate" gift this Christmas, one may be less generous next Christmas, but if a college graduate does not "return" support to his retired parents, they are in no position to "adjust" his college aid. Nevertheless, there is good social-science reasoning to maintain that this behavior is more deeply affected by what is considered right than by the fear of economic retribution.[55] Hence, what is needed, above all, is to clarify what is expected in the new age, rather than concern oneself with shortening the term or increasing the frequency of reciprocal relations as a way of increasing the opportunities for adjustment.

Even with clarified and strengthened mores, even following reconstruction of the nuclear or extended family, there are sharp limits to the social services the family can provide. Social services will have to be provided in large part by neighborhoods, voluntary associations, religious and ethnic groups, and local communities, and, as a last resort, by the government. To reiterate, the family's first mission is educational.

CHAPTER SIX
Schools: Educational Experiences First

Schools are the second educational institution, second to the family in the sequence of personality development. Their contribution to mediation tends to be small, because schools typically are not in a position to act on behalf of pupils, or even staff members, to countervail the state. The schools' pattern-setting and service-provision tend to be limited to those tasks related to their prime preoccupation: teaching, the transmission of knowledge and skills. Their essential mission is education, which many do not carry out, although, as we shall see, hardly for the reasons usually given. Education, to reiterate, the development of personality and character, is the process by which newborns, in effect barbarians, are humanized, acquire the capacity for mutuality, civility, and performance (whether studying, working, or serving in the armed forces).

CURRENT STATUS OF THE INSTITUTION

It is a commonplace to suggest that American schools are a diminished, hollowed institution. Reports abound of rampant violence, drug abuse, and alcoholism; of teacher "burnout"; of disappointed parents and resentful taxpayers; of declining test scores; of both long delays in adopting new teaching materials and methods (said to require a generation) and a rudderless pursuit of unproven fashions in the teaching of subjects from math to reading. Some reports stress differences among schools, e.g., seeing more merit in private than in public schools

131

(without maintaining that all is well in the private ones). Others see misdirection across the board.

The public feels that schools in general are doing a rather mediocre job. A minority (28 percent) of the public expressed great confidence in the schools in 1980. Asked to issue a report card for schools, 35 percent of the public accorded schools a high A or B, while the proportion of those who rated the schools a failing F or a D was 18 percent; 29 percent settled for a middling C.[1]

My readings of the data on school performance suggest that the criticisms of schools are, on the one hand, too sweeping, and on the other hand, misfocused. Violence and highly disruptive behavior, for instance, are concentrated in about 15 to 20 percent of the schools, mainly inner-city public schools. A nationwide study of the scope of violence in schools, conducted for Congress by the National Institute of Education, used several measurements to assess the extent of the problem. One was simply to ask principals their judgment. Principals of 75 percent of the schools studied responded that vandalism, personal attacks, and theft were not a problem in their schools, or only a minor one; 17 percent, that they were moderately serious problems, and 8 percent, a serious problem. A second measure was the number of illegal incidents that occurred in a month; five or more per month was defined as a "serious problem." These data paralleled the judgments of the principals.[2] In short, violence is a serious problem in a small minority of the nation's schools.

Another segment of the schools, whose number is very difficult to estimate, are seriously damaged by poor teaching, a high degree of bureaucratization, and what we shall see is the educational equivalent of the ego-centered mentality. At the same time, at least half of the schools seem to be doing a creditable to excellent job.

The lament of declining reading, writing, and other school achievements, as well as declining SAT scores, has reached the level of cliché. However, the low point may well already have been passed, with both local and national scores slowly starting to mend. For instance, the percentage of correct answers on reading tests administered nationwide has gradually risen over the last decade for students aged nine (the percentage of correct answers was 64.0 in 1971, 65.2 in 1975, and 67.9 in 1980) and has not declined in the two other groups studied, ages thirteen and seventeen.[3] Declines in other scores, such as the SATs, continue, but they may reflect the fact that improvements in achievement so far are concentrated in younger groups and have not yet worked their way up the age structure.

All this is not to deny that scores are low nationwide compared to other advanced countries, and that whatever improvements are discernible began at rather low levels. Still, these data do not show that "young Americans" are functionally illiterate, or that "Johnny can't read," or that "Johnny can't count," or that, as John R. Silber, the president of Boston University, has put it, "today's high school diploma is a fraudulent credential."[4] Such statements and many similar ones about schools in general are much too sweeping. It is bad enough that maybe as many as half of the nation's schools do not function effectively; we need not go beyond that and declare that the schools *in toto* are failing.

Aside from being too broad, the criticisms commonly focus on the wrong issue. Cognitive learning is the preoccupation of most school critics. The continuing exposé of why "Johnny" (who stands for American kids in general) can't read, for example, not only overstates the cognitive deficiency of young Americans but rests on the assumption that the schools stand or fall on their ability to teach cognitive skills.

This cognitive preoccupation is revealed both by those who urge that kids not be graduated, nor promoted from class to class, unless they demonstrate "minimum competence" in certain skills, and by those who oppose such educational policy on the ground that it is biased against minorities or enforces an all-too-low standard. It is the focus of those who favor a "core" curriculum as it is of those who favor plenty of electives; of those who see the salvation of reading in the use of phonics (the fervent belief of Rudolf Flesch, the author of *Why Johnny Can't Read* and *Why Johnny Still Can't Read*[5]) as of those who advocate "sight reading." It sustains the proponents of "mastery learning" and modular units, of the new math and the old, and so on through all the various teaching panaceas.

This preoccupation with cognitive achievements was engraved in my mind when I took my youngest son to his kindergarten class at Dalton School in New York City and heard a fellow parent—after waiting impatiently for the teacher to finish explaining her agenda for the term, crowned with helping the children learn to relate to one another and to the school's routines—unable to contain herself anymore, exclaim: "But when will they teach him to read?" Books with titles such as *Kindergarten Is Too Late* scare parents into demanding more teaching of formal academic subjects to very young children. According to one source, some parents end up piling word-association flash cards in their child's crib.[6]

CHARACTER FORMATION, MUTUALITY AND CIVILITY

In evaluating the status of American schools and contemplating reconstruction, the criteria one brings to bear are even more crucial than in dealing with families. Quite unlike families, schools are subject to public policy; they have elected boards and are accountable to parents, taxpayers, or churches. Hence, while the criteria one applies to the family affect largely one's assessment of its condition, in the case of schools the criteria one uses affect not only the way they are assessed but also the public policy that is to govern them.

The first criterion I suggest we ought to use is contribution to personality development, to character formation. This requires special attention to school-generated experiences, which educate young Americans in the broadest sense.

To put it briefly first, a significant proportion of the children who enter American schools each year seem to be psychically underdeveloped. Their families have not helped them mature to the point that they can function effectively in a school, relate constructively to its rules, authorities, and "work" discipline. It might be said that to relate well to many of the nation's schools—to their burned-out teachers, uninspiring principals, arbitrary rules, and tedious assignments—would itself be a mark of maldevelopment on the side of the young generation. However, I refer here to a *general* incapacity to deal with authority, rules, and "work," a deficient capacity to mobilize self and to commit it, whatever the setting. Just as no wind will sail a boat without a keel and rudder, so underorganized persons cannot function effectively in any institution, though they may seem to do better in those which expect least of them.

Many schools—I estimate roughly a third*—seem to add psychic

---

* My estimate that roughly a third of the schools turn out largely underdeveloped persons is impossible to justify by hard data. (Such schools graduate some well-formed persons, and properly structured schools turn out some underformed persons.) Such data simply do not seem to exist. I "guesstimated" the size of the group by calculating backward from the proportion

damage to the psychic deficiencies new pupils import from their homes. These schools do little to develop underdeveloped personalities and quite often provide opportunities for further maladjustment. As a result, many young people are unable, for psychic reasons, first to learn effectively in the schools and then to function effectively in the adult world of work, community, and citizenship. Thus, the root problem is not that millions of high school graduates have great difficulties in reading, writing, and 'rithmetic; these all-too-common deficiencies are *consequences* of insufficient self-organization, of inadequate ability to mobilize self and to commit. These graduates enter the adult world *twice* handicapped. They suffer both from continued psychic underdevelopment *and* from the inadequate cognitive preparation this underdevelopment helped to cause.

The significance of psychic deficiencies for cognitive learning, for the acquisition of skills, can hardly be overstated. The relevance of personality development to the ability to work is elementary; young persons who cannot cope effectively with authority figures, rules, and routines in schools cannot be expected to do so on most jobs.[7] Its significance for civility and mutuality needs a bit more elucidation.

At the foundation of civility and mutuality is a capacity to control impulse and mobilize ego's energies *in part* for acts other than the satisfaction of biological needs. The newborn infant has next to no such capacity; it is preoccupied with its immediate biological needs. The process of education, starting with the family, channels some of these drives to "energize" a regulator, to modify behavior by introducing a "personality" or character. This is achieved by tying biological satisfaction to socially acceptable gratifications (sublimation, if you wish); by relating satisfaction to sensitivity to others and deriving satisfaction from the affection and respect of others, the psychic basis of mutuality; and by building ego-restraints, the basis of playing by the rules, and ego-involvement in the transcending (public) realm and issues, the basis of civility.

It is possible to overeducate and draw too much of ego's energies into these spheres, a process that has concerned social scientists in the past and that has led to a call for less education and more freedom for ego.[8] However, the historical context of present-day America seems

---

of schools viewed by the public as poor or mediocre, deducting the proportion classed as violent, and so arrived at one third. At best this should be viewed as a first approximation.

to require the opposite: schools that, making up for undereducation in the family, lay the psychic foundation for mutuality, civility, and work in the adult world—and in the schools themselves.

THE PSYCHIC FOUNDATION

There is no solid, incontestable evidence to prove that large parts of the present generation of Americans are psychically underdeveloped, that they have insufficient ability to control impulse, mobilize ego, and be involved in transcending circles and causes, the bases of mutuality, civility, and the work-ethic. An account of the reasons no such data are available would require a long aside about the problems of social science research in general, and psychological and educational studies in particular, including such issues as the tendency of theory and empirical work to diverge, the difficulties involved in conducting experimental work with human beings and in generalizing from labs to "field" (*i.e.*, reality) conditions, and the shortage of resources available to the social sciences. Once that had been undertaken, another even longer "review of the literature" would be required, to see what various limited studies do suggest, why the findings do not necessarily complement one another, and what further lines of investigation must be followed before solid conclusions can be drawn. All this needs to be done, but it cannot be done here, in the context of another pursuit. Because of this limitation, my discussion of the psychic underdevelopment of many young Americans, its effects on schools, the effects of schools on it and in turn on the adult world must be treated as largely an hypothesis. While I will indicate which occasional, limited data, observations, and reports led me to develop my position, they clearly do not suffice to confirm it beyond reasonable doubt until more research is done.

To return to the substance of my argument, let us look first at a simple incident. A young secretary, recently hired, was asked to use the Yellow Pages of the telephone directory. When she was unable to do so, it became evident that she did not command the alphabet nor understand the principles of categorization and subcategorization involved.

Such inability would usually be counted an example of a cognitive deficiency, of poor teaching if not low IQ. However, if one asks why it is difficult to teach someone a list of twenty-six items and the principles of a very simple classification, one soon realizes that something more is amiss than that no one ever provided the needed time and effort. Nor could it be a question of IQ for most pupils, because so little comprehension or intelligence is involved.

Think what it would take you to memorize, say, a telephone number of 26 digits—a considerable amount of effort, but *not* cognitive; instead, concentration, control of impulse, self-motivation, ability to face and overcome stress (in order to resist distractions and accept the "routine" work involved in memorizing). This element of psychic organization, or capacity to mobilize and commit psychic energy to a task, is what those who are not learning well seem to me to be most lacking. It is what seems to account for their "inability" to do elementary computation (i.e., to memorize a few rules and discipline oneself to adhere to them), or to write a coherent paragraph (*i.e.*, to remember the rules of punctuation, that sentences have nouns, and so on—we are not dealing with effective writing, but straight English exposition.)

While the common preoccupation with the cognitive agenda thus focuses on consequences rather than on the prime cause, a parallel concern with discipline is much closer to the mark. In one public opinion survey after another, teachers and parents rank discipline as the number one problem of the schools. This attention to discipline is highly relevant: It focuses on the school as a structure in which learning is to take place, and suggests that in a classroom where the proper relationships between pupils and teachers, and between students and rules and routines, cannot be developed and maintained, learning is not possible. Violent schools, the public correctly perceives, are not only unsafe but also provide institutional conditions under which schools cannot discharge their teaching duties.

So far, so good. Unfortunately, the focus on discipline itself is partially misdirected, although at least it calls attention to the right issue, the psychic one. Discipline, as most people understand it, is highly external: Teachers and principals "lay down the law," will not brook any talking back; students "show respect" (rise when the teacher enters the room, do not speak unless spoken to, and so forth). What the pupil—and the future adult—really needs is *self*-discipline, *self*-organization, the ability to mobilize and commit self. This in turn is developed in structured conditions, but not in authoritarian ones.

The line between structure and authoritarianism is easy to illustrate but not to define with great precision. Basically, what is needed is not close, continuous external supervision, but a school structure—authority figures, rules, and organization of tasks—that will build up the capacity of the student to regulate self. This is achieved best, it seems, when what is required of the student is clearly stated and the link between requirements and educational goals is clearly and fully explained, rather than arbitrarily announced, changed at will and whim, and aimed as much at teachers' egos as at educational enhancement. Advancing self-organization requires that assignments be "do-able," appropriately checked, and rewarded. When they are excessive and mechanical (such as excessive memorizing) or when rewards are allocated by irrelevant criteria (such as being teacher's favorite or having influential parents or minority status), requirements become dictates, not sources of involvement and ways to build commitments.

Kenneth D. Benne puts it in terms of desirable versus undesirable forms of authority. Undesirable forms are authoritarianism, which overemphasizes the demands of the bearer of authority, and anarchy, which overemphasizes the subject's right to autonomous action. Desirable forms are those that result from a working interaction of teacher and subject.[9]

How quickly these matters can be confused is apparent in the following statement by James O'Toole:

> Because of the American school system's commitment to mobility and equality, there is now a shortage of working class people, individuals socialized for an environment of bureaucratic and hierarchical control and of strict discipline. Employers are correct in their observations that the schools are failing to provide enough men and women who are passive and compliant, who seek only extrinsic rewards for their labors, and who have the stamina and stoicism to cope with the work technologies and processes developed during the industrial revolution.[10]

Strict discipline and hierarchical structure will tend to produce passive, compliant workers, at best suited for some crude jobs. Most work, especially in a high-technology society, requires people who are more actively involved in their work, care about the outcomes, and show a measure of initiative and creativity—all the hallmarks of the self-disciplined and committed person, not the industrial cog.

STRAWS IN THE WIND

Schools that provide creditable to excellent education inform us whether or not the factors we consider essential are present. There are some studies of such schools, though much work is yet to be done.

To start with a newspaper account, in one school system student responsibility was made the cornerstone of the educational program. A special program launched in Modesto, California, a school district with nineteen thousand students, starts the elementary grades with "character education" rather than focusing exclusively on so-called academic achievements. According to a school official, in this part of the program the school "spells out, as a regular part of the curriculum," its expectations of students' behavior. Each grade has a written conduct code explaining students' rights and responsibilities and the penalties for violations of the rules.[11]

The significance of this approach is multiple. By being explicit, it avoids the transgressions that arise from vague guidelines and the alienation caused by arbitrary ones, which are typically unstated. By covering both duties and rights, it addresses both sides of human motivation; and by tying behavior to explicit sanctions and rewards, it increases the likelihood that students will follow the code.

Modesto's high school juniors and seniors learn "citizenship accountability," which here does not amount to learning the three branches of government or the number of justices on the Supreme Court, but the criteria for discharging one's obligations to the school and for participation in its activities. Students are graded for their citizenship performance. Ultimate sanctions are suspension and expulsion, even though these are public schools. The net result reported was a decline in "unsatisfactory citizenship" scores from 35 percent when the program was initiated to 18–20 percent three years later. Far from welcoming suspensions, students plead for their right to study. More than three fourths of the elementary students test at or above grade levels on standard tests; on the college boards, high school seniors score 20 percent above the national average in verbal skills and 15 percent above in math.[12]

This picture is of course incomplete. It does not tell us whether the codes were merely imposed on the students or the students were involved in forming them; how strict they are; or to what extent acceptance has been merely "instrumental," to what extent deeper, including some internalization of the values promoted by the school. Also, programs that start with good results due to original enthusiasm and commitment often deteriorate over the years, though a three-year record at Modesto is reported to show some ability to sustain success. While we clearly do not know enough about the Modesto program, and it cannot and should not be mechanically copied elsewhere, it serves to illustrate an approach that is compatible with the focus on school-generated experiences as a basis for character formation, which in turn sustains learning and teaching.

Another informal account comes from an observer who visited successful elementary schools (at least half of the sixth graders were reading at or above grade level) in poor neighborhoods (at least 60 percent of the kids were eligible for free lunches). These schools, he found, showed unmistakable marks of structure: clear goals, high expectations, monitoring of students' progress, and frequent use of tests.[13]

A quite different set of observations arises out of a grand tour of 750 "alternative schools." The two educators who visited these schools are alternative-school advocates and hence are not suspect of antagonism to this type of school. Despite the popular notion that alternative schools never require a student to do anything he doesn't want to do, these observers report that "*no* public alternative school that has survived more than two years gave students such a veto. Successful public alternative schools . . . soon learned that they needed rules about behavior, attendance, graduation requirements, respecting rights of others, etc." At the same time, in alternative public schools "students have had opportunities to help make, review, and revise many rules." However, in schools that survived two years or more, these opportunities did not include a right of students to ignore rules.[14]

A paper on vocational education prepared for the National Institute of Education comments:

> During the height of the war on poverty it was a common observation of those employers who were making a good-faith effort to train disadvantaged workers that it was easy

to teach cognitive job skills (how to run the machine), but next to impossible to teach good work habits (show up on time, do not cuss the boss, work hard, etc.).[15]

Also possibly relevant is the finding of the National Assessment of Educational Progress that as reading scores have improved somewhat, the ability of high school and junior high school students to draw inferences and to apply knowledge to problem-solving has declined.[16] There are no compelling data—in fact few data of any kind—to explain this decline. Among the possible causes nominated by the research team are excessive TV viewing and a focus on "basics" at the cost of more advanced skills. My hypothesis is that this development also shows lack of intellectual self-discipline. Interpretation and application, much more than basic reading skills, require following certain rules (e.g., check out all main options, avoid premature closure) and a measure of patience (i.e., control of impulse). The data suggest to me that these attributes declined. This is not to deny the possible role of other factors; for example, under most circumstances extensive television watching develops neither self-discipline nor the ability to think.

The large-scale comparative study of public and private schools conducted by James S. Coleman and his associates[17] stirred up a major controversy, which Coleman admits he helped to generate by stressing in his interpretation of the data the virtue of private over public schools and elsewhere calling for granting them taxpayer support.[18] What this study of 58,728 sophomores and seniors in 1,016 public, parochial, and other private schools suggests is that effective schools, both private and public, had two features in common: Their structure enables them, first, to impose discipline, and second, to uphold academic standards. Schools with these attributes graduated students with significantly higher knowledge and skills than those without them.

The single most important difference between more effective and less effective schools was the disciplinary structure. While Coleman relied on such measures as enforcement of a dress code and strictness in dealing with those who cut classes, are absent, or attack teachers, he also drew on student-based measurements. These indicated that in the more effective schools, discipline was not merely imposed but by and large was accepted as legitimate—that is, the majority of students perceived discipline not as a set of dictates but as worthy of their commitment. Thus in these schools the majority of the students found the discipline "fair"; they believed teachers' interest in them was relatively high; they did a significantly larger amount of homework than students in the other schools (a difference that both affected their achievements and reflected the effectiveness of the disciplinary structure); and, maybe most revealing, they had a high degree of self-esteem.

The reason Coleman's analysis comes out favoring nonpublic schools is that private schools are more commonly able to maintain these structural prerequisites of learning; however, when they are available in public schools, they work there too. That is, the critical factor in school structure is not the mode of ownership. Private schools without the appropriate structure will not educate or teach well, and public schools that do have it will tend to be "high performers," all other things being equal. Statistically, private schools do more often have the needed structure, but public schools can and do develop it; they are not congenitally unable to do so.

It has been suggested that the differences Coleman found in the schools' achievements are due to differences in the parents who send their children to the two kinds of schools. But Coleman's findings held even when he controlled for this factor, although he points out that "despite extensive statistical controls on parental background, there may very well be other unmeasured factors in the self-selection into the private sector that are associated with higher achievement."[19]

An aside is called for: At first reading it may seem that Coleman's findings combine the psychic agenda with the cognitive one, since they stress both discipline and academic standards. However, the second most important factor determining high performance, after disciplinary structure, is also more a structural item than a cognitive one. This is the proper authority relationship between teacher and student, the ability to compel task-relevant behavior and to have the class, peers, and parents support it, or at least not negate it.

Another large-scale study relevant to the question of what makes schools effective was conducted in Britain. *Fifteen Thousand Hours* reports a longitudinal study, from 1970 to 1974, of twelve secondary schools, all in London's inner city but differing widely in other respects.[20] Holding constant the social background of pupils, the authors found substantial differences among schools in students' learning and behavior. The single most important factor in these differences was the school's character as a social institution—its structure and the processes that administrators and teachers establish. In the schools that provided clear incentives and rewards, that had a strong academic emphasis and gave priority to student learning, that expected students to carry out clearly defined responsibilities, students not only did better in school and attended more regularly, they also were less involved in delinquent behavior outside of school. And schools with clear and well-established standards of behavior and discipline did better than those where teachers had to struggle alone to establish these standards.

The more successful schools in this study provide a good illustration of the difference between creating the structural conditions for evolving self-organization and self-discipline, and merely imposing discipline from the outside. The better schools created a climate of respect for students as responsible individuals and held high expectations of both their behavior and their academic work. Students accepted specific "supervisory" tasks in corridors, classrooms, and assemblies, for example. Teachers provided many occasions for students to work independently, during class or in the library, in effect saying to them, "We trust you to use your time for productive, self-guided work." At the same time, the results of work students do on their own must be checked, and some students need help to develop study habits that are up to independent work. The point, though, is that expecting students to take responsibility and work independently encourages self-regulation rather than reliance on constant close supervision; the latter contributes to inadequate internalization of impulse control.

Another important finding of *Fifteen Thousand Hours* is that appreciation and praise—that is, positive sanctions rather than merely negative ones—were highly effective, although teachers did not use these tools often. Indeed, what "discipline" brings to mind most immediately is restraining and setting limits, not encouraging or promoting any particular behavior. As reported earlier, my own study shows most clearly that involvement based on positive feelings is psychologically much more productive than the same degree of compliance attained by fear, pressure, or negative sanctions.[21] Educators must use both sides of the motivational scale—in view of the paucity of tools available to them, to give up either would undercut their capacity to discharge their duties. However, the more they can use the positive side, the more likely the result will be students' self-organization rather than compliance limited to the time and scope of actively present disciplinary agents.

Of course, other factors affect teaching. A community uninterested in or hostile to learning, one lacking in successful role models (or rich in the wrong ones, such as "making it" by circumventing school and being a numbers runner or drug peddler), one ravaged by unemployment, crowded housing, garbage and rats—such communities dampen learning. Teachers who are underpaid and who do not feel respected will not be paragons of education. Extensive TV exposure seems to be a negative factor. And there are some pupils—in all classes and races—who do have low IQ's or severe learning disabilities. However, so far as the effective working of schools is concerned—holding constant, so to speak, their environment and the cognitive abilities of the pupils—school structure is in my view the prime factor. Cognitive deficiencies are secondary and often reflect in part the other factors. True, the circle closes: Once cognitive deficiencies accumulate, they tend to pose personality problems, as evident in learning-disabled pupils who become disruptive. But the main vector points the other way: Studies of effective schools suggest that even children with cognitive problems learn when they can mobilize and commit.

POP PSYCHOLOGY IN EDUCATION

Deficient self-organization—and school structure that neglects its development—is by no means limited to inner cities, or to public schools, or to schools where violence and disruptive behavior are prevalent. Indeed, many suburban schools, schools in upper-middle-class parts of cities, and private schools suffer, as do the families that form their communities and are the source of their pupils. *What Really Happened to the Class of '65?* provides a vivid description of one such school in Pacific Palisades, California, a rich suburb of Los Angeles.[22]

Structural weakness in these schools is often promoted by an educational version of the ego-centered mentality. One version is a bastardization of Freud, which calls for "working out," "letting go," "expressing primordial urges," "listening to one's inner feelings" as needed for ego-growth. In schools these notions provide the ideology for an understructured social environment and the withdrawal of authority both in practice and principle.

Two minor incidents provide quick, vivid illustrations. A kindergarten on New York City's West Side: Freddy, age four, bullies and brutalizes other kids for better than a week. The teacher does nothing to restrain or dissuade him; she firmly believes Freddy is "going through a stage" and must "work out" his hostilities. After that, she says, there will be an opportunity for some other kid to "find his victim." Lesson imparted: Yield to your impulses; others will have to make way; society is a sequential jungle in which victimizers and victims take turns, as opportunity arises.

A primary school in Montgomery County, Maryland: Jim, age twelve, sticks a pencil through the lip of David, age twelve, in the course of a fight; David requires some stitches. Teacher next day explains to parent: "First of all, it was a very hot day—and Jim's parents are just in the middle of the worst divorce fight ever." Implication: What can be *explained* from the viewpoint of ego psychology is taken care of. And attention is focused on ego rather than the needs of mutuality and civility. Lesson imparted: Do not rely on shared rules; take "the law" into your own hands.

The enthusiastic following won by popularized developmental psychology does not help. Particularly relevant in education have been the theories that portray children's learning as a natural unfolding from within, a process initiated and basically carried out by the child her- or himself.

Among the most influential of these educational pop psychologies is that based on the theories of Jean Piaget. Piaget's exploration of the way children's language and thought evolve rests less on large, systematic studies than on his inferences from detailed observation of a very small number of children. As is usually the case, in popularized form his theories are made less complex, more extreme. As generally interpreted, Piaget suggests to educators that from birth children are internally programmed to grow and learn in natural stages. They take to learning as a duck takes to water, as a sunflower follows the sun's light. The stages cannot be hurried: On their own, children will learn what they are ready to learn; efforts to teach what the child is not ready to learn are doomed. The educational message: Passive teachers are fine, and unstructured learning "occasions" are "in."

In a book introducing Piaget to teachers, Hans G. Furth explains that the purpose of a school that embodies Piaget's theories "is to provide the setting in which the child's natural intelligence can develop to the fullest. Such a school is in no particular hurry about the development."[23]

Another educator put the essence of Piaget's message as follows:

> The most fundamental of Piaget's insights for education is that the child literally builds his own intelligence, that he is in fact the architect of his own growth. . . . It is the idea to which education must attend if it is to promote the optimal development of the child.[24]

A parallel view of emotional and social growth, with similar consequences, was incorporated in pop psychology from the work of child-development specialists such as Arnold Gesell and his colleagues at Yale. Their careful description of "normal" development for children at successive ages was welcomed by parents and teachers alike as a guide to reasonable expectations and a source of comfort ("It's just a phase"). While Gesell and his co-workers emphasize the importance of the child's environment and culture, their starting point is the individual: "The reactions of the child are primary: he must do his own growing."[25] Maturation, the innate process of growth, and acculturation, the acquisition of a social heritage, "interact and interfuse," but "maturation is most fundamental."[26] The educational impact of popularized Gesell is felt even in relatively traditional classrooms, where the style of the teacher often reflects this picture of the discerning mother: "She aims first of all to be perceptive of and sensitive to the child's behavior. . . . He is a living, growing organism, an individual in his own right to whom the culture must attune itself if his potentialities are to be fully realized."[27]

John Holt, a prolific educational writer and critic, echoes the view of education as an ego-centered process:

> True learning—learning that is permanent and useful, that leads to intelligent action and further learning—can arise only out of the experience, interests, and concerns of the learner. . . . Education is something a person gets for himself, not that which someone else gives or does to him.[28]

Holt believes that "children are by nature smart, energetic, curious, eager to learn, and good at learning."[29] And he would leave educators quite passive. Consider his picture of the teacher—as travel agent:

> We teachers can see ourselves as travel agents. When we go to a travel agent, he does not tell us where to go. He finds out first what we are looking for. . . . Given some idea of what we are looking for, he makes some suggestions. . . . He does not have to take the trip with us. Least of all does he have to give us a little quiz when we get back to make sure we went where we said we would go or got out of the trip what we hoped to get.[30]

As I see it, this approach imposes too much on the child, too little on the educators and the schools. Moreover, this sunny view ignores the elementary fact that what children are when they begin school is not what children are by nature. At birth, when their "nature" is most evident, children are unformed creatures who, left to their own devices, will learn little. And what schools and teachers face is not children's unadulterated nature, but what families—and neighborhoods—have made of it. Schools cannot ignore the fact that many of the children who reach them are neither eager to learn nor good at it; they must first be won over to learning, in effect rehabilitated, and helped to develop learning habits.

I say "habits" deliberately. Not all learning can be made fun and games, and it should not be even if it could, because it would then provide a poor preparation for the post-school world. There the ability to defer gratification is required; not all work, not even all thinking, calculation, writing can be made intrinsically rewarding.

Educational pop psychology's focus on ego and on immediate satisfactions rather than self-organization is also evident in the open-classroom movement, with its planned lack of structure. Open-classroom education is in effect a counterculture concept. Students initiate their own "learning experiences" according to their interests and capabilities; the role of the teacher is to facilitate and encourage rather than to guide. For the pupil, enjoyment and spontaneity are said to be as important as growth and achievement. The open-classroom movement explicitly repudiates deferment of gratification and ability to play by the rules, and advocates instead the educational equivalent of "do your own thing."

Critics of existing schools and advocates of alternative approaches often zero in on valid problems exhibited by traditional and bureaucratic schools, but then go overboard in their criticisms and, above all, in the reforms they suggest. Thus, critics correctly see many schools as too large, insensitive to children, and teacher-oriented. But their more extreme corrections—such as making schools and teachers heed kids' cues almost exclusively, or closing the schools and letting each kid learn by following adults around ("the way they did in primitive tribes")—take reform too far, both practically and conceptually. Learning needs structure (if only to rebel against eventually), and learning in the streets of most inner cities—or affluent suburbs, for that matter—is much less educational than following a preliterate farmer or fisherman. And what our society must teach is just a bit more complex.

Both valid criticisms and the tendency to carry them too far are illustrated by proponents of "informal education," an umbrella term for approaches, such as the open classroom and the free school, that emphasize the quality of the school experience in its own right and the interests and desires of the learner, and that play down rules, routines, and organization.

Charles E. Silberman, a teacher and journalist who has labored long in the educational vineyards, outlines the case for informal education in *Crisis in the Classroom*.[31] Far from a fanatical advocate of the virtues of informal education, he presents a balanced view of the case for it, citing its champions at length.

The foremost weakness of existing schools, according to advocates of informal education, is their excessive concern with structure, order, and control. Silberman says this results in part from school people's view of the school as "a collective experience requiring . . . subordination of individual to collective or institutional desires and objectives."[32] He quotes Willard Waller's statement in his classic *The Sociology of Teaching:*

> It is only because teachers wish to force students to learn that any unpleasantness ever arises to mar their relationship. . . . We have defined the school as the place where people meet for the purpose of giving and receiving instruction.

> If this process were unforced, if students could be allowed to learn only what interested them, to learn in their own way, and to learn no more and no better than it pleased them to do, if good order were not considered a prerequisite to learning, if teachers did not have to be taskmasters, but merely helpers and friends, then life would be sweet in the school room.[33]

It is typical of the hedonistic undercurrent in the ego-centered mentality to seek for life to be "sweet" in the classroom, as if there are not other values that take precedence, as if a certain amount of tension is not constructive. Thus, while Silberman, and Waller before him, raise a valid concern—that teachers with rigid, pre-set agendas, indifferent to children's interests and pace, will not be effective— they overlook that teachers who see themselves first and foremost as kids' pals and "helpers" may do harm in their own way. Recognition that teachers command superior knowledge and represent the adult world, that children are immature and often must be prodded to grow, and that not all growth is enjoyable and self-propelled must balance the proper rejection of teacher authoritarianism.

Charlie Chaplin made the clock a symbol of factories in modern times; Silberman sees in it the symbol of slavish adherence to routine in the schools. A rigid timetable, he says, not only wastes time; it means that activities, as Philip Jackson puts it, "often begin before interest is aroused and terminate before interest disappears. Adherence to the schedule also means that lessons frequently end before the students have mastered the subject at hand."[34]

Again, there is merit in concern that the preoccupation with routine and schedules is excessive. At the same time, without some structure, how is one to teach a very large number of students a variety of subjects, using specialized teachers for each? (Much of the writing on informal education is implicitly elitist, assuming not only eager, able students but very small schools, small classes, and highly skilled teachers, assumptions none of which is quite realistic in the age of mass education.) Having one teacher teach a variety of subjects would allow greater flexibility in scheduling. For example, if everyone were keyed up about literature, the class could continue with that and delay math, and there would be no need to rush to another teacher's class. But this would sacrifice specialization. The tradeoff of specialization for flexibility, which is common in the lower grades, becomes ever more costly in intellectual rigor as students advance to higher grades.

While structure in schools is often excessive, the basic reason it is there is not the one advocates of informal education advance, what Silberman calls "the reluctance to turn children free—to let them follow their own curiosity." Silberman, again with an assist from Waller, states their position:

> At the heart of the schoolmen's inability to turn responsibility over to the students is the fact that the teacher-student relationship in its conventional form is, as Willard Waller states, "a form of institutionalized dominance and subordination. Teacher and pupil confront each other in the school with an original conflict of desires, and however much that conflict may be reduced in amount, or however much it may be hidden, it still remains. The teacher represents the adult group, ever the enemy of the spontaneous life of groups of children."[35]

This misses the point. Schools have not been established to provide children with additional opportunities for "spontaneous life," and to take schools to task for failing in that aim is to ignore what they can do: provide more opportunities for creativeness, a reasonable number of "electives," consultation with students—not eliminate the structure but make it more effective for education. Personality and structure must meet each other; only in utopias can structure yield to personality, especially to young, unformed personalities.

The horror with which grades are viewed provides one more example, if one more is needed, of both a valid criticism and an exaggerated conclusion of the informal education approach. Grades should indeed be an educational means, not a goal in themselves, and they should be allocated according to achievements; without doubt, they often fall short of these ideals. There is evidence that the specific information transmitted by grades is often very unclear.[36] Students are often vague about the standards by which they are being evaluated and to which their achievements are compared. Moreover, they often question, appropriately or inappropriately, whether grades are given on the basis of merit. Nevertheless, to argue therefore that grades should be merely "diagnostic," never used to reward or punish, is to ignore both human nature and the need of the school to motivate its pupils.

The deepest link between informal education and the ego-centered mentality is in the implicit view of the relationship between children and the community represented by the school, the notion that the school should be shaped to suit individual children. After all, only in one-on-one teaching could scheduling, for example, be carried to the logical conclusion toward which informal education drives it, where no child learns a subject (or learns it longer) other than what that child on his or her own wants to do at that time. Elementary as this idea may be, scheduling is not primarily an instrument of domination by the school, but a way of accommodating the needs of hundreds of pupils simultaneously.

Similarly, to teach the values and skills and knowledge that work and life in the community require may well not be fully responsive to human nature as it presents itself raw. But only when the community is unjust and oppressive, and one seeks to undo it in order to redo it, might one educate a generation of children to follow their own instincts to the disregard of shared and community needs and values. In all other situations, as one seeks to reform society one must learn to participate in it.

RECONSTRUCTION: SCHOOL AS AN EXPERIENCE

I have tried to show how the ego-centered mentality feeds into the tendency of numerous American schools to neglect psychic development and character formation. If we are to turn about, to recognize the need to balance self with a renewed capacity for membership in the community, where must we go from here?

The first step toward reconstruction of the schools from the inside will require a higher level of awareness and analysis of the school as a *set of experiences*, as a system of rewards and punishment, as a structure. When you look at a school, don't see teachers, pupils, classrooms, curriculum. See, instead, young people being rewarded for work well done, finding that self-organization and achievement are a source of social gratification, as long as students abide by the rules (*e.g.*, compete fairly) and are sensitive to others (*e.g.*, do not deride slower learners). Alternatively, see teachers dictating to pupils assignments they are unable to handle or are not motivated to do, vandalism going unpunished, drugs sold openly, pupils being rewarded or punished according to criteria other than achievement—whether staying out from underfoot, obeying without question, or coming from an affluent or otherwise socially preferred background.

Some educators refer to the merits of "learning by experience" rather than by lecture, evoking the work of Dewey or Montessori, for example. This is quite a different matter. They refer, by and large, to teaching methods that enhance cognitive learning. A child is said to learn more about Egyptian pyramids, for example, by building a small one out of toy bricks than by a teacher-talk, even if it is backed up with visual aids. The educational experiences I refer to are as a rule imparted by life in school, and they affect most immediately personality development, not task-oriented learning.

With typical disregard for this aspect of schools, David Thornton Moore, writing in the prestigious *Harvard Educational Review,* seeks to discover the "pedagogy of experience" outside of school, in "community settings" that require one to be "engaged in activities in the real world."[37] (A similar position is advanced by Ivan Illich.[38]) Moore goes on to suggest, quite correctly, that "social encounters" outside of school help participants learn to "organize their behavior,"[39] but like many other educators, he overlooks the significance of the comparable experiences that school itself generates.

The significant effect of such experiences in school *has* been widely recognized in one area. Sports have often been held up as the arena in which character is formed. In sports—and other "extra"-curricular activities—the noncognitive dimension is obvious. Hence, the opportunity sports provide for education (as distinct from teaching) has been recognized since the ancient Greeks. The British evolved the dictum that the playing field is where you learn that how you play— cooperating with your own team and, above all, being fair to the other—is more important than whether you win. In other words, learn that a commitment to shared rules outweighs personal—or group—gains.

It is symptomatic of the American condition that in forming character, sports in schools are often not geared to this element of civility, but to Nixon's favorite quote from football coach Vince Lombardi: "Winning is not the most important thing; it's everything." A common lesson is, hence, that violating rules, often with impunity, is the shortest way to personal and group gains.

My point is not that sports with this emphasis form people who are willing to vote for politicians on the take, who adopt a cynical view of no-holds-barred interest groups, or who embark on unbounded quests for personal and corporate gain. My point is that *all* school activities are like sports in two pivotal ways: First, the experiences generated—not by what teachers say, but by the way they conduct themselves, deal with students, with each other, with assignments, and so on—affect pupils' characters. Second, like sports, these experiences are often counterproductive in many, maybe as many as half, of America's schools.

In about 15 to 20 percent of the schools, especially public schools or schools in large cities, the dominant issue is custodial maintenance (*i.e.,* coping with violent or disruptive students). In many other schools, especially suburban or private schools, a variety of ego-centered psychological approaches hinder education. Since most educators, parents, and citizens seem to think about schools in terms of academic achievements, content of teaching, and teaching styles— or to think about personality-shaping experiences as a matter reserved for extracurricular activities, not the whole school—the first step to correction must occur through a change in awareness of how schools affect personality development, the direction on their current effect, and how it might be redirected.

Britain's Tavistock Institute of Human Relations, under the direction of Elliott Jaques, developed for industrial management a strategy for enhanced self-awareness and change that might well be applied to schools.[40] In this strategy, Jaques does not attempt to introduce changes either from the outside (on the basis of directives, expert advice, and so on) or by meeting with some of the staff (say, the foremen). Instead, self-analysis and change are "dialogued" from the top down. The process starts with sessions with top management and works its way down the corporate hierarchy. This approach greatly increases the probability that the higher levels will support rather than hinder change and that all levels will be involved and won over. Group therapists or other facilitators may participate, but to enhance the process, not to dominate it.

In schools, this approach might entail working first with school boards and groups of superintendents, then principals, then teachers, then parent-teacher organizations and students. A good way to start might be to determine what experiences the school now generates and ask what they ought to be from the viewpoint of the desired educational outcomes. The next step would be to ask how the desired changes can be achieved. Outside facilitators might be required to prevent self-analysis from turning into defensive self-justification or mere gripe sessions.

The New Whigs have a suggestion for fixing what ails the American educational system. They favor educational vouchers or tax credits for private-school tuition payments. (Not every New Whig does, but these educational schemes are philosophically compatible with the New Whig position.) It would be naive to assume that the only reason these ideas are promoted is philosophical; for instance, they are particularly attractive to parents who send their children to Catholic schools—and to politicians who seek to appeal to them. But every philosophical position has some such background. Here the focus is on the inner intellectual merits of such positions, whatever their political or other roots.

The philosophical kernel of tax credits for tuition and of educational vouchers is the notion that the individual knows what is best for him; in this case the individual is not the actual consumer but the parent. It is further assumed that the result of creating a "marketplace" for education would be competition to provide effective education, both among individual schools and among sectors, such as the public and the private. A full examination of the merits of this approach would require, to begin with, asking if parents are in a position to judge what good education is, an issue that similarly arises with regard to other professional services such as legal and medical, although education of course is not as highly specialized. I am personally inclined to believe that a mixture of professional and client judgment is more effective than mere judgment by the consumer. Another relevant issue is whether there are factors that would restrict fair and free competition among schools in such a marketplace; still another, what effect such a system would have on the more vulnerable groups in society. Here, though, my focus is elsewhere. Whether such a change is or is not introduced does not matter to my key consideration, that attention must be paid to character formation, not merely, or first, to cognitive learning. If parents come to play a larger role in the schools than they currently do, all that means for the issue at hand is that they too—not merely teachers, principals, students, and educational policymakers—will have to invest more, promote more, even fight more for the use of the schools for character development.

At the same time schools heighten their awareness of character development, factors external to the schools will have to be tackled. The schools have been overloaded with assignments, from making up for the pre-school education millions of families do not complete to scores of educational goals promoted by various interest groups, from sex education to religious teaching, from foreign languages to "non-competency-based" promotion. According to Gene Maeroff, education writer for the *New York Times,* the chief problem with the public schools is that adults have burdened them with too many good intentions—for which the kids pay the price.[41] The question is not the merit of these assignments; when each is viewed in isolation from the others, many are quite valuable. But if one looks at the schools' ability to carry out all of them, or even a fair share, they clearly overwhelm the schools to the point that many have stopped trying to be effective and just "cope."

Correctives might come from several directions. I have already suggested that the schools' load could be eased if families do more of their educational duty before their youngsters reach school. In addition, it would be helpful for families to work more closely with schools, and especially for the schools to make greater efforts to involve parents in their work rather than either shut them out or manipulate them in PTAs and other such groups.

Another corrective would be for the general public to raise its public involvement somewhat, to countervail single-issue and other interest groups. More broadly based public pressure would make it easier for the schools to avoid the costly and ultimately counterproductive programs to which they have been pushed, for example, by extreme advocates of bilingual education, who want almost everything taught in a child's native language, and not merely for a transition period.

As a result of greater mobilization of the public, interest groups would have to moderate their demands on schools, if only because they would be made to recognize that unless the schools are allowed to attend more actively to their first business, nobody's goal will be served. They might also be more inclined to work *with* the schools to find mutually satisfactory ways of meeting legitimate needs. Thus, the American Civil Liberties Union, to protect students' civil rights, has insisted that schools meticulously observe due process in suspending students. As Roland S. Barth of the Harvard Graduate School of Education put it, as of early 1980, "the courts have established that students are now entitled to virtually the same due process rights as an accused felon."[42] He then cites forty lines of tight text that describe the protocol. The result has been procedures that are so cumbersome and time-consuming that in practice very disruptive students often stay in school. The urgent need is to work out ways to make it easier to remove from public schools truly disruptive students, without opening the door to wanton violation of their civil rights.

Some deregulation and reduction of the role of state and federal agencies would also help. In the matter of suspending students, for example, procedures prescribed by state and federal agencies push schools in the same direction as the safeguards urged by the ACLU—toward protecting the rights of a disruptive student at the expense of the need of all students for the school to sustain an educational environment.

Reducing state and federal intervention would also serve to reduce the mountain of paperwork that now takes time and energy away from the schools' primary task. In the state of Maryland, for example, for the principal to take one student out of a regular class and for that period assign him or her to a resource teacher for school-paid tutoring to help the kid catch up, parental consent in writing is required, and this in turn requires a meeting with the school's "educational team," the filing of a written report, and several other bureaucratic steps.

Secretary of Education T. H. Bell reported that by eliminating thirty sets of "cumbersome, burdensome, and unnecessary regulations," the equivalent of 118 printed pages in the *Federal Register,* he reduced the size of a year's grant applications by two hundred thousand pages, dropped seven thousand pages out of financial reports and twenty thousand pages out of programmatic reports.[43] The deregulated bliss may have been exaggerated by a few pages, but nobody doubts that a keen search would find more regulations and forms that could be cut with little harm and much relief.

OTHER RECONSTRUCTION MEASURES

In addition, there are several major shifts in public policy (not necessarily limited to governmental and certainly not to federal policy) that would help to reconstruct schools. These include a major "downward" shift in educational resources; more opportunity for combining work and study for students aged sixteen to eighteen; and a year of national service. It is my purpose here not to explore these items of public policy in detail, but to illustrate the approach to which the preceding analysis leads.

A "Downward" Shift of Educational Resources

If one looks at American schooling as a whole, one sees that it is top-heavy. A very high proportion of the young population stays much longer in the educational sector, especially in colleges, than in other societies. For instance, as many as 50 percent of Americans in the relevant age cohorts attend college, compared to about 10 percent in countries such as West Germany or France. (This is not to suggest that the United States should have as few of its young in college as these countries, but just as 10 percent may be much too restrictive, 50 percent may be too expansive.)

This overeducation is slowly gaining recognition as college graduates no longer find that a college degree is a secure ticket to a job, let alone a good job. Unemployment rates for college graduates under age twenty-five, though nowhere near those for inner-city youth, run quite high (5 percent to 8.3 percent between 1974 and 1977); more important, an estimated one fourth to one half of graduates hold jobs that do not require a college education.[44] In the view of the Carnegie Commission on Higher Education, overeducation on the college level is both a misuse of scarce resources and a political time-bomb.[45]

One reason for overeducation is that colleges, especially junior and community colleges, are doing work not completed in the high schools, so-called remedial education. Colleges are often used as a remedial educational tool because many metropolitan high schools are written off as beyond remedy. Thus, for example, in New York's City College, high-powered, expensive professors of comparative literature teach remedial English to people who graduated from New York City high schools unable to write a simple statement correctly.

Moreover, as concern for the scarcity of resources has increased in recent years, the time is ripe to try again to complete more of the educational task at earlier age levels, where it is most cost-effective. A downward shift of resources could be achieved by adding no new public resources to colleges, especially four-year ones, and instead adding resources to primary and high schools.

Two other considerations also lead to the same conclusion, that resources should be shifted downward. One is prevention versus correction. It is much more efficient to teach a subject effectively the first time around than to allow pupils to waste high school, acquire poor study habits, and grow in alienation, then try to correct for all these later.

A study of low-income children who attended preschool in the 1960s suggests that, regardless of their background and intelligence, these children were far less likely to require special education, be retained in grade ("fail"), or drop out of school than similar children without preschool experience. Social scientists located some of the original preschool students, by then aged nine to nineteen, and examined the long-term effects of the early childhood program. Irving Lazar and Richard Darlington of Cornell University coordinated the Consortium for Longitudinal Studies. They report:

> We can safely conclude that low-income children benefit from preschool programs—in being more likely to meet the minimal requirements of later schooling—and that this finding is not due to initial treatment/control differences in sex, ethnicity, early intelligence level, or early family background.[46]

Preschool graduates did markedly better in later schooling than their nonpreschool counterparts, scored higher on achievement tests, and were more likely to express pride in specific achievements.

Most important, since we stress the role of personality in these matters, personality is shaped early and is particularly difficult to reshape once it is misformed. Some data suggest that little progress on this front occurs after the sixth grade, roughly age twelve.[47]

Greater Work-Study Opportunities
A more radical reform would start schooling at age four and continue it until age sixteen, to be followed by two years of mixed work and study. Schools could either recognize certain kinds of work as providing educational experiences equivalent to classroom time (*e.g.*, work as an apprentice instead of in the schools's carpentry shop) or provide internships in voluntary or government agencies on a part-time basis. This is one of the recommendations of the National Com-

mission on Youth, whose report has the telling title *The Transition of Youth to Adulthood: A Bridge Too Long.* The Commission would also lower the age of mandatory school attendance to fourteen.[48] Taking a different approach, a Carnegie study, *Giving Youth a Better Chance,* suggests that school could be cut back to three days a week—in effect leaving half time for regular (rather than "educational") employment, without necessarily any loss to education.[49]

The work-study years should be aimed at easing the transition from the school to the work world, and at adapting the last years of schooling to a large variety of needs, *e.g.,* allowing some pupils a more vocational and less academic mix. This would work best if the work were meaningful and properly supervised, *i.e.,* more educational.

This is certainly not always the case. Social psychologists Ellen Greenberger and Laurence Steinberg found that young people receive little on-the-job training in many of the jobs they typically hold. Few develop relationships with adults (potential role-models) on the job, and students who work use more alcohol and marijuana than those who do not.[50] On the other hand, when Northwestern High School of Baltimore sent six hundred students to work one day a week as volunteers in hospitals, offices, and primary schools, the pupils gained in maturity, insight, and reality of expectations, as well as involvement.[51]

A Year of National Service

A year spent serving the country, interrupting the "lockstep" march from grade to grade, right into and through college, has been widely recommended.[52] While the suggested programs vary in detail, many favor a year of voluntary service, with options including the armed forces, Peace Corps, VISTA, and Conservation Corps. Some would make it the senior year of high school; I prefer for it to follow high school, replacing the first years of college for those who wish to continue, or providing a year between school and work for those not college-bound.

The merits of a year of national service range from primarily pragmatic to normative ones. To begin with the pragmatic: In an average month of 1979, while the unemployment rate was 5.8 percent for all workers, it was 9.0 percent for those aged twenty to twenty-four and 16.1 percent for those sixteen to nineteen.[53] High unemployment among teenagers and young adults is generating a demoralizing experience for the many individuals involved. It is also undermining the rest of society, since young unemployed persons make up a sizable part of the criminal population, violent street criminals in particular. A year of meaningful national service might well help many unemployed youths avoid enticement into crime. Much of the potential impact lies in psychic development, in enhancing the individual's self-respect, sense of worth, and outlook on the future. A year of national service could provide a positive, constructive experience with which to start one's post-school life.

In terms of future employment, a year of national service could furnish young people with an opportunity to try their hands at a skill they might later want to develop. For those planning to go on to college, service after high school would provide a break between "work" in two institutions, and time out to consider their goals in a setting that is largely noncompetitive.

On the normative side, national service would provide a strong antidote to the ego-centered mentality as youth become involved in vital services for shared needs. Thus, an important criterion for including a particular form of service in the program should be its societal usefulness; that is, promotion of values that transcend the mere advancement of self-interest. This could encompass myriad possibilities, from improving the environment and beautifying the land to tutoring youngsters having difficulty in school or visiting nursing homes, schools for the retarded, and other such institutions to check on the quality of services. At the same time, forms of service that infringe on the rights of others would be excluded; for example, volunteers would not be given responsibilities that would, in effect, take away jobs by providing a pool of cheap labor.

Finally, one of the most promising payoffs of a year of national service for young Americans is that the program could serve as the "great sociological mixer" America needs if a stronger national consensus on fundamental values is to evolve. That is, national service could fill a role somewhat similar to that once served by the march toward the western frontier. At present, America has few of the structural opportunities for shared experience to develop shared values that are essential if the polity is to reach agreement on courses of action with sufficient speed and without disruptive conflict.

One of the major reasons for America's low consensus-building capacity is that the schools are locally run; they do not subscribe to a common national curriculum, and they transmit different sets of values of a regional, racial, or class nature. A year of national service, especially if it were designed to enable people from different geographical and sociological backgrounds to work and live together, could be an effective way for boys and girls, whites and nonwhites, people from parochial and public schools, North and South, big city and country, to get to know one another on an equal footing while working together at a common task. The "total" nature of the situation—being away from home, peers, and "background" communities, and spending time together around the clock—is what promises the sociological impact. It is the reason such a year may be more effective than several years of casual contact in high school or college, cafeterias, pool halls, or bowling alleys.

The costs of such a program are formidable. If every American who reaches eighteen were to participate—a very far-fetched assumption—it would cost an estimated $21 billion a year ($7,000 per person times 3,000,000). However, one must deduct from this the costs, such as salaries, for young people who would be serving in the armed forces anyway; the cost of fellowships and grants-in-aid from public funds to college freshmen; the cost of unemployment and welfare for eighteen-to-nineteen-year-olds, itself a hefty sum, as unemployment in this group is particularly high; savings from an almost certain reduction in crime, police work and jail sentences. Moreover, at least 10 percent of the cohort can be expected to be mentally or physically unable to participate. Even so, the program has a multibillion-dollar net price tag; it can be seriously considered only if there is great public support for it, and parallel commitment by Congress and the administration.

IN SUMMARY

To state the obvious, that the first duty of schools is education, turns out not to be self-evident. First, there is a strong tendency to equate education with teaching, transmitting skills and knowledge, which it is not; at least that is not the school's only major task. Second, there is a lack of understanding of how important character formation, education's core subject, is *in itself* for the purposes for which teaching is usually sought—as a source of basic skills for work, for mutuality, for membership in a civil community, and for effective teaching.

The single most important intra-school factor that affects education is not the curriculum or the teaching style, at least not as these terms are normally used, but the experiences the school generates. In many schools, perhaps as many as half, these experiences are not supportive of sound character formation, mutuality, and civility. While many factors combine to account for this weakened condition of many American schools, the ego-centered mentality is probably the easiest to reverse; it is almost certainly a good place to start the reconstruction of the schools, by providing legitimation for a structure under which self-organization will be more likely to evolve. Reconstruction must also draw upon other factors, many external to the schools, ranging from greater parental support for the schools' primary educational mission to a reduction in the number of other missions, which currently dissipate their resources and blur their focus.

CHAPTER SEVEN
Regionalism and Nation-Rebuilding

The centrifugal forces we have seen so far, the forces that pull the American society apart because they are not sufficiently balanced by the centripetal forces of mutality and civility, are those of interest groups, both the old garden variety and the newer single-issue type. Much additional pulling apart is generated by the decline of mutuality among the country's regional groups, which find their expression chiefly in state governments and in local representation on the national level, especially in Congress.

The retreat from nation and the consequent need to shore up the bonds that make America a nation is not an issue that is currently "fashionable." The public's and policymakers' attention tends to focus on a few issues at a time. Inflation, crime, pollution, and the Soviet threat have all gained top attention at one point or another. In contrast, the deterioration of national bonds, the rise of regionalism and tensions among the states, is not on the list of problems that preoccupy Americans these days. That does not mean Americans are unaware of the issue. It is occasionally discussed in academia and the media, and fellow citizens I interviewed were vaguely concerned about it. But it is not as much on their minds nor has it commanded the same kind of search for solutions as, say, the energy crisis or inflation.

This relative neglect ought to be changed. The retreat from nation is a serious one, rising in severity, and reconstruction in this area is particularly difficult to achieve. What is the problem? Why have the national bonds deteriorated? What is to be done?

THE WIDEST CIRCLE

It is my recurrent theme, far from novel but in need of reiteration, that no individual can function unto himself, to the disregard of others; individual needs and shared concerns both require mutuality. But how far does the circle of mutuality extend? Parents and their children are the most elementary circle; friends, neighbors, classmates, or workmates the next; the community one lives in—another extension of the circle. But what about those beyond community borders? How far is one to extend the reach of mutuality?

People have dreamed, at least since the days of the Old Testament, of a brotherhood that would embrace all people and, in recent generations, of worldwide peace firmly established under world law. However, generation upon generation of tribal, feudal, religious, and world wars, bitter disappointments first with the League of Nations and then with the United Nations, have left the dream of a worldwide community-circle a pale vision. The international reality is dominated by nations, which constitute the widest circle to which most people extend their mutuality and commonweal concerns. This is as far as their effective commitment reaches. Beyond the nation, there are limited tokens of charity (some milk for foreign kids via UNICEF, some food packages via CARE, some Peace Corps volunteers) and some special ties (such as that between the United States and the United Kingdom). The prevalent mode, though, is for national borders to define the limit of the main bonds of mutuality, and with it, the limit of main commitments of civility. Few Americans seriously subscribe to the notion that they owe allegiance to a world community, or that they should treat foreigners according to the same legal and moral rules Americans are expected to abide by in dealing with one another. Hence, I will focus on issues of mutuality within this nation, because that is the most encompassing effective community for most Americans, and because civility is typically extended only to those whom mutuality embraces.

My main point is not the familiar regret for the weak status of worldwide bonds—but the deterioration of the national bonds.[1] While my focus is limited to the United States, many other nations are also losing in mutuality, not to a world community but to segments within themselves, thus shrinking rather than extending the circle of mutuality. As individuals lose in national perspective and commitment, narrower loyalties and commitments rise, pitting regions against each other. In Canada, French-speaking provinces are highly disaffected, even exploring secession. In Britain, Scottish and Welsh regionalism has risen. In Belgium, Flemish and Walloons are in intensified conflict. In the United States, in recent years, the Northeast and the Midwest have moved in different directions from the South and the West and away from each other and nationhood. (Whether it is true that in other nations the rise of tribalism has a strong ethnic component, while in the United States it does not, in all countries the shared key factor is the geographic foundation of the newly enhanced divisiveness.)

The immediate danger in the United States is not the ultimate breakdown of the national community or the secession of one region, but less willingness to attend to shared concerns and growing regional and state "egotism," which make it more difficult for the nation to act in unison and to share burdens. Indeed, many of the difficulties the United States faces as a nation, regarding issues ranging from welfare to energy to national security, are directly affected by the weakened status of national mutuality. In the area of welfare, for example, a major block to attempts at reform is the strong regional divergence of views between the more conservative South and Southwest and the more liberal Northeast as to how charitable one should be, even as to who the welfare clients are, as well as differences in the economic status of those not on welfare.

Tensions created by such divergences have been compounded by the fact that public assistance programs such as welfare and Medicaid have traditionally been funded disproportionately by the northeastern states, as southern and western states were considered relatively poor. Each state could set its own benefit levels, and the richer states generally provided much higher payments. Moreover, richer states paid about 50 percent of their higher public assistance costs, while poor states paid about 20 percent of their lower ones.[2] As the economies of the poorer states improved, they did not correspondingly increase their contributions. In 1979, the average monthly payment to families with dependent children was still two to four times as high in the northeastern states as in some southern states. The average payment in Massachusetts, for example, was almost four times that in Mississippi.[3] (Note, though, that the cost of living has been higher in the Northeast and the opportunity for income-in-kind smaller.) Some northerners contend that the southern states have been keeping public assistance payments low in a deliberate attempt to encourage poor southerners to move north.

Demographic shifts during the 1970s also intensified the interregional strains. From 1970 to 1979, the population increased in the West by 17 percent and in the South by 14 percent, in the Midwest by less than 2 percent and in the Northeast not at all.[4] In some western states, the population increase was dramatic–42 percent in Nevada, for instance, and 37 percent in Arizona.[5] Much of the population increase was caused by the migration of people from the Northeast and Midwest to the South and West in search of better jobs, lower taxes, or a warmer climate. The shift further aggravated interregional debates over public assistance costs because, as one observer put it, "After absorbing millions of rural poor from the South, the North is sending its skilled workers and its tax base back to the South."[6]

The dust has not yet settled on this migration to the Sunbelt— and a new one is reported on the rise. A new study projects a 27 percent increase in the 1980s in a second Sunbelt, ranging from the Rocky Mountain states through the Southwest to the southern Appalachians. Growth in what is now called the Sunbelt will pale in comparison—it is projected to be only 13 percent.[7]

M. S. Forbes, Jr., puts well another sign of rising conflict among the states. Under the heading "We're Supposed to Be One Country," he writes,

> When it comes to tax laws, the states of the United States seem to be losing sight of the fact that they are part of a federal union. They are considering or are passing discriminatory levies designed to help themselves at the expense of the rest of the country—and ultimately themselves.[8]

Among the numerous examples he cites: A 1974 Minnesota law (since overturned) that heavily fined employers who offered pension plans if they closed a Minnesota office; an Iowa corporate income tax law that openly favors home state manufacturers at the expense of manufacturers who sell in Iowa goods produced in other states; a duty levied by Ohio on out-of-state low-sulphur coal to force local utilities to buy Ohio's high-sulfur coal. Different observers have pointed to other examples. Seventeen states, for instance, place a severance tax on the lumber they export, and several others—including Iowa, Illinois, and Indiana—were considering imposing a "corn tax" on agricultural exports as the 1970s ended.[9]

Other reports detail the way states try to pull industry away from other states by proffering a large variety of privileges and grants, in an escalating tug-of-war. Northeastern states fought to change the allocation of federal resources to benefit their region. In 1977, for instance, the House passed a Northeast-backed bill that would favor pre-1939 housing in the distribution of federal aid for housing and community development, although representatives from the South and West objected that this would channel more money to the North than to their regions.

On the other hand, northerners contend that the South has received an unfair number of military installations and contracts. Rhode Island Senator John Chafee, dismayed by what some in the state refer to as the "second Pearl Harbor"—the 1974 decision to shift the Navy's headquarters south from its traditional home in Newport, Rhode Island—complained in 1973:

> The southern group is extremely well organized. It is no coincidence that you see Charleston, South Carolina, brimming with defense facilities and Strom Thurmond sitting as ranking Republican on the Armed Services Committee. Or the lovely Naval Air Training facility sitting in Meridian, Mississippi, near where [Senator John] Stennis [also on the Armed Services Committee] lives.[10]

Another sign of pulling apart is the question, which seems to be asked with growing frequency, what did "my" state pay into the national kitty and what did "we" get out of it?[11] Aside from the near impossibility of honestly calculating what a state gets out of the federal government (How does one "allocate" national security? What are the blessings—or damage—of national fiscal policies?), the question itself reflects a dismembering tendency. In a well-integrated community, members may seek an equitable basis for contributions to the commonweal and a fair share of disbursements according to some principle (*e.g.*, favor vulnerable members or children or senior citizens). However, any attempt at mechanically equating members' inputs and payouts undermines the ability of the community to invest in shared endeavors and reallocate resources among the members.

In other words, it belies the acceptance of membership in a community, and the foundation of mutuality.

Even national security is not spared. Thus, Nevada and Utah rallied against placing MX missiles in *their* states, not on the grounds that they considered these missiles unnecessary for national defense against nuclear attack, but because they did not want to spend "that much" of "their" land and water on a national need. Also, they did not wish to be a prime target in case of nuclear attack, even if the national defense required it.

SOURCES OF DECLINE OF NATIONAL BONDS

The deterioration of national mutuality in recent American history (1950 to 1980) is a relative one: American national bonds were never very strong, nor have they recently "fallen apart"; they have merely weakened again—and further.

American nationhood has been weaker than that of, say, Britain or France for many good reasons. The very size and complexity of American society, as compared to most other nation-states, agitates against a high level of unity. The federal constitution left the states with considerable power and made the national government less important in early generations than it would have been under a unitary government. Throughout most of American history there has been no unifying enemy at the gate. The national legislature is composed of local and state representatives, not nationally elected members. And there is no common national educational system to promote shared values, sentiments, and ideals.

This far-from-high level of national unity (raised during periods of U.S. involvement in world wars) was sufficient in previous generations, when many economic decisions were made locally and there was little pressure for shared national action on most fronts. The demand for national management of the economy in the United States dates largely from the 1930s, in response to the Depression; the development of a sizable standing peacetime national military force, from the emergence of a Soviet threat in 1947–48; and the rise in national social services, from the 1960s. The 1973 energy crisis added to the call for national action. In short, *since World War II the need for nationwide actions, and for the mutuality and civility to sustain them, has increased substantially.* It is my thesis that *at the same time the United States* has faced this growing *need* for nationhood, it has *experienced further weakening of national bonds that were not strong to begin with.*

Almost every major societal development is propelled by a variety of forces, not one primordial drive. Consequently its course is difficult to chart and to explain. This is the case with the deterioration of national bonds in recent American history; several factors must be considered. The most recent is the nation-tearing effect of the new energy world that emerged in 1973.

The Northeast and Midwest, already disadvantaged by rugged winters, suffered disproportionately as a result of the energy crisis of the 1970s. New England has been hit hardest, since it is 85 percent oil-dependent, whereas the rest of the country is about 45 percent oil-dependent.[12] Partly because of this dependence, by 1976 energy costs for the northeastern metropolitan areas ran 97 percent higher than the average for the rest of the country.[13] Other regions did not suffer as much; indeed, some prospered. For the nine American states that are net energy exporters—Louisiana, Wyoming, New Mexico, Kentucky, Alaska, Oklahoma, West Virginia, Montana, and Texas[14]—increased energy prices after the 1973 oil embargo brought large benefits, both in increased revenues from their "raw" energy resources and in improved economies, as the increased demand for domestic oil promoted oil drilling, pumping, refining, and shipping.

Not only must the Northeast rely heavily on high-cost OPEC oil, it does not have an ample supply of natural gas as an alternative. In the mid-1970s, industry in New England was using natural gas for less than 20 percent of its energy needs; in Louisiana and neighboring states, on the other hand, natural gas supplied 52 percent, and in the Texas region 81 percent. Moreover, what natural gas is available in the Northeast is much more expensive than in other regions. In early 1976, a million BTUs of heat from natural gas cost $1.23 in New England, only $.33 in the Southwest.[15]

Adding to the gap between regions is that many states in the West and the South have been able to increase their government revenues by imposing "severance taxes" on oil and coal exported to other states. At the top of the group is the American Saudi Arabia, rich in oil, thinly populated—the icy deserts of Alaska. The state has calculated that by the year 2000 its annual royalty and tax income from oil and gas may be as high as $10 billion, a prospect that so delighted the state's voters that in 1980, by referendum, they established an

Alaska Statehood Commission to study the advantages and disadvantages of remaining a state and to consider seceding from the United States.[16] Coal-exporting states have also added to their coffers by imposing severance taxes on coal sold in other states. Montana levied a tax of 30 percent, for example, and North Dakota 33 percent.[17] Each year, Illinois residents pay Wyoming enough money in severance taxes to cover the salaries of the members of the Wyoming legislature, the governor, his cabinet, the highway patrol, and the Department of Revenue.[18] As Wyoming Governor Ed Herschler put it, "They call us the blue-eyed Arabs of the West. I don't like to be called a blue-eyed Arab, but I see the point."[19]

In 1980, seven states raised more than 20 percent of their revenues through severance taxes on minerals, mainly oil, gas, and coal; just one had raised that much a decade earlier.[20] The Midwest Governors Conference estimated that residents of its member states paid roughly $700 million in severance taxes in 1979 and would pay more than $2.5 billion in 1985.[21]

Different rates of economic growth in various regions of the United States have paralleled differences in the impact of the energy crisis, dividing the nation into two high-growth regions and two laggard regions. The South and West outpaced the rest of the country during the 1970s both in job growth and capital investment. Between 1967 and 1977, while the West added 14.8 percent and the South 19.6 percent to manufacturing employment, the Midwest lost 1.4 percent and the Northeast 15.5 percent.[22] Between 1970 and 1977, service jobs grew twice as fast in the West and South as they did in the Northeast. During the same period, investment in capital equipment increased 43 percent in the Northeast, but it shot up 96 percent in the West and 131 percent in the South.[23] One observer discerned not two or four regional economies, but nine different and competing Americas.[24]

A colleague who read an earlier draft of the manuscript of this book suggested that regional differences have always been a hallmark of the American society and that sharp economic differences among the regions, e.g., between cotton growers in the South and textile mills in the North, played a key role in the Civil War, for instance. While this is true, studies by Karl W. Deutsch and others suggest that after the Civil War, especially after the age of reconstruction— say, as of the 1890s—the United States was becoming increasingly one nation. And while it never achieved the same level of integration as countries such as Britain,[25] the level of national bonds was significantly higher in 1950 than, say, in 1850. However, national bonds diminished in the 1960s and 1970s.

Beyond the effects of this new energy situation, national bonds are strained by the general retreat from commitment and from institutions. Most Americans continue to be proud of being Americans and believe "the U.S. is the very best place in the world to live in."[26] Few would choose to emigrate, although their ranks had risen from 4 percent in the 1950s[27] to 12 percent by 1971.[28] At the same time, there is a crisis of confidence.[29]

The retreat from nationhood was further spurred by two developments that have been captured by code names, one a faraway country, Vietnam, one a building complex in Washington, Watergate. The much disputed war in Southeast Asia and the specter of constitutional violations by the President himself, along with the resignation in disgrace of a Vice President and a President, were not the prime sources of widespread national disaffection, but they did add to and amplify the retreat from nationhood.

Three other developments had fed into the deterioration of national bonds by the late seventies: The decline of the cold war, cessation of the growth of the economic "pie," and a sense of national incompetence, especially incompetency of the national leadership. As these are all quite familiar, they need be only briefly discussed here.

The cold war served for decades as a leading unifying, rallying theme for America. In active opposition to communism, perceived by most Americans as an evil global force seeking to conquer the world by any means available, divergent groups found a common cause beginning in the late 1940s. For more than two decades it provided a basis for national consensus. However, beginning with President Kennedy's 1963 "Strategy for Peace," which deliberately sought to defuse cold war tensions, and continuing through the various détentes and Nixon's "open door to China," an American psychological disarmament took place. As a result the anti-communist unifying theme weakened, though it far from disappeared. It was not replaced by any other theme with comparable power to draw the nation together.

Economic growth benefited the American society for decades, indeed, a century and a half. Aside from satisfying ever more needs, it allowed the great majority of Americans to sense that they personally were successful. It also enabled newly active groups, such as minorities and women, to improve their condition without directly cutting into the take of other groups; and it was conducive to peaceful resolution of conflict. The slower economic growth of recent years, the largely stagnant standard of living, the end of expansion of the economic "pie," reversed all this. Reslicing the "pie" is much easier when it's growing, and is highly tension-provoking when it's not.

The sense of a nation that "can't do," reflecting inability to "win" the war in Vietnam, "roll back the tidal wave of crime," slow down inflation, or make most social programs work effectively, fed into a sense of frustration with the national government and the national leadership.

Everett Carll Ladd, Jr., a leading analyst of American public opinion, puts it well:

> Poll findings aplenty since the mid-1960s have in fact seemed to indicate a big change in national self-perception and self-confidence. During the Vietnam years, for example, according to Harris polls, Americans began expressing markedly diminished confidence in the "people in charge of running" the various central institutions of the society. There has been no recovery. Over the 1960s and 1970s, according to surveys conducted by the Institute for Social Research of the University of Michigan, large majorities of Americans came to see their political leadership as incompetent and insensitive to the public interest.[30]

Ladd cites some quite impressive shifts in public opinion to substantiate his point:

> In 1958, only 18 percent of respondents told the Michigan interviewers that "the government is pretty much run by a few big interests looking out for themselves . . ."; in 1980, however, the proportion had risen to its all-time high of 76 percent. . . . The proportion of respondents to the Michigan surveys professing to believe that "quite a few [of the people running the government] don't seem to know what they are doing" stood at 28 percent in 1964, jumped to

45 percent in 1970, reached 52 percent in 1976, and stood
at 63 percent in the last asking of the question, during
campaign '80.[31]

From 1965 to 1979, the proportion of Americans who viewed "next
year" as likely to be difficult economically grew from a minority of
22 percent to a majority of 69 percent.[32] On the whole, at the end
of 1980, 81 percent of Americans were dissatisfied with the way things
were going in the country, though only 17 percent were dissatisfied
with the way things were going in their personal lives.[33]

The public seems to project its frustration and ambivalence about
the nation onto its leaders. Very large segments of the public have
been displeased with each of our recent presidents; each was found
deeply deficient in one way or another by the majority of his country-
men and -women. Ford was considered slow, uncharismatic, falling
all over himself. Nixon was considered a crook. LBJ—manipulative
and scheming. JFK—a fine speechmaker who confused his words with
reality and accomplished very few things. Ike—a do-nothing president
who left the White House at three o'clock in the afternoon to play
golf and let his staff run the country.

Individuals, local communities, and regions have increasingly fallen
back on their own initiatives. They have scaled down their expectations as to what the nation can do as a community and what can
be achieved through public policy. The corollary has been weakened
nationhood—a lower level of commitment of the parts to each other,
a decline of national mutuality and civility—which is standing in
the way of whatever business must be discharged nationally.

RECONSTRUCTION

The Need to Relegitimate National Policymaking

The reach of citizens' commitments and the foci of public policymaking tend to parallel one another. Thus, as attention focuses on
a particular set of policymakers, people identify with them and build
loyalties around them and the communities they represent. Take Europe, for instance. Attempts to build a United States of Europe floun-
dered again and again as the national capitals of Germany, France,
Italy remained the foci of policymaking, identification, and loyalty.

A measure of *Europa* as a community evolved when *its* capital, Brussels, became a site of policymaking for the members of the European Economic Community, especially once the representatives of the rising community were allowed to deal directly with corporations, labor unions, and even individuals in the member countries, rather than only via their respective governments. In the United States, national loyalties evolved with the rise of Washington, DC, as a national capital alongside the capitals of colonies and later those of the states.

Theoretically, and only theoretically, one could boost American nationhood by a constitutional convention that would abolish the federal structure and replace it with a unitary national one. Such a change would abolish all state government and state legislatures, as well as local and state representation in Congress. It would move their policymaking power to Washington. Members of Congress would be elected on national ballots, as the President is now. They would be nominated by the national political parties and committed to them. This is, of course, the pattern followed by countries such as Israel, Italy, France, Sweden, Norway, Denmark, Austria—indeed, the majority of the world's democracies.

Such a constitutional change would work to shift attention, loyalty, and power to the national level, away from local differences. Other lines of conflict would remain—*e.g.*, among workers, consumers, and employees, or among corporate groups—but these cut across localities, and are less divisive than geographically based loyalties. A state or region can, in principle, take the ultimate step of breaking away from the union, but no class of workers, employers, or some other class, can seriously contemplate such an act.

All this is theoretical. In the American context, local power bases and regional differences in values, perceptions, and interests are too strong to tolerate such centrism. On the contrary, the trend is to reduce national policymaking and shore up local decision-making. While the fifties and sixties saw many attempts by the federal government to impose itself on local decision-making, in recent years the move has been to cut federal intervention and restore states' rights, powers, and discretion.

The Reagan administration's championship of states' rights and its "new federalism" are well known. It openly and actively seeks to turn over policymaking powers, missions, and control over funds to the states. (Critics depict the "new federalism" as a form of budget-cutting sugar-coated by promises of greater state freedom to allocate whatever funds they do get.)[34] However, this does not constitute as sharp a departure from previous administrations as the media often make it seem. Previous administrations referred to a federal-local "mismatch" due to the fact that the federal government collected most of the nation's tax revenues, while local governments managed most of the domestic social programs. While some early attempts to correct this mismatch involved greater national management, the main thrust, at least since the early seventies, has been to transfer funds to state and local governments under what has been called "revenue sharing." The federal government often attached strings to these funds, demanding that they be spent in ways that would promote its own social goals, such as increased numbers of minorities in local vocational training. However, as a matter of practice, these strings were often ignored, circumvented, or cut by Congress.

Thus, while Reagan's approach extends and accelerates the trend away from national policymaking on most domestic matters, the trend started at least a decade earlier. Indeed, since 1975, the much-criticized growth of government has occurred almost completely on the local and state level, not the federal one. In effect, the civilian *federal* labor force ceased growing as of 1975, when it reached 2,890,000 employees. In 1979 it numbered 2,869,000, of course serving a larger nation. At the same time, the number of state and local government employees continued to grow, from 12.1 million in 1975 to 13.1 million in 1979, constituting 82 percent of the total of government employees at all levels.[35]

This decentralizing of national policymaking provides a partial solution of sorts to the problems posed by the weakened national bonds. If a truck's engine is aging and needs an overhaul, one way to cope with it is not to spend resources on fixing it but to reduce the load the truck is carrying. If, indeed, the national government could be reduced in future years largely to matters of defense and foreign policy, as many New Whigs pray, the transfer of policymaking power to the states would reduce the nation's missions to the point that it might be able to make do with a relatively low level of national consensus and commitment.

There are, however, several limitations to this approach, each more serious than the last. They encompass the social agenda, interstate business, the social consequences of the defense budget, and above all economic decision making. First, the social agenda. In the United States the national government has often been the main lever for social change; this is, of course, one main reason those opposed to such change wish to curtail, if not abolish, its domestic power. It was the federal government that weighed in against local governments to promote the extension of effective (as distinct from nominal) voting rights to minorities, to fight against racial segregation, and to professionalize the jobs of prison wardens and postmasters (once chiefly political rewards).

Sociologist Nathan Glazer warns us not to take too simple or one-sided a view of the role of the federal government in promoting social change. He points out that many rights were guaranteed in several states before federal action. And not all states opposed social change; some even championed it.[36] Nevertheless, *on average,* the states have been and are less keen to change. While Glazer notes, as one should, some instances of "progressive" work by some states, there is no denying that if all are taken together, despite whatever early initiative this or that state has shown, the federal government has been the chief engine of social change.

The current trend to roll back the national government in effect assumes that in the future there will be no social issue on which the nation as a community will become sufficiently aroused to demand national action. It seems more likely, however, that the current return toward more local management of social programs is a reaction to excessive, poorly managed, alienating national intervention. If this is true, one would expect that after a period of adjustment a demand for a renewed national role in local social matters would reassert itself.

One early straw flying in this direction is the active local demand for a national role in the resettlement of refugees, especially Cubans, Haitians, and Southeast Asians. Overwhelmed localities say that since the national government, through its immigration policies, created local refugee problems, it ought to help solve them, not merely by turning over funds to the states, but by actively helping to spread the refugees among various potential settlements, a typical national duty.

Another harbinger is the growing demand for a national ID card, issued and verified by a national authority, to reduce cheating on Social Security, welfare payments, unemployment insurance, tax refunds, and immigration laws. Most revealing in terms of future social issues, the New Tories are not content to leave social matters such as abortion to state and local governments (which they correctly perceive would leave the United States with many localities open to legal abortion) but demand instead a national law banning abortion.

Such renewed demands for a national role in social matters may well favor new modes of national "intervention." For instance, it might draw more on economic incentives and less on administrative decrees and regulations. But, in view of U.S. history and the experiences of other countries, for the nation to refrain completely from a national social role seems unlikely. However, this is the least compelling of the four limitations on the extent to which one can curtail national government late in the twentieth century.

The second of these limitations is that interstate business transactions are considerable and growing, due to factors no one can control. Rotten beef, polluted air, criminals, guns, and so on flow easily from state to state, and require interstate collaboration. To evolve such collaboration on a state-by-state basis turns out to be extremely difficult. The national center is the most obvious and effective way to work out matters that involve many if not all of the states.

Third, national security policymaking is not and cannot be socially neutral. Thus, if one relies on a "volunteer" army (in effect, one of hired hands), one tends to draw heavily on lower classes and minorities, while the draft—especially if it is effectively and equitably enforced—tends to distribute the burden more equally among the classes and races. Other socially loaded questions must also be decided on a nation-wide basis—for example, whether women should be included in combat duty.

Similarly, the relative size of the defense budget is a major *social* decision. This has often been put in terms of "guns versus butter," or, in recent years, "guns versus social services." Obviously, as the economy at any one time produces only a given level of resources, the more the nation allocates to defense, the less is available for all other uses. Less obviously, national security is not a matter that can be defined with any precision; one cannot say, for example, that granting X billions to missiles and Y to destroyers means that national security will be reasonably taken care of. How much one spends on national security reflects how deeply one values some unclearly defined additional margin of safety versus other matters. This is clearly a national decision, and one of greater importance the larger the share defense takes of the GNP and the national budget. These are all decisions that cannot be made by fifty state legislatures, not to mention thirty-eight thousand county governments.

Last and most compelling, a modern nation cannot turn over economic policymaking to local authorities. Basically there is but one economy, which is deeply affected by such matters as the amount of money in circulation, the size of the federal budget and deficit, the magnitude of the national debt, decisions to act or refrain from acting to defend the value of the national currency, the imposition or removal of import restrictions. On all of these matters only one national policy is possible. It makes little sense to refuse Japanese auto importation to Oregon, but allow it to California; one cannot protect the dollar for the Northeast but let it drop for the South, and so on.

Wherever there is a need for national policy, there is a need for national consensus concerning the purposes of the policies to be advanced and the means to be used. If such consensus is not available, national policymaking becomes difficult if not impossible, as our problems in formulating a national energy policy from 1973 to 1980 amply illustrate. National consensus, in turn, rests on national bonds. Where they are weak, it cannot be strong. Continued undiscriminating attacks on the legitimacy of the national government may delay the day we attend to the need for nation rebuilding.

Extending the Circle

It is easy to describe the weakened status of national bonds, the reasons for it, and the need for more national mutuality and civility. How to promote nation rebuilding is a much more difficult question. Nations, despite the frequent analogy to ships (the President being the captain) do not turn about—let alone reconstruct—simply because someone tugs at a steering wheel, however wise the direction he pulls. If nations are like ships, they are like heavy barges caught in strong currents, equipped with weak outboard engines; their crews know precious little about ship-rebuilding and do not agree with one another as to what is to be done. Nations change only slowly, not always for the better, even when policies are well-intended; they never change at anyone's easy command.

To apply this sociological generalization to the situation at hand, the future of national bonds depends not on decisive leadership, even if national leadership added nation-building to its agenda. What is required first is a change in mentality that would enhance individuals' commitment to the commonweal at the national level—citizenship—to countervail excessive regionalism. Renewed citizenship, in turn, depends on the reversal of the general retreat from society by millions of individuals who, sensing the void, recommit themselves to mutuality and civility. While such recommitment will not by itself automatically benefit the national circle, without it there is little hope for a reaffirmation of citizenship to countervail the intensified regional pull. In a world where everybody is encouraged to work only for self, whether that means ego, my interest group, or even, yes, my community, the nation is most unlikely to be cared for. Only in a community where concern for ego is balanced by a fair measure of mutuality and commitment to the commonweal might this orientation be extended to encompass the nation.

If this change in mentality does come about, it will arise out of individual disillusionment with egotist pursuits, and intellectual and moral leadership pointing to the need for recommitment. Within this context, public leaders, above all the President, have a role to play as *agenda setters.* The President cannot dictate, prescribe, or set national values or mentalities, as he is often expected to do. What the President and other public leaders *can* do, though, especially if the public is already moving in that direction, is call attention to an issue that needs attention and to ways of dealing with it. Thus, Kennedy and Johnson focused national attention on social issues, Nixon on "law and order." Reagan in his first year in office focused on economic issues. The turn of nation-building has yet to come, in all the relevant realms: the concern of individuals, intellectual and moral leadership (which needs to precede and pave the way for others), and public/political leadership.

Institutional Change

Beyond a change in mentality, institutional changes might contribute to nation-building. Particularly helpful would be changes in the institutions that promote shared values and in those that provide a national focus for policymaking and loyalties.

One main force that binds communities, whether local or nationwide, is the sharing of basic values. If the members of a community subscribe to the same basic beliefs, it is much easier to work out specific agreements on a course to follow when action in unison is required. Thus, for instance, in the early 1950s the belief of most Americans in "standing up to Communism" served as the basis for doubling the U.S. defense budget and sending Americans to fight in faraway Korea. And recently, the *divided* view as to the status of blacks, with about half of Americans believing the nation has done enough or too much for them, half the opposite, has been one reason public policy has steered away from questions of racial equality to more consensual areas.

While families are the first educational institutions, they are not the first basis of consensus-building. On the contrary, they are the bases of diversity, the sociological loci of different perspectives and values. It is the schools that are theoretically the first line of consensus-building. They can introduce youth to a shared set of values, concepts, and ideals. However, in the United States, they do not fulfill this role, at least not well, mainly because schools are locally controlled and reflect local and regional values more than nationally agreed-upon values, perceptions, and symbols.

The main American "common school" is television. Thus, while school kids are exposed to divergent views about Darwinism and creation, Martin Luther King, Jr., the Civil War, and Roosevelt, they are exposed to basically the same comics, sitcoms, and commercials. Network television, which beams basically the same programs nationwide, could be the great unifier, at least an important source of shared bases for unity, but it is not, largely because its content is so vacuous. Thus, even if all American children ate the same cereals and admired the same cartoon figures, from Tom the Cat to the Amazons, little substantive consensus would be achieved.

Occasionally network television does create a shared frame of reference and normative experiences, suggesting how this consensus-building mission can be achieved. For example, in the 1960s, network news, less directly dependent on commercials and closer to the public arena, played a major role in building a consensus for civil rights reforms by televising the burning of Freedom Riders' buses in the South, the unleashing of police dogs against peaceful marchers, the burning of black churches, the ominous activities of the KKK. In the early 1970s it showed Americans what the war in Vietnam was really like, culminating in a consensus to withdraw from Vietnam. Television broadcasts of the hearings on Joe McCarthy are widely credited with building the consensus to curb his abuse of power, and finally with his unmaking.

This role of network TV raises many questions concerning the decisions about what to televise and the slant in effect accorded the news. (The notion that news can be objective, without any bias, has little to commend it.) It also raises the question whether network television should be protected, or whether the recent trend to localize television, turning it into a medium more like current radio, should be welcomed.

Without dealing with these important questions, from the viewpoint of the issue under study here, certain facts are clear. In the absence of a nationally guided school system, effectively providing shared bases of consensus, television is the only major alternative, and the more localized TV becomes, the less consensus-building power it has—for good or evil. Moreover, as it is, network TV's first use is to promote consumer products, its second to divert and entertain. At best its third contribution is to consensus-building.

Another institution which could weigh in for consensus-building is national service. A truly effective, enforced universal military draft of young Americans or a year of national service, of the kind already depicted, would go a long way to generate a set of experiences among young Americans, experiences of the kind which bind many of those who served in the Peace Corps.

But even if the U.S. introduced national service (unlikely in the near future because of the high costs involved) or a military draft, there still would remain the question of how to bring together older Americans, those past their youth. Only two institutions that could serve come to mind. Both are so familiar that they elicit no measure of enthusiasm, but they may nevertheless be essential, especially in view of the weakness, limited scope, or unavailability of alternatives. These two are political parties and voluntary associations.

For most, political parties bring to mind divisiveness, not unity. The parties seem frequently to place their partisan goals before national needs. Their bickering seems to delay national policymaking. And they often agitate Americans against each other, even to the point of implying that the other party is full of people disloyal to the country, or bloated with warmongers or profiteers. Despite these excesses, by the very fact that there are only two main parties, and that to win they must gain majority support—the parties work to reduce all dividedness other than that they themselves represent. That each party contains factions and important differences of opinions further illustrates their consensus-building role. Finally, despite their important differences, they often end up working out shared national policy on the foreign front and finding ways to compromise on domestic matters. And they combine members and viewpoints from different parts of the country into national organizational loyalties, and thus act to countervail divisive regional forces.

I discussed earlier some suggestions which have been made to restore vigor to the political parties; others need to be evolved. Reconstruction of the parties may well be possible only within the context of a general return to institutions and recommitment to civility. Once such a context is formed, it should be easier to add specific steps to enhance the recovery of the parties, for instance by providing financing for local candidates via the party system.

If the merit of political parties is far from widely acknowledged, few Americans question the virtues of voluntary associations. Indeed, forming them and joining them has historically been something of an American specialty, a feature foreigners have come to study, admire, and try to emulate. In the next years, the need for voluntary associations will be greater than ever. The needs to rebuild community, to involve more individuals in shared concerns, and to reduce reliance on government all point to greater need for and opportunity for voluntarism. In the present context these associations have a crowning virtue: With few exceptions, they are cross-territorial; like political parties, they involve Americans from different parts of the country, and thus help foster unity instead of regional divisiveness.

IN SUMMARY

National bonds have deteriorated in an era when they require strengthening. Above all, regional forces have arisen which undercut the ability of the nation to act in unison. American schools, TV, and national service can each contribute, but they cannot be relied upon to provide sufficient nation-rebuilding even if the scope of business which is to be conducted nationally is significantly reduced. Political parties and voluntary associations provide a perhaps dull but a much needed antidote to regionalism. They themselves are likely to be revitalized best as part of a general reconstruction of community as individuals become more committed to mutuality and civility.

THE REINDUSTRIALI-ZATION OF AMERICA

PREFACE TO PART TWO

The Reindustrialization of America

A person is competent—but competent in what? A person is able to function maturely, is "well put together"—to do what? A society and its members require mutuality and civility for sheer survival. Unless the retreat to ego is overcome and community and institutions are reconstructed, the level of conflict and frustrations will rise, and the limited energy channeled to shared concerns will make for an ineffectual, "can't do" society, continued deterioration, and even, ultimately, the possibility of destruction. However, assuming that these centrifugal processes, this retreat from society, will be reversed and that personal renewal as well as community reconstruction will be successfully advanced (as I firmly believe they must and can be), there will remain the question of the purposes toward which the American society, its leaders, its public-minded citizens will direct themselves in the next decade. The inescapable answer, in my judgment, is the reconstruction of the economy, the reindustrialization of America, not only to secure the means for a decent standard of living and for America's ability to compete in the world's markets, but also to provide for national security and for social services.

The basic reason the reconstruction of the American economy must be made the number-one priority, at least for a decade or so, is that the economic, psychic, and social underpinnings of the American economy, once the most affluent in the world, have deteriorated, together with the nation's total institutional structure. The United States has become a new kind of country: not developed, not developing, but underdeveloping, a modern economy in reverse gear. (Britain is even further down this road.) This occurred within an historical context of unprecedented external economic pressures and escalating threats to national security; in other words, the United States is undergoing a measure of internal erosion in the face of mounting external challenges. The diagnosis is not "The End of America," a "decline and fall of the West," but an accumulation of difficulties, which, if not attended to, will eventually lead to a crisis. Indeed, the recent partial regression is as much a basis for a new or renewed start as for a breakdown.

What are the options? Theoretically, there are three main avenues: continued drift and erosion; a transformation to a different societal system; or an age of economic and societal redevelopment.

At stake is the core project. Most societies dedicate themselves first and foremost to one overarching accomplishment. Medieval societies, in the period of the Crusaders, made holy wars their core project; ancient China, the *literati* activities of stylized poetry, Confucian philosophy, and brush painting; the Jewish community in the middle ages, the study of the scriptures. Developed America, in non-war years made its core project providing a high standard of living for millions, including not merely consumer goods and services, but also abundant provision for health, education, and culture. No society dedicates all of the resources and energy not needed for sheer survival to its core project. All societies dedicate some resources to other activities. However, most have one dominant purpose; service to this purpose, the core project, commands priority on resources and is *the* source of identity and meaning, the society's organizing and mobilizing principle.

Contemporary America is largely shaped by a core project of economic development that lasted from the 1820s to the 1920s. Both the high level of productive capacity and the basic societal framework evolved in those years. After two "interruptions" (the Depression and World War II), the golden age of consumption, private and public, economic and social, set in (1950–1980), though in the last five years of this era much erosion was already evident.

By 1980, fifty years or so had passed since productive capacity, and the societal bases that support it, had been a matter of first priority, a core project. These were, increasingly, years of overconsumption and underinvestment in the economic and societal foundations of productive capacity. The neglected productive base was strained not just by the growth of the public sector and social services, but also by the private consumption spree. Not only was the high-production core project neglected; its resources, psychic energy, legitimacy, and projection into the future were being challenged by an alternative project. This alternative, it is claimed, puts social progress above economic and strives for greater harmony with nature, others, and self than the productive core project provides. I will refer to this alternative vision as the quality-of-life society.

For many Americans, what started as a vision of an alternative society, less well-endowed materially but richer in humanity or spirit, deteriorated into a retreat from society and a celebration of ego. (Truth to tell, some intellectuals and quite a few other Americans moved into an ego-centered mentality without first embracing a vision of a quality-of-life society.) Both the alternative vision and the hollowing of society—the preoccupation with ego and its parallel, the growing dependence on the government—undermine the high production project.

As the high-production project was challenged from within, it was also challenged from without, above all by the wealth drain from the United States to the oil-exporting countries, by the renewed expansionism of the Soviet Union, and by the increased competitive power of previously semi-destroyed former U.S. enemies, Germany and Japan. The issue is hence not merely whether the high-production project should be maintained, but how this is to be done under the changed external conditions. To put it differently, even if there had been no *maintenance gap* due to internal erosion, there would have been an *adaptation lag,* inadequate adjustment to the new energy, security, and competitive world.

Theoretically, the main options for the near future are these: Steady as she goes, which means continued economic, social, and national deterioration; or transforming America to organize itself around a new core project, the quality-of-life society; or rededication to the high-production project, which requires a decade or so of reindustrialization, strengthening of the relevant institutions, and attention to national security.

Practically, it is the thesis of this book, America has no choice. Continued erosion will serve no project and is self-destructive in the longer run. A focus on the quality-of-life society now (rather than after reindustrialization, say in the 1990s) may not be economically practical, and it certainly is not reconcilable with the country's international challenges. A decade or so of reindustrialization, paralleling individual renewal and community reconstruction, seems the indicated course.

Reindustrialization does *not* entail a *re*run of the first industrialization of America. Communications satellites may replace the old Western Union wires, jet trains, the canal barges, and so on. Nor, obviously, does it call for a return to an age of robber barons, police shooting down striking workers, young children sent to mine coal, and the other social horrors of an earlier century. On the contrary, a much higher sensitivity and responsiveness to human, social, and environmental considerations should be the hallmark of the second industrialization of America. However, if reindustrialization is to be, economic, technological, administrative, and security considerations will have to take on, for a decade or so, the status of high values, priority, and—core project.

In the following pages, I explore first the historical factors that contributed to the first industrialization of America. I then ask to what extent they have deteriorated in the period of economic erosion. This leads us to the critical juncture. While America might choose to transform itself into some other kind of society, a commitment to production, for reasons spelled out below, is almost inevitable. The book closes with a review of the strengths and limitations of the 1981 Economic Recovery Tax Act and suggestions of other steps needed to shore up the economy. Last, the corollary societal developments, which no one can commandeer but which must be evolved if economic reconstruction is to be effective, are charted.

CHAPTER EIGHT

The Seven Elements of Industrialization: An Historical Flashback

What went into making America's the strongest economy in the first place? The United States was hardly born with a major productive industrial economy. On the contrary: In 1789 America fully qualified as an underdeveloped country. I turn next, drawing on a branch of economics that specifies the elements of development, to ask how we did it the first time around. Developmental economics is less abstract than the economics relied upon most by American academicians and policy makers. It provides down-to-earth insights into what makes an economy grow. The review of the "first," founding elements will lead to an examination of their current status. Most important, a concept of development, I suggest, provides a guide to *re*-development.

STAGES OF ECONOMIC DEVELOPMENT

The Housing Development Analogue

Building a housing development provides a useful analogue for an accounting scheme for the elements that provide for economic development. At the beginning, there is a piece of land, often part of what used to be a farm. The builder begins by leveling the ground, laying water and sewer lines, running power lines, and constructing a road. Also, in this preparatory period, legal and financial matters must be attended to, from zoning regulations to securing credit. And qualified workers must be recruited or trained.

These steps, which in combination have not yielded even a single building, are what is referred to in the theory of economic development as preparing the infrastructure, (or "social overhead capital"), which economist Albert O. Hirschman defines as the services, *not* directly productive, that "facilitate, or are in some sense basic to, the carrying on of a great variety of economic activities."[1] He adds that while a variety of items might be included, from water supplies to education to supportive laws, the hard core of the concept is transportation and power. Other experts emphasize that the infrastructure prepares for more efficient economic activities, especially by providing the opportunity for economies of scale.

That these preparatory elements are indeed needed for a solid development is demonstrated when builders skimp one or more of them; the result is a deficient development (*e.g.,* basements leak if workers are poorly trained) or higher costs (*e.g.,* if major pipes must be laid *after* the buildings are built). Supply bottlenecks and noncompetitive industries are the parallels in a country's economic development.

The builder's preparatory steps are followed by construction of the buildings themselves, the analogue of the capital goods stage in economic development, when heavy investment is made in plants and equipment. These production elements are not themselves consumable, but they can be used to generate mass consumer goods and services in the next stage of economic development. In the analogue of the housing development, this third stage is represented by the residential apartments, ready to rent.

Development economists hence point to three main stages in the transition from an "undeveloped" farming country to a modern industrial one: evolving the infrastructure, accumulating capital goods, and mass production of consumer goods and services. Some distinguish within the third phase the rise of individual or private consumption from the rise of public consumption (increase in the government sector, social services or "welfare capitalism").

These stages deal with foci of efforts and commitment of resources—with the core project. They should not be regarded as exclusive shifts, a common error when one deals in periodization. Thus, a country that is developed in the "proper" sequence does not cease to invest in the infrastructure while focusing on capital goods nor—in Stage III—is it dedicated only to consumption.

The construction project analogue is again useful here. A society is like a complex, sizable lot; tenants may be moving into some buildings, while others are still under construction and for still others the ground is just being readied. Indeed, the revenues generated by one segment (*i.e.*, selling consumer goods and services) help to provide the financing for the other segments. And, of course, some important advances in consumer goods were made in the early industrial era. Tinned utensils instead of copper, the enclosed stove, and piped water supplies are cases in point. Phases are thus a matter of focus, not exclusive dedication.

It is indicative of the American mentality that if I stopped my account of economic development at this point, many a reader would find nothing amiss. Despite all the recent setbacks, ours is an optimistic, youthful culture. But there is at least one more stage: that of a mature and aging project. Depending on how well the buildings have been maintained, the aging housing project may require ever greater maintenance costs and, after decades of use, require replacement of worn-out elements. Moreover, to keep pace with changes in the surrounding world, the owner may have to introduce new elements, say energy-saving devices, to adapt to the different circumstances. If maintenance is continually neglected, the project's yields and, ultimately, its safety will suffer; if either maintenance or adaptation is neglected, the project's competitive status will decline.

America's economic development, I will show, has reached this fourth stage. The country began as a predominantly farming society. In a century that began about the 1820s, the elements of an industrial society were gradually assembled, with the focus first on the infrastructure, later on capital goods, eventually on mass consumption leading to the affluent society. Over the last decades (1950–1980), it is my thesis, overconsumption—public and private—and underinvestment have created a maintenance gap, and an adaptation lag, due to insufficiently innovative response to changes in the outside world.

Industrialization

It is both difficult and unnecessary to find a precise starting point of America's first industrialization. Economic historian Victor S. Clark places the beginning of American factory production in the period 1790–1815.[2] Some put the initiation date after the War of 1812, when they see a change in mentality; Jefferson noted in an 1816 letter: "We must now place the manufacturer by the side of the agriculturist."[3] A recent study by Thomas C. Cochran emphasizes the fifteen years before the Civil War as the critical period in American industrialization.[4]

For my purposes here, however, the issue is not to search for early signs of industrialization; my concern is with a fully developed industrial system. This concept suggests that until and unless the preparatory elements have been accumulated to provide sufficient momentum for industrialization to be self-sustaining and to continue, early industrial activity will be stunted and the society will continue to be mainly a farming one, like an airplane rolling down a runway with insufficient speed for takeoff.

The question hence is not when some of the necessary elements first began to evolve, but when sufficient accumulation occurred to make a societal difference, inevitably at a later stage than sheer initiation. Thus, when a historian states that before the Civil War the United States was already second only to Great Britain in most areas of industrial production, this simply means that it was second in a race of two, not that it was running very fast. Indeed, as late as the 1850s, the United States was still overwhelmingly a farming society; agriculture employed more than half the total labor force, more than three times as many workers as in manufacturing; and the value added by agriculture was almost twice the value added by manufacturing. As late as the 1870s agriculture employed more than half the labor force and accounted for more value added than did manufacturing.[5]

Moreover, in the initiation stage, much of the "industrial" production was processing of agricultural produce, such as meat packing, food preserving, or lumbering. Even in 1860, American industry was still largely dependent on farm and forest products. Fundamental as steel is to industry, commercial steel production did not begin in the United States until the 1860s. While it is true that mechanization of agricultural processes provided some of the capital needed for industrialization, and the rising productivity of agriculture released labor for industry, these steps did not constitute the building of industry itself, nor of the industrial infrastructure. While many elements of industrialization (canals, railroads, steelmaking) began to be developed and even advanced before the Civil War, as I see it, the full development of the industrial system is properly dated in the generation that followed that conflict.

The behavior of prices further supports this relatively late dating of American industrialization. As long as production was centered in localities or neighborhoods, widely discrepant price indexes in different markets were apt to result; a degree of harmony in these indexes would point to the national integration of the market. "For five urban centers wholesale price indexes show a wide discrepancy before 1850 and 'a sharp increase in the measure of harmony in the succeeding decades.' "[6]

THE SEVEN ELEMENTS OF INDUSTRIALIZATION

Compared to many historians, I am less concerned with the past-as-it-was and more anxious to learn from it for the future. I attempt this by suggesting that behind numerous specific, concrete developments, one can see certain systemic needs. Thus, I am interested not so much in the excavation of new canals as in what it points to: the need for more efficient transportation of goods. And the initiation of Western Union brings to mind not singing telegrams nor the genius of Morse but the need for more expeditious communication. Later, one may ask if cargo planes and data-phones can answer the same needs more efficiently, as long as one has a clear conception of the needs of the system, of a developed economy.

The purpose of the following discussion is to introduce the specific elements that made for an affluent America. They are not the prime causes, but the component elements. Thus, to say that the United States had, roughly as of the 1880s, rapidly increasing cheap sources of power helps explain what made up its infrastructure—*not* where the cheap coal came from. The task here is to provide a design of components and relations among them, not a list of historical suppliers.

As there is no agreed-upon list of the needs of economic development, the following discussion accounts briefly for the inclusion of each of the seven elements of industrialization: *transportation* of resources and goods; *communication* of knowledge and signals; secure supplies of *power; human capital* (the mobilization and preparation of labor); *innovative capacity; supportive legal/financial institutions;* and the accumulation of *capital goods.* While these elements are introduced one at a time, historically of course they evolved in overlapping sequences.

Transportation of Goods

The Need

A developed economy requires expeditious, large-scale movement of raw materials, parts developed at different locations, and finished products. General Motors assembles passenger cars in more than twenty locations nationwide, using components manufactured in more than eighty of their own plants as well as in the plants of thousands of outside suppliers. Most GM assembly plants have on hand only enough components to operate for a day and a half; the rest of their "inventory" is in some twenty thousand rail cars and thousands of trucks, en route over the vast conveyor belt of the nation's transportation system.[7] Material and products in transit, like inventory, add to costs—not to production. All other things being equal, the slower and less reliable the transportation, the less developed a country.

Historical Illustration

In early farming America, transportation was quite undeveloped. Roads were narrow, dusty in summer, often impassably muddy in wet weather. Most simply connected farms and local markets. The few built for longer-distance travel were still crude, making transport slow and unpredictable. Even over the National Road from Cumberland to Wheeling, a rarity with its crushed-stone surface, the average speed was 5½ mph. Water transportation was better and cheaper, but reliance on natural waterways limited the routes and the direction of travel.

Initiation of industrialization was associated with the development of canals as an important means of transportation. Construction of trunk canals began not long after the War of 1812, and by 1860 a network of canals linked East Coast ports and the developing areas of the Great Lakes region and the Ohio Valley. Except during the winter freeze, canals could carry freight in larger volume, faster, and more reliably than roads, and they brought much lower transportation costs. Before the Erie Canal was built, the charge for freight from Albany to Buffalo is reported to have been eighty-five to a hundred dollars a ton; between 1830 and 1850, freight charges on the Canal averaged less than eight dollars a ton.[8]

Even as the canals were built, railroads began to overtake them.

Railroads could be built where steep terrain or uncertain water supply made canals impractical, and they could provide an integrated nation-wide transportation system. Moreover, trains could run all winter and travel faster than mule-drawn canal boats. Faster, more direct, year-round service, accompanied by lower costs, quickly attracted shippers. By 1860, forty-two hundred miles of canals had been out-stripped by thirty thousand miles of railroads, connecting all the major eastern cities.[9] By 1920, over a quarter-million miles of track criss-crossed the continent; four-fifths of intercity freight moved by rail.[10]

The next round belongs to the motorcars, still quite insignificant in the beginning of the twentieth century. By 1909, a New York–to–San Francisco trip—4,106 miles—took twenty-two days for the fastest car. Only in 1916 did the Congress pass an act leading to a national system of highways, which led eventually to mass trucking, offering shippers new flexibility and speed, especially for short hauls. Still later, air freight entered the transportation mix, playing a small but important role for light, high-value shipments. In 1939, railroads carried 62 percent of American freight ton-miles, trucks 10 percent; 18 percent moved on the Great Lakes and inland waterways, and 10 percent through pipelines.[11]

Communication Systems

The Need

As transportation moves raw material, goods, and people, communication moves symbols. They contain information and control signals, as well as expressions of sentiments and values. Information is an important input for productive decision-making, and expeditious transportation of control and other signals, such as those from headquarters to plants, is of course vital for large-scale organizations—national corporations, financial institutions, and markets.

Most studies of the subject focus on the generation of information, not its communication. Indeed, the costs and difficulties of transporting information were often ignored in earlier economic writings. Now it is widely agreed that inaccessible information may just as well be nonexistent, and that the costs—or efficiency by which information is transmitted—matter a great deal.

The significance of communication of values and sentiments is that they help broaden people's horizons and loyalties from the village to the nation and beyond. They also allow public policymakers to gauge what the populace will support, tolerate—or resist.

Historical Illustration

American colonists were largely preoccupied with local events and chiefly identified with Virginia or New York or Massachusetts. It took a century or more after federation for a strong sense of national identity to evolve, one that could compete with and supersede local loyalties. Some see in the Civil War the turning point. Before it, the Supreme Court used to refer to the nation in the plural ("the United States are")—only after it, in the singular. Indeed, even today rather strong state and regional loyalties persist, hindering national policymaking and implementation, and fostering localization.

In contrast, many economic decisions are at least in part national in nature, from how much to limit imports to the fate of the gold standard. When national bonds were weak, these decisions were difficult to reach and sustain. And, conversely, as nationhood grew, so did a nationwide economy and the ability to fashion nationwide policies. During much of the nineteenth century, for example, the United States currency system was complex and fragmented. Policy fluctuated, and controversy was intense regarding such issues as paper versus hard money, silver versus gold, and the proper monetary role of the federal government.

Improved communication technologies played an essential part in the process of nation-building, as well as in the transmission of information and control signals. Early communication depended on slow surface transport. The Overland Mail, established in the 1850s to provide fast mail and passenger service to the West Coast, pared down the mailcoach trip from the Mississippi to San Francisco, but still required twenty-two days. A decade later, a message could travel the same distance in a matter of minutes by telegraph. By 1848 the telegraph reached from the East Coast to St. Louis, and it spanned the continent in 1861.

Toward the end of the century, the telephone further advanced communication. By 1892, fifteen years after Bell patented the telephone, the telephone network reached from the Atlantic coast to Chicago, and by 1900, almost 2 million miles of telephone line interlaced the entire country. Later, radio made it possible to address the entire nation at once.

Power

The Need
Oxen and buffalo will not do for a modern economy. Mass production requires massive, routinely available, reliable, easy-to-stockpile, highly concentrated sources of energy. These qualities suggest heavy and growing reliance on extra-human and extra-animal sources.

Historical Illustration
Early American factories depended primarily on water power, available at a limited number of sites. After 1840, the use of steam increased rapidly, and by about 1860, steam surpassed water as the chief source of power.

Fuel for the increasing use of steam power came from increasing production of coal. Early in the nineteenth century, anthracite from Pennsylvania provided fuel for industry and for transportation. By 1870, it had been largely superseded in industry by bituminous coals, found in deposits that were larger and more widely distributed than those of anthracite. Bituminous coal production grew from 20.5 million tons in 1870 to 568.7 million tons in 1920.[12] The mechanical power available in manufacturing plants grew from 2.3 million horsepower in 1869 to 5.9 million in 1889 and 18.1 million in 1909.[13]

Through the 1870s, electricity was used primarily for communication—for the telegraph, for example; steam and water power continued to be the dominant power sources for industry. With the introduction of central generating stations in the 1880s, electricity gained importance in transportation and industry. By 1902, production of electricity was 6 billion kilowatt hours, and from then on it rose rapidly, reaching almost 57 billion kilowatt hours in 1920.[14]

Research and Development, Innovative Capacity

The Need
Economic growth is propelled not merely by larger "inputs," increases in the *amounts* of productive elements available, but also by combining them in new, more efficient ways. Hence, the role of innovation, which in turn is fed by research and development, is

central. The shift from hand tools to mechanization, and from the use of muscle power to high-energy inputs, both required technological innovations. Indeed, some leading researchers, such as Edward Denison and John Kendrick, have pointed out that new knowledge outweighs all other factors in contribution to economic growth.[15] (Denison's studies of long-term U.S. economic growth indicate that about 50 percent of measurable growth between 1948 and 1969 derived from advances in knowledge.)[16]

Historical Illustration

Many innovations crucial to American industrial development were encountered in the preceding discussion: the internal combustion engine, the vacuum tube, the electrical transformer, to name only a few. Some innovations were imported, in part or in whole, from Europe, especially from England, and adapted to American needs; others evolved in the United States. The cotton gin, the power loom, the sewing machine all contributed to the development of the New England textile industry, which had a fully developed factory system before the Civil War. The steamboat opened up the Great Lakes region, and adaptation of the steam engine was the base of the railroads. The process developed by Henry Bessemer in England and by William Kelly in the United States made large-scale steel production possible. A rough measure of America's growth in innovative capacity is the number of patents issued for inventions: 544 in 1830, 883 in 1850, 12,137 in 1870, and 25,313 in 1890.[17]

Innovation was important to systems as well as to machines. Eli Whitney, at the beginning of the nineteenth century, began to apply the principle of standardization and interchangeability of parts in the manufacture of firearms. The "Waltham system" advanced the factory production of textiles by bringing together all the processes of spinning and weaving. Alexander Holley designed a floor plan that improved the utilization of Bessemer converters and that became the standard layout of American steel plants.

Engineering, before 1850 largely the province of the military, gained rapidly in industrial importance in the latter part of the nineteenth century. Rensselaer Polytechnic Institute, at Troy, New York, and the Columbia University School of Mines pioneered in nonmilitary engineering instruction. In 1862, the Morrill Act furthered the "practical education of the industrial classes" by a grant of public lands to each state for support of a school to teach agriculture and the "mechanic arts"; many state-supported schools of engineering resulted.

Financial/Legal Institutions

The Need

So far we have examined the elements of industrialization, the "inputs," one by one, as they expand and improve, laying the foundations for a higher level of economic growth. However, each of these elements is affected by the encompassing society within which it is nestled. As Gustav Ranis, Yale's renowned developmental economist put it,

> In modifying the simplified view of how the world operates, we must take into account not only more realistic notions of the role of labor, factor substitutionability, and technological change, but also the heretofore neglected changes in the institutional milieu within which an economy operates.[18]

Key among these factors are, first, the financial/legal institutions, such as institutions that can amass large amounts of capital or regulate the amount of money in circulation; can condone, promote, or retard the development of corporations that are legal entities chartered by the state, and so on.

The changing nature of these financial/legal institutions, in turn, rests on the development of the societal context in which they are imbedded. For instance, the more the society is divided into separate political-cultural-territorial entities, the more difficult it is to evolve the financial/legal framework required by high economic growth, because the divisions prevent economies of scale and the rational division of labor. Typically, at least a measure of de-feudalization, of nation-building and unification, preceded or accompanied industrialization.

Historical Illustration

In nineteenth-century America, the national financial system developed with great difficulty due to the low level of nation-building. Canals, even railroads, can be built locally and pieced together later; the pattern may not be completely rational, but it may be tolerable and can be improved. Finances are a different matter; without a nation-wide, easily mobilized flow of capital, large-scale development is severely set back. Until savings were no longer dispersed in thousands of banks, inaccessible to large borrowers, specialists such as Pierpont Morgan, Edward Harriman, and Jacob Schiff were required to improvise *ad hoc* the linkages to secure enough capital for large projects.

For twenty years prior to the Civil War, the paper currency consisted largely of bank notes issued by local banks—some sixteen hundred in 1862—operating under diverse state laws. From 1863 on, as the nation sought to resolve the divisions accompanying the war and the economic crises following it, gradually a greater degree of uniformity and national collaboration evolved. In 1913 Congress established the Federal Reserve System, which provided a basis for national coordination of banking activities.

A crucial development in building the nation was the adaptation of the British institutional framework to one less aristocratic, more favorable to free-market capitalism. As historian Jonathan Hughes puts it: "No feudal remnants, no quitrents, entails, primogenitures, land titles, patents of nobility, or what have you would be allowed to exist. Property rights were 'sacred,' contracts were inviolable."[19]

While these words describe the North more aptly than the South, the Civil War, in effect, secured northern institutional domination. Its direct effect on industrialization is a subject of great controversy among historians. It seems though, that the Civil War marked the beginning not only of northern institutions as the predominant national institutions, but of northern industrialists rather than southern planters as the dominant political force. It thus opened the way for a national banking system, high tariffs against imports, a tax system favorable to industry, and easier immigration that brought cheaper labor. The abolition of slavery also accelerated the need for machines in the South. Furthermore, both the Civil War and the wars against the Indian tribes, though not the high points of American history, served to integrate the country into one peaceful territory, a prerequisite of successful commerce.

Practically all economic historians of the United States stress the supportive role of government—in the nineteenth century, primarily state governments—toward business in general and economic development in particular. Financial aid, direct and indirect, was common. Governments invested in railroads and other transportation facilities;

they favored the banks, and the banks in turn financed railroads and industrial enterprises. Regulations that protected young industries were introduced. Lotteries were conducted and their proceeds used for the construction of bridges, roads, and paper mills. Government franchises were used to spur the building of bridges, aqueducts, and dams, and to protect builders against damage claims resulting from consequent floods or diversion of water.[20]

While the majority of financial/legal developments between the 1860s and the 1920s were basically favorable to industrialization, not all pointed in this direction. In sizable segments of the American public, concentration of wealth and economic power tended to evoke fears, sometimes leading to regulations that benefited all concerned, and sometimes to irrational interventions in the economic process.[21]

Between the Civil War and World War I, the public was becoming aware of big corporations. Newspapers and magazines helped stir up sentiment with articles and cartoons that attacked trusts and such trust-builders as John D. Rockefeller and J. P. Morgan. By 1888, both political parties were attacking trusts in their platforms.

In his popular history *Our Times,* Mark Sullivan notes that the *Boston Globe* defined mergers in this fashion: "Mergers are monsters of so frightful mien, that to be hated need but to be seen; but when they're seen, despairing of a cure, the public has to whistle—and endure."[22]

Public opposition to "combinations of capital" was so strong that the Sherman Antitrust Act was passed *unanimously* by the House in 1890; in the Senate, there was only one dissenting vote. Many states passed their own antitrust laws. Prominent politicians built their careers largely on promises to bust the trusts. While the antitrust laws were ineffectually enforced, and most corporations worked their way around them, they had a nuisance value and illustrate instances of populist misgivings about the new industrial world. They did not stop or significantly slow down industrialization but they sniped at it.

Human Capital

The Need

Industrialization requires a labor force motivated, educated, and trained for the new factories, offices, financial institutions, and laboratories. This brief statement covers a lot of ground. It encompasses the need for "bodies"—a sufficient number of people to staff positions, a problem those preoccupied with the population explosion tend to overlook when dealing with "underpopulated" areas, Sub-Sahara for instance. And people must be motivated to put up with the regimens of industrial work; simply paying them well will not suffice, as early factories discovered. Workers who had relatively set wants took off as soon as they got their first pay. The need for self-discipline and commitment, aside from "basic skills," is spelled out in Chapter 6.

Historical Illustration

In the United States, unlike many other developing countries, the very availability of persons was a major problem. Industrialization was not largely propelled by "surplus" farm labor, though farms were one source of industrial workers. The large majority of the new millions were immigrants. In 1790, the population of the United States is estimated to have been less than 4 million; in 1860 it was just over 30 million; by 1914 it had risen to almost 100 million.[23] From 1860 to 1914, more than 25 million immigrants came to the United States, most of them from Europe.[24]

Farm hands and immigrants had to be educated, acculturated, and trained. This was done rather effectively. By 1840, for instance, 90 percent of white adults are reported to have been literate, a higher rate than in most countries.[25] Expenditures on education grew from 0.6 percent of GNP in 1840 to 1.7 percent in 1900; since GNP was climbing rapidly, actual expenditures are estimated to have increased thirtyfold.[26] By 1920, 83 percent of Americans aged five to seventeen were in school for at least some part of the year; and although only about one in six graduated from high school, that proportion was increasing.[27]

Beyond elementary and, later, secondary and college education, was technical training. At first, curricula in civil and other branches of engineering were regarded as "inferior" by "cultural" colleges, but this did not stunt their development. Even in those early days, one way to overcome the snobbishness of "cultural" parts of colleges was to increase the theoretical, "basic science" part of engineering training, even though science had not reached a stage when it had many practical applications.

In addition to technical education at the college level, specialized schools for specific industries, such as textiles, were established, and vocational training was introduced into elementary and high schools, with some support from the federal government after 1917.

An industry is more than machines, materials, and workers; it is an organization and management system with a division of labor, authority, and communication. This concept was introduced in a very preliminary fashion in the early textile mills; later the ideas of "scientific" management, championed by Frederick W. Taylor in the 1890s, were introduced and advanced. A major corrective, viewing workers as persons and not as cogs, even if only to try to manipulate them, was introduced by Elton Mayo and other founders of the human relations school. This school pointed to the importance of taking into account the nonrational, personal relations between foremen and workers. Workers' bonds to one another were also important; these could be mobilized to support production—or, if ignored and violated, could alienate workers.

Capital Goods

The Need

The six elements introduced so far together constitute the "infrastructure." Creating an infrastructure suitable for a modern economy is a prerequisite for the takeoff of industrialization. However, before it can provide for a modern, growing economy, for an age of mass production and mass consumption, one other element must be added: capital goods. These are assets that cannot themselves be consumed but that serve in the production of consumer goods; they are the plants, their machinery and equipment—steel mills, cranes, lathes, shipyards, assembly lines, and so on.

As most industrializing economies already have a labor force (although often it must be transferred, motivated, educated, and trained for industrial work), attention tends to focus on accumulation of capital, invested in the infrastructure and in capital goods, to lay the foundations for industrialization. A society that consumes all or most of its product, and does not set aside a growing proportion of its savings for capital goods and the infrastructure, will not industrialize, or will industrialize only as much as foreign investments and contributions will carry it.

Historical Illustration

Before 1860, as we have noted, much of the American industrial effort was piggybacked on the produce of field and forest. But in the era that followed, new sources of power and important innovations in iron and steel production were major factors in making industry less dependent on growing things, more dependent on minerals and on capital goods. As historian Edward C. Kirkland has put it: "The age since 1860 may have been the 'age of coal and iron' or the 'age of petroleum' or the 'age of electricity.' It was unquestionably the 'age of the machine.' "[28] Air-driven power drills and steam shovels were introduced in the coal mine, suspended rotary drills in the oil fields. The Bessemer process reduced the cost of steel so that its widespread use became practical, and later the open hearth process made it possible to use lower-grade ores.

While steel can be used to make both capital (producer) and consumer goods, early in industrialization much of it is typically used for capital goods, and the capacity to make steel reflects a rise of capital goods. Hence the amount of steel produced is often used as a gross measure of the potential of the capital goods sector. In 1860, raw steel production in the United States was 13,000 tons; ten years later, production was 77,000 tons. By 1910, production had grown to more than 28 million tons.[29]

The production of other capital goods also grew rapidly. The value of output of industrial machinery and equipment increased from $99 million in 1879 to $512 million in 1910.[30] In general, manufacturing production multiplied twelve times from 1860 to 1914,[31] and output per workhour in manufacturing doubled from 1869 to 1914.[32]

Another measure of industrial growth in the "age of the machine" is the increase in the amount of capital invested in U.S. manufacturing facilities. From 1850 to 1880 it grew from $533 million to almost $3 billion.[33] It reached $8 billion in 1900, then climbed sharply to nearly $40 billion in 1914.[34]

The importance of capital accumulation is emphasized in studies that relate the takeoff and acceleration of industrialization to the increase in capital/output ratio. Between 1850 and 1900, it grew from approximately 1.6:1 to 2.9:1; capital per worker grew from about $2,100 to $5,000 or more.[35]

THE LOOSE SYSTEM

As all these preparatory elements of industrialization were adequately developed and articulated, the economy was ready for the next step, mass production of consumer goods and services. It is important to keep the analytic elements distinct from the particular historical forms in which they have been introduced: We are accustomed to thinking of a car, for example, as a vehicle with wheels, a gasoline engine, a radiator, and so on; these are "historical" forms of the car's elements. Analytically, one would see instead that a car has a friction-reducing mechanism to facilitate movement over the ground—which might take the form of wheels, or caterpillar treads, or an air cushion. It has a means of propulsion—an internal combustion engine, a steam engine, an electric motor—which in turn is fueled—by gasoline, alcohol, storage batteries. Unwanted heat is dissipated—by water, air, refrigeration coils. Furthermore, these parts are assembled, not willy-nilly, but according to a system design, which secures that they are compatible. A steam engine will not typically be fueled by storage batteries.

So with the elements of industrialization: Their historical form—whether the primary power source is steam or electricity, for instance—is relatively unimportant for our analysis. The important questions are whether these elements meet the system-needs of industrialization; whether they provide the critical elements that can sustain modern mass-production, or industrialization; and whether they fit together in a loose system pattern. A high rate of innovation is futile if appropriately trained workers are lacking; supersonic jets add relatively little to the speed of transportation by "regular" jets if the access roads to the airports are congested.

I refer to a "loose" system, because one element can be advanced before others as long as they do not lag too badly (*e.g.*, one can improve jet transportation between airports before one fully develops access roads to airports). No precise links are needed (*e.g.*, while it makes little sense to speed up intercity air transport even further if freight unloading remains slow, there is no exact speed required of each link). However, the concept of a loose system sets a *guide* for relations that in the longer run cannot be ignored.

THE BOTTOM LINE: A POWERFUL ECONOMIC MACHINE

Rapidly Rising GNP

The assembly of the seven elements of industrialization, and their continued development in a loosely patterned mix, generated a very powerful economic machine. By 1913, the United States produced over one third of the world's manufactured goods, more than twice as much as its nearest rival, Germany.[36] Manufacturing production continued to grow after World War I, increasing in real value by over 50 percent from 1920 to 1929.[37] During the same period, manufacturing output per workhour, in constant dollars, increased by more than 60 percent, and real per capita GNP rose 27 percent.[38]

After the twin interruptions of the Depression and World War II, America's high production machine continued to work its economic wonders. (Actually, during World War II, productive capacity continued to grow rapidly. From 1941 to 1944 GNP increased, in 1958 dollars, from $264 to $360 billion, and 1944 industrial production was two and a half times the depressed pre-war level. Output of durable manufactures rose three and a half times. But nearly half of the production—$160 billion out of $360 billion in 1944—was used for the war.[39]) In the twenty-five years following World War II, manufacturing production, in constant dollars, increased at an average rate of almost 5 percent per year.[40] GNP, measured in 1972 dollars, rose from $533 billion to $1,202 billion;[41] per capita GNP increased by almost 60 percent.[42] All this provided the economic foundation for the age of mass consumption.

Consumer Goods and Services

In the golden age of consumption, which stretched roughly from 1950 to 1975, median real family income increased by 85 percent,[43] and per capita disposable personal income, the standard measure of consumer purchasing power, rose 69 percent, from $2,386 to $4,025 in 1972 dollars.[44] The standard of living in America rose steadily. While in 1950, 34 percent of occupied housing units lacked some or all plumbing facilities, by 1974, only about 3 percent were subject to such indignities.[45] The outhouse ceased to be a fixture and became a butt of jokes. At the time of World War II, about half of American households had a refrigerator; by 1975, virtually all did.[46] Ice carriers virtually vanished.

Beyond such basics, possessions that once would have been counted luxuries came to be taken for granted. In 1950 about 9 percent of households had a TV set, then the latest in home entertainment; by 1975, 97 percent had TV, 40 percent had more than one set, and 66 percent had color.[47] Hi-fi and stereo equipment, ten-speed bicycles, power lawnmowers became commonplace; for a wide segment of society, there was not only a chicken in every pot but a steak on every grill.

The centerpiece of this golden era of consumption was the automobile. In the fifties and sixties, Henry Ford's vision of a car for everyone "making a good salary" became part of Americana. By 1975, 84 percent of all American families owned a car, and 33 percent owned more than one.[48] The cars themselves became more reliable, more convenient, even luxurious. Thus, while only 7 percent of new cars had factory-installed air conditioning in 1960, ten years later 61 percent had "factory air."[49]

Affluence was not limited to material goods. More and more young people were attending college. In 1950 about 40 percent of each high school graduating class enrolled in college; by the early seventies 60 percent were entering college.[50] Part of this increase was achieved through the great increase in the number of public junior colleges, especially in the late sixties. Consumers' real per capita expenditures for health services and supplies grew by almost 80 percent between 1950 and 1975.[51] At the same time, life expectancy increased by more than four years, from 68.2 years in 1950 to 72.5 years in 1975.[52]

Leisure activities mushroomed as well. Leisure spending in real terms (after allowing for inflation) was up 47 percent from 1965 to 1981.[53] Personal-consumption expenditures for recreation, in constant dollars, were more than two and a half times as high in 1975 as in 1950.[54] In the same period, while watching TV became a favorite leisure activity for nearly half the population,[55] recreation outside the home also gained. The number of bowlers quadrupled;[56] attendance at pro football games quintupled;[57] the national park system recorded more than seven times as many visits.[58] Recreational activities once associated primarily with the upper classes came within the reach of a widening circle—the number of golfers nearly quadrupled,[59] and attendance at concerts by major symphony orchestras more than doubled.[60]

Public Expenditures

As private consumption increased, there was rapid growth in public expenditures for human services—education, social insurance, public aid, health and medical programs, veterans' programs, and so on. Between 1950 and 1975, these expenditures increased, in 1976 dollars, more than fivefold, from $54.5 billion to $302.8 billion.[61] During this period social welfare expenditures under public programs grew both as a proportion of GNP—from 8.9 percent to 19.7 percent—and as a proportion of all government expenditures—from 37.4 percent to 57.9 percent;[62] real per capita public expenditures for education almost quadrupled,[63] for health and medical services, almost tripled.[64]

A substantial part of the increase in public expenditures was in "transfer payments," technically defined as government funds paid to individuals, other than payments for current salaries or purchases of goods. Often these were in effect a transfer of funds, collected via taxes and distributed by the government, from well-off parts of the society to those less well-off, although part of the funds transferred spilled over enroute into unintended pockets, those of people on the take or simply of middle-class constituents.

Transfer payments gained momentum with the "war on poverty," begun in 1964, and eventually covered over 180 programs on the federal level, from family assistance to child nutrition to Medicaid. In 1960, federal transfer payments totaled $28.9 billion, not quite a third of federal budget outlays; by 1975, they totaled $178.2 billion, 55 percent of federal budget outlays. They accounted for 7.2 percent of total personal income in 1960, 14.2 percent in 1975.[65]

While the golden age of consumption started earlier than that of social services (the former might be dated as of 1950, the latter as of the early sixties), the private consumption spree started to slow down somewhat earlier, as the economy weakened in the late seventies. Public consumption continued to barrel ahead for a few more years, and became the symbol of America's "excessive" consumption. Thus, from 1975 to the end of 1979, transfer payments rose from $178.2 billion to $266.7 billion,[66] a rise of 49.7 percent, while the registration of passenger cars, for example, rose by only 13 percent in the same period.[67]

Two Views of Poverty

While it is widely recognized that the United States experienced an age of abundance and high consumption, based on a high level of economic growth, there are considerable differences of opinion about how widely this prosperity was shared.[68] Especially in the sixties, poverty became a focus of concern and debate. Some stress that throughout the consumption era, all income groups shared the rise in real income; in fact, during the fifties and sixties, the situation of families with money incomes in the lowest fifth improved slightly more than average.[69] Others point to the fact that in 1975 one American out of eight was below the official poverty level, and this proportion was much higher among previously disadvantaged groups, especially blacks and other minorities.[70]

Looking at poverty in terms of ability to maintain some minimum standard of living, some observers emphasize that poverty diminished considerably between 1950 and 1975. During the fifties, the proportion of families with money income (in 1967 dollars) under three thousand dollars decreased by about a third.[71] In the sixties, the proportion of persons below the federally defined poverty level fell from 22.2 percent in 1960 to 12.1 percent in 1969. (It varied little from then on.)[72] From this point of view, it appears that while some were still poor in 1975, they were markedly fewer than in 1950 and substantially better off. Moreover, even the poorest in America enjoyed a much higher standard of living than the poor in most other countries.

A different point of view focuses not on real dollar income or standard of living as the criterion of poverty, but on relative income. From this perspective, it appears that while the entire pyramid of wealth was lifted up the scale of real income, it only slightly flattened. As the poor gained more income, so did the rich, and the distance between poor and rich (a measure of inequality) remained essentially unchanged. Families with money incomes in the lowest fifth received 4.5 percent of aggregate income in 1950, 5.4 percent in 1975; families in the highest fifth received 42.7 percent of aggregate income in 1950, 41.1 percent in 1975; in the middle three fifths, change was even less.[73]

Inequality between races also persisted, although it declined somewhat. The median income of nonwhite families, in constant dollars, was 54 percent of that of white families in 1950; by 1975, this ratio had risen—to 65 percent.[74] In 1975, the percent of blacks and other minorities below the poverty level was only about half as high as in 1959, but just as in 1959, it was over three times as high as that of whites.[75]

IN SUMMARY

In short, while in some sense, poverty clearly continued, during the quarter century following World War II American society as a whole enjoyed consumer goods and services in unprecedented volume and variety. This golden age of consumption and social services was the "payoff" of an arduous process, stretching over more than a century, through which the elements of a national industrial infrastructure were assembled and the capital goods accumulated to support a thriving economy.

CHAPTER NINE

The Seven Elements of Industrialization Revisited

SIGNS OF GENERAL DETERIORATION

What happened to the U.S. economic machine—which once provided for the richest and most powerful nation in the world? As I see it, a generation of underinvestment in the seven elements of industrialization, in the infrastructure and capital goods sectors, coupled with a generation of overconsumption, threw the U.S. economy into reverse gear. In this chapter I first review the familiar signs of economic weakness and then reexamine the seven elements, to show that they deteriorated in the period from 1950 to 1980, especially in the last decade of that era. Their decline was gradual, uneven, *not* a collapse, but in accumulation it accounts for the weakened productive capacity of America. On top of the strains caused by this internal maintenance gap came those generated by the external challenges of the oil-exporting countries, rising international competition, and new security needs. As these challenges were met with an utterly insufficient commitment of resources, the problems caused by the resulting adaptation lag were added to those caused by inadequate maintenance.

The deterioration of the U.S. economy did not start suddenly, nor did it encompass all elements to the same extent. Many of the early signs came amidst the golden age of consumption and were largely ignored. Indeed, throughout a good part of the seventies, consumption continued to grow rapidly, while productive capacity was growing at a slower and slower pace. This was made possible, "achieved" if you wish, by eating up resources accumulated by previous generations. It's fun while it lasts, which is never very long.

One may call the pattern a disendowment process. It is quite familiar to those who deal with campus economics. You have a deficit one year; you finance it by selling off some of your endowment. Next year your yield from the endowment is smaller, your deficit is bigger, and your need to dip into the endowment is greater. You do this for a few years in a row and you learn the power of geometric retrogression: Your economic base narrows at an accelerating pace.

How can a nation consume more than it produces? It performs a national equivalent of the campus trick: It undermaintains, it runs down the infrastructure and capital goods; in effect, it lives off the national economic endowment left by the work and savings of previous generations. The disendowment was reflected in high obsolescence of major segments of the industrial plant and machinery (especially steel, textiles, rubber), in a deteriorating infrastructure (especially railroads, bridges, dams, and ports), and in low savings rates and high borrowing. The declining yield was reflected in slower GNP growth, high inflation, and lower productivity growth.

Some often-cited figures illustrate the point. The average annual growth in real GNP (after "deducting" inflation) was 3.9 percent from 1960 to 1970. It slowed to 3.3 percent from 1970 to 1978; in 1979, it was 2.3 percent.[1] However, these discouraging figures are misleadingly optimistic. They disregard the fact that not only were there more Americans than before (due to population growth), but a much higher proportion than before were working outside the household and hence required tools, equipment, capital. That is, while the total GNP continued to grow a bit between 1970 and 1978— 3.3 percent per year—average family income, in constant dollars, increased only 0.8 percent per year.[2] Similarly, GNP per employed worker increased 1.9 percent per year from 1963 to 1973, a meager 0.1 percent per year from 1973 to 1979.[3] This latter rate of growth was estimated to be not only well below that of Germany and Japan but also below that of France (2.7 percent), Italy (1.6 percent), and even the United Kingdom (0.3 percent).[4]

Another sign that not all was well was the declining growth in productivity. Productivity is one of the most important indicators of an economy's vitality, since it is increasing productivity that generates new wealth and higher living standards. From 1947 to 1967, private sector output per worker-hour in the United States grew about

3.2 percent per year, a rate that came to be considered normal.[5] John Kendrick's data indicate, in fact, that U.S. productivity had been increasing significantly since 1800.[6] During the period from 1967 to 1973, however, growth in productivity slipped to 2.1 percent per year, and from 1973 to 1979 it fell to 0.6 percent per year.[7]

Rising inflation is another indication of disendowment. Through inflation, saved resources are used up by the government or those it favors. Inflation reduces the value of assets—savings, funds tucked away as nest eggs for the kids' college or for retirement, pension funds—and finances government spending, such as the war in Vietnam, growing social services and transfer payments, payments to OPEC and government employees themselves. Steadily climbing inflation is shown in the steady increase in the consumer price index, which averaged 1.3 percent annually in 1960–65; 4.2 percent in 1965–70; 6.7 percent in 1970–75; 7.8 percent in 1975–79.[8]

The government is depicted by most American leaders and citizens as the number one culprit and cause of the disendowment process. This is true enough in the sense that the public sector grew especially rapidly in the disendowment years, as did social services and regulatory costs imposed by government on the private sector. However, quite a few labor settlements that were lavish in both wages and fringe benefits, vastly exceeding increases in productivity, also contributed to the problem. Leaders of the United Auto Workers concede in private conversations that they helped price their industry out of the market in those days. Other aids to disendowment were high dividend payments by some industries, accompanied by low investment in productive assets (causing deteriorating plants and machinery) and in innovation (as measured by R&D statistics). The old Penn Central Railroad Corporation (which went bankrupt although it was later revived) and several major steel corporations come to mind as cases in point.

In addition, individuals learned increasingly to live on credit, which means that, in proportion to their incomes, they spent more than they used to. Americans' willingness to work hard and save declined, although the data on increased use of credit and reduced saving are much clearer than those on the decline of the work ethic.

The government may have contributed heavily to these developments in labor, industry, and personal habits, but these other sectors participated avidly in the overconsumption pattern. From 1950 to 1979, while the national debt more than tripled (growing from $257 billion in 1950 to $834 billion in 1979),[9] consumer debt multiplied more than eighteen times (growing from $73 billion in 1950 to $1,327 billion in 1979).[10] It is important to keep this in mind as we turn to correctives, lest preoccupation with the number one culprit distract attention from the accomplices, and they be left free to do their inflationary/disendowment thing.

More immediately, the question is—if it is true that America owes its economic development to a rich endowment, created by a successful combination of seven specific elements, what happened to those elements in the disendowment process? The answer is important for two reasons: First, it allows one to "test," in a way, the notion that these elements deserve the productive potency we attribute to them. If as economic yield deteriorated they did not, clearly something else was at fault. If they did deteriorate simultaneously, this increases the plausibility of our contention that these elements are essential to sustain productive capacity.

Second, the answer to this question points the direction for reconstruction. If these seven elements are all needed, as I maintain American economic history suggests, *merely spraying the economy with generalized stimulants may not rain sufficient incentives on some of the essential elements.* I return to the implications after the revisit, our next stop. What happened to the elements of industrialization in the golden age of consumption and public services?

An aside on what might be called the horse-and-buggy problem is unavoidable when one deals with historical lessons for analytic schemes. To show, as I am about to do, that certain historical elements deteriorated does not necessarily indicate a neglect of the analytic elements. A decline of the horse-and-buggy business does not spell neglect of transportation needs—because there has been a rise of the automotive industry. Nevertheless, the starting point must be the condition of the historical elements. When little has replaced their declining service, obviously an economic deficiency or gap is caused. The rest is a matter of details: which elements deteriorated *without* replacement, and which grew obsolete as their economic role was taken over by other elements.

TRANSPORTATION: EXTENSIVE DETERIORATION, LITTLE REPLACEMENT

Americans tend to think about the U.S. transportation system in personal terms: people speeding on highways in their cars, or through the air in jet planes. However, the economy's first concern is expeditious transportation of raw materials, semiprocessed goods, and finished products. For these purposes, the economy relies first on trucks, heavily on railroads, and to a lesser extent on waterways and pipelines. In 1976, trucks carried 38.0 percent of American freight tonnage, railroads 29.3 percent; 14.6 percent moved on the Great Lakes and inland waterways, 18.0 percent through oil pipelines; less than 1 percent of freight tonnage was air cargo.[11]

Rails

By the end of the 1970s, the condition of American railroads, despite some local exceptions (especially in the West and South), was particularly poor. As much as 50 percent of the track was estimated to be defective.[12] In 1976, trains had to reduce speed on more than 15 percent of the total rail mileage, sometimes as low as ten miles an hour.[13] The rate of accidents attributable to defects of way or structure almost quadrupled between 1966 and 1976.[14] Equipment also deteriorated; the proportion of unserviceable freight cars, for instance, almost doubled, increasing steadily from 4.4 percent of cars on the line in 1966 to 8.0 percent in 1976.[15]

This poor condition is attributed to the failure of the railroad industry since the 1950s to keep up with what is considered "normal" maintenance. Tie replacement, for instance, was 33 percent below normal rates from 1956 to 1965, and 23 percent below normal from 1966 to 1975. Since many ties were installed in the 1930s and 1940s, the U.S. Department of Transportation estimated in 1978 that 50 percent of all ties would have to be replaced within ten years in order to maintain 1978 conditions of track use and speed, already low. Likewise, the replacement rate for rails was below "normal" from 1953 at least through the mid-seventies.[16]

Overall, expenditures for maintenance of way were $5.4 billion less than they should have been for the decade 1966 to 1976, according to the U.S. Department of Transportation.[17] Although no estimate is available of the resources needed for a complete overhaul of the railroad system, a partial estimate was given in a study done in 1977 for the Federal Railroad Administration. The study concluded that the industry would have to expend $40.5 to $43.8 billion between 1976 and 1985 in order to maintain facilities at "appropriate" levels and gradually overcome deferred maintenance.[18]

Roads

Highways have not deteriorated to nearly the extent that railroads have, but failure to maintain them properly is beginning to erode this important element of the American transportation system. Highways are designed to last only a certain number of years; federal highways, for example, were built to last twenty years, and an increasing number are reaching that age. Meanwhile, the number of registered vehicles and the total miles traveled both increased by 50 percent or more in the decade 1967–77,[19] increasing the wear and tear on highways. Yet real expenditures on road maintenance declined during that period. According to a 1981 Federal Highway Administration report, capital investment in highways, in 1967 dollars, decreased from $9.8 billion in 1967 to $5.0 billion in 1979,[20] a drop of roughly 48 percent.

One of the problems caused by aging, improperly maintained roads is potholes, which have become more common over the years. In 1979, there were an estimated 93 million potholes in the nation's roads. In Illinois, the state's chief maintenance engineer, Ed Kehl, noted: "When it's not snowing, all 2700 of our maintenance people are filling potholes."[21] In Pennsylvania, the surface of one interstate highway deteriorated to the point that a thirty-mile-an-hour speed limit was put into effect in some sections.[22]

Bridges, which of course are a vital part of any road system, are probably the weakest link of the American system. The U.S. Department of Transportation now considers many bridges either structurally deficient or functionally obsolete. (A "structurally deficient" bridge is open to light vehicles only, or is closed or needs immediate rehabilitation to keep it open. A "functionally obsolete" bridge can no longer safely serve the road system because of its deck geometry, load carrying capacity, clearance, or approach roadway alignment.)[23] In 1980, the Department of Transportation reported that of approximately 255,000 bridges on the federally aided road system, almost 57,000—more than one in five—were considered deficient in some way. The proportion of deficient bridges outside the federally aided system was estimated to be even higher: nearly 83,000, or roughly 49 percent.[24]

Waterways

If bridges weaken the highway system, ports hold back transportation via waterways, inland and ocean. The bottlenecks created by slow modernization of ports have been highlighted by the problems of shipping coal. Coal, which the United States has in great abundance, has been increasingly in demand worldwide as the high price of oil has made the use of coal attractive. However, U.S. ports were unable to respond to rising demand for transporting coal. At one point in 1980, 122 ships were reported waiting their turn at the nation's two largest coal ports, Norfolk and Baltimore. These ships cost an average of $20,000 a day in demurrage (waiting fees), and they waited an average of thirty-five days to load; on the average the delay added $700,000 to the price of their cargo—an addition of $14, or 23 percent, per ton of coal, which was then going for $60 a ton.[25]

Aside from having antiquated, insufficient, or unsuitable loading and storage facilities, many ports are not deep enough to handle the large ships that are used in the worldwide coal trade. Most U.S. ports have depths of forty to forty-five feet, while the large ships require about fifty-five feet. Dredging just four major coal ports would cost an estimated $1.5 billion.[26]

Coal is but one example. Overall, the poor condition of many of its ports has inhibited the United States from reaching its full exporting capacity. Although U.S. exports to foreign countries increased by 41 percent from 1979 to 1980, experts estimated the increase could have been as much as 100 percent if the ports had been operating more efficiently.[27]

To summarize, the nation's transportation system has generally deteriorated in the past decades. One comprehensive study sponsored by the Council of State Planning Agencies concluded:

> America's public facilities [of which transportation facilities are a major component] are wearing out faster than they are being replaced. Under the exigencies of tight budgets and inflation, the maintenance of public facilities essential to national economic renewal has been deferred. Replacement of obsolescent public works has been postponed. New construction has been cancelled.[28]

Now it is time to return to the "horse-and-buggy industry" problem. The fact that this or that transportation element deteriorated is not the troubling condition, by itself. The trouble is that no new, efficient element was introduced (in the transportation of goods and raw materials) as the old ones weakened. This is evident if we reexamine the transportation mix: It continues to rely largely on rail, road, and waterways, and these all weakened, albeit not evenly. True, some gains were made through less reliance on particularly weakened rails, and greater reliance on less deteriorated roads. But as roads too were pointed downward—and are energy-inefficient—the total picture was of a weakened system making do, not one in which new, vigorous elements were replacing obsolescent ones, a development that did take place in the transportation of persons through the growth of the airline industry.

COMMUNICATIONS: A "MODEL" SECTOR

Just as transportation could well stand as a symbol of the problems of the U.S. economy, so the communications sector could well symbolize what a strong U.S. economy would be like (with some notable exceptions, especially that of the U.S. Postal Service). The communications sector is a vigorous, basically competitive, fast-growing sector. Innovations follow rapidly one after another and are widely implemented.

Taken as a whole, during the period 1950 to 1980, the communications industry showed steady growth. The value of the industry's product increased from about $4.5 billion in 1950 to $61.3 billion in 1979; its share of GNP grew from roughly 1.6 percent in 1950 to 2.6 percent in 1979. (This compares with a decline in the transportation industry's share of GNP, which was 5.6 percent in 1950 but only 4.0 percent in 1979.)[29]

In 1950, the communications industry was spending about half as much as the transportation industry on new plant and equipment ($1.1 billion, compared to $2.4 billion); by 1979, however, the communications industry was spending twice as much as the transportation industry ($20.6 billion, compared to $10.1 billion.)[30]

Generally speaking, the parts of the communications industry that have grown most since 1950 are those that have benefited most, in decreased unit cost and increased efficiency, from technological innovations. Three technological developments revolutionized key segments of the communications industry and serve to illustrate the general thrust of this sector: large-scale integrated circuits, which sharply reduced the cost of processing and storing messages; communications satellites, which offer efficient, high-capacity distribution of signals; and computer networks, which transmit messages and data almost instantaneously.

Before 1948, the basic electronic components of communications systems were tubes and relays; both provided amplification of electrical signals. They were large—the smallest tubes about an inch long—and each cost several dollars. The invention of the transistor in 1948 was the first of several steps in reducing the size and cost of electronic components. Next, about 1960, an integrated circuit was developed, allowing several transistors to be combined on a single small chip of semiconductor material. Several amplifying elements could then be purchased for a dollar.[31]

During the 1960s, researchers worked to develop large-scale integrated circuits, and by 1970 had achieved this goal; the result was a semiconductor chip that held thousands of amplifying elements. By 1978, Texas Instruments had developed a semiconductor chip that was approximately the size of a 1940s miniature tube and cost ten times as much—but held approximately seventy thousand times as many amplifying elements.[32] As one observer noted:

> If the motor car of 1950 had followed the same line of development as the transistor and its micro-circuit successors, it would now cost less than a cent and be the size of the thimble.[33]

Similarly, the cost of transmitting messages decreased as satellite technology took off. Satellite technology has two elements—one in space and one on the ground; the costs of both dropped. When the first commercial satellite, *Early Bird*, was launched in 1965, it cost $23,000 per voice channel per year to operate.[34] By 1979, the cost of satellite operation had dropped to $1,250 per voice channel per year.[35] In 1962, an earth station that received signals from AT&T's *Telstar* satellite cost $50 million;[36] by 1979, earth station costs ranged from a high of $5 million to a low of $10,000, depending on antenna size.[37]

Finally, the refinement of "interconnect" systems between computer terminals in the early 1970s provided an alternative to communicating by mail. Such systems allow one computer terminal to send data and communications to another terminal via telephone cables. Related to this was the development of facsimile networks that can transmit graphic and pictorial information.

Technological innovations in components used by the communications industry helped make it a high-growth industry throughout the period from 1950 to 1980. As unit costs decreased, so too did the costs of many of the products of the industry, in an economy in which most other prices seemed to know only one direction—up. A black and white television set cost, on the average, $190 in 1950 but only $84 in 1975. A color TV cost about $500 in 1955, but had dropped to $341 in 1975.[38] Telephone toll rates also generally decreased; for instance, a three-minute daytime station-to-station call between New York and San Francisco cost $2.50 in 1952, $1.30 in 1979.[39]

The Postal Service is a weak element. Until 1958, the cost of mailing a letter had stayed at two or three cents an ounce since 1885.[40] In contrast, between 1958 and 1979 first-class rates were raised seven times, and the price of a stamp rose from three cents to fifteen cents.[41] Throughout the same period, the Postal Service experienced deficits ranging as high as a billion dollars (in 1976).[42] And the service hardly improved.

As the seventies ended, there were indications that the communications industry would continue to benefit from a large number of technological innovations, rushing one on top of the other. For example, high-technology private companies were trying to establish nationwide computer-to-computer networks using high-frequency microwave transmission. Since capacity grows with frequency, microwave transmission offers increased communications capacity. This technology had been in use since the 1940s, but primarily by radio and television stations to broadcast programs, and by AT&T to transmit long-distance calls. Technological progress, providing access to a greater range and use of frequencies (following the FCC's decision in 1959 to begin allocating microwave frequencies to private as well as regulated industries), led companies such as IBM and Xerox to enter the microwave transmission field.

Another technology being opened to more and more uses is cable television. Often used to bring television signals to areas where, because of topography or other factors, they do not travel effectively through the air, it is now being adapted to richer purposes. One is to bring large bodies of information to people working at home, to investors following their stocks, to school kids who thus have access to electronic libraries and data banks. Another is to turn all those linked by cable TV into a community of sorts, able to conduct a dialogue via cable TV somewhat the way they can on a shared telephone trunk line. There is even serious experimentation with cable TV as a means of conducting public opinion polls and elections.

At the same time, several companies are investigating fiber optics technology, the process of transmitting information by bursts of light through glass fibers. Such fibers are smaller than the copper-wire cable that is generally used, but can carry more communications— theoretically, millions of telephone conversations per glass fiber. Many other examples could be listed, but the main point seems evident: basically a "model" industry.

POWER: ADAPTATION LAG

The first American industrialization was propelled by concentrated, cheap, reliable power (or energy). So much has been written and said about the changed energy world after 1973 that one often wonders if anything of merit can be added to characterize our predicament or state our needs. As to the future, energy seers have proved to be even more disappointing than other futurists. No sooner did they finish explaining—in 1974—why OPEC would "soon" collapse, "as all other monopolies did," than OPEC proved its staying power. And soon after they got used to escalating oil prices and projected them into the future, the 1980–82 glut slowed down the price escalation.

For the purposes at hand, only two statements need to be made. Both benefit from being strictly hindsight. First, the United States has not shown, in the period 1973–80, the commitment needed to come to terms with any one of the numerous aspects of the problem, from the dangers of international blackmail to those of supply interruptions, from dangers to the economy to those posed to national security. That is, the adaptation lag is most evident in this sector.

Second, energy (from oil or the BTU equivalent from other sources) has become significantly more expensive relative to other means of production in the 1973–80 period, compared to the pre-1973 era. Those who suggest that the oil price increase has not exceeded other price increases simply use as their starting point a post-1973 price, already highly inflated. The increase in the price of oil, from $2.59

a barrel in January 1973 to $26.00 in January 1980,[43] was not matched by an increase in other production costs. While the price of oil increased tenfold, other prices did not even double.[44]

The change from cheap to costly energy has several implications that need highlighting after all that has been written on the subject. It causes a major transfer of capital, of wealth, from the United States to oil-exporting countries; in 1980 this transfer was $82 billion. Financier Felix Rohatyn put it dramatically:

> The value of all companies listed on the New York Stock Exchange is approximately $900 billion. The idea that over the next five years we would mortgage to OPEC half the productive capacity of this country, built up over 200 years, to pay for oil is obviously absurd. This situation is as dangerous to our system, and as unacceptable to our security, as would be a Soviet presence in Saudi Arabia.[45]

While the wealth transfer was slowed by the multi-country recession and economic slowdown in 1980–81 and the resulting oil glut, as well as by increased conservation and production, it is unlikely that the problem has been licked. It results in the removal of hundreds of billions of dollars' worth of assets from the American economy, especially since a large proportion of these funds is not reinvested in the United States by the oil-exporting countries. (A good part of their riches flows to other nations; and the part that flows to America tends to be in short-term "paper," such as T-bills, which is not a suitable base for investment, as these funds might be called back on short notice.)

Expensive oil imports also worsen the real terms of trade for Americans, as measured by working hours. That is, Americans have to work longer to buy a barrel of oil, and oil-exporting countries have to work less to buy American products, from bushels of wheat to machines.

Of particular concern in the context of this analysis is the effect of the need to "rewire" most of the American economy on the availability of capital for other purposes. Since most American machines were designed, developed, mass-produced, and placed when energy was cheap, they tend to be energy-inefficient. This puts great pressure on producers (as well as consumers, as the owners of autos, air conditioning, appliances, and so on) to replace machinery and equipment *even* if it is *not* otherwise obsolete. This generates the need for a gigantic capital outlay, which comes on top of the huge outlays needed to develop sources of energy other than oil or to find more oil, often from deeper or less accessible—*i.e.,* costlier—sources. For example, commercial jets by and large are not obsolete, but they need to be replaced because they are fuel-inefficient; Delta Air Lines alone planned to spend about $7 billion over a fifteen-year period for fuel-saving planes.[46] To produce more fuel-efficient cars, General Motors, the industry leader, was expected in 1980 to spend more than $38 billion on new plants and equipment over the next five years. That is $10 billion more than it spent in the entire decade of the seventies,[47] when restyling was the main change introduced.

According to the overall estimate of the U.S. Department of Energy at the beginning of 1980,

> The domestic oil and gas sector will need to invest an average of $25 to $30 billion annually during the 1980s for exploration, development, production, and refining capacity just to achieve the lower share of energy supply that has been projected for it. Other private estimates range as high as $35 billion per year. Comparable expenditures were less than $13 billion in 1972 and approximately $20 billion in 1978. . . . The domestic coal industry will have to invest between $5 and $6 billion annually during the 1980s if it is to increase its output as forecast. This compares to actual investments of less than $1 billion in 1972 and $2.4 billion in 1978.[48]

It had been estimated in 1974 that a full-blown energy development and conservation drive would cost between $906 and $1,026 billion by 1990.[49]

The main reason these projections deal with future years, rather than the period under study (up to 1980), is that the necessary investment and adaptation did not take place. The task left to be done is a measure of the task left undone. The task is not to make the United States fully energy–self-sufficient or to return to cheap pre-1973 energy costs. The task is to adapt the American economy, through coordinated conservation and development, to more efficient use of energy and less reliance on oil; the goals must include ensuring that economic pressures due to disproportionate rises in energy costs cease to be a major disruptive force, and significantly diminishing the security-vulnerability posed by high energy dependency. Admittedly these provide no precise cut-off points, only a rough guidepost both for what is missing and what is needed.

INNOVATIVE CAPACITY: UNEVEN EROSION

According to one wit, there is one file at the National Science Foundation for "rosy" R&D indicators, another for gloomy ones. According to the political need, one or the other is used to make the case for "our strong science and technology" ("We are all to be proud of . . .") or to point out signs of decline and fall (". . . calling urgently for additional infusions of funds and talent"). Whether this tale is true or tall, it reflects the ambiguous status of this sector.

One often-used indicator of innovative capacity is the proportion of GNP dedicated to research and development. As a percentage of GNP, total R&D expenditures fell from 3 percent in 1964 to 2.3 percent in 1979.[50] However, as R&D specialist John Logsdon has pointed out, much of the decline was due to reductions in space and weaponry R&D, which is relatively costly; the overall figure does not necessarily reflect an across-the-board decline in R&D activities.[51]

While neither percentage of GNP nor any other measure provides a reliable yardstick for the health of innovation in the United States, several indicators are troubling. For example, it is widely agreed that the pace of America's technological development has slowed. A Commerce Department economist found one major technological development in the United States during the 1970s: the microprocessor, or silicon chip. In contrast, he listed at least six from the period between the late 1930s and the late 1940s, including the transistor, nuclear power, and synthetic fibers.[52]

America's position in the world technological market has grown more precarious as other industrial nations, particularly West Germany and Japan, have pumped more and more funds into their own R&D. While America's R&D expenditures were falling relative to GNP, West Germany's increased from 1.6 percent of GNP in 1964 to 2.3 percent in 1978, and Japan's from 1.5 percent of GNP in 1964 to 1.9 percent in 1976.[53] Studies by a U.S. Labor Department economist have indicated that Germany overtook the United States in 1977 as the leader in high-technology exports and that Japan is likely to do the same.[54]

The need to depend on innovations from other countries—thus giving their products a leg up—seems to have increased. In the 1950s, according to an analysis by the Stanford Research Institute, 82 percent of the major inventions brought to market were developed in the United States, but by the late 1960s, 55 percent originated here. This decline contributed to America's low productivity growth compared to that of most other industrial nations.[55]

Aside from drawing a smaller slice of the GNP pie, American R&D is believed to have suffered from disincentives due to excessive regulation. Businesses are said to have had to allocate considerable resources to compliance with these regulations, to work such as checking the toxicity of chemicals and their carcinogenic effects. Funds and skilled personnel have been diverted from developing new products and from applied research to meeting mandated standards. This is sometimes referred to as "defensive research." A vice-president of General Electric stated in 1979 that about 12 percent of G.E.'s $1.3-billion R&D budget was absorbed by defensive research.[56] Many of these expenditures seem highly justified from a human and social viewpoint (just as some seem excessive), but at the same time, given a smaller R&D sector, defensive work has further reduced the resources available for innovation. Moreover, for some firms, especially small ones, the high cost of defensive research has made it (and thus innovation) appear economically not worthwhile, or has driven them to carry it out in other countries, thus contributing to foreign R&D sectors.

Besides regulation, another source of disincentives, especially until 1978, has been the tax system. Because modern R&D requires rapidly increasing sophistication in facilities, R&D facilities become obsolete more rapidly than do plant and equipment used directly in production. Thus a relatively large investment of high-risk capital is necessary.

Although this necessity affects even large manufacturing firms, it is much more significant for small, high-technology businesses, and for individual innovators who are trying to raise the money to develop and market their inventions. A 1976 study found that between 1953 and 1973, smaller businesses (those with fewer than a thousand employees) accounted for almost half the nation's innovations.[57] The National Science Foundation estimated that, during the same period, these firms produced more than three times as many innovations per research and development dollar as did larger firms.[58] However, the access of these small firms to the capital needed to develop new products declined precipitously through much of the seventies. The capital acquired in public markets by firms with net worth less than $5 million is reported to have dropped from $1.5 billion in 1969 to $15 million in 1975, and to have remained at a very low level through 1978.[59] That more risk capital became available following the 1978 reduction in the maximum capital gains tax suggests that, from the viewpoint of venture capital, the tax was too high during most of the period under study.

Other reported R&D-related problems range from growing "scientific illiteracy" among school pupils to a shortage of engineers and computer programmers. Each of these has an "on-the-one-hand-but-on-the-other" quality. True, schoolchildren should know more about science—but the effect of lack of such knowledge on the nation's innovative capacity and R&D yield is slow and indirect. And in the past, engineering shortages (and other such) soon were followed by gluts. All in all, R&D seems (in areas other than communications and computers) to have weakened, but not nearly so much as transportation.

LEGAL/FINANCIAL INSTITUTIONS TURN CONSTRICTIVE

While during the first industrialization of America, the institutional context was basically supportive of economic activity and growth, in the golden age of consumption and social services, the institutional context grew less supportive, more inclined to impose noneconomic priorities and to intervene in private market decision-making. Indeed, a large segment of the business community came to perceive the institutional context as hostile not merely to businesses or "capitalism," but to economic activity in general.

The pace and scope of the government's regulatory apparatus, already encountered in the context of its effects on R&D, similarly restricted all other economic activity. The number of regulatory agencies grew from about a dozen before 1930 to fifty-eight by 1979.[60] Between 1950 and 1978, the *Code of Federal Regulations* expanded from about 23,000 pages to almost 84,000 pages, and the *Federal Register* grew from about 9,500 pages to more than 61,000 pages.[61] By the late seventies, completing the more than 4,000 different forms required to comply with federal regulations was eating up more than 140 million hours of executive and clerical effort each year.[62]

Even if one fully grants the need to regulate, say, the safety of nuclear plants, or to require examination of the environmental impact of a new utility, if the process (including challenges in court) takes several years, the costs of regulation multiply. Suggestions for "fast tracking" failed, and up to the late seventies, deregulation was largely an idea in some intellectuals' minds, tried out in a few areas.

Aside from causing costly delays, regulations were said to interfere with the "proper" matching of jobs and people, and the most effective allocation of resources among various uses. This is, of course, from the viewpoint of maximizing production. As the very purpose of various regulations is to advance other outcomes or values, from worker safety to environmental protection, this problem is caused not so much by regulation per se as by the increased scope and power of noneconomic values. Either way, regulation often hobbled production.

In addition, extensive and expanding regulation introduced a new measure of uncertainty for investment, and indeed all other business decision-making. Regulation often reflected a tug-of-war between the regulators and the various interests affected by them, resulting in prolonged efforts to get the government agencies to modify their regulations, and thus making it next to impossible to know what regulations would prevail a few years later.

Another side effect has been the sizable amount of paperwork generated by federal agencies. The Commission on Federal Paperwork estimated in 1977 that the federal government's requirements alone cost business between \$25 and \$32 billion each year.[63] Of course, not all this paperwork is "superfluous"; it includes, for instance, tax forms. Also, it results in part from firms' unwillingness to allow information provided to one agency (*e.g.*, the IRS), to be transmitted to others (*e.g.*, Commerce). Even so, the economic cost of paperwork is far from trivial.

By far the largest part of the cost of regulation seems to have been that related to the cost of compliance by the private sector. In a study of the cost of regulatory compliance conducted by Arthur Andersen & Co. for the Business Roundtable, forty-eight Roundtable member firms provided information on the incremental costs generated by six regulatory agencies or programs. These costs totaled \$2.6 billion in 1977, equivalent to about 16 percent of the companies' net after-tax income, 10 percent of their capital expenditures, or 43 percent of their R&D costs.[64]

A widely cited estimate of nationwide regulatory costs was prepared by Murray L. Weidenbaum (now Chairman of the Council of Economic Advisers) and Robert DeFina, when both were at the Center for the Study of American Business at Washington University. They estimated that in 1976, the federal regulations they studied cost the economy $66.1 billion—$3.2 billion to operate the regulatory agencies, $62.9 billion to comply with the regulations. Specifically,

> federally required paperwork contributed the largest share—$25 billion, as estimated by the Federal Paperwork Commission—followed by "industry-specific" regulation (of the airlines, for example, by the Civil Aeronautics Board) at $19.9 billion. Regulation of energy and the environment . . . cost $7.8 billion; consumer safety and health, $5.1 billion; and job safety and working conditions, $4 billion.[65]

By extrapolating from the results of the 1976 cost-study, Weidenbaum calculated in 1978 that federal regulation would cost at least $102.7 billion in 1979.[66] While some have claimed that these estimates are high, an Office of Management and Budget estimate runs higher: OMB estimated that in 1975 the total costs of regulation were between $113.3 and $135.4 billion.[67] Give or take $20 billion, these costs clearly imposed a major drag on the economy.

This is not to say that all regulatory costs constitute an economic drag. The Environmental Protection Agency, citing a study it had sponsored at the University of Wyoming, estimated the gains achieved through reducing air pollution as $5 to $16 billion a year by reducing death rates and $36 billion a year by reducing sickness rates. The Wyoming researchers arrived at the $36-billion figure by estimating the value of time lost from work, particularly in areas with high pollution rates.[68] Another major study of regulatory benefits, issued by the Corporate Accountability Research Group, estimated that in 1978 five agencies that imposed costs of $31.4 billion produced benefits of $36 billion, and that benefits would increase to $80.6 billion in 1985.[69] Nobody maintains that these estimates are more precise than those of the regulatory costs. They serve mainly to remind one that regulation is not sheer economic loss.

Antitrust laws were initiated long before the golden age of consumption. However, during that age their interpretation was expanded and, while they were rarely effectively enforced, staving them off added to business costs. And there is some reason to believe that fear of antitrust actions stopped corporations from actively considering many steps they believed would be productive and would otherwise have undertaken—collaboration in research, for instance.

Until 1980, U.S. antitrust laws prohibited collaboration among corporations in R&D activities, even in developing safety or antipollution devices; in other countries, corporations could collaborate in these matters easily, and with government encouragement. This limitation multiplied the costs of U.S. corporations. During the Carter administration, when I asked a Department of Justice official in charge of antitrust about this matter, he replied that allowing U.S. corporations to collaborate rather than compete could lead them to "lock into" a "bad" technology. I thought one need not worry about this possibility; a group of firms that clung to "bad" technology would soon feel the salutary effect of competition from overseas R&D—which, in the past, competition in the national market would have secured.

Furthermore, American antitrust laws, up to 1980, were said to hamper the ability of the United States to compete in international markets. Under the Webb-Pomerene Act of 1918, manufacturers may bid collectively on certain foreign projects (something they are not allowed to do in the United States). But problems stem from the interpretation of which types of projects are open to collective bidding. "As a result," Paul MacAvoy of Yale University explains, "there is a tendency for U.S. companies to play it safe, and they end up operating in Jakarta in the same way that they do in the U.S."[70] This limitation, it is said, curtailed the ability of U.S. firms to compete with foreign companies, which face no such restrictions. (Trading companies do exist in the United States, but most of their activity has been on the import side; there has been little success in developing large, export-oriented trading companies such as those that trade many Japanese exports. Legislation favoring American trading companies has been opposed on the grounds that it would "encourage local cartels and allow banks to own an interest in industrial enterprises.")[71]

All this is not to suggest that antitrust enforcement was not needed to preserve competition. A case in point is the overt monopolistic practice of price fixing, which merely enriches producers while harming consumers, with no broader economic justification. Even this "best case" argument for antitrust enforcement is questioned by some.

The dry breakfast cereal business illustrates the problem. The Federal Trade Commission charged that Kellogg, General Foods, and General Mills had created a shared monopoly that limited competition among themselves and prevented new competition from entering the market. The FTC estimated that this monopoly cost the consumer an additional $1.2 billion between 1958 and 1972. However, MIT economist Lester Thurow points out, this amounts to only about a tenth of a cent per breakfast, "hardly one of the nation's more pressing problems." Thurow continues:

> Consumers can buy no-name corn flakes, or a breakfast alternative, like bacon and eggs . . .
>
> Consumers may have been convinced of this very small extra psychic utility from branded cereals because of advertising, but so what? Needs determine very few of our spending decisions. . . .
>
> Individual consumers may be making silly decisions, but it is hardly the appropriate role of the antitrust laws to stop them. People seem willing to pay large amounts to have brands located in conspicuous places on their clothes. Should we use the antitrust laws to correct this irrationality?[72]

Besides regulations and antitrust laws, other legal and financial developments during this era have hampered U.S. productive capacity. For instance, take the debt/equity ratio. The Japanese government has encouarged banks to take risks by allowing investment in corporations that have piled up debts as high as eight or nine times their equity; U.S. banks have been "encouraged" by the Comptroller of the Currency, *i.e.*, the government, not to exceed significantly a one-to-one debt/equity ratio, to protect investors. Similarly,

> West German . . . , banks with equity interests in industry, are much more aware of their responsibility to promote industry as opposed to "just making loans." If American industry is to survive, it has to have the same kind of all-out support from its financial system.[73]

To complete the picture, one would have to compare the role played by monetary policy (presided over by the Federal Reserve System) and fiscal policy (formed by the various administrations and Congress) in this era to their role in the first industrialization of America; all by itself this would require a very major study, which I cannot undertake. It is widely agreed that in the last decade, budget deficits and expansionist monetary policies contributed to rising inflation, which in turn undermined the sources of investment (by undermining the motivation to save, the bond and stock markets, and public confidence, and by encouraging extensive credit use by consumers). But it does not necessarily follow that between 1820 and 1920 either the banking system or Congress and the Presidents of the time followed wiser economic policies. Indeed, severe bouts of inflation and of recessionary bust were far from unknown. That over the centuries the economy did so well is probably more because the interests committed to industrialization had a freer hand in those days than after World War II, and because the government, being much smaller in size, scope, and powers, caused less damage even when its economic policies were no wiser.

As for the changes that occurred gradually from 1950 to 1980 in the financial and legal framework of the American economy, they seem to have turned less accommodating, either because they increasingly promoted other values than economic growth and efficiency, or because the government grew bigger, more bureaucratic, and more restrictive.

HUMAN CAPITAL: SIGNS OF WEAKNESS

There is no general agreement that the quality of human capital was lower at the end of the post-war generation than it was at the end of the first century of industrialization, but there are some signs of weakening within the period under study.

Demographics

One factor was demographic change. The average worker in 1979 was younger than in 1950.[74] There were somewhat more minority workers in the labor force, and many more women. (Between 1960 and 1979, the proportion of minorities among the employed rose from 10.5 per cent to 11.3 percent; the proportion of women rose from 33.3 percent to 41.7 percent.[75])

The influx of women and minorities is said to have diluted the labor force because, on average, both groups were less well-prepared than white males. This is no aspersion on their innate ability, but reflects centuries of discrimination and less educational preparation as well as different psychological histories. Also, proportionately more women than men go to work outside the home compelled by economic pressures, not because they want to. A national survey conducted by the University of Michigan's Survey Research Center in 1971 found that 41 percent of the women questioned, compared to 26 percent of the men, would not work if they didn't need the money.[76]

The tie between workers' background and productivity is also suggested by Edward Denison, a leading expert on productivity. He found that the introduction of masses of less well-prepared persons into the labor force caused a reduction of productivity, albeit not a major one.[77]

Education

The thesis that a sizable segment of the graduates of America's schools are psychically underprepared for the adult world has already been advanced, in Chapter Six. The implications for the world of work are dual: Many new workers do not have the capacity to cope with routines, rules, or authority. And since they had the same basic incapacity in school—due as well to other factors ranging from school "overload" to "burned-out" teachers—they are deficient in cognitive preparation (both in ability to read, write, and compute, and in specific work skills, from reading a blueprint to dealing with a computer).

Motivation/Work Ethic

Among the most popular explanations for the decline in productivity growth throughout the period 1950–80 is the decline in worker motivation and the waning of the work ethic. Productivity expert Edward Denison is "skeptical that a sudden drop in willingness to work is responsible for the recent retardation of productivity, whether that is dated after 1966 or after 1973."[78] He explains that his skepticism is

> largely attributable to having heard similar generalizations all my life and having read them in the works of observers who wrote long before my birth. It was well before 1967 that I wrote, "Like the supposed decline in the spirit of enterprise, there seems always to be a popular belief that

people are less willing to 'put in a hard day's work' than they used to be, but this is scarcely evidence."[79]

Denison's analysis leads him to conclude that "it is quite possible that a decline in work effort contributed something to the retardation of productivity, although this has not been demonstrated; but it is unlikely to have been a major cause of the suddenly retarded growth . . . after 1973."[80]

The difficulty in assessing the changing quality of the labor force is, in part, a measurement problem. Denison writes that an "inability to answer the simple question—how hard do people work?—and to compare different places and dates, is probably the most serious gap in my measure of labor input."[81]

This difficulty is further illustrated by two studies, conducted at roughly the same time, early in 1981, that asked rather similar questions of highly similar national samples of adult Americans. The first asked respondents to agree or disagree with the statement, "People should place more emphasis on working hard and doing a good job than on what gives them personal satisfaction and pleasure." Two thirds of Americans (64 percent) agreed, while a minority (20 percent) disagreed, and the rest expressed mixed feelings or no opinion. The second asked, "Which do you think is more important in life: working hard and doing what is expected of you . . . or doing the things that give you personal satisfaction and plesaure?" While 38 percent stressed hard work, nearly half (49 percent) of adult Americans stressed personal satisfaction (14 percent evaded the question by answering "both equal").[82]

Obviously this is an area in which findings might vary considerably, and not much weight should be given to any one study. Still, if the available studies are put back-to-back, a suggestion of change arises. The research firm of Yankelovich, Skelly and White, studying worker motivations, discovered two groups of workers—old-values and new-svalues workers. Some of the differences between the two groups:

> To the old-values group, external cues are everything. They derive their sense of how they're doing and what they want out of life from the way people react to them.
> With new-values people, the cues are internal. It's part of the focus on *self*. Second, the work and the job define

old-values people. The new-values people are defined by what gives them psychic kicks. . . .

Third, respect for authority is almost automatic among old-values people. Skepticism about authority and self-confidence is part of the new-values lifestyle—especially with respect to work. . . .

Focus on the department, the company, a larger social unit are an expected part of life for the old-values people. Focus on the self is the rule for the new-values people.[83]

Daniel Yankelovich has called this new-values group the "New Breed." He describes their different motivation:

For the New Breed, family and work have grown less important and leisure more important. When work and leisure are compared as sources of satisfaction in our surveys, only one out of five people (21 percent) states that work means more to them than leisure. The majority (60 percent) say that while they enjoy their work, it is not their major source of satisfaction.[84]

Yankelovich suggests that if the incentive system were changed from emphasis on the "old" incentives, the carrot and stick of money/success and economic insecurity, to greater reliance on "new" incentives revolving around the "preoccupation with self," the "new breed" might work as hard as the old one.[85] However, as of 1980, most corporations seem not to have shifted to reliance on "new breed" incentives, although there was a growing interest in Quality of Work-Life programs.

Some insight into the status of the work ethic is provided by comparative data and by indications of changed habits and emerging problems. None by itself is compelling, but together they help to illuminate the condition of America's human capital.

Data from Japan show that the average auto worker in Japan turns out 40 to 50 cars a year, compared to 25 in the United States; a steelworker in Japan turns out 421 tons a year compared to 250 tons in the U.S.[86] Japanese employers in the U.S. compare American workers unfavorably to Japanese in attendance, turnover, ability, and morale, and also in their education and even language. While all the workers in Japan are fluent in their tongue, a Japanese manufacturer who opened a plant in Los Angeles found that 70 percent of its employees were "native Spanish speakers"—and others spoke mainly Korean or Vietnamese.[87]

One study found British construction workers "leaning on the shovel" and "walking around" more than their American fellow workers.[88] Little wonder: the United Kingdom is farther down the road to underdevelopment than the United States—by a country mile.

Concerning changed habits, a study of worker absenteeism by two Purdue University researchers found that

> perfect attendance is no longer necessary to keep a job or win promotions. In fact . . . company policies that allow for more frequent absences provide a basis for *greater* satisfaction. Liberal leave policies and a decline in the work-ethic have made skipping work much less risky. Only supervisors who directly control schedules and promotions seem to induce faithful attendance. In companies with ample sick leave and seniority systems, even the happy employees have little reason to work every day.[89]

Other data indicate that rising thefts at work, vandalism, and alcoholism and drug abuse on the job were serious problems by the end of the 1970s. Estimates in the late 1970s indicated that roughly 9 percent of all employees stole regularly from their employers and that 30 percent of business failures were directly attributable to employee theft. The National Retail Merchants Association found that while shoplifters took about 35 percent of all stolen goods, employees took 45 percent. (The rest was considered "accounting error.")[90]

An example of the effects of rising thefts, vandalism, and absenteeism has been provided by the Ford auto plant at Mahwah, New Jersey. Ford executives describe some sources of the plant's reputation for poor quality, which they claim was a main reason it was closed:

> In 1978 and 1979, the troubles reached a climax. Late in 1978 it was discovered that a half-dozen employees were looting the plant. Members of the theft ring, which included

security personnel, had been driving a truck into the plant at night, loading it with parts such as radios and electric motors for power windows, and driving out.[91]

Vandalism was continuing. Some workers would "get upset over something and they would take a drift pin (a heavy metal pin) and drive it right through the trunk or hood," said a car repairman at the plant.[92]

Absenteeism soared. According to a director of the quality-assurance program at Ford, "20 percent of employees were out some days. That meant workers had to be switched around on a day-to-day basis to fill gaps."[93]

Some workers turned to drugs. "You could walk through certain parts of the body shop during the night shift (when many younger men work) and get high just from breathing" the marijuana smoke, said one UAW official. [94] The number of companies that had formal programs to help employees with drug or alcohol dependency increased from only a few at the beginning of the decade to about two thousand by 1979.[95]

Other studies have concentrated on the attitudes and activities not of workers, but of American managers. Two Harvard Business School professors claim that a good part of the responsibility for economic problems falls on the manager's shoulders. Robert H. Hayes and William J. Abernathy write of the "new managerial gospel . . . that has played a major role in undermining the vigor of American industry."[96] They continue, "Responsibility for this competitive listlessness belongs not just to a set of external conditions but also to the attitudes, preoccupations, and practices of American managers."[97] Problems stem from what Hayes and Abernathy call "new principles" that "encourage a preference for (1) analytic detachment rather than the insight that comes from 'hands-on' experience and (2) short-term cost reduction rather than long-term development of technological competitiveness."[98] They say that by preferring short-term returns, "servicing existing markets" instead of creating new ones, and following a "management by the numbers" strategy, managers have, in effect, sacrificed "long-term technological superiority as a competitive weapon. In consequence, they have abdicated their strategic responsibilities."[99]

As an example of the problem Abernathy and Hayes see, they cite a manager who said, "In the last year, on the basis of high capital risk, I turned down new products at a rate at least twice what I did a year ago. But in every case I tell my people to go back and bring me some new product ideas."[100] Abernathy and Hayes argue that if companies are to maintain or recapture international competitive status, more risks, not fewer, must be taken in innovative production and market development.

A recent management survey likewise suggested that while U.S. workers are only two-thirds as productive as their grandfathers were, the fault lies with managers, not workers. According to the study, 30 percent of a workday is lost through "scheduling problems, unclear communication of assignments, improper staffing and poor discipline."[101]

The preceding overview has focused on internal indicators of the status of human capital. These seem to suggest a growing weakness. The quality of human capital is also affected by the prevailing societal mentality and by the educational institutions (family and school), which, we shall see shortly, have quite clearly turned less favorable to high economic growth.

CAPITAL GOODS: GROWING OBSOLESCENCE

As far as one can tell, major segments of the capital goods sector were seriously undermaintained during the period from 1950 to 1980. Plants, machines, and equipment in several key industries grew in obsolescence and did not keep up with the installation of new machines by competitors overseas. This seems to be the case in such major American industries as autos and steel as well as rubber, textiles, and, for different reasons, shipbuilding. One survey found that at the end of 1978, although some industries had made considerable progress in modernization during the previous two years, the proportion of technologically outmoded plant and equipment was 26 percent in iron and steel, 25 percent in rubber, 18 percent in mining, 17 percent in autos, trucks, and parts.[102] Other industries, such as petroleum and chemicals, showed stronger innovative signs. The manufacturers surveyed reported that it would cost $126.4 billion to replace all technologically outmoded facilities with the best new plants and equipment.[103] Since this figure excludes all nonmanufacturing industries as well as the manufacturers which did not reply to the survey, the total outlay needed for modernization would obviously have been much greater.

It might be said that the decline of some industries and the rise of others is part of the adaptation of the economy to changing conditions. There is a considerable measure of truth in this argument. For instance, in a world of rising oil costs it might serve well to "reduce capacity" in auto manufacturing and to build up energy exploration. At issue is not drawing up a master plan but accepting the market's way of adjusting to changed circumstances. At the same time, it is clear that on balance the total American capital goods sector did not fare well between 1950 and 1980. Its share of the investment plowed back into the economy declined, while the share channeled into residential housing, actually a consumer good, rose. No good data are available, but very crude estimates suggest that at the height of the first industrialization of America, say in 1870, sixteen dollars of every hundred dollars invested were dedicated to housing, compared to nearly thirty-three dollars in the post–World War II generation.

Also, a growing segment of investment in capital goods has been dedicated to pollution abatement and safety.

> In 1978, these expenditures amounted to $6.9 billion, more than 4.5 percent of the total investment in the surveyed industries, with a projected increase to $7.3 billion for 1979. For certain industries the share in 1978 was higher: primary metals (12.6 percent); electric utilities (10.1 percent); petroleum (8.3 percent); and chemicals (7.8 percent). And these data omit the annual operating costs of complying with pollution abatement regulations.[104]

Stanford economist Michael J. Boskin writes:

> The U.S. gross investment rate in physical tangible capital has fallen. . . . Of our $386 billion of gross private investment in 1979, the bulk went into housing and replacement of wornout capital as well as into pollution abatement and safety programs; real net addition to plant and equipment was about $40 billion, less than 2 percent of GNP.[105]

While the proportion of investment in capital goods to GNP did not change much between 1950 and 1980, remaining roughly 10 percent of GNP, the labor force grew, and thus the capital available per worker (and hence probably the capital goods) declined.[106] The capital/labor ratio is considered a better measure than investment as a percentage of GNP, since it accounts for growth in the labor force as well as the change in the capital stock. The capital stock/labor force ratio peaked in 1974 at $10,604 (in 1972 dollars) per person. Since then investment has not matched the rapid growth of the labor force, and the ratio has fallen by nearly 3 percent.[107]

While from 1960 to 1973 the net amount of plant and equipment per U.S. worker in the private sector was increasing at an average annual rate of 2.3 percent, since 1973 this rate has declined to 0.1 percent. Between 1973 and 1980, there was virtually no increase in the net stock of manufacturing plants.[108]

In the 1970s, high rates of inflation reduced the incentive to invest in new plant and equipment. Depreciation of plant and equipment for tax purposes is based on historic cost. As inflation pushes current replacement cost above historic cost, current depreciation allowances (and therefore current expenses) are understated, especially for long-lived investments, and current profits are overstated. Thus the amount of tax paid is in effect increased, and dollars that would otherwise be available for investment are diverted into taxes. Indeed, between 1965 and 1979, the average real economic rate of return on capital investment for nonfinancial corporations declined from 10 percent to about 5 percent.[109]

Two other factors, already discussed, seem to have required additional investment. One was the need to "rewire" American industry in response to the energy crisis. The second was the rise of competing nations that channeled much more of their GNP into capital in general and capital goods in particular.

Although cross-cultural comparison can be misleading, it does suggest that the United States was lagging behind its major competitors in this sector. In 1978, while total U.S. investment was 17.6 percent of GNP, that of West Germany was 21.6 percent and that of Japan, 30.5 percent.[110]

IN SUMMARY

Of the seven elements that accounted for the successful development of the infrastructure and the capital goods sector in the first industrialization of America, we have found that by 1980 only one is still in vigorous health, the communications sector. The transportation sector is particularly rundown, with railroads, bridges, and ports worse off than other weakened segments, and no new means for transportation of goods have been widely introduced recently. The energy sector has been causing numerous well-known problems, not due to a maintenance gap, which characterizes many of the other elements, but due to utterly insufficient adaptation of policies, technologies, and investments in the 1973–80 era. The R&D and human-capital sectors show signs of decline, but not as clearly and certainly not as severely as some of the other sectors. Legal and financial institutions have clearly turned against economic development in the era under study, if an across-the-board generalization is to be made. The status of capital goods has varied a great deal from industry to industry, with a fair number showing the signs of rising obsolescence and relatively few new, vigorous replacement.

By 1980 the cumulative results of the maintenance gap and the adaptation lag, of high consumption and insufficient plowback into the economic foundations, were the multiple signs of economic weakness that are all too familiar—from falling productivity to declining growth rate, from high inflation to difficulties competing overseas.

CHAPTER TEN
The Rational Mentality and Its Challengers

Industrialization is not merely a matter of amassing capital and labor and combining them in new ways. It is also a matter of a mentality, a way of thinking about oneself, others, and the world—a mentality that seeks to open the world's resources and use them to make stronger instruments and increase output. The outlook on the world that is central to industrialization is hardly a passive orientation, accepting of fate, nor one indifferent to wealth, preoccupied with inner values or inner self.

Social scientists and assorted intellectuals have debated for more than a century how important the "proper" mentality is for industrialization. Marxists tend to play it down, while many Western social scientists emphasize it. I try to circumvent this important but, for the purposes at hand, unnecessary issue. Changes in mentality may cause or accompany or follow industrialization (frankly, I believe the answer is "all three"); the "right mentality" may be a pivotal cause or merely supportive. In any case, the initiation, advancement, and sustaining of industrialization are closely related to the development of a compatible mentality: specifically, a rational mentality.

THE RATIONAL MENTALITY

Rationality Defined
Rationality is the capacity to subject the selection of means in pursuit of a goal to logical and empirical considerations. Nonrational

or irrational persons allow emotive considerations ("sentiments") and normative elements ("value judgments") to intrude on, if not submerge, logical/empirical considerations. A simple example: During Manhattan's rush hour, someone in a hurry, acting rationally, will use a subway instead of his auto. A nonrational person "loves" his car and would rather sit in it than switch.

Nobody is completely rational; in moments of high stress, for example, most people allow emotions to cloud their considerations. Similarly, nobody is completely nonrational; even members of primitive tribes who exorcise evil spirits so that their crops will grow plant seeds first. However, there are great differences in the role accorded rationality in different societies, historical periods, and even subcultures. In the mentality supportive of industrialization, a high level of rationality is a fundamental attribute, one that outweighs all others.

Industrialization and the Three Realms of Rationality

Industrialization requires a higher level of rationality than traditional farming and home manufacturing primarily because it requires a more efficient, output-oriented economic system. In a sense, what industrialization is all about is developing a set of means for production that, compared to previous production systems, results in much higher output at much lower cost ("mass production"). This, in turn, requires greater openness in the selection of means to be used; institutionalization of the open search for means so that it is carried out systematically, not merely occasionally; and logical organization of tasks and sub-tasks, and allocation of resources (capital and labor).

To put it differently, the pro-industrialization mentality encompasses much more than mere effective/efficient economic activity, production and distribution of goods and services ("economic rationality"). Industrialization also benefits from a greater body of knowledge, more effective use of technology and science, and more supportive institutionalization of innovation than traditional farming societies. (Rationality is, of course, as essential for modern agriculture as for modern industry; modern farming is no more akin to traditional farming than a modern steel mill is like an early nineteenth-century iron works.) The evolution of a growing body of knowledge and its systematic application to productive purposes are what makes for "better" instruments. The mentality element involved is dedication to a rational search, an acceptance of the scientific method and its findings—fewer almanacs, more weather forecasts; less trial-and-error tinkering, more a priori testing. (This might be referred to as the technological-scientific realm.)

In the same vein, rationality plays a central role in the division of tasks and their combination into more encompassing entities—the foundation of modern administration, especially within corporations, but also among them and within government. If workers are hired, assigned, reassigned, and fired according to tribal ties, kinship, political loyalties, or payoffs, production suffers. And if executive (or government) decisions are deeply affected by "irrelevant" (nonempirical, nonlogical) considerations—if they yield to bribes, for example, or are governed by political back-scratching—production, technology, and modern administration will not flourish. On the contrary, industrialization advances when economic, technical, and administrative activities are allowed a rather wide leeway to unfold their own logic. (This is the administrative realm of rationality.)[1]

I choose my words precisely when I say, "a rather wide leeway" rather than a more drastic phrasing, say, "to have their way." This narrower wording is a reminder that rationality need not be all-powerful for industrialization to advance, and advance well. After all, rationality concerns instruments; it is properly bounded by normative goal-setting. Why be rational? Rationality itself does not explain. It is the "best" means to an end—an end set by other considerations, such as the quest for affluence or national security, or some other goal.

These normative goals (and the "rewards" for the psychic discipline entailed) do not violate rationality; they are, so to speak, at the *end* of the open process that rationality entails. Rationality is undermined only when normative considerations penetrate and interrupt the process of selecting means—say, if nationalism curtails international trade and thus limits the ability to get the most effective and least costly resources.

The goal considerations set the context within which rationality is practiced. As long as they do not penetrate into the selection and application of means, whether economic, technical, or administrative, rationality can thrive. Indeed, even some limitation in the selection of means is not debilitating. No international trade is or ever was completely free, and concern for human values and needs typically limits some means-selection at work (*e.g.*, holidays are granted not just to rest the labor force, but also out of religious or patriotic concerns). But as long as the scope of these constraints remains limited, rationality can function quite effectively.

SELF-DISCIPLINE, DEFERMENT OF GRATIFICATION, AND RATIONALITY

Self-discipline, as we have seen, is the foundation in the personality for mutuality and civility. Lacking self-discipline, a person is unable to deal with impulses or to relate properly to others, to rules, or to the community. Self-discipline is what allows people to function as mature persons, persons who are both reasonably autonomous and also "connected," "looped-in."

Self-discipline is also a basis of rationality; like mutuality and civility, rationality suffers when the personality is underdeveloped. But while a high level of self-discipline is valuable for a wide variety of pursuits (highly disciplined persons make fine violinists or long-distance runners, not just entrepreneurs, scientists, or administrators), the activities that are fundamental to industrialization require not simply self-discipline or self-organization per se, but, more specifically, rational conduct based upon self-discipline.

Mobilizing self-organization for rational behavior, as previous writers have emphasized, is important in preparing farm workers, used to irregular and varied work, to provide the highly routinized, dependable labor that industry requires. Likewise, instead of consumption, it encourages savings and investment, which are essential in the early stages of industrialization to generate the resources required by the infrastructure and the capital goods sectors.

A main link joining self-discipline to rationality is the capacity to defer gratification, to wait for the fruits of labor or savings rather than spend money as soon as it's earned or quit work after every few days of earning. Self-organization provides the capacity to control and channel psychic energy and to use some of it for superego purposes. The same capacity is at the root of scientific work; the willingness to search, to be open to evidence rather than adhere to prejudice, and to carry to their conclusion the logical implications of findings. Similarly, it is fundamental to administrative work: the ability to deal with logically relevant attributes of a clientele while disregarding others that might be emotionally relevant, *e.g.*, to decide among job applicants according to their qualifications rather than their personal appeal or political connections. In short, the capacity to defer gratification, with its inherent orientation to the future, is the psychic trait that self-organization "provides" for rationality, and thus in turn for a high level of economic, scientific-technical, and administrative activity.

Another side of the psychic basis of rationality is suggested by the work of cardiologists Meyer Friedman and Ray H. Rosenman. Since the late 1950s they have focused attention on a behavior pattern they call "Type A," characterized as competitive, controlling, preoccupied with work and achievement, tense, driven by a sense of urgency. In contrast, "Type B" personalities are unhurried, tranquil, relaxed, more easily satisfied.[2] These types are not unequivocally defined; findings of studies identifying them have been contested, and reports that suggest that Type A behavior is related to heavy smoking, high blood cholesterol, and high incidence of coronary disease are controversial. There is, however, a clear conceptual correspondence between Type A behavior and the rational mentality: The highly focused pursuit of achievement, to the partial exclusion (or "deferment") of extraneous pleasures, is characteristic of both. The work of Friedman and Rosenman, and others who have followed this line of study, reminds us that the rational mentality is far from cost-free.

While there are, of course, no data on how many Americans were of Type A versus Type B in 1820, nor for that matter in 1920, many social scientists would expect that Type A personalities prevailed in these earlier eras. It is widely agreed among social scientists that the capacity to defer gratification was common even earlier, among preindustrial Americans, largely because of Protestant religious beliefs, which were predominant among those who emigrated to America from Britain and the northern parts of Western Europe. Their minds were set on future rewards; moreover, to work hard and to save, two useful kinds of conduct for industrialization, were blessed and encouraged as signs of being chosen by the Lord. In addition, the escape from dogma; the selective process all emigration, but especially voluntary emigration, entails; the relative weakness of traditional clan, tribal, and class bonds; the open frontier—all encouraged an open, rational orientation in the early stages of American history. Sociologist S. M. Lipset attributes much of the rapidity of American economic growth to "a particularly productive, symbiotic relationship between economic growth and the American value system . . . a set of values that enshrined 'the good life' as one of hard, continuous work, frugality, self-disciplined living, and individual initiative."[3]

One need not be a professional historian to recall that not all Americans had or welcomed these attributes. There was, especially in the South, a landed aristocracy with other traditions, more anti-commerce and more consumption-oriented, and among the slaves and the American Indians quite different psychic and cultural mentalities were common. Nevertheless, although other groups and mentalities continued to exist as subcultures, the rational mentality seems to have been widely embraced by the main groups that launched industrialization in nineteenth-century America.

FROM GOD TO CONSUMER GOODS

As secularization set in (a decline in the power and scope of religion almost always accompanies the rise of industrialization), the domination of the rational mentality continued, despite the loss of religious legitimation, in the kind of sociological inertia that would continue to expand a highway to a city that has lost most of its population. The resulting abnormality is of great importance for the issue at hand. Rationality concerns relations among means and goals. While it is occasionally obsessively followed as an end in itself, psychically it is but a tool, not an end-state satisfying in itself. True, there is some psychic income in the search process, in finding a "better" means or pattern, but basically, the psychic payoff comes at the end of the chain: a "large" reward (and anticipation of it) that is not rational in itself—such as salvation, or community approval. Without such an end-state, rationality is "irrational" (as Max Weber put it) or "mad" (David Riesman's term). Why asphalt the road to nowhere? The *present* joys of deferment of gratification and rational conduct are secondary and, usually, quite slim. Secularization thus undermined the Calvinistic religious "reward," cutting rationality off from its ultimate anchor.

Psychic dynamics abhors such severed moorings. As secularization intensified, a new ultimate purpose had to tie in the rational mentality, or it would gradually drift away. For reasons that are not well understood, God was soon replaced by a new ultimate purpose: consumer goods and services. Gradually the justification for working hard, saving, and otherwise being rational came to be not the Lord but "the good life," defined as a high standard of living. Factory workers stuck to their drudgery because they expected, after years of work, a house of their own, a boat, a rocking chair on the front porch.

Most important for America's first industrialization, while the justifying goals were replaced, the basic approach was not: The goals were still to be reached at the end of a chain of deferred gratification, rational behavior, effort and saving.

The Great Depression did very little to shake this new god. That economic earthquake was widely perceived as an aberration, just as unemployment was viewed by most Americans as either bad luck or their own fault, not as a systemic flaw. Indeed, the consumption goal, far from losing, gained in luster. A "survivor" of the Depression tells his grown children, accustomed to affluence: "You can't imagine what it was like to walk home every night to a dinner of canned fish and potatoes. I dreamed of being able to eat steak."

World War II was another temporary deflection. For the time being, the first priority for instruments, for the industrial-technological-administrative complex, was the service of the national goal of winning the war, but high consumption remained an ideal, the more celebrated because it had to be partially deferred. People were waiting for the day when they could get all the Camel cigarettes they wanted, replace their aging cars, and forget about ration books.

The end of World War II brought the end of constraints and the beginning of a generation-long consumption spree. Instead of waiting, more and more Americans bought on installment credit—*now*—what had once been luxuries earned by decades of hard work and scrimping. "The American way of life" came to mean not only the promise of liberty and ultimate rewards after a lifetime of labor, but contemporary affluence. The United States was the richest society in the world, and Americans enjoyed it and found purpose in affluence. Other societies might speak of their culture, history, conquests; Americans bragged about their liberties—and their flush toilets, large cars, and color televisions.

For my argument, it is essential to recapture the mentality of, say, the mid-1950s, when mass consumption both flourished and was celebrated. One may savor it by recalling that a main concern of the day was that Americans had developed such a powerful, efficient, and productive economic system that the ever-larger avalanche of products it generated might not find takers. Marxists had argued that the capitalist system would collapse under its own weight as ever fewer owners amassed ever more of the capital, or "surplus value," leaving the ever larger proletariat less ability to buy; the conquest of other societies (imperialism) would secure additional markets only temporarily before capitalism killed itself off. But few Americans concerned themselves with these notions. They paid somewhat more attention to Joseph A. Schumpeter's critique of capitalism, which noted the possibility that since people's wants are not endless, ultimately they might be so satiated that there would be little incentive for productive effort; entrepreneurs would have nothing to do, and capitalism would become atrophic, the victim of its own success.[4]

In those faraway days, John Kenneth Galbraith wrote *The Affluent Society*, widely remembered for its notion that Americans were gaining an ever-higher standard of living, rather than for its key thesis, that there was one sector, still poor, that would help alleviate the fear of over-production: the public sector. Galbraith argued that the surplus of products individuals could not absorb might be channeled to schools, hospitals, museums.[5]

David Riesman was more imaginative. He envisioned a "Nylon War" against the Soviet Union, in which the United States would "bomb" Russia with stockings and washing machines, both softening the fanatic regime (as preoccupation with consumer goods tends to do to austere, tyrannical regimes) and providing American assembly lines with new outlets. And as American productivity rose still higher, he proposed that New Orleans be made a national park, its 1950s lifestyle conserved and subsidized as bear are protected in Yellowstone.[6]

A sense of born-to-affluence, not merely a great rise of social consciousness, was at the basis of the "social era" of the 1960s and beyond. If you were rich, growing richer by the day, why not share? Thus President John F. Kennedy sought to help develop and democratize scores of nations through the Alliance for Progress (both before it was understood what it takes to develop one nation and before our own limitations came to light). President Lyndon B. Johnson, before he got more deeply entangled in the Vietnam war, launched an incredible 435 domestic social programs, seeking to fix practically every social facet of American life from poverty to highway billboards, from the condition of blacks to that of public parks.

In short, the preoccupation of the late fifties and early sixties was finding outlets or takers—consumption, not production. Scarcity, as a mind-set, was unknown. The long view, rationality, deferment of gratification, self-discipline, all receded in value as, more and more, the future seemed at hand.

CHALLENGES TO RATIONALITY

Extending versus Violation of Rationality

The rationality that was central to America's first industrialization was rather narrowly focused. Whether the goal of "the good life" was seen in terms of religion or consumption, the selection of means, from where to build a railroad to the hiring and firing of workers, was based quite strictly on economic, managerial, and technical criteria. Suggestions that considerations other than profits, efficiency, or empirical evidence should enter into economic decisions received only a limited hearing. When these "intrusions" were tolerated, they were generally seen as special limited cases, *e.g.*, when child labor was grudgingly terminated. The basic assumptions, linking hard work and savings to the end-state of high production and consumption, remained essentially undisturbed. Indeed, they gradually gained in power during the first half of the industrializing century and withstood growing challenges from populist and socialist sources in the second half.

However, out of the golden age of consumption and social services came *major* challenges to this highly focused, "narrow," rationality. These challenges called into question both the rationality of the means by which production and consumption were to be achieved, and the legitimacy of the economic goals used to justify the self-discipline it required. As the consensus of the value of production and consumption as the end-goal weakened and alternative goals gained support, this underpinning of modern America began to falter.

It is not that a new vision took over; rather the old vision paled and other visions demanded attention simultaneously, as well as sought to compete to be the prime source of legitimation. For individuals, the dilemma of pursuing more than one goal at a time is familiar. A person may want to get downtown not just in a hurry, but in reasonable comfort and at low cost; in deciding how to go, he weighs the speed and low fare of the subway against the greater comfort of a taxi. Similarly, the multiplication of societal goals makes rationality not impossible, but much more difficult. To extend the scope of rationality to encompass multiple goals requires not merely comparing two or more sets of means leading to one goal, but also ordering the goals themselves and maintaining a balance among them. Various intellectual techniques are available to deal with these difficulties. However, the judgment of what is rational is never as straightforward with reference to multiple goals as with reference to one.

One response to the combination of multiple, sometimes conflicting goals with diminished support for logical, empirical selection of means was to modify rationality while seeking to preserve its essence. Narrowly focused rationality was *extended* to accommodate goals and normative considerations other than efficient production and rising consumption. However, as normative considerations penetrated deep into the selection of means, rationality was *violated*, allowing nonrational criteria to take priority.

The extension and ultimate violation of the previously dominant, narrowly focused rationality requires some elucidation. Limited challenges to the goal of high production/consumption, and to rational pursuit of it, were by no means unknown in the nineteenth century. There were, for instance, scores of efforts to retreat from the rationality of modernity into a more primitive setting within early industrial America. The Shakers, the Mennonites, the Owenites based their communities on a different vision. While industrialization proceeded apace, Henry David Thoreau wrote eloquently in *On Walden Pond* of a simpler, more contemplative life. And some early socialist following developed among America's intellectuals, immigrants, and workers. But these early challenges were, by one criterion or another, at the margin of society. They were limited in duration, in the number of their adherents, in the breadth of their appeal among various segments of society. While they represent fascinating byways of American history, none of them amassed sufficient force to undermine the core high-production project or its supportive rational mentality.

The Depression left deeper marks, but they, too, concerned subgoals, not core values. In this era, the *social* value of keeping people working was widely accepted, the role of government as employer of last resort was initiated, and Social Security was introduced. While these developments placed limits on economic logic and extended the rational selection of means, they did not call into question the basic merit of the core project or of the rational mentality; they did not present new core values nor an alternative conception of the way to relate means to goals. Instead they extended the list of means-considerations that were viewed as necessary or prudent, thus extending or moderating rationality while preserving its domain and status.

Similarly, while the increase in workers' rights—to strike, to organize "closed shops," and so on—was seen by some as an intrusion of alternative social values into the rationality of production, it was perceived by many others as contributing to production through the development of a more satisfied, better motivated, more peaceful labor force. Thus, it could be justified in terms of a new sub-goal of production, "good labor relations." Indeed, most corporations came to prefer the usually orderly process of dealing with labor unions over the wildcat strikes, sabotage, and violent outbreaks that are common when there is no institutional channel for personal and collective grievances. In short, although these new labor practices set some new limits on the selection of means (by excluding the use of strike-breakers, for example), they made some new means available (*e.g.,* drawing on the labor union to help secure regular attendance). On the whole they did not challenge the essence of the system in the way, for instance, nationalization of the means of production, favored by socialists at the time, would have.

To put it differently, the narrow, focused rationality of production was extended to a degree to encompass other considerations, in the case at hand, that of workers' rights, labor peace, and a view of workers as fellow citizens, not merely tools. But this extended rationality was merely that. It either incorporated other values and, using logical/empirical criteria, selected means that were appropriate both to these values and to production, or it made limited room for "other" considerations.

The same may be said about the other significant pre-1950s "intrusion," Social Security, at least as it was originally proposed. Social Security is based on a different set of assumptions from those underlying rationality narrowly focused on high production. Instead of granting the rewards of consumption exclusively for productive work and saving, Social Security assumes that some members of society, the old and infirm, are to be accorded some support regardless of their contribution to production.

It is, of course, no accident that the issue was clouded: Social Security was initially introduced as an insurance scheme, to make it seem that the potential beneficiaries paid for their benefits, and thus that it was compatible with narrowly focused production/consumption rationality. Not until later was it widely understood that Social Security, an idea lifted from socialist-democratic Fabian thinkers in Britain, was instead a transfer of payment: Payouts were not directly based on pay-ins. For example, according to an analysis by Donald O. Parsons and Douglas R. Munro, in 1940, when Social Security payments began, the average annual benefit to a male aged sixty-five was $270.60, while a private annuity based on the same contributions would have paid only $6.59; in other words, 98 percent of the annual benefit represented a transfer payment.[7] This proportion declined as the system matured, but even in 1970, they estimated that the "welfare component" of the average benefit to men retiring at sixty-five was 68 percent.[8]

The "intrusion" of other elements of "welfare capitalism" was resisted much more vigorously. The most prominent example of these is national health insurance, which was adopted by other industrialized societies but has been repeatedly rejected in America.

In the late fifties and, especially, in the sixties, the balance between the leading theme and the intruding ones changed significantly. Three *major* onslaughts on the mentality of focused rationality and the core project of high production came in rapid succession, each new one rising before the previous one crested. Coming first in the name of social justice or equality, second from the counterculture, and third for the environment's sake, these challenges culminated in the vision of an alternative society, with an alternative mentality and source of legitimacy: a society whose first priority and core project was social growth or the quality of life.

This vision was based on both a different set of goals and different criteria for the selection of means. For example, meditation, as a major activity, is hardly a new, more enlightened, socially more responsible way of production; it is part of a new world of purposes—and defines utterly new ways of getting there.

Three Challenges to Focused Rationality

Equality
The ideal of equality is hardly a mid-twentieth-century revelation; it was obviously on the minds of the framers of the United

States Constitution, and it played a key role in the early formation and later reform of American political institutions (*e.g.,* in the Jacksonian era). However, until the late 1950s, it did not play a key role in legitimating the ways economic rewards (consumption) were allocated, nor in practices governing access to choice jobs, which generate the income for high consumption and carry rewards of their own, such as high prestige and attractive working conditions.

S. M. Lipset has examined the complex interaction of equality with the prominent value of rationality—achievement. He found that while achievement and equality have sometimes reinforced each other, sometimes conflicted, during the period of America's first industrialization the emphasis, not surprisingly, was on achievement. Moreover, equality was interpreted primarily as equality of opportunity: All Americans, equally, should have the opportunity to work hard for a rich future, not be *provided* with equal futures.[9]

With the maturing of the industrial economy, the equality/achievement dynamic shifted toward equality, particularly toward concern for those who were at a disadvantage in gaining rewards through effort alone. As sociologist Herbert J. Gans wryly observes, "Rich and poor . . . have an equal opportunity to work as common laborers, but the poor rarely obtain the education and social contacts that provide access to executive positions."[10] The concept of equality was enlarged to encompass both equality of opportunity and equality of treatment, or equal access to resources; school desegregation from the 1950s on provides a vivid illustration. Still, Gans reminds us, treating the disadvantaged uniformly with the advantaged only perpetuates their disadvantage: "The only truly egalitarian principle is equality of results, which may require unequal treatment for the initially disadvantaged so that they eventually wind up equal in resources or rights."[11]

Increasingly, in the social sixties, equality of *results* was emphasized over equality of opportunity and access, let alone the undiluted achievement criteria.[12] The difficulties of overcoming the effects of past and cumulative disadvantages convinced more and more Americans of the merit of allocating rewards—consumption, jobs, even wealth—by status rather than achievements (*e.g.,* granting certain proportions of construction jobs, highly desirable apprenticeships, housing, college fellowships to minorities on the basis of race—and little else). And the ranks of those deemed entitled to allocations based on status vastly expanded to include not just a few senior or frail citizens, but minorities, women, the handicapped, children, the majority of Americans.

Unequal treatment came to be accepted in a growing circle as a means of equality of results. The *actual* distribution of rewards changed much more slowly; but as equality of results became more widely considered legitimate, the other principle, that effort and the deferment of gratification (means) are the legitimate basis of al-locations (access to goal-states), weakened. Many of those who were previously under-rewarded could now hope to draw on new ways to gain a share. And many of those who were previously fully re-warded for their efforts came to feel that their work and saving were disparaged, because others received the same rewards for much less effort.

Counterculture

The counterculture movement cut even deeper into the rational mentality and the legitimation of the core project. It seriously ques-tioned both the value of the payoffs (or "outputs"), the high standard of living, and the merit of the inputs, hard work and savings. Indeed, it openly and directly challenged the virtue of deferment of gratifica-tion, self-organization, and rationality. It elevated to the level of virtue psychic satisfaction derived from little work, low consumption, and direct relation to others, nature, and self, relations not mediated by objects. Growth was to be found not in the economy but in harmoni-ous relationships and deeper understanding of self and others. What-ever its form—"flower children," the drug culture, communes, certain cults—the counterculture sought in immediate pleasure, in making way for impulse, in nonrational and irrational behavior, in preoccupa-tion with personal rather than production needs, the vitality people missed at the end of the long chain of rationally combined means that is the basis of "materialistic" efforts. Technology, science, and administration were viewed no more favorably than economic endeav-ors.

While the counterculture's most visible carrier, the hippie sect, quickly burned out and largely vanished, like that of many other extreme sects before it in social history, its cultural and psychic impact persisted. The counterculture fed into the retreat from rationality and the vision of an alternative world and mentality.

The Environmental Movement

A third wave of challengers was rolled into the environmental movement, which championed, among other ideas, the conception that high production and consumption were destroying the natural world. It suggested that the high production/high consumption core project was self-contradictory, both in that it was gradually destroying the base of the rational/productive society and in that it was undercutting other important sources of satisfaction, such as open space and clean air, for the sake of plastics and chemicals, dubious goods at best.

Some concern with conservation and husbanding of resources is compatible with, may even complement, a high level of economic activity. However, to the extent that the environmental movement won support for the idea that only slow economic growth (or none at all) is compatible with environmental goals and greater harmony with nature, it challenged the very core of the high production/high consumption project and violated the rational mentality associated with it.

Stretching Rationality: A Case Study

The lines that separate focused from extended from violated rationality can perhaps be most easily traced in a specific example: the treatment of the handicapped. In the 1920s, even in the early 1950s, it was common practice that a person who could not do the work—in school, factory, office, lab—on the same terms, with the same equipment, as everybody else did not get the job, or the education. A person who because of some handicap needed extra attention, special equipment, or a different system received sympathy, and treatment or custodial care in a segregated world, but few concessions in the dominant one: Jobs and job-related education were allocated according to narrowly production-focused rationality.

Gradually it came to be acknowledged that this approach was unnecessarily limiting; that many handicapped people could learn productive skills, that the workplace could be adapted to use the skills and abilities they had, at no or little net cost. This would be a case of rationality extended. Why? Because the needs of the handicapped are encompassed without any major sacrifice of rationality. From the viewpoint of a narrow rationality of production, the employment of the handicapped is not an issue at all, at least not as long as other employees are available or there is no evidence that the handicapped are *more* efficient than regular employees.

A broader perspective contains the costs to society. It is argued that it costs the taxpayers less if handicapped persons are employed than if they must be supported through welfare or disability payments. One federal training program, for instance, reported that it placed five thousand handicapped persons in private-sector jobs at a cost of about $1,000 per person. It was estimated that in a full year of employment, even at the minimum wage, they would earn at least $35 million and pay $7 million in taxes. In contrast, it costs the government an estimated $5,000 per year, and perhaps twice that for the severely disabled, to support unemployed handicapped persons.[13] This is thus one more consideration for extending rationality.

Aside from decreased cost to society, there are also human benefits, in dignity, autonomy, and self-esteem, to the handicapped person who is able to participate more fully in the economy and in the society. As long as these are "additional" benefits, and employment and taxpayer benefits are the main criteria, reducing the segregation of the handicapped and training them and otherwise helping their employment are a matter of extending rationality.

Such extended rationality led to programs designed primarily for handicapped adults whose qualifications promised a high and reliable economic return, and for children and young people with non-intellectual handicaps, even fairly severe physical disabilities, who without extreme measures can be prepared for employability. That is, the selection of means was still predominantly subject to logical, empirical criteria, and the logic was economic logic.

However, at the height of the social era, the emphasis in dealing with the handicapped changed again. The new theme became "mainstreaming" (a metaphor associated especially with education): making it possible for handicapped persons to do the same things, in the same way, as "normal" persons—ride buses, use subways, study in any classroom, and so on. The scope of programs was broadened to include all kinds of handicapped persons, with little regard to the nature or severity of the handicap, and to include many areas of life that are not directly related to production, such as college education and entertainment. Thus considerations other than economic gained priority in the selection of means, and the core goals were not economic, but social/human.

In education, for example, mainstreaming has meant that by law recipients of federal funds (that is, virtually all public schools) have been prohibited from discriminating against qualified handicapped people, and states have been required to provide a "free, appropriate public education" to all handicapped students in the "least restrictive environment" possible. In practice, the former has meant eliminating physical barriers by installing ramps, toilets accessible to wheelchairs, and so on; the latter has meant integrating handicapped children into regular classes.

The cost of compliance has been considerable. Removal of physical barriers in existing buildings has been estimated to cost colleges alone $1 billion to $1.8 billion.[14] On the elementary and secondary level, the special education budgets of local school districts have risen about twice as fast since 1976 as their instructional budgets.[15] National expenditures for educating handicapped children increased from $4.8 billion in fiscal year 1975 to an estimated $9.3 billion in fiscal 1978.[16] The Department of Health and Human Services (HHS) has estimated that the total "excess" cost for twelve years of special education ranges from $4,100 for a speech-handicapped child to $60,200 for one with an orthopedic handicap.[17]

Proponents of mainstreaming defend its cost first by stressing the importance of its human and social goals, such as justice and human dignity, not economic value. Some argue, in addition, that the cost will be dwarfed by the long-range economic contributions of handicapped people who are enabled to become self-supporting. On the basis of various economic models, HHS suggests that in most categories of handicap, the "excess" costs of mainstreaming a handicapped person will be recouped, and there will be long-term savings to society, if that person is continuously employed at the minimum wage during a working life of forty years.[18]

However, other evidence indicates that many of the handicapped will not attain this degree of self-sufficiency, nor a forty-year worklife. Two analysts reported in 1977 that in any given year, the level of employment among the disabled is little more than half that among the able-bodied. According to a 1972 study, even among handicapped college graduates, 30 percent were unable to work regularly.[19] Moreover, for the handicapped, "employed" is not necessarily "self-supporting"; many work in nonprofit, federally aided sheltered workshops.

Without question, mainstreaming has brought significant personal and social benefits to handicapped persons. And in education, it has improved access to education for the estimated 45 percent of handicapped students who formerly lacked special services or even a basic education.[20] In many instances, to some degree, it has also generated productive gains for the economy. But in good part through mainstreaming, social/human values have intruded into the selection of means and goals to the point that logical, empirical criteria of service to production can no longer be said to govern. Economic rationality has been violated.

The question is not whether it is "good" or "bad" to violate the rationality of production in general, or for a particular group. That is a value judgment. What the preceding discussion seeks to highlight is the difference between extending rationality to incorporate secondary services to other goals and other criteria for the selection of means, versus violating rationality in the service of an alternative, *governing* set of goals and criteria. It is my thesis that during the sixties and seventies, violation grew in scope, strength, and following. Rationality was much weakened, but not knocked down; it remained a relatively strong principle for guiding the selection of means, tied to the much-challenged but not defeated core project of high production and consumption.

A colleague who read a draft of the manuscript suggested that at issue is not violation of rationality but the substitution of social rationality for productive rationality. "Nothing is irrational *per se*; what is one person's rationality, is irrational to another." My response is that there are some matters which are irrational (even if the sentiments behind them are noble). To seek a risk-free society is irrational; not only is the goal completely futile, but vainly pursuing it squanders resources that could be used to reduce high risks. These stand out only if one realizes that since not all risks will be abolished, one must concern oneself with rational analysis—focusing first on the highest risks with the greatest disutilities and greatest frequencies. Similarly, it is not possible anymore to do "all one can for one's loved ones" because, in the age of new medical technology, this may mean keeping bodies on machines for decades, affordable for a few but destructive for a community. And one simply *cannot* spend one and one half times the GNP, which is about what it would take, to remove one chemical, benzene.

Nevertheless, my colleague has a point. Beyond these extreme situations, each core project has its "rationality." One could talk instead of violating the rationality of production—about the dominance of social rationality. Different words, but the same point: the replacement of the criteria of a mentality supportive first-of-all to production—by another.

THE "QUALITY-OF-LIFE SOCIETY"

Cumulatively, the demands for equality, the counterculture, and the environmental movement raised a new vision of America, the "quality-of-life society." There is no generally accepted definition of the term. I define it as a society dedicated to increasing the satisfaction of its members not by increased production and mass use of material goods, but by greater harmony with self, others, and nature. Some other definitions include a higher income per capita, or better products, such as mahogany instead of Formica, tailormade suits instead of off-the-rack. Inclusion of such materialist items or criteria confounds the distinction between the high production/high consumption, affluent American and the quality-of-life society, and for that reason I do not include them in the definition followed here.

From the viewpoint of recent American history, of course, the issue is not a precise definition. The point is that the quality-of-life ideal as an alternative vision and legitimating principle did not extend rationality but sought to supersede it. A community preoccupied with social justice (defined as equal sharing of what is available), with near-term nonmaterial satisfaction, with harmony with nature, is not one to put high on its approval list the merits of strenuous efforts to find ever more efficient production means, to save for greater future economic growth, to labor for higher but deferred consumption. It is more interested in astrology and psychics and psychotherapy than in science. And it puts "good" interpersonal relations above "efficient" administration. A society dedicated to the quality-of-life idea welcomes Type B behavior—less achievement-oriented, less demanding, more relaxed, more oriented to the present.

It is impossible to assess precisely the scope and depth of the appeal the quality-of-life ideal had to Americans in the sixties and seventies. The answers to public opinion polls vary a great deal, and data often confound mere retreatism with positive commitment to an alternative world. However, judging both by Americans' expressions of opinion and by behavior changes, the quality-of-life society was more than a limited fad or the ideal of a small, deviant social movement. Teaching people to live with basic essentials was rated more important than reaching higher standards of living by a large majority (79 percent to 17 percent) in a national poll in 1977. Three fourths of those sampled preferred to draw pleasure from nonmaterial experiences rather than satisfy the need for more goods and services; two thirds chose "breaking up big things" and returning to more "humanized" living over developing bigger, more efficient ways of doing things.[21] Asked what kind of presidential candidate they favored in 1976, 43 percent of a national sample of Americans preferred a qualify-of-life candidate, compared to 17 percent who preferred a liberal, 15 percent a conservative, and 13 percent a moderate.[22] A 1978 poll that put the two ideals in direct opposition to each other found 30 percent of Americans "pro-growth," 31 percent "anti-growth," and 39 percent ambivalent.[23]

Behavioral data provide another measure of the appeal of the quality-of-life society. There was a significant increase in the number of male Americans who retired before they were required to do so. Many of these did so because they were willing to sacrifice salary and future pension income for more leisure. Among men aged fifty-five to sixty-four, the number not in the labor force grew from 871,000 in 1950 to 2,232,000 in 1975, reflecting a decline in labor force participation from 86.9 percent to 75.8 percent.[24] A study by the Institute of Social Research at the University of Michigan found that as of 1976, 40 percent of working family heads from age thirty-five to sixty-three planned to retire before age sixty-five, and one out of four of those thirty-five to fifty-nine, before age sixty-two.[25]

While some who retired early did so for health reasons, an estimated one-fifth did so because they wanted more years for non-income-producing purposes or for more fulfilling activities. The number of Americans who elected to leave one career for a less lucrative, but, in their view, more self-actualizing "second career" is estimated to be in the millions. We have already discussed Yankelovich's data, indicating that about 63 percent of Americans were affected to one degree or another by the retreat from high production, rationality-first America, and that an estimated 17 percent were "strongly" out of it.

Clearly, then, the weakening of the production base has gone hand in hand with a weakening of the rational mentality. Neither has been destroyed, but each has been hollowed, and an alternative vision has been actively introduced.

CHAPTER ELEVEN
The Pro-Industrial Coalition and Institutions

The institutional context of industrialization has remained in the background while we focused on its economic foundation and the supportive mentality. Now I turn to bring into the picture the changing societal context—in particular, changes in power relationships and in the institutions of education and the family. In what ways did they support the first industrialization of America and then lose their capacity to sustain it? This, in turn, will suggest under what conditions they may assist economic reconstruction.

RISE AND SLIPPAGE OF INDUSTRIAL POWER

The transformation of societies is most directly propelled not by changes in economic factors or mentalities, but by one or more social groups, the agents of change. Some call these groups "elites," which suggests a select few; some speak of "classes," which suggests a cast of thousands; others point to "social movements" as the force behind change. Whatever the term, the focus is on social groups that provide the changing vectors of power that promote, sustain, or undo societies in general. Here, the focus is on the dynamics of power that account for the rise of the first industrial America and its subsequent weakening. Who favored industrialization? Who opposed it? Who won, and why? And what is their leverage now and in the foreseeable future?

Power in the First Industrialization

A full account of American political history in terms of changing power relations cannot provide the much needed foundation, because it has yet to be written. Here a few selected points are highlighted to suggest how industrialization was advanced.

The first industrialization of America was propelled by, and in turn promoted, a new set of classes and elites, led by merchants, bankers and financiers, and industrialists, in that order; that is, with industrialists initially playing the smallest role. In a typical American view of history, these groups tend to be personified in such late nineteenth-century figures as Marshall Field, J. P. Morgan, and John D. Rockefeller. But these men and their earlier counterparts—Stephen Girard, Nicholas Biddle, Moses Brown—are but the most visible members of powerful social groups whose interests favored industrial development. The merchants developed markets and sources of supply, and fashioned trading patterns. The bankers and financiers extended credit, provided nationwide networks of connections to put together large sums of capital, and managed—or mismanaged—the currencies. The early industrialists moved production from the home into the factory, systematized work, and encouraged and applied new technologies. While these groups did not deliberately form a coalition, their interests were, for the most part, mutually supportive and supportive of industrialization.

These pro-industrial groups were not most prominent among the founders of the American society in the seventeenth and eighteenth centuries, nor were they dominant among those who framed the Constitution and shaped the union, though they participated with others in these institution-setting endeavors. The founders and framers were to a greater extent representative of large landowners and freeholders, groups whose interests were more strongly agrarian. Throughout the nineteenth century, particularly before the Civil War, these groups frequently opposed the pro-industrial groups on such issues as protective tariffs and the gold standard.

In the decades after the initiation of industrialization, the industrial groups gradually rose in size and power, while the relative power of the other groups declined. The pro-industrial coalition reached its full strength after the Civil War, and by the last two decades of the nineteenth century, it was dominant in American society.

The pro-industrial groups were not always in full harmony; on the contrary, they quite often collided with one another. Thus, when most of the pro-industrial groups favored tariff protection for the young textile industry, New England maritime interests joined Southern cottongrowers in opposing higher tariffs.

But even when they were divided on specific issues, the pro-industrial groups continued to share the dominant thrust in favor of industrializing America. While traditionally prestigious groups, such as the clergy, scholars, statesmen, and the military, still commanded a fair measure of respect, business groups shaped more and more of the fundamental structure of the society, and, as S. M. Lipset puts it, "the entrepreneur became a cultural hero."[1]

In part this was true because business was the way not just to fortune but also to power and even prestige. In 1854, Washington Irving pointed to "the almighty dollar" as the "greatest object of universal devotion throughout our land."[2] In the 1890s, when grand entrepreneurs were flaunting their wealth and their power with little restraint, William Dean Howells put in the mouth of a fictional banker the observation that since the Civil War, "in any average assembly of Americans, the great millionaire would take the eyes of all from the greatest statesman, the greatest poet, or the greatest soldier."[3] But even on more workaday levels, business enterprise was the focal point of American society. Calvin Coolidge laconically stated this view in the often quoted line: "The business of the United States is business."

The dominance of business at the peak of America's first industrialization is well illustrated in Robert and Helen Lynd's classic study, *Middletown*. Observing this small midwestern city in the mid-1920s, they noted its "overwhelming preoccupation with business"; "just as the high school 'professor' has been surpassed in salary and prestige by the vocational teacher, and the dominance of the professional man has been largely usurped by the business man, so the prestige of the judge in the legal profession has yielded to that of the corporation lawyer."[4] When the Lynds returned to Middletown a decade later, they found that the business-class control system had grown tighter, and that while business control was often public-spirited or even unconscious, it operated "at many points to identify public welfare with business-class welfare."[5] They show in detail how, by direct control, through philanthropy, or in indirect ways, one prominent business-class family influenced Middletown's industries, credit sources, real estate, schools, churches, charities, local government, and press.[6]

What has been said so far concerns the axis of power along which organized social groups, arranged in a shifting hierarchy, compete to shape both political decisions and the format of the polity itself. For example, in nineteenth-century America two loose coalitions, one of agrarian groups, one of merchants, financiers, and industrialists, disputed at length both the relative merits of "hard money" and paper currency and the extent of federal authority in matters of currency and banking.

At the same time, we have seen, there is in all societies another power axis, that of national bonds, along which forces that seek to weaken these bonds face those that seek to sustain them. Historically, the groups that supported industrialization in general also favored nation-building. Those groups that opposed stronger national bonds and championed localism or regionalism were in general farm-oriented; they opposed changes that advanced a modern industrial economy. What usually joined industrialization and nation-building was a common interest in larger and freer markets, in economy of scale, and in the free movement of labor and capital within the national confines.

The interrelationship of these two axes of power is neither simple nor static. In the tug-of-war between French and English Canada, for instance, where cultural differences are powerfully symbolized by language, the English-dominated provinces are more committed to continued union and they are also more powerful in the hierarchical sense: They have more leverage in the polity and command more resources. And, as would be expected, they are more supportive of industrialization. But the French-dominated provinces include the major Atlantic trade routes and several important industrial centers; moreover, the western provinces, long rich in agriculture and forestry, are predominantly English. In Britain, where the class hierarchy was relatively well defined and slow to change, Scotland was united with England and Wales in one polity by essentially land-oriented social groups well before industrialization. And, in mature industrial Britain, a Scottish separatist movement has continued; its argument for independence is based, in part, on Scotland's industrial and commercial strength. Thus, while nation-building and promotion of industrialization have often gone hand-in-hand, the association is not automatic or inevitable.

In the first industrialization of the United States, however, nation-building and industrialization basically did follow the expected pattern of mutual support. Early in the nineteenth century, sharp sectional differences among the North, the South, and the developing West were a dominant feature of American politics. Gradually, after much struggle, a more national orientation emerged, promoted by the same groups that favored industrialization. Traders and manufacturers sought wider markets; regions became more interdependent; financial institutions grew in their reach; and the pro-industrial groups themselves developed nationwide constituencies. On the other hand, those who maintained a regional outlook and resisted stronger national union were largely those more committed to the ways of life associated with traditional farming and a less entrepreneurial society.

The convergence of nation-building and industrial interests is evident in the Civil War. It entailed a conflict of opposing economic interests: free labor versus low tariffs, factories versus plantations—and the differing mentalities and political directions of the groups on either side. At the same time, it involved a conflict about the strength and direction of the national union; at issue was not merely states' rights versus federal control, but also, for instance, whether developing areas to the west would be aligned with the South or with the North. The Union Army's victory signaled the ascendancy of groups favoring strong national bonds and groups—for the most part the same groups—supportive of industrialization, even though in both respects opposing forces continued to exist.[7]

Power in America's Mature Industrial Economy

As industrialization matured, the patterns of power relationships changed on both axes. The hegemony of the industrial groups was gradually undermined and nation-building slowed as groups that previously had been small or passive grew in size, mobilized, and gained increasing say in the marketplace and in the polity. The first of these were the industrial labor classes and labor unions.

Farm labor was—and is—hard to organize and activate politically, even after the modernization of agriculture. The first major base for labor as a political force was the massive group of blue-collar workers created by the establishment of the industrial system. Between 1870 and 1920, the number of gainful workers in nonfarm occupations grew from 6 million, or 47 percent of the work force, to 31 million, or 73 percent of the work force.[8] The number of workers in "manufacturing and hand trades" alone grew from 2 million to 11 million.[9] These industrial workers gradually built up their self-awareness and learned to act in unison. Early attempts at labor organization were strongly, systematically, even ruthlessly resisted by employers; sometimes violence resulted, as in the Haymarket affair in 1886 and the Homestead strike in 1892. From World War I on, and especially from the mid-thirties through World War II, labor organizers became much more successful. While in 1920 about 19 percent of nonfarm workers were organized, most of them in the American Federation of Labor, by 1945 almost 36 percent of the nonagricultural labor force belonged to unions.[10]

As labor unions grew in power and legitimacy, they acted, first of all, directly in the marketplace; they used or threatened strikes, slowdowns, or boycotts to win recognition and to negotiate higher wages, better fringe benefits, shorter hours, and improved working conditions. Attention tends to focus on the dramatic: the long sit-down strike in 1937 that in the end forced General Motors to deal with the United Automobile Workers; the United Mine Workers' militant insistence on portal-to-portal pay and its repeated strikes during World War II (which won wage increases of almost 50 percent in 1941–43); the rash of strikes immediately after the war—nearly five thousand in 1946 alone. However, at the same time, the routine use of power through bargaining—backed by the possibility of direct action—became increasingly important in building and applying the power of the labor unions. One study indicates that from 1933 until the beginning of the 1960s, unions increased the wages of their members, relative to the wages of all labor, by 10 to 15 percent.[11] In some trades, the differential was larger. Unionized construction craftsmen and carpenters, for instance, in 1970 earned on the average 40 percent more than their nonunion counterparts.[12]

To reduce the effect of the graduated income tax as well as the bite of inflation, organized labor increasingly demanded and gained new fringe benefits: insurance plans, sick leave, holidays, vacations and others. By the early 1970s, over 90 percent of plant workers were covered by at least partially employer-paid hospitalization and life insurance, and over 75 percent participated in pension plans.[13] Union activity is only one of the elements contributing to labor's gains, of course; and union contracts have, to some extent, set patterns for the wages and benefits of nonunion employees, if only due to management efforts to forestall additional unionization. For all full-time workers, average real compensation nearly tripled between 1920 and 1970; its annual growth slightly exceeded the growth in real GNP per capita.[14]

At the same time unions gained in the marketplace, they also gained in power to act indirectly, by affecting the polity. The attitude of labor organizations toward political activity varied, from early aversion to a policy of "reward your friends, punish your enemies" to broad-gauged activism. And as a wider social coalition emerged, labor often joined with it. Much early labor legislation, for instance, was pushed not just by labor unions but by a variety of other social groups, such as the Progressive movement and the General Federation of Women's Clubs. Moreover, labor organizations themselves were not always of one mind; for example, the Wagner Act brought sharply differing responses from the AFL and CIO, and a still different one from John L. Lewis, the feisty president of the UMW, who suggested repealing all labor legislation and depending solely on the unions' economic power. However, whether standing alone or acting in concert with other groups, the labor movement was united on many political issues. For example, organized workers repeatedly advocated legislation limiting immigration (except in the case of displaced persons after World War II) and preventing restriction of union activity; they backed unemployment insurance after 1932 and vehemently opposed the Taft-Hartley Act. On many of these issues—though certainly not all—they achieved substantial success in affecting the course of public policy.

Even in its earliest, officially nonpartisan, political activity, labor tended to ally itself with the Democrats; in later years, the unions became a major, recognized power in the Democratic Party. Union leaders were involved, for example, in the selection of Harry Truman as Roosevelt's running mate in 1944, and union funds contributed significantly toward Truman's re-election in 1948. In addition, labor organizations acted often directly to influence individual senators, representatives, governors, and mayors—including Republicans, *e.g.* Governor G. Mennen Williams of Michigan.

Gradually, and with increasing effectiveness after World War II, other social groups followed labor into the direct action realm of demonstrations, strikes, and boycotts, into political action to win a larger share of the nation's power and wealth. Blacks, activated by younger blacks and by white liberals, made gains in voting rights, educational opportunity, choice jobs, other civil rights, and political representation. Wage differences between blacks and whites declined.

"Minority" once meant "black," but beginning in the late 1950s, many other ethnic groups came to the fore as self-aware, organized, increasingly active minorities: Hispanic-Americans, native Americans, Asian-Americans, and others. Groups representing women (despite suffrage still a minority in power though not in numbers) broadened women's self-awareness, public commitment, and power. Senior citizens fielded several powerful organized groups; consumers found new advocates, as did handicapped persons.

The various groups differ in many ways from the labor movement and from one another. For instance, their "base" was not occupational-economic, although most, like labor, drew on groups that were economically disadvantaged. However, all, like labor, increased their power in the political arena during the era 1950–80, although they "peaked" before the very end of the period. And all, like labor, gained both directly in the marketplace and indirectly via the polity, drawing both on the legitimation of their claims and on their capacity to act as organized groups.

Volumes have been written on the rise of each group and much more could be said; for our purpose, only a few points need be flagged. The most important is that as these groups gained in economic and political power, others lost some of both. Increasingly, through the golden age of consumption and social services, from the fifties through the sixties and into the seventies, the losers were the pro-industrial groups, the corporations, banks, other investors, producers, and distributors.

This statement, pivotal to the following analysis, is open to misunderstanding: Saying that a group lost in power is easy to misread as saying that it grew weak, while another that is said to have gained in power might be understood to have become powerful. This is not what happened, nor what is implied. In fact, as Edward S. Herman's careful study of corporations concludes, despite the rise of public pressures and government regulations, "the large corporation in the United States has preserved its autonomy to a remarkable degree during the twentieth century."[15] Herman provides case studies and other data in support of his conclusion, as well as detailed explanations of the way corporations retained much of their power even in the "down" period. He makes the important point, for example, that many government regulations either turned out to be ineffectual, or were introduced at the request of the corporations and helped them maintain their power, for instance by limiting competition among them.

The change that did occur was *relative.* The weak grew less weak and exacted concessions, registered gains; the powerful became less powerful and lost privileges. The latter continued to rule and to gain a lion's share of all that was allotted, from higher pay to capital gains— but they were significantly less dominant than before, and their status and take diminished as the social era unfolded.

Other qualifications must be colored in, or the picture drawn, deliberately general, will turn misleading. One concerns the role of legiti mation. The pro-industrial coalition lost not only power but also legitimation. This loss was due to increased questioning of the priority of economic values (challenges to the rational mentality were discussed in the preceding chapter) and also to a fair measure of social insensitivity on the part of important members and sub-groups. Early entrepreneurs invited social criticism, for example, whenever they emulated the predatory tactics of a Jay Gould, who watered stock and used bribes to build a nineteenth-century railroad empire, tales of which persisted long after the actual events. And during the Great Depression, the business community's stubborn, wide-based resistance to government action not only fueled support for the New Deal, but also legitimated a bigger role for government and a lesser one for the pro-industrial groups.

Moreover, the history of power in America is hardly limited to the story of a two-sided affair, with a well-formed industrial coalition confronting a solid front of "social" groups. There have been many pro-industrial groups and many social groups, and over time their alignment has shifted and their ability to act in concert often changed. Thus, while employers and labor unions constantly vied with each other, in many instances they were as one in discriminating against black workers. Big and small businesses frequently did not support the same legislation, and the social coalition of labor, minorities, women, was on-and-off, and limited in the scope of issues they worked on together.

These and other qualifications would need elaboration if our purpose were a history of power in America in recent generations. Our point is much more limited: To suggest that as the rational mentality was first extended, then, increasingly, violated (although never dethroned), as the economic underpinnings eroded unevenly, so did the *relative* power of the pro-industrial coalition.

At the peak of their power, the various groups favoring increased social programs, transfer payments, and consumption were strong enough to outweigh the coalition favoring production and industrial development on several key issues, though not across the board in the political arena, and even less consistently in the marketplace. These social groups dominated the Democratic Party, holding its more conservative wing at bay on numerous issues, and they were able to get their way in Congress even when there was a Republican in the White House. In 1973, for instance, when Nixon, having won re-election, moved to dismantle the Office of Economic Opportunity, Congress voted to continue its programs, although in other agencies, and for the time being refused to close OEO itself.

In those days, the Republicans, traditionally closer to industrial and business groups, could not ignore the social groups. Even though backlash against social programs grew, the social groups were still sufficiently strong that Nixon's administration found it politically necessary to strengthen some social programs. Affirmative Action employment practices, for example, had been required of most government contractors since 1965, but when Nixon took office, the means to achieve these goals had not yet been specified. His administration established "results-oriented" implementation procedures, requiring institutions receiving federal funds to establish goals and timetables for hiring specific numbers of women and minorities. The Philadelphia Plan, passed during the early months of Nixon's administration, required employers with large federal construction contracts to hire minimum percentages of minority workers in six skilled trades. Colleges and universities with federal contracts were also subject to Affirmative Action requirements; some of the nation's most prestigious universities, including Harvard, Columbia, and Berkeley, were threatened with suspension of government contracts because they had not set acceptable guidelines.

Environmental protection measures followed a similar pattern through Nixon's administration. During the first two years, the Environmental Protection Agency was created; more stringent legislation governing air quality was signed into law; a program of federal grants to develop solid-waste disposal programs was instituted. In his 1970 State of the Union address, Nixon called the environmental cause "the great question of the Seventies." By 1972 momentum was slowing but it was far from lost. Through much of the seventies, some programs were being scaled down, industry was becoming more vocal about the costs of antipollution laws and regulations, and administration representatives were urging that environmental goals be weighed against economic reality. Yet the environmental program continued to grow, as measured by direct government expenditures, regulatory bite, and compliance costs to the private sector.

Shift on the National Axis

This account of the weakening of the power of the pro-industrial groups and the rise in power of the social groups, and the implications for industrialization, has concentrated on one axis of power, the hierarchy of groups that compete to shape the polity and the allocation decisions. As industrialization matured, there was also an important shift on the other axis, between centrifugal and centripetal forces affecting the national bonds. After a long period in which the progress of industrial development went hand-in-hand with stronger national unity, the interests of the industrial groups and those of nation-building diverged, leading to a near-reversal of their mutually supportive relationship by the end of the social era.

The indications that national bonds were straining and centrifugal forces rising have already been outlined.[16] What needs to be added is the reason the pro-industrial groups allied themselves more and more with state (and regional) rights, against the national government and national decision-making, while the social groups often found Washington much closer to them than the state capitals.

While there are many reasons the pro-industrial groups turned increasingly to the states, there is one main reason: Corporations found they had more clout in most states than in Washington, while the social groups found they had more influence with the national government. Minorities, for instance, can be easily outvoted in most states, but they form a powerful lobby in Washington. Consumer activist Ralph Nader urged federal chartering of corporations, to impose nationwide standards tighter than the state standards now on the books; the corporations fought for continued state chartering, which lets them choose the most lenient states (*e.g.*, Delaware) as their legal home. As the *Wall Street Journal* put it: "The corporations control huge numbers of jobs and the prospect of more—or less. It's relatively easy for them to play off one community against another, threatening to close or open plants on their terms."[17]

Similarly, often when business failed to block new legislation favoring consumers, the environment, or workers, it sought enforcement on the local level, typically less strict than the federal—partly because major corporations often have more clout locally. Thus, car makers have more influence in Michigan, not to mention Detroit, than in the national capital. Citibank is much more at home in Albany than in Washington; the Bank of America may be big in Sacramento, but not on the shores of the Potomac; and steelmakers would rather deal with Pittsburgh and Harrisburg than with Capitol Hill.

In addition, while neither level of government has been free of corruption, it has been much easier to find one's way illicitly with most state assemblies, enforcement agencies, DAs, and judges than with federal authorities. Compare, from this viewpoint, the FBI to local police, or state judges to Supreme Court justices.

IN SUMMARY

All said and done, in the sixties and seventies the shift in relative power from pro-industrial to social groups, and the dissociation of industrial interests from nation-building, paralleled the economic developments as well as the changes in mentality. Gone were the days in which pro-industrial groups had a high concentration of power and largely controlled national public policy. On the rise were groups that had different priorities and visions and that made the national government take into account their preferences. The pro-industrial groups, far from being overrun or counted out, responded by transferring more and more public policy-making where they could control it more—to the states; they actively supported the conservative movement, ideas, and candidates calling for reducing the powers of the national government. Ultimately, they recaptured the national government, but this occurred when the social era had ended and the golden age of consumption had come to a halt.

SCHOOLS AND FAMILIES AND INDUSTRIALIZATION

We have already seen the diminished capacity of the family and the schools, over the last generation, to develop in individuals self-organization and the qualities required for mutuality, civility, and sustaining the community they share. Throughout the rise and deterioration of America's economic productive capacity, these institutions too changed their contributions to industrial America. To see clearly the changes that occurred, and their implications, I need to step back briefly to origins.

In simple, preliterate, farming societies, the family is the central social entity. "Everything" takes place within the family, which is often "extended" to include numerous related persons. The family is the unit in which work takes place, the main basis for the division of labor, production, and consumption. Education, religious ritual, conflict resolution are first and foremost intrafamily matters.

Education, at this stage, is almost completely absorbed into other social activities. Children learn while they follow their parents at work in the fields or at home, join in family meals, or squat at the periphery of tribal councils. There are no separate, specialized educational institutions, no schools. The values the society subscribes to and the limited core of existing knowledge are transmitted from generation to generation by the family and the community (in the sense of clan, tribe, or village).

As a society grows in complexity and size, some activities come to be partially or wholly invested in separate institutions, such as schools, churches, courts, and factories. This process of *differentiation* has profound effects on the family itself, and on each of the activities involved. It reduces the centrality of the family, and it introduces social units organized by different principles. In preliterate families, for example, education flows naturally from the authority figures, the elders and parents, to children. In modern schools, authority has no natural base; the appointed staff must continuously earn the respect of the pupils. Similarly, in preliterate families, work is typically carried out in the context of closed, personal bonds; factories, offices, and other specially organized work units require a different social relationship, more open and rational.

The "Industrialization" of Education

American education in the pre-industrial, farming age was light-years more "advanced" than the preliterate, family-based process.[18] In New England, where the Protestant standard of an educated clergy and a literate congregation was dominant, the settlers were quick to establish schools. As early as 1647, the Massachusetts Bay Colony required towns of fifty or more households to appoint a teacher of reading and writing; larger towns had to provide instruction in Greek and Latin as well.

Throughout the colonies, though, particularly under frontier conditions, much education was still carried out informally by the family and in the community. Especially in the sparsely populated South, where prosperous families might hire tutors for their children, schools were slow to emerge. What schooling there was hardly resembled modern education: The typical "school year" was only a few months; secondary education was rare; and the curriculum was very narrow, its main goals literacy and a basic understanding of religious and civic principles. The total core of knowledge to be transmitted was after all quite limited, and the scope of education was further circumscribed by the European tradition of classical education, and by the primacy of religion in shaping colonial education. In what has been called the first American schoolbook, *The New-England Primer*, even the alphabet was taught through religious rhymes.

Though Massachusetts required town schools in part to thwart "the old deluder, Satan," it was also concerned that the colony's children become responsible, self-supporting citizens. With the expansion of commerce and the gradual emergence of an ethic of success through work, merchants increasingly demanded education that would prepare individuals to function in the world of trade. Well before the Revolution, private schoolmasters began to teach "practical" subjects, such as arithmetic and navigation, and sought to improve on apprenticeship as a way of teaching trades. Soon after the colonies gained independence, secular goals gained rapidly in education.

At the same time, the political needs of the new nation called for education that would unify the former colonies behind new shared principles. Reading books, for example, began to contain more patriotic selections, fewer religious ones. In addition, the idea that all men are created equal gave impetus to more encompassing schooling and, eventually, to the principle that education should be available to "the common man," regardless of status or intellectual potential.

Public financing of schools was a hard-fought issue through most of the early nineteenth century. The usual practice had been to charge parents for their children's schooling; lotteries, philanthropy, and state aid supplemented parents' fees. Advocates of tax-supported schools, led by Horace Mann, argued that if schools were to be open to all, they must be removed from the control of vested interests (usually religious), and that publicly supported schools would be an investment by society in its own welfare. By mid-century, the concept of tax-supported elementary schools had been formalized in state law. Its acceptance underscored the dwindling of religious influence in the schools.

With advancing industrialization came great changes in the social fabric of the United States, as the cohesion and stability of small, agrarian communities gradually gave way to the secular, heterogeneous society of the urban melting pot. The population grew rapidly; a major factor in this growth was the great influx of immigrants. The population became increasingly urban, as immigrants and American-born alike gravitated to factory work in the cities. In 1820, less than 10 percent of the population lived in urban areas, and even by 1870, only about 25 percent; but throughout the century of industrialization, the urban population was growing much more rapidly than the rural, until by 1920 over half of the population was concentrated in urban areas.[19]

As the industrializing society became more heterogeneous and more urban, and as the body of knowledge to be transmitted grew, the family and local communities—both in transition—were less able to educate for industrial life. More and more parents worked away from the home rather than in it. Many immigrant families lacked modern cultural elements that were integral to life in industrial America. At the same time, in densely populated cities, where work was little affected by weather and agricultural cycles, more students were available for formal schooling, and for longer school terms. Even in rural areas, mechanization made it possible for children to spend more time attending school, less time working on the farm.

These changes were reflected in changes in the character of schooling. Enrollment increased: The average daily attendance in public schools quadrupled between 1870 and 1920;[20] from 1900 on the proporton of school-aged youngsters enrolled in school climbed steadily.[21] At the same time that enrollment grew, school terms became longer; the number of days the average pupil attended rose from 78 in 1870 to 121 in 1920.[22]

Higher rates of enrollment in more densely populated urban areas meant larger schools, and thus graded classes became the standard. By the last decade of the nineteenth century, the educational "ladder," an orderly sequence of educational "work," was firmly established.

School curricula also changed. In the early nineteenth century, as industrialization was first initiated, nine-tenths of a child's school time was devoted to the three R's. As industrialization took off, new subjects—such as science, drawing, geography, physical training—reduced that proportion, to about 60 percent by 1900.[23] By this time, the needs of the industrial labor force had also led to vocational training programs in many schools.

At first, all these changes mainly affected the elementary schools. The existing secondary schools, mostly private, did widen their curricula to include science, mathematics, and other "practical" subjects, but secondary education remained almost exclusively preparation for college, and enrollments were small. Toward the end of the nineteenth century, just 15 percent of fourteen- to seventeen-year-olds were enrolled in secondary school.[24] Not until after World War II did graduation from high school become the educational norm.

College education was even more limited. Nine colleges, all private, all but one church-related, had been established in the colonies, their initial mission the education of ministers. Although by 1870 the number of undergraduate colleges approached five hundred, they remained relatively narrow in scope. In the last decades of the nineteenth century, especially with the establishment of the land-grant agricultural and mechanical colleges, higher education began to reflect more clearly the secular and commercial society, but its growth continued to be slow. In 1870, just 1.7 percent of those aged eighteen to twenty-one were enrolled in undergraduate-degree credit studies; in 1920, it was 7.9 percent.[25] The great explosion in college education also awaited the consumer age that followed World War II.

Such a sketchy and limited overview of American educational history suffices to point out certain important movements: Toward secular content and control, especially public financing; toward a curriculum both broader and more "practical" (i.e., useful for the industrial labor force); toward the inclusion of more and more young people for more and more extended periods at more levels of education. But it leaves out other aspects, including some of particular importance to the links between education and industrialization.

We have already seen the importance of schools for character-building, specifically for self-organization. The same basic capacity to control impulse, especially coupled with a capacity to defer gratification, is, as we have also seen, the basis of the rational mentality, and of the ability to deal with rules and authority and carry out routine tasks for later reward. In short, the schools play a crucial part in helping individuals develop self-organization and lay the psychic foundation for rational behavior. The formal character of the school, as distinct from the more fluid family and community, in itself provides a transition between the home and the factory or office. The relations to teachers and principals, the completion of assignments, the allotment of grades are all analogues to work in industry, a kind of educational dry run. Typically, teachers are "halfway" supervisors: less personally involved than parents, but more than factory supervisors. Homework is in some ways akin to overtime; grades are toy money.

Moreover, the school is internally designed to increase worklike pressures as the pupil advances in age and grade levels, so it serves to ease the transition to higher levels of self-organization and rationality. In short, schools are "compatible," supportive to industrialization, to the extent that they help evolve self-organization (as the psychic base for a general ability to act) and rationality (the ability to act in ways compatible with industrialization). Specific skills, and cognitive preparation for acquisition of specific skills, are also useful; even if not provided in school, they can be developed more readily on the job if the school has helped lay the personality foundations.

There seems to be no body of data that would demonstrate to a modern social scientist that in the industrializing century, American schools did increasingly serve these educational missions, enhancing not only self-organization but also the capacity to act rationally. However, many of the pupils entering the schools were the sons and daughters of farmers and immigrants, and the graduating labor force by and large served well the increasing needs of the industrialized society. These facts strongly suggest that on the whole the schools were effective in contributing to the first industrialization of America. They may have done less, much less, for cultural sophistication, emotional empathy, and other values dear to present-day educators, humanists, and adherents of the quality-of-life vision; at issue here is not a general evaluation of the schools of 1820 to 1920, but their contribution to industrialization. It seems to have been considerable. Indeed, a common criticism at the time was that the schools were too attuned to industrial needs and not sufficiently attentive to other values.[26]

Deindustrialization of Education

With the rise of the affluent America after World War II, education became less a preparation for an industrial/productive society, more and more an end in itself, a consumer product. By 1960, the proportion of eighteen- to twenty-one-year-olds enrolled for undergraduate degrees was more than double what it had been in 1940;[27] increasing importance was attached to the college degree itself, rather than to the specific skills that might go with it. The ideal of liberal education—development of the whole person, education not for its narrow vocational usefulness, but for a more cultivated and civil person—spread more widely through colleges and into high school as well.

Historian Daniel J. Boorstin comments that, in contrast to European universities, where the majority of students were preparing for a profession,

> The characteristic American college was less a place of instruction than a place of worship—worship of the growing individual. . . . Increasing numbers of Americans agreed that any citizen who had not been sent to some institution of higher education had been cheated of his opportunity for maximum growth. . . . Generally speaking, American colleges and universities were meant to be Hotels of the Mind, providing for each American community's mental and cultural activities many of the democratic conveniences which its hotel provided for their social and commercial activities.[28]

"Non-useful" education was hardly the invention of the postwar era; it existed well before industrialization. The traditional classical education, emphasizing language and philosophy, was the fare of the privileged in America's early colleges and academies. Jefferson's idea of a classical education as the proper training for potential leaders carried over into the industrial age, broadened by Jacksonian egalitarianism. And even at the height of the industrial/production age, schools were never run merely as industrial preparatories; an element of investment in "non-useful" education reflected the society's need to draw on schools in educating for mutuality and civility and in transmitting cultural values. Finally, with the onset of the golden age of consumption, some elements of a liberal education gained in practical usefulness. The growth of international trade and multinational corporations, for example, conferred greater economic importance not only on language skills, but also on sensitivity to the political and cultural nuances of societies different from our own.

Nevertheless, the main function of the rising emphasis on liberal arts in both secondary and higher education after World War II, with the accompanying explosion of four-year liberal arts colleges, was not to serve production purposes. In growing measure it served as a basis for consumption and the use of leisure; as a source of satisfaction through the cultivation of literature, music, and the arts; and as a base for commitment to the quality-of-life society and preoccupation with self. This role of education is evident in the conception of lifelong learning, or continuing education. Some of it serves production ends by preparing people for second careers or updating their professional knowledge, *e.g.*, enabling physicians to stay up to date in their professional knowledge. For many, however, continuing education is an end in itself, part of a *literati* life or a life of sophisticated consumption.

The distinction between studies that are production-oriented and those that enhance the quality of life is not clearcut. Some can serve both ends, and some that appear nonproductive may serve production purposes, and, to be sure, vice versa. Actually "scoring" an educational course or program from this viewpoint would require a detailed content analysis and a study of its effects on the life of the participants.

Nevertheless, it is safe to assume that, on average, for most students a study of Shakespeare, Homer, or archaeology is not as production-oriented as a study of the use of computers, applied statistics, or management techniques. This is not to judge one content as of more value in some absolute sense, but to assess the second category of learning as more directly relevant to industrialization than the first. Qualifications come to mind: A person highly trained in today's techniques may not be as open to new ones in a rapidly changing world as one not trained; being widely cultured may be quite essential for some high executive posts. Nevertheless, the generalization holds— as a generalization.

As to mass involvement in liberal arts through college education as primarily part of the age of consumption, there is, of course, a world of difference between courses that are clearly consumption-oriented, such as wine-tasting or antiques buying, and studying, say, comparative literature or the culture of ancient China. But, from the limited viewpoint of the balance between production and consumption of goods and services, a preoccupation with liberal arts is primarily consumerist even when it is highly cultural.

As the consumption age advanced, and social programs rose, schooling was increasingly imbued with noneconomic purposes: to advance equality (of classes, races, sexes, the handicapped) and to enhance insight into self, relations to others, and harmony with the environment. Horace Mann, the "father of the common school," had envisioned the school as the "great equalizer" that would free students from the inequities of their origins, from the economic and social effects of their parents' status, and send them on their way according to their proven merits. However, by the 1960s it was evident that schools were not that powerful; they tended more to reflect than to overcome economic and social differences. Consequently, special programs and measures were introduced to further social purposes, especially equality. Several of them may be quickly recalled to illustrate this development.

Compensatory education, introduced as part of the Great Society and the New Frontier, attempted to serve both social purposes and industrial needs. Past discrimination had underprepared many minority children for schooling and tended to make schooling itself less effective for them. Compensatory education was intended to help them catch up, graduate with comparable skills, and participate on an equal footing in the industrial society. As it turned out, most compensatory education programs—with the important exception of Title I—did not work. First of all, the accumulation of past discriminations was too big. It is difficult to make up for three years or more of deficiency in reading, writing, and arithmetic. It is even more difficult to do so in an environment of continued deprivation, substandard housing, high unemployment, and lack of assurance of meaningful jobs.

Emphasis then shifted to procedures and processes that would provide some of the same economic and social benefits for minority children without full schooling. *Automatic* (or social) *promotion* moved pupils from one grade to the next, or graduated them, even if they had not acquired the requisite skills and knowledge. This practice helped greatly to equalize graduating classes in racial composition, but it could not but have adverse effects on students' actual preparation and on the self-organization/rationality nexus. What automatic promotion and graduation did for high school, *open admission,* which either removed or greatly diluted college admission standards, did for entrance to higher education, particularly in junior colleges.

De-credentialism argued that education-based certificates (*i.e.,* attesting to successful completion of specific training) were neither appropriate nor necessary for many jobs, that people should be hired for these jobs (*e.g.,* teaching) without any formal credentials, or be granted credentials on the basis of "life experiences" (*e.g.,* having worked in the community). The de-credentialing movement was another step in the same basic direction as automatic promotion and open admission, that of detaching reward from specified, standardized, and verified achievements.

Another instance of education that tended away from productive capacity toward other goals is to be found in the direction taken by *federal support of vocational education.* Although the federal contribution was a relatively small part of the total expenditure on vocational education, federal dollars, regulations, and signaling had an important influence on the entire vocational education system. Beginning in the early 1960s, federal support sought to pull the system toward social goals. Increasing the participation of minorities and women was stressed. And quite often the federally supported training programs—CETA—provided very little training and were but thinly concealed workmaking, a source of public jobs for groups in need. Among the many arguments advanced in favor of these approaches, the two perhaps most typical of the era have been that social justice is more important than short-term economic efficiency, and that human considerations ought to replace stringent technical criteria.

As these various programs were introduced and took effect nationwide, many students "graduated" underprepared for the industrial/production world. As we have already seen, this was not solely the work of changed schools. They were often unable to make up for deficiencies that were generated by the family and the neighborhood, let alone generations of discrimination and economic disadvantage. By the end of the 1970s, less effective preparation of the future labor force by the schools seems to have become one factor in declining productivity.[29]

To sum up: By the 1970s, education was abundant. The United States was the only country in the world to send nearly half its young people to college; the nation's expenditures for education had risen from 3.3 percent of GNP in 1950 to 7.6 percent of GNP in 1975.[30] But schooling had become more multipurpose, and it was divided against itself. In part, it was used increasingly as an end in itself, or as a means to social, psychic, and cultural ends. In part, it simply deteriorated as schools became less effective institutions.

The Family

In pre-industrial America, economic activity was an integral part of family life. All members of the family but the youngest joined in the productive tasks that sustained the family and the community; having a large number of children was valuable as a pool of farm labor. With advancing industrialization, just as education came to be largely separated from the family and invested in schools, many of the economic tasks historically attended to by the family were transferred to new, distinct social units, especially factories.

Some early industrial work was still carried out in the context of the family—spinning and weaving, for instance, and small foundries. Also, skilled craftsmen supplied a variety of goods to their neighbors. Some of the first oil wells were run by families, and some ironworks, flour mills, and brickworks were family affairs. But before long these became exceptions to the rule. The essence of the transition to industrialization was not just moving workers from farm to factory, but moving work itself out of the family into specially organized work units.

Hand in hand with this change went a significant reshaping of the family and a decline in its importance. It lost not only work and education, but also, to some extent, virtually every socially important activity except child-rearing and mutual emotional support. At the same time, a smaller family emerged, with fewer kin and kids. More and more, the nuclear family succeeded the extended family (although by no means all families had been "extended" before industrialization),[31] and the number of children in the nuclear family declined. While experts disagree whether industrialization "required" a smaller family, it seems that the smaller family contributed to industrialization in that it significantly increased the geographic mobility of the labor force, freeing it to be distributed on a nationwide basis according to economic demands.

In the postwar era, the question once centered on the extended family—does it restrict mobility?—came in effect to be raised about the nuclear family. The nuclear family was highly mobile, so long as it followed the traditional pattern of the husband as breadwinner, the wife and mother in the home full-time. As this pattern increasingly gave way to one in which both spouses were employed outside the home, the nuclear family became less mobile. And the tension job-required relocation causes the two-income family, often pitting one spouse's job against the other's, was added to other factors weakening the family.

Frequent relocation of corporate executives, as often as every three years, is a clear example. When one spouse in a two-career family is asked to relocate, the confrontation between loyalty to spouse and response to corporate demands is far from theoretical. Long-distance marriages are unlikely to work well for most couples in the longer run; the majority of married couples reject that possibility. More commonly, the choice is for the corporate executive to sacrifice advancement in order to stay put, or for the spouse to sacrifice a job in order to move along. The resulting tensions have forced many corporations to modify their policies of reassigning people so often, and have increased the costs to the corporation (for example, for financing housing as an added inducement for those who will agree to relocate). It is hard to determine to what extent frequent reassignment is due to genuine corporate needs or merely a ritualistic tradition. To the extent it represents a true need, the two-career family is less able to serve it in full traditional measure.

The main role of the family, for the economic realm as for the society as a whole, is educational. We have seen that in the consumption, ego-centered age, the traditional nuclear family became less able to contribute to self-organization and to lay the psychic foundation for rationality, a mainstay of a committed and able labor force. A less-committed labor force, indicated by signs that are far from clear but nonetheless detectable, reflects changes in parenting as well as other factors.[32] It follows that just as family reconstruction—if it took place—would serve mutuality and civility by providing the psychic foundation for self-organization, such reconstruction would also lay a foundation for a labor force more oriented toward rationality.

The other activity that in the industrial age remains primarily the task of the family is mutual emotional support of its adult members, relief of the tensions worklife inevitably generates, especially in highly industrialized societies. In this respect too the family seems to have become, on balance, less effective. Greater acceptance of divorce and increased turnover of partners may in some ways strengthen this aspect of the family, but they also mean that more and more workers return to homes in which there is no dependable partner, or no other adult at all. Even in more stable families, as attention has turned more toward individuals' inner needs and self-actualization, mutuality has declined. In many families, the adult members are simply less available to one another for mutual emotional support.

As one looks at the relationships between these institutions and industrialization, the objection might be raised that schools and families should not be used to serve industrial needs. Certainly no one should view education, parenting, or marriage as a tool for greater rationality, efficiency, and productivity; their human importance is far broader. Indeed, they are, as we have seen, the first building stones for a mature, effectively functioning personality and society, whether industrial or otherwise. Nevertheless, education, parenting, marriage, and productive activity are inextricably linked in the societal system. Changes in one reverberate in the others; and just as their deterioration adds to the strains of the industrial sector, so their reconstruction will make the reconstruction of the economy more likely and more sustainable.

CHAPTER TWELVE
Junction America

EROSION—NOT "THE END"

The American society entered the 1980s with a weakened productive capacity, a tendency to underdevelop, a kind of industrialization in reverse. The rational mentality had lost vitality; the supportive power base had weakened; national bonds and the institutional framework were straining. It is worth repeating that this erosion had not proceeded to a crisis point. The high-production society did not collapse, America was not "ending." Indeed, precisely because America's retreat from industrialization started from such a high level of production, and because societies can withstand a considerable amount of conflict of forces and of mentalities, America's production project was still quite strong; it was, though, significantly less so than it used to be—and sliding backward.

Part of the blame is properly put at the feet of external forces, such as the rise of OPEC and renewed Soviet pressures both in the strategic arms race and in expansionary policies (in Afghanistan, for example). However, external challenges do not dictate a society's own response. Faced with similar challenges, Japan chose to work harder, export more, neglect its defense, and maintain its high-growth project. Whether Japan will be able to maintain its economic achievements remains to be seen; having very few energy sources of its own, it is being tried particularly heavily. Britain, on the other hand, did for a while embrace a version of the quality-of-life society, accepting a less "hyper," less productive, relatively more genteel and socially comforting lifestyle.[1] (It has been referred to as the "British disease" by those committed to a higher level of production.) More recently, under the stewardship of Margaret Thatcher, Britain has been trying to recapture the high-production project.

The United States, we have seen, tolerated an erosion of the foundation of the production project without fully embracing any new project. It neither abandoned economic growth nor made the quality-of-life society its new core project. A measure of ambivalence, retreat, and drift best characterizes the American "response" of the middle to late 1970s. Ambivalence is evident in the combination of a measure of commitment to the old high-production project (though insufficient to sustain it) with a weaker, partial involvement with the quality-of-life project. Retreat was reflected not merely in partial abandonment of the core project, but also in the rise of the ego-centered mentality, weakening institutions, lower mutuality and civility, and intensification of the government. That is, the retreat encompassed not only the core project, but also the society and its members themselves— and not merely what they do, but what they are.

There followed a period of attempts by the Carter administration to bandage the problems through such limited treatments as partial and gradual decontrol of domestic prices of oil (to encourage conservation and production), a very weak system of voluntary restraint of price and wage incentives (to slow inflation), and six weeks of some measure of credit control, from mid-March to May 1980. The Reagan administration tried a much more comprehensive change of direction and effort. But before the Reagan American economic recovery program can be assessed, one must ask: to what purpose?

Societies like that of America, whose core project has begun to disintegrate, basically face three options: Allow erosion to continue; transform themselves to embody a new vision; or reaffirm some selected part of their past and build on it. The following review of these options suggests that in effect there is no choice.

AMBIVALENCE AND RETREAT

Continued ambivalence, accompanied by additional retreat, is the course most societies find easiest once erosion sets in, because it entails less pain than recommitment or a major mobilization for change. To illustrate from the all-too-familiar energy scene of the 1973–80 period: A major and costly push to reduce the use of energy would have been compatible with the quality-of-life society but would have entailed a lower level of economic activity, a lower standard of living; a major push to develop new energy sources would have been compatible with reindustrialization, but would have cut deeply into the resources available for other purposes. Instead, the earmark of American energy policy in that period was a hodge-podge of minor steps that were less taxing, required fewer changes in American institutions, mentality, labor force, investment, and so on, than either transformation to a high conservation mode or commitment to high production.

The reluctance of society to mobilize for a major, multifaceted change in direction reflects not only a deep aversion to pain, but also the difficulty of predicting the future. Policymakers and citizens alike are accustomed to the wails of crisis-mongers, which have been followed time and again by precious little crisis. During the time of campus riots, it was widely foretold that the students would destroy academia, but they soon returned to their books and studies; in the early sixties, blacks were said to be ready to "burn down the cities" unless they were granted encompassing social changes "now," but they settled for much more modest changes. A renowned British scholar, C. P. Snow, predicted in the late fifties that unless there were nuclear disarmament, there was *sure* to be a nuclear war within ten years; neither disarmament nor nuclear war followed. Thus, if societies were to mobilize for massive change, or restructure their core project, every time the prophets of doom sing out "crisis," there would be endless turmoil. As a result, policymakers and citizens tend to find it not only less demanding but also wiser to mobilize in a big way only in response to clear and present dangers, and to hedge their commitments as long as possible, even if this means that when a true crisis hits, the initial response is anemic.

It is my thesis that by 1980 the underdevelopment of the American economy and the retreat from society had reached such a level that the signs of deterioration unmistakably required a massive and comprehensive commitment of reconstruction. To await further erosion, with even clearer signs of deterioration, would be sure to multiply the difficulties of reconstruction.

Aside from growing and accumulating signs of strain in the economy, institutions, and national bonds, there were also indications of rising public discontent; of the lack of a clear direction, a sense of progress, and a sense of mastery of the future.[2] These reflect psychic pressures to reduce the ambivalence between the old core project and its challenger, and to overcome the sense of void and drift, which is as troubling as the sense of loss of economic vitality.

In short, while ambivalence and drift could have gone on for quite a while longer before the United States faced an economic, institutional, and national breakdown, the mounting indications of strain and the growing sense of foreboding provided the needed basis for a major mobilization for change, against continued drift. But change in what direction?

A QUALITY-OF-LIFE AMERICA

People who live in a society dedicated to one core project, even when it is weakened, tend to find it difficult to see how their society— in effect, their lives—could be recast as deeply as it would be if it were transformed and dedicated to a new core project. Nonetheless, societies can be and are transformed, albeit infrequently. For example, America was a predominantly farming, rural, small-town society of less than four million people, and it turned into a mainly urban, industrial, mass society. Societies can change their core project. A quality-of-life society, one dedicated to greater harmony with self, others, and nature, would entail such a turnabout for America.

What was the extent of support for a new core project, the quality-of-life society, as of the late seventies? There is no precise measure. We have seen that the available data that speak directly to the issue tend to measure jointly the retreat from the old core project and the commitment to an alternative, new one—that is, they show both commitment to and ambivalence about the quality-of-life society.[3] A minority showed considerable commitment, while much more sizable segments of the public revealed varying degrees of involvement and ambivalence. Although some elements of American life were actually reconstructed around the new project, these were far from enough to constitute a basis for a new core project.

For quality of life to become the core societal project would entail deliberately slowing down economic activities. Activities that are capital-, or labor-, or energy-intensive would have to be substantially curtailed: no $20 billion for fusion research, $35 billion for renovating steel mills, or $60 billion for making synthetic fuels. True, one cannot say that any specific item would have to be avoided; one could cut some others and keep synthetic fuels or fusion research or whatever item is particularly favored. The point is that shifting to quality of life as a core project would require major, far-reaching, encompassing cutbacks, involving lessened productive capacity and output, and hence lessened public and private consumption. People would have to derive more "psychic income" from activities that are not related to material consumption or work, such as culture, social life, interpersonal interaction, and contemplation. Some communes provide an extreme example of such a life.

Two important attributes of human and social nature, it should be mentioned, suggest that a more moderate but nevertheless substantial shift toward such a project is not completely inconceivable. One attribute is due to the fact that culture and knowledge are scarcity-free. These realms of human activity are highly atypical from this viewpoint. In the typical world of objects, the raw materials used to make any one item, say an auto, are not available for any other, and the gasoline one driver burns will not fuel anybody else's car. The same holds for the other objects that make up the high production/consumption, "materialistic" way of life; they are "scarce" in the sense that more people wish they had more of them, and there are not enough to go around, which, as economics textbooks explain, is the basic reason objects have prices. (Non-scarce items, such as air, are "free," have no price.) The need to pay and the ability to purchase are, in turn, what motivate people to work, to compete, to make a profit—the basis of the modern economic project, at least in the West.

In contrast, culture and knowledge "products" are basically patterns of symbols, such as arrangements of tones, colors, words that make symphonies, paintings, novels. (There is always present as well a small nonsymbolic element, such as the pulp that goes into a book or the plastic into a record, but its cost is usually relatively trivial.) Now, symbol patterns can be multicopied in very large numbers without losing their psychically satisfying quality. Not only can A "have" Beethoven's Ninth while it is still fully available to B, but also a billion copies can be made—and the symphony can still be "had," in full.

True, the non-symbolic carrier—the quality of the recording or the book's printing, the texture of the canvas—makes a difference to enjoyment. For instance, the first hundred thousand copies of a record may be of somewhat better quality than the next hundred thousand, and an expensive hi-fi set may provide somewhat better sound than a less costly one. However, a cheap print provides a fair copy of a Picasso, and a $1.98 paperback edition of Homer or Shakespeare is identical in content to a leatherbound copy of the same text.

The point: A society that can increase the satisfaction its members gain from culture and knowledge can satisfy them despite lower output or productivity, an achievement that is not possible if their satisfactions are focused on typical, material, "scarce" objects.

The other reason a transformation to a quality-of-life society is not so extreme a societal change as it might at first seem is that quite a few of the activities of high-production societies are aimed at symbolic satisfactions, not at biological/physiological needs. The main difference is that in a high-production society, these satisfactions are often mediated by objects, while in a quality-of-life society they are achieved more directly.

The core source of satisfaction in a mature high-production society (as distinct from the early, formative stages) is amassing a large quantity of consumable objects. Only a small proportion of them are dedicated to elementary biological/physiological needs, Maslow's "creature comforts," such as the needs for liquid, caloric intake, and shelter. Most go to "secondary," derived, socially defined needs. Thus, we need protein, but we could get it from cheap soybeans; we seek it in steaks because they are culturally prescribed and tend to be associated with prestige, *i.e.*, are a source of respect. Indeed, at its high point the consuming society judges people largely by their consumption.

Persons who subscribe to the quality-of-life project may eschew steaks, either because for them a less costly object (fish?) has become the symbol, or, more to the point, because they have learned to express appreciation and approval directly by hugs and cheers, not through objects. The resulting psychic income is quite similar, or greater. It is not that people well integrated into the high-consumption society do not hug or cheer, but in this society, especially in its heyday, these direct expressions of feeling are less dominant and those mediated by objects are more common. Thus, a typical high-consumption spouse presented a birthday gift composed of an extensive embrace, an evening of family togetherness, and a paperback copy of a long-missed book would not find it appropriate, while a member of the quality-of-life society would. For the collectivity, this means that a quality-of-life society would not have to "invent" satisfactions from relationships, only free them from frequent mediation by costly objects.

Advocates of the quality-of-life project correctly point to a neurotic aspect of mediating human relations by objects. A typical figure from high-production America is the father/husband who works long hours and has no time or energy left to "relate" to his wife and kids, to develop relations and to express affection; he works hard to get them the objects that he senses they "need," that his neighbors' approval requires, and that will show his dedication, affection, and status. "Sick," say the quality-of-life people.

The other side of the coin, though, must also be shown. Dislodging objects from the main language of satisfaction not only undermines the motivation to work and save but also has its own neuroses. Gestures and words work well only as long as relationships are "good," anchored in strong mutuality. Objects, while they may mediate and to some extent even stand in the way of "good" human relationships, also make relationships more workable when mutuality is less than strong.

This discussion is not a psychological case for one type of society over the other. The point is that each type of society has its own built-in strengths and strains; both types are "possible," and the two are less remote from each other than the difference in satisfaction from objects versus satisfaction from symbols and from unmediated relations might at first suggest.

A transformation to a quality-of-life society would entail more than a change in the sources of human satisfaction; it would also require a major change in human organization. The high-production society centers around corporations as the bases of work, exchange, and other economic activities. Most of the day's energies and time is spent in their confines; they are the bases of power and status (*i.e.*, respect). A quality-of-life society would have to downgrade these corporations by weakening their power; by lowering the priority they accord economic goals, using various regulations and controls aimed at increasing their contribution to shared needs that are not production-related; and by promoting other bases of power and status—from colleges to social movements, from voluntary associations to intellectual groups.

Which new bases would be advanced would depend on the focus

of the particular quality-of-life society. If it were relatively highly *literati,* investment in schools, museums, operas, and other educational/cultural institutions would gain in role, power, and status; if its focus were empathetic, "therapeutic communities," personal growth movements, and institutions would rise; and so on, as long as the institutions and activities celebrated were not intensive consumers of material objects, labor, or energy.

The question has been raised whether production, science, technology, and administration could be contained in a subculture, as would be necessary if quality of life became a society's core project; or whether, once downgraded, they would continue to deteriorate to the point that society could not maintain a reasonably strong sector of these rational activities. As it's sometimes put, if such a society did not slide all the way back to the Stone Age, would it return to pre-industrial, medieval levels, a standard of living its members would find unacceptable? As such a partial downgrading of the rational realms has never been deliberately attempted in a democratic society, the outcome is hard to tell. For reasons that will become self-evident once we discuss the international implications of a transformation to a quality-of-life society, the question may not need to be answered.

REINDUSTRIALIZATION

Reindustrialization—an active reaffirmation of the high-production project—is a second option for mobilization for change. It would involve, for a decade or more, shoring up the economic foundations of America by investing heavily in the infrastructure and capital goods sectors and proportionately reducing consumer goods and services, public *and* private. ("Proportionately" because, as the GNP grows, they might grow in absolute terms, but not as a proportion of national production.) Limited fixes would not do; massive investment and an encompassing approach would be needed.

Parallel developments would be necessary in noneconomic sectors. If human capital is to be improved, education and training need to be more closely related to the economic priority. If administration and technology are to be shored up along with the economy, rationality, the logical-empirical element of our mentality, must be relegitimated. The same holds for the national unity.

Some of these needed developments are properly subjects of public policy (*e.g.,* tax incentives for higher productivity, modification of the antitrust laws); some are a matter for the private sector to sort out (*e.g.*, larger investment in R&D; smaller dividend payouts); some will respond to consensus-building as to where the nation should be headed, but cannot and should not be engineered by the government.

Reindustrialization would draw on a segment of the historical past of the country as a source of future-vision, legitimacy, and analytic design, in the sense that the same basic elements that buttressed the original industrialization now needed to be shored up. It would *not*, however, require or benefit from a rerun of the same substantive items. Reindustrialization would require a secure, abundant flow of energy, as the United States learned in the 1970s, but it need not be energy from the same sources as before. Indeed, the first time around oil grew in importance second to coal; this time coal could grow second to oil, and both might eventually be surpassed by some still-undeveloped source. Similarly, reindustrialization would require expeditious communication: not Western Union telegrams, but their late-twentieth-century equivalents—data phones, satellites, and computer networks. The same holds for noneconomic features: not a return to child labor in mines, for example, but avoidance of excessive regulation of the workplace, which multiplies costs and grievances while adding little to workers' safety.

Finally, in some important ways the vision would differ from its origins. It would have to be more socially sensitive than the first industrialization, because of both ethical considerations and political facts. Ethically, very few indeed wish to recapture the abuses of civil and human rights entailed by slavery, segregation, and child labor. Politically, the newly mobilized social groups have weakened, but they are not down and out, and they would hinder, if not block, any major societal drive in which they did not share the purposes, the design, and the fruits.

CHOOSE WE MUST

"Can't we have both social *and* economic progress?" is a question I have been asked whenever I have discussed the conflict in contemporary America between those who seek a quality-of-life society and those who favor rededication to economic growth. Cannot America develop new energy sources, increase productivity, keep consumer products flowing, *and* at the same time use its growing wealth to purchase healthier and safer consumer products, workplace, and environment? Cannot America both keep its economy growing and enhance harmony with others, within self, and with nature?

My answer to these questions is "In the short term, no." For both economic and social-psychic reasons, we must choose one core project or the other. Either quality-of-life or reindustrialization must be accorded first priority, not irrevocably but for a decade or so. After this period, priorities may be re-examined and reaffirmed or changed. To accord first priority to economic growth, as I advocate, does not mean sacrificing the vision of a quality-of-life society, but it does entail deliberately deferring major new steps in this direction to a more distant future. And during a decade of reindustrialization, one need not "forget" about quality-of-life (nor need one "forget" about economic growth, if the priorities are ranked the other way). What *is* essential is to establish one of the two projects as the first priority and the other as secondary, and to make the parallel commitment of resources and will power.

The reasons a firm choice is needed fall under three rubrics: costs, psychic needs, and international considerations.

Costs

Estimates of the costs exacted by a full-blown reindustrialization drive run as high as 6.7 percent of GNP in an average year of the decade of reindustrialization, with the first, startup years costing less and the later ones more. This calculation is based on channeling new funds at the rates of 0.14 percent of GNP for railroads, 0.46 percent for highways, 0.57 percent for bridges, 2.68 percent to 3.03 percent for energy, 2 percent "additional" on capital goods, and 0.5 percent "additional" on R&D.[4] These estimates are, of course, strictly illustrative. For instance, one might seek to invest less in railroads and more in slurry pipelines or ports, and so on and so forth. In terms of billions entailed, these cannot be readily specified as it depends on when the decade of reindustrialization starts, and of course on the future level of GNP growth, inflation, and other such circumstances. However, to provide a sense of the magnitudes involved, if the decade were the eighties and 1985 GNP rose, as has been projected, to $4,500 billion,[5] the reindustrialization costs for an average year would amount to $301.5 billion.

Thus, while a precise estimate cannot be formulated costs would run into the hundreds of billions of dollars a year for ten years. Such investments simply do not leave room for equivalent, or even similar, amounts for quality-of-life projects, especially if one takes into account the expenditures to which the United States is legally committed (interest payments on the national debt, for instance), not to mention expenditures for defense.

The extent of difficulty in proceeding vigorously on either front, and certainly on both, depends on how much strength is left in the economy, how much growth—*i.e.*, new resources—it will provide in the next decade. Terleckyj, in calculations for the period 1974 to 1983, estimated that new resources would total $101 billion for the first four years, then rise, reaching $400 billion by the tenth year, but he assumed an average rate of growth in GNP of 4.8 percent per year, a rapidly growing totality of resources.[6] This high growth was not in fact achieved during the first eight years of that period. Moreover, even on this optimistic assumption, reindustrialization in addition to a high-power quality-of-life project could not be fully funded for the first five years.

In short, it seems reasonable to conclude that because of the high costs involved, it is not possible to advance both projects *on a high-priority basis*, even under quite optimistic assumptions about growth in GNP and the size of "discretionary" resources (those which can be dedicated to either project).

What about "mixing" the two core projects, allotting to each say $50 to $70 billion from real economic growth (after "deducting" inflation) and some funds switched from third projects? "Third" programs to be cut do not exactly jump to mind. Most social programs directly affect quality of life; hence, cutting them is not compatible with progress on two fronts. To increase some social programs and cut others would not generate a net saving in resources, although some efficiency might be gained (or lost). Something might be gained by reducing government fraud, abuse, waste, and mismanagement, but past experience and study suggest that both because of the technical difficulties and high resistance to measures that must be taken, the amounts that can be actually saved are a far cry from what rolls off so glibly from politicians' tongues, press releases, and newspaper editorials. Defense spending may well be stretched out to some extent; we will explore shortly why sufficient savings are unlikely to be found in this sector.

The funds available from real economic growth, if divided equally between the two core projects, might allow significant incremental improvement in the quality of life, with presumably larger improvement in later years. However, such an allocation would not suffice to close the maintenance gap, eliminate the adaptation lag, or shore up the infrastructure and capital goods sectors. Cumulative weakening of the economy would continue, or even accelerate, and would pose mounting problems pertaining to the GNP's ability to grow even at a relatively slow rate. Hence, to accord quality of life equal status with reindustrialization implies, in effect, *an acceptance of underdevelopment.* For an economy already on a downward path, a decision not to grant redevelopment first priority until it is restored is, implicitly, a decision for a slow-(or no-)growth society—although one can, of course, neglect growth in varying degrees. Practically speaking, the choice is for a high-power redevelopment drive and a rather thin quality-of-life program for the next decade—or for a quite effective quality-of-life program with growing underdevelopment.

Psychic Needs

A relatively clear choice of projects is also necessary because "mixing" is psychically less compelling. The thesis that America must choose for psychic reasons may at first seem abstract, but it has clear practical foundations. Every society has one or more sets of values and meanings that indicate which patterns of behavior are approved and disapproved, and among those approved, which are most desired. These, in turn, are actively promoted by schools, the media, and churches, and serve as a source of guidelines for the laws and concepts of justice that the courts and police uphold.

Societies vary a great deal as to how actively and effectively they set such guidelines. Some express few expectations of their members, others articulate numerous demands, and still others have several sub-sets of expectations (in addition to a core, or dominant, set), among which members can choose which to follow. Nevertheless, all societies have some mechanisms for the continous formulation and promotion of values and meanings that provide one main source of the purposes members seek to serve or incorporate in their own lives, and that color their self-view as well as their expectations of others. One mark of decomposition of a society is precisely that most members do not heed what the society prescribes, and that the society promotes incompatible main themes (as distinct from subculture variants). It is then that schools have difficulty deciding what to teach; parents, what values to pass on to their children; and police, which laws to enforce rigorously. The result is a "mixing of signals," which in turn promotes deviation, withdrawal, uncertainty, and ambivalence.

The strains resulting from a high degree of what might be called "core project ambivalence" are well known, so I refer to them here only briefly to flag the psychic stress that emanates from such ambivalence and that, in the long run, tends to promote clearer commitment to one project over the other.

Without a clear indication of the society's direction, parents are often unsure what values, meanings, and behavior to promote: say, the old virtues of self-discipline, deferred gratification, achievement, and the work ethos; or the "new" virtues of relaxation, openness, and the social ethos; Type A or Type B behavior.

Similarly, schools oscillate and are internally divided between emphasis on specific skills and preparation for the labor force versus concern with "total" personality growth, liberal arts, self-guided development, and social justice.

At work, an emphasis on efficiency and productivity competes with the demands of self-actualization, work rights, and Affirmative Action. Police and courts are often neutralized by the conflict between pressure from the "uptight" part of the community to enforce "strict" laws (*e.g.*, against the use of marijuana) and the demands of the "untight" part at least *not* to enforce them.

Another indication of rising ambivalence, as distinct from sheer rejection, is that the continuous decline of the proportion of Americans who define themselves as "very happy" has *not* been accompanied by a rise of those who are unhappy—only of those who feel "pretty happy."[7]

These tensions themselves tend to pull the society toward a clearer pattern by impelling it to set priorities, so that young persons know what is expected of them, even if many rebel against such expectations for a while (and fewer, for a lifetime); so that the community and its leaders know what to extol, even if many rarely fully live up to these ideals themselves; and so that authorities know what standards to uphold.

International Considerations

When Napoleon returned from the Battle of Waterloo, he is reported to have asked his artillery officer: "Why didn't you give me any cover?" The officer responded: "I had six reasons. First of all, I had no shells." Retorted Napoleon: "Never mind the other reasons." There is one argument concerning the choice between core projects that I find so compelling that the others pale in comparison, and that is the all-too-infrequently mentioned link between economic vigor and national security. A no-growth economy will find it much more difficult than a high-growth one to allot the resources needed for defense, especially if it is not to shortchange all other needs. This lesson was driven home shortly after President Reagan discovered that the United States was entering a recession, in the middle of 1981. He had entered office ten months earlier with a very strong commitment to a high-powered progran to "re-arm America." However, as soon as the cutbacks of social programs, rising unemployment, and the slowing economy started to pinch, the demand rose—even among his supporters in Congress and in the country—to slow down defense spending. (Other reasons included the very steep increases the Reagan program called for, which may well have been steeper than the Armed Forces could sensibly absorb;* the poor strategic justification for several key items; and the excessive focus on nuclear versus conventional forces.)

Aside from the general close connection between what the economy can afford and what people are willing to set aside for defense, there are specific links between the strength of the economy and the strength of defense. *The same elements that make for strong infrastructure and capital-goods sectors also make for strong defense.* Thus, the railroads that move commodities at ten miles an hour cannot move tanks any faster. The underprepared worker and the underprepared foot soldier are recruited from the same societal cir-

---

* Typically, David Wood reports in the *Los Angeles Times* ("Rapid Defense Buildup May Hamper Economy." March 14, 1982):

> Economists and defense analysts from a wide variety of backgrounds are beginning to warn that:
> • Injecting too much money too fast into the Pentagon pipeline could lead to an unproductive bidding up of prices for scarce materials, equipment and skilled workers by defense contractors, creating what economists call "bottleneck inflation."

cles and homes. To illustrate: During a tank maneuver, a radio dispatcher was unable to pass on an urgent message because he could not read it.[8] Similarly, a sailor who could not read the operating instructions for an engine did a quarter of a million dollars' worth of damage to it.[9] The same "human capital" that is "stoned" on the assembly line is "stoned" on guard duty on the border between West and East Germany.* And the weakened condition of R&D cuts into our ability to provide engineers, technologists, computer programmers for both defense and industrial innovation, in an era when the arms race with the U.S.S.R. is, to an important extent, one of upgrading weapons on the basis of R&D. In short, a reindustrialized America is needed for national security.[10]

There are those who feel that the claim that we must invest heavily in defense has been exaggerated, that the U.S.S.R. is not an aggressive, expansionist power but is merely responding to the U.S. arms buildup, and that we already have enough bombs "to kill every man, woman, and child in the world three times over, so why buy more?"

I cannot, in the confines of an aside, examine all these issues. But let me briefly say that, first, to argue in favor of a stronger American defense is not to favor every multibillion-dollar item the defense industry and the Pentagon are promoting. For instance, the arguments for heavy investments in an MX system and B-1 bombers, both said to be at best useful for a few years, make one wonder if these outlays are justified. Second, a world of *effectively verified* mutual arms limitations (not to be confused with the dream of worldwide general and total disarmament) is certainly preferable to an arms race.[11] Unfor-

---

* A 1980 study of nonmedical drug and alcohol use among U.S. military personnel throughout the world found that during the year preceding the study, half of the junior enlisted personnel (pay grades E1–E5) had used marijuana or hashish; a smaller proportion, roughly one-fifth, were using it once a week or oftener. Nearly one-fifth reported that they had been high on drugs while working, and of that number, almost half said they had been high while on duty on forty or more days during the preceding year. Moreover, 28 percent of junior enlisted personnel were heavy beer drinkers (eight or more drinks a day) and 14 percent were heavy drinkers of hard liquor; 31 percent reported some impairment of their work during the preceding year because of alcohol use. (Marvin R. Burt and Mark M. Biegel, *Highlights from the Worldwide Survey of Nonmedical Drug Use and Alcohol Use among Military Personnel: 1980* [Bethesda, MD: Burt Associates, Inc., 1980].)

tunately, so far it has not been attainable. Third, for the last decade, the U.S.S.R. has been spending heavily on strategic armaments and has vastly improved its position. Some say it has overtaken the United States, others say it is merely close, but it is obviously racing. As long as there are only few mutually agreed-upon limitations, the United States must keep up its side of the balance of nuclear terror on which the strategic deterrent system is based, or the system will become unhinged and wreak its terror on us. Fourth, to say that we have "enough" bombs is both true and quite misleading, because at issue is not the number of bombs, but updating and protecting the means of delivering them on target in the face of continuous efforts by the U.S.S.R. to find ways to render them useless, *e.g.*, by hitting our missiles in their cement silos.

Next to the strategic system is the need for conventional forces. When we do not think about a Soviet first (nuclear) strike, we tend to worry about a conventional Soviet attack in Europe, especially in Germany. It seems to me that it would be foolhardy for the Soviet Union to attack in an area where we are best prepared, are sure to respond, and might well use tactical nuclear weapons. It would be much less risky for the U.S.S.R. to try to pull off additional Afghanistans; for instance, to send its troops to support a left coup in Iran or in western Pakistan. The West would find it impossible to declare war on the Soviet Union and risk its survival for such an act, as we have seen in the case of Afghanistan. However, such steps could lead the U.S.S.R., drawing on its allies in Syria and South Yemen and maybe Iraq (if the regime's direction changes one more time), to capture important segments of the Middle East's oilfields. This would suffice to cow Japan and Western Europe, because for at least the next decade they could not do without this oil, and the United States could not replace the lost supplies from its sources. The best and often the only way to deter such Soviet expansion in the Middle East (and elsewhere) is by credible conventional forces.[12]

The point illustrated by the Middle Eastern scenario is more general: In a world in which super-powers use armed forces to back up their foreign policies, the United States cannot protect its vital interests and those of its allies without adequate conventional forces. As of the end of the seventies, the United States did not command such forces.[13] The Rapid Deployment Force was but a plan, without a command, troops, or the necessary overseas bases. American divisions, ships, and air bases were understaffed, and their munitions stores were often inadequately stocked. (Funds to supply them were in effect diverted to pay for cost overruns on new high-technology big-ticket items.) This meant that American foreign policy lacked the necessary backup in areas in which only conventional forces are credible, and the temptation to resort to nuclear blows was unduly high. (Frustration with the inability of conventional forces to free our fifty-three hostages in Iran led to the slogan "Nuke Iran," an extreme example of the point at hand.)

In short, while one may well favor a less frenetic pace and a mix that includes relatively more conventional forces, one can readily see that the United States needs a stronger defense than it commanded in 1980. A stronger defense, in turn, rests directly and indirectly, in general and in detailed ways, on a reindustrialized America.

CROSS-COMMITMENTS

If reindustrialization is defined as the core project for a decade or so, one can still expect considerable desire to see social growth as well. Concern about the quality of life will not vanish, for political reasons—major social groups will continue to push for it—and, it should not be ignored, for ethical reasons. Hence, one should make reindustrialization as compatible as possible with quality-of-life needs, without losing sight of its higher priority. One main way to accomplish this is to accord much more attention to a strategy of "cross-commitments" in general, and especially to cross-commitments between these two projects.

The idea involved may be so elementary that it escapes the attention of most policymakers and of the attentive public that follows these matters. The idea is that given a scarcity of resources and public funds, *one and the same set of resources should be made to do two or more tasks,* and a systematic and continued effort should be made to find new ways of evolving and implementing such strategies of cross-commitment.

To start with a simple example of a project already working: In New Mexico a score of welfare mothers were trained to serve as home-health services staff. Home-health services include some household help, shopping aid, visits to overcome isolation and loneliness, and some nursing services, such as changing bandages and giving injections. Cross-commitment is achieved here by using one program *both* to reduce the welfare rolls *and* to reduce the Medicaid/Medicare costs that are incurred when people are institutionalized to receive services that could be provided at home. According to one estimate, the cost of home-health services is no more than one third that of nursing home care. While such comparisons are very difficult, most experts agree that a significant proportion of the nursing home population, say 40 percent, could receive better services at lower cost at home. Care at home also lowers the human costs that institutionalization often exacts of patients: Their loss of contact with family and community; abuses due to profiteering; and inadequate medical care, which characterizes too many nursing homes. Moreover, training welfare mothers to work as home-health aides alleviates the human costs of being on welfare. Often, however, we lack suitable personnel for home-health programs. Hence the idea of training welfare clients for those jobs. This is not to suggest that every AFDC mother can or should work. But among the hundreds of thousands of AFDC clients in the nation, there might well be thousands in other states who could be involved in similar programs based on the strategy of cross-commitment.

Another cross-commitment idea involves several (rather than merely two) uses of the same set of resources. Relatively small expenditures to conserve energy in public buildings, such as public schools—to install storm windows and otherwise improve insulation, to install more sensitive thermostats—would at the same time reduce the skyrocketing taxpayer bills for operating these institutions and create employment in an often depressed industry, construction. To keep the program simple, each public institution should determine for itself which items from an approved list of energy-saving devices it will purchase or install; and funds should be allotted not on the basis of costs (which would generate an open-ended bill, likely to lead to gross overruns and waste, à la Medicaid), but on the basis of a fixed amount per pupil (in schools), or per bed (in public hospitals), or some other appropriate unit.

Roger Starr and James Carlson, comparing the jobs generated by expanding programs in housing, education, and employment, found that by far the highest proportion of work opportunities for unskilled labor (which most unemployed are) would be generated by introducing the necessary improvements in American sewer systems. (Some of the nation's sewage is dumped raw or inadequately treated into the streams and water resources of the nation, and storm drainage overloads many systems.) The authors recommend "the deliberate interaction of two programs"—create jobs for the unskilled, treat sewers—"aimed at different goals because each may be important to the goal of the other."[14]

A particularly attractive cross-commitment idea, my favorite, is to serve security needs by expanding conventional forces, a course which at the same time has desirable educational, social, and economic consequences. Thus to have fewer MX missiles and B-1 bombers, and several hundred thousand more troops, would provide the United States with a better national defense mix. It would also create jobs for youth—who are particularly short of jobs—and an opportunity to educate and train those schools failed.

The range of other possible cross-commitments is practically endless, from those minor in scope and consequences to those national in scope. What cross-commitment takes is unconventional thinking, "license" from regulators and labor unions, and a willingness to cross agency lines (rather than each agency's guarding a "turf"—housing, police work, welfare, health services—as "its own"). In an age of growing awareness of the limits of public resources, cross-commitment should receive more attention: It does provide a way to reduce the strain of having to focus on the core project and delay commitments to other projects. True, it will not resolve this tension, but it can to some extent mitigate it.

A SOCIAL SCIENCE PERSPECTIVE ON REDEVELOPMENT

Functional Differentiation

Three ideas touched upon in the preceding analysis find their anchor in a social science conception, which deserves to be explicated. The ideas are: (1) that after retreat there might be transformation to a new society or recommitment to a vision based on a previous historical experience; (2) that recommitment does not entail retracing but is a form of renewal itself, a return to an earlier theme, modified and presumably improved; (3) that societies are complex systems and, hence, that major changes in one element, say economic policy, must be accompanied by roughly parallel changes in other elements, such as mentality, institutions, and power (although these elements are much less subject to public policy than economic matters, more a matter for individual and community action).

The social science perspective I have drawn upon and will explicate shortly, which accounts for the position I have taken, is not an infallible guide. The social sciences are hindered by the openness of human actions. Unlike the planets in their movements or radioactive materials in their decomposition, persons are ultimately free to change their direction (especially if they act in unison); their actions are only to a limited extent predetermined. Furthermore, the social sciences are younger, weaker, and more open to value judgments than the natural sciences. Within the social sciences, moreover, forecasting the future is generally one of the least advanced specialities. At best, one can offer optional futures, rather than try to foretell "the future," and explicate the social science grounds for the alternative scenarios advanced.

The sociological scheme on which I have drawn is my adaptation of a model technically known as "functional differentiation."[15] According to this scheme, societies in their small, nascent stage are structurally highly compact and undifferentiated, with one entity attending to most if not all societal needs (which sociologists term "functions"). If these needs are not met, a society will not survive. Thus, if some sort of production is not organized to replenish perishable resources—even if it's only hunting or collecting berries—the members of that society will starve; if youngsters born are not introduced to the values of the society via some form of education, their inability to play by whatever social rules there are will breed mass deviance and violence; and so on.

Societies that survive differ in how and how well they attend to these various shared needs. Some, like the Athenians, emphasize internal needs: spiritual matters, social harmony and some; like the Spartans, conquest of others. Some, like the Israeli society at the high point of the pioneering era, are highly mobilized in pursuit of their goals; others, like some Central American republics, are much less so. A major factor in determining what societies focus on and how well they attend to their needs is the level and nature of functional differentiation.

Historically, societies grow not merely in size, but also in complexity; they differentiate. An analogue may be helpful here. There are tools that try to be at once a hammer, screwdriver, pliers, and drill.

These multipurpose tools are compact and in this sense convenient, but they are not very efficient at any one of their tasks; they are used mainly by novices or for simple home repairs. Professionals use a differentiated set of tools—hammers of different weights and shapes, various screwdrivers and pliers, each dedicated to one mission and designed with that particular task in mind. Similarly, as societies grow, they evolve differentiated institutional "tools" to serve specific societal needs—more effectively.

In the process of differentiation, no new basic needs are served; the basic needs continue to include production, education, social order, and tension management. The significant new development is that activities to serve each need are now parceled out to one or more specialized units, each with its own "suitable" structure. Differentiated societies have factories for the organization of work, schools for education, courts for conflict resolution, families for character formation and tension management, and so on. This is not the work of master planners any more than the evolution of species Darwin uncovered is the work of a genetic engineer; it is an historical development that social scientists observe. Policymaking can built on it or try to fight it, but it cannot command functional differentiation.

For the purposes at hand a corollary observation is quite crucial: Each specialized unit, each "differentiated structure" develops—as part of the differentiation process, as it separates out of the "original," all-encompassing family-community—its own mentality and power base. Factories, banks, and offices are more rational and more competitive than families and constitute the basis of corporate power; universities, laboratories, and think tanks tend to be more open-minded than churches and provide the power base of science, and so on.

Differentiation vastly increases the "productivity" of each unit, since each is freer to follow its own logic, norms, and authorities. Take work within the "original" family and work in a factory. In the family, the father, who doubles as a foreman, needs to weigh both intra-family considerations and work logic; say, dare he assign the firstborn to work "under" his younger brother if the latter is more competent? Can he ask grandpa to work under the instruction of junior? and so on. Indeed, these problems arise when members of a family work in the same factory. However, in a typical factory the supervisors are not kin of their employees and are comparatively free to relate to them as the logic of work requires.

Historically, differentiation was favorable to industrialization; it provided a supportive societal context. It is through the process of differentiation that economic institutions (including production and distribution as well as technology and administration) were "freed" from kinship, community, and the religion-magic nexus and gained their own structures and hence opportunities to develop their productivity.

Here the typical account of differentiation ends. It leaves unanswered a core question: *What are the relationships among the differentiated societal sectors (or units)?* Precisely because each differentiated sector follows its own logic and promotes its own mentality and power base, the relations among them, and the relative strength each commands within the societal whole, are of great importance for societal cohesion and direction. Thus, a very strong productive sector means that within the society-wide allocation of resources, rewards, and psychic energy, high priority will be accorded to rationality in general and to the logic and means of instruments in particular. Moreover, this societal sector will *tend to penetrate others, attempting to organize them to its purpose, and in its image.* As a result, other societal needs will be neglected. Similarly, a very strong sector dedicated to quality-of-life pursuits will tend to neglect productive capacity, technology, and administration.

Theoretically, a well-balanced society would be one in which each sector is kept in place by all the others, a society of checks and balances. In practice, there is no blueprint for a well-balanced society; neither is there an effective centralized societal regulator to correct consciously for societal imbalances, although to some extent the government fulfills that role. Furthermore, external forces—changes in the environment, the spread of new ideas, new developments in science—render all existing balances obsolete. Thus, a continual rebalancing of the relationship among the segments is necessary, or one or more societal needs will be neglected.

Because of the inherent limits of public policy (quite evident in the weaknesses of those public policies employed in adapting society to its inner imbalances and to external changes), societies show a considerable tendency to correct only after the fact, and to tilt in one direction or another—until correction takes place. Therefore, instead of following the straight, precisely mapped theoretical path of balanced service to all segments, societies tend to follow a pendulum course, or to stagger through history, leaning first to one side, then another.

Viewed in this perspective, the period of America's movement toward independence was one of great attention to political institutions, to nation-building, and to the definition of societal identity and shared values. (This does not mean that other societal needs received no attention, but that they were accorded lower priority.) Independence was followed by a period of growing concern with the economy, directly related to maintaining independence. As economic historian Samuel Rezneck puts it, in the early years of the federal government, patriotism impelled a new wave of industrial zeal: "Manufacturers, like the Constitution, were expected to strengthen the country and help it achieve true independence."[16] This emphasis on economic development continued, indeed, grew, through the first half of the nineteenth century. Then the rift that culminated in the Civil War returned the nation's first attention to matters of unity, identity, and polity.

Following the Civil War, emphasis returned to industrialization, and economic activities absorbed much of the national resources and attention all the way to the late 1920s, although in the 1890s the question of labor's place in the polity began to heighten concern with social issues and unity. With the Depression and the New Deal, social issues—questions of social management, distribution of income, the role of government—gained first priority until U.S. involvement in World War II renewed emphasis first on national unity—and then, on production. After the war, consumption came to the fore, and it remained the American preoccupation until the early sixties, when it was joined by social issues in an era of joint emphasis on consumption and on social and, later, environmental problems. Production, technology, and administration were relatively neglected.

Regression and Recommitment

The transition from one societal focus to another is frequently a time of societal and personal stress. Thus, independence, the Civil War, the Depression, the United States' involvement in World War II mark not merely changes of focus, but also high points of stress. Stress is particularly high when the shift in societal focus is forced upon the society following a period of mounting difficulties in a neglected sector, as if a societal unconscious were signaling that a change of core projects is overdue. Transitions are often accompanied by a period of regression, of de-commitment and rise in impulsive behavior, *as if societal energies must first be released before they can be rechanneled.*

Personality development might provide a fruitful analogy. As children grow up, their personality structure "differentiates." The very young child, unaware of self or others, is immersed in the relationship with a core parent, typically the mother (biological or social). As the child matures, he (or she) first separates his own self from the core parent, then differentiates between the parents, and later among other relatives, peers, and so on, until the child is able to maintain and balance a complex set of relationships. If this process is not sufficiently advanced, the child cannot relate to different persons or can relate only immaturely (treating all close adults as mothers, for instance). At the same time, differentiation involves channeling some psychic energies, initially free-floating, into internal control functions (superego and ego). If investment in control is too weak, impulses break through; if it is excessive, the remaining psychic energies are inadequate for other needs, and the person becomes obsessed with rules and compliance, rigid or low in affect.

When the personality is under strain—because of some inner imbalance or because the individual is out of step with a changed society or culture—there is often a period of regression to lower levels of differentiation, with less self-control, more impulsive behavior and dependence. A young child's regression when a sibling is born is a typical example. The same process may occur in an adult who loses a spouse or job, or who emigrates.

Similarly, when a society needs to readjust the balance among its differentiated sectors, it frequently regresses to a lower level of differentiation. The specialization of some parts may become blurred (*e.g.,* schools and corporations come under pressure to do *extensive* family and community work). Periods of regression or transition are periods of partial breakdown of rules and mores; of rising violence, deviance, and messianic and other social movements.

There is no guaranteed outcome to a period of personal or societal regression. A person who regresses may remain in a dependent, "infantile" status, or recommit (*e.g.,* pick up his job, marriage, although usually with some modifications), or transform (*e.g.,* embark on a second career, remarry). Similarly, societies that regress may continue for a considerable time to wallow in their regressed status. Eventually, if the society is not conquered by a more mobilized one, the societal and personal strain of the regressed status either propels societal re-commitment (as Britain experienced during the reign of Queen Victoria) or transformation (as Russia underwent in 1917 when the breakdown of the Czarist regime opened the way to a Communist one).

Industrialization and the societal developments that supported it in the United States were followed by a period of focus on consumption and social growth, accompanied by the relative neglect of production, technology, and administration; erosion of support of societal institutions, from family to school to nation; and the rise of an alternative societal vision. For reasons we have discussed, transformation to a quality-of-life society is unlikely. A period of continued regression is possible, but under increased strain. In the longer run, recommitment is the most likely course. If it does not involve retracing our steps and is more attentive to social needs, it would lead not to another abrupt swing of the pendulum to the social priorities, but to a more balanced program. Thus, while some zigzagging probably cannot be avoided, a steadier balance of economic and social growth is possible, once the recent economic neglect is addressed.

CHAPTER THIRTEEN
Reindustrialization Policies

What specific public policies would advance reindustrialization? To what extent does the Reagan economic program provide for these— or undermine them? In dealing with these questions I proceed from principles to specifics. First, I outline the reasons the general approach of reducing government and unleashing the market is insufficient. It must be supplemented by setting a supportive context so that, for a decade or so, the market channels more resources to the infrastructure and capital goods sectors, less to public and private consumption. Next, I examine from the viewpoint of these considerations, specific actions already undertaken. Last, I list additional policies that seem called for, especially elements not now covered, not to provide a catalogue of all possible measures, but to further illustrate the basic approach advanced here.

THREE POSITIONS ON GOVERNMENT/ ECONOMIC RELATIONS
At issue are competing conceptions of both what ails the economy and what prescriptions are called for. The advocates of all the varying positions despair, albeit to differing degrees, of Keynesian theory and policies based on it. All agree that in the American economy of recent years, something more is amiss than unduly high readings on some indicators (*e.g.,* inflation, unemployment), poor productivity growth, and low savings, that the problem is more severe than just one more downturn of the age-old business cycle, soon to swing up again. All

concur that the recent inflation has not been merely or even mainly demand-driven (or OPEC-caused). All agree that the foundations of the American economy have weakened and need shoring up.

The differences are best viewed as divergent conceptions of the proper relationship between the polity and the economy, and where the levers for correctives are. The positions taken do not directly parallel those taken by political parties, or the conservative-liberal dichotomy. They may be arranged, for convenience of presentation, on a continuum from laissez-faire conservative to moderate-centrist to left-liberal.

Non-Targeted: Supply-Side Economics

The well-known laissez-faire, New Whig position is that what ails the economy is mainly an excessive level of politicization, reflected not merely in the polity's use and allocation of an unduly high proportion of the GNP and in excessive regulation of private decisions, but also in the revolution of entitlements, in attempts to deal with all social and many personal needs via the polity rather than the market.

The remedy that follows is to reduce the scope and intensity of the polity as much as possible, by releasing resources to the private sector, deregulating, and letting the market do its wondrous things. The most radical of the lot, such as Professor Arthur Laffer, Congressman Jack Kemp, and Senator William Roth, hold that the revenue lost via monumental tax cuts will be restored by the higher tax yield of a more productive economy. Other laissez-faire conservatives, say Milton Friedman, are satisfied to cut back government expenditures and taxation drastically, without assuming a *proportionate* gain in the economy and tax revenues.

In terms of the second defining issue, *where the levers for change are,* this approach is wholly non-targeted. It sees no need to direct, aim, or guide the public resources released to the private sector in any particular way. Indeed, freeing them to go wherever the market will take them is the kernel of the approach.

Targeted: Industrial Policy

At the other end of the spectrum is the notion that, far from being reduced, the polity's role should be intensified. Here the diagnosis is that, compared to other highly successful economies, especially

West Germany and above all Japan, American institutions provide insufficient guidance and support for the private economy. The market, it is implied or openly stated, has shown its inability to invest enough in new plant and equipment, in innovative and competitive capacity. Executives have grown risk-shy and dividend-happy. Steel mills, auto plants, the textile and rubber industries are crumbling. Computers face a government-orchestrated attack from Japan, while the response of American computer firms is anemic and divided against itself.

According to this view, correctives are to be found in emulation of "Japan, Inc.," above all its MITI (Ministry of International Trade and Industry). The solution lies in government-guided collaborative efforts, in which business and labor pull together, with government agencies and experts serving as the sources of analysis, tax incentives, capital, and informal if not outright control. Attempts by the Carter administration, on its last legs, to turn around the U.S. auto and steel industries according to the suggestions of tripartite committees were viewed as early-bird American industrial policy.

Beyond this, advocates of this highly targeted approach see the Department of Commerce transformed into a Department of Trade and Development (or some new agency, the Americanization of MITI) with a desk and a committee for each industry, from ball bearings to industrial diamonds. The trade desk would analyze the industry assigned to it, say, shoes, and determine whether it is a "winner" or a "loser," whether it has a promising future, in terms of productivity, export-ability, technology/innovations, labor intensiveness, and other good things in life. "We must not only 'reindustrialize' but emulate the proper model—which turns out to be West Germany or Japan. 'We have two ways to go,' " an advocate of industrial policy warns, " 'the way of the British or the way of the Japanese.' "[1]

A Harvard sociologist topped it all when he declared Japan the winner, number one. Professor Ezra Vogel finds Japan first not only in economic achievement, but also in education (Japan scores high on international math tests), crime control, equality of income distribution, environmental protection, and health (life expectancy in Japan is among the longest in the world). Above all, Japan is said to offer a model for the United States to emulate in dealing with industrial problems. Specifically, Vogel would have the United States learn from Japan by forming a "comprehensive" industrial and trade policy;

by creating a national center of top administrators to implement that national policy; by turning our large corporations and other "large organizations" into "something people enjoy," the way the Japanese loyally adhere to their corporations; and by increasing cooperation between government and business.[2]

Similarly, Frank A. Weil, lawyer, investment banker, and Assistant Secretary of Commerce under Carter, called for a cabinet department for International Trade and Industry with "the responsibility for gathering and developing a reliable and specific information base about all industrial sectors"; the department would "shape trade policy, take the lead on tax policy as it relates to and affects industry, direct import and export controls."[3] (Other advocates of industrial policy include Gar Alperovitz, co-director of the National Center for Economic Alternatives, Ronald E. Müller, the author of *Revitalizing America*, and Ira C. Magaziner and Robert B. Reich in their *Minding America's Business*.)[4]

The designated "winners" would be showered with government-provided subsidies, loans, loan guarantees, tax incentives, a measure of protection from international competition (as in a trigger price or import quotas), R&D writeoffs, and what not. The "losers" would be "sunset." The government might provide the losers' workers with "trade adjustment assistance" to help them move from parts of the country where the losers congregate (Detroit, Pittsburgh) to where the winners roam (the Sunbelt, coal states), but basically the losing industries are to be doomed, and government help is to be withheld.

This policy might be called "national planning," but as the term tends to raise fears of socialism, most of its advocates avoid the label. Instead, the term "industrial policy" is in favor. It is quite appropriate, because the assumption is that the unit at which the levers of policy are to take hold is not "the economy," or a major sector of it, but the specific industry. Also, "industrial policy" is the label used for such detailed government planning and direction of corporate efforts in other countries.

That such approaches may work in other lands does not mean that they are suitable for the American society. Many elements that go into these efforts in other societies are not available in America, nor producible, nor desirable if producible. Take the growing tendency of U.S. executives to play it safe, while the Japanese are more prone to take risks and hence come up with more innovations. Our business schools, from Harvard to Stanford, are told to rework their teaching fast and train less risk-averse executives, "as the Japanese do." But being risk-shy and profit-oriented runs deep in our business system. It reflects, in part, our much greater reliance on the stock market to raise capital, while Japan uses more bonds. Stocks are more quickly dumped than bonds if the corporation's earnings drop.

Similarly, while Japan's government is knee-deep in allocating capital to industry, Americans consider such government intervention an anathema. As we noted earlier, Japan's government encourages banks to take risks by allowing investment in corporations that have piled up debts eight or nine times their equity; U.S. banks are delicately nudged by the Comptroller of the Currency not to exceed significantly a one-to-one debt/equity ratio, to protect investors. Before American executives become significantly more venturesome, all these factors would need to be reversed.

Even if this were done, attempts to "redo" American executives would face a second set of factors, rooted in the American mentality, upbringing, and organizational culture. The Japanese pattern is for an executive to stay with one corporation for life; the loyalty expected is high, as is the corporation's commitment. Are American executives ready to submit to a highly paternalistic corporate bondage? Is greater willingness to take risks worth that much less mobility and flexibility?

All this is not to say that U.S. executives could not become somewhat more venturesome. But they would have to be encouraged in ways that are compatible with our own culture, mentality, and capital structure, not Japan's. More generally, most of what goes under the name of industrial policy in other countries is alien, un-American; not in the McCarthyite sense, but in a technical sociological sense: not suitable for the American context.

Aside from being alien, industrial policy prompts other objections from critics: (1) we do not have the analytic capacity to determine correctly who will be a winner, who a loser. Our record suggests that we would misidentify industries and sink vast amounts of public resources in tomorrow's Edsels.[5] (2) Our polity, in which government tends to be weak compared to business, labor, and local communities, especially when these work together for their Chrysler, would tend to channel resources not to those who merit them by some rational analysis, but rather to those who have political clout. Interest groups are a major factor in determining, for instance, where the United

States places its military bases, builds highways, digs waterways. (3) The country is unwilling to accept more politicization, less reliance on the marketplace.

Semi-Targeted: Reindustrialization

At the center of the continuum, between laissez-faire supply-side economics on the right and industrial policy on the left, is the conception that what ails the country is overconsumption (public and private) and underinvestment, resulting in a weakening productive capacity. Signs of deferred maintenance and lack of adaptation to the new environment of expensive energy can be seen in most of the elements that make up the infrastructure and capital goods sectors.

The suggested cure is *semi*-targeted: Release resources to the private sector, but channel them to the infrastructure and capital goods sectors, away from both public and private consumption. For example, if we cut government revenues by $50 billion through across-the-board cuts in personal income tax, the funds released might well be used mainly to spur private demand for consumer goods and services; little rejuvenation of productive capacity might occur. On the other hand, if those resources are guided to the productive sectors of the economy—*not* to specific industries—reindustrialization is much more likely to follow. Thus, if tax revenues are "lost" not just through tax cuts for individuals but in part by allowing companies to take accelerated depreciation when they replace obsolete equipment, or replace oil-based or energy-inefficient equipment with equipment that is energy-efficient or that uses alternative energy sources, the released resources will revitalize, *without* determining which specific industry will benefit: steel or textiles, rubber or rails. The polity will set the context; the market will target.

Similarly, providing tax incentives for greater R&D expenditures spurs on all such efforts; it does not require any government trade desk or tripartite committee to decide *which* R&D project is desirable. And if workers are provided with productivity-based incentives, so they can share directly in renewed economic growth, Washington need not be involved in determining which group of workers is eligible or to what extent; this is best done by the management and the workers within each corporation.

Critics suggest that such reindustrialization will return the country to the nineteenth century and focus on "basic" or "smokestack" industries rather than on post-industrial high-technology industries. The prefix "re-" does point to a return, but it should not be taken literally. A return to strong infrastructure and capital goods sectors does not require a return to the same mix of specific industries. The return implied is to higher investment and innovation in the productive sectors, not to anachronistic details.

On another count, though, reindustrialization must plead guilty as charged: It does favor mitigating the criteria of "comparative advantage" with considerations of developmental economics, social sensitivity, and national security. Studies of developmental economics show that a measure of government-provided incentives and support, even short-term import limitations, is often essential for developing a new industrial base; the same might hold for renewing one. Social considerations provide many reasons why we should not export all blue-collar work to Third World countries; to start with, we have plenty of unskilled labor of our own. National security requires us not to grow so dependent on imported coal, steel, and shipbuilding that we are unable to withstand boycotts or other supply interruptions.

Reindustrialization thus stands between supply-side economics and industrial policy; it is semi-targeted, and the context it seeks to advance is a stronger productive capacity.

TWO ECONOMIC-POLICY PACKAGES

Two main policy positions that competed with each other during the 1980 election provide concrete illustrations of the underlying options. Neither position was cut from one cloth; each mixed elements of the three main policy positions.

Carter's Revitalization

Carter's revitalization mixed much reindustrialization with some industrial policy. Thus, Carter favored reducing labor costs (by offsetting part of business's contributions to Social Security) and helping replace obsolescent plants and equipment (by faster tax writeoffs), two reindustrialization ideas. Programs to retrain workers and thus reduce the resistance to technological innovation were also in accord with reindustrialization. The same might be said about the American Revitalization Board, which aimed to increase *general* collaboration among business, labor, and the government. Touches of industrial policy were to be found in the suggestion to grant investment tax credits to unprofitable firms, tailored to help auto and steel manufacturers, and in industry-specific tripartite committees.

Altogether Carter's revitalization plan hardly left an indelible mark on American political-economic thinking, partly because it was pieced together and released very late in his administration, as his policy positions were being overshadowed by other matters—especially the situation of the hostages in Iran and Senator Kennedy's electoral challenge. Also, Carter firmly believed that balancing the budget was both the best cure for America's economic malaise and the soundest political posture for himself. Since a full-blown revitalization drive would delay that goal by increasing government outlays and by reducing tax revenues, he preferred an anemic revitalization plan, which had neither economic scope nor great appeal, over a more encompassing, but much more costly program.

Reagan's 1981 Economic Recovery Tax Act

Reaganomics is more ambitious than reindustrialization. It seeks not merely to restore the productive capacity of the United States but also to reduce inflation, substantially increase military spending, balance the budget, and change the social profile of the government by doing less for groups that traditionally were Democratic constituencies (such as the poor, minorities, and labor) and more for groups closer to the Republicans (big corporations and small business).

In the following discussions I focus on the steps taken that are relevant to reindustrialization (of which there are quite a few) and their expected consequences for this goal.

New Tax Incentives for Saving and Investment

The best way to encourage a substantial increase in saving and investment, essential if the capital needed for shoring up the infrastructure and the capital goods sectors is to be available without savaging other sectors (military, consumption), is to reduce inflation. The way a successful fight against inflation would affect investment is highlighted if one considers for a moment the effects of a few years of *declining* prices combined with the expectation that they would continue to decrease. With the expectation that one can both collect some interest (probably not more than 2 or 3 percent per annum, under these circumstances) and buy things more cheaply later, the incentive to save and to invest is obviously very considerable. From this view all the components of Reagan's American economic recovery program are relevant, including deregulation, the cut in government expenditures, the supply-side cut in personal income tax, and the size of the budget deficit. To the extent that this program is successful in substantially reducing inflation for extended periods, not merely during a recession, it would provide the soundest base for capital formation.

However, from the beginning, the Reagan administration itself found it unwise to rely only on these across-the-board, generic measures. It topped them with a large set of additional *specific* measures to encourage saving and investment, which might add to capital formation if the general program works, and might spur saving and investment even if the general, non-targeted measures fall short of their goals.

Reduction in Capital Gains Tax. The first step here was actually taken by the Carter administration. In 1978 it reduced federal taxation of capital gains realized from assets held for more than twelve months. Before then, 50 percent of such "long-term" gains was subject to ordinary-income tax rates that could run as high as 70 percent; as a result, top-bracket investors might have had to pay as much as 35 percent tax on any net long-term gains realized during a given tax year. In 1978, a change in the law required only 40 percent of such gains to be taxed at ordinary-income rates. That amounted to a 20 percent tax cut for profits on assets held for at least a year.

The 1978 tax cut is believed to have played a significant role in sparking greater demand for equities, one main way capital flows from savings into investment. The 1981 tax law promised to provide a similar spur to investment. To begin with, for investors in the upper brackets it further cuts taxes on net realized long-term capital gains by slashing the highest marginal tax rate from 70 percent to 50 percent. Result: The maximum tax on long-term gains after June 9, 1981, dropped from 28 percent to 20 percent—a reduction of 28.6 percent, coming on top of the 20 percent tax cut implemented three years earlier.

IRAs and Keoghs. Another boost to investment springs from the new tax law's liberalized provisions for Individual Retirement Accounts (IRAs) and Keogh plans, which now make it possible for virtually all workers to shelter part of their income from ordinary income tax. Tax on contributions to these long-term savings plans and on the interest they earn is deferred until retirement. The 1981 law substantially increased the maximum tax-deductible contribution to Keogh plans, available to the self-employed, and to IRAs. Moreover, while previously IRAs could be opened only by workers not covered by a private pension plan, the new law allows those who already have such coverage to open them.

From a narrower reindustrialization viewpoint, the Keogh and IRA provisions have two particularly welcome features. First, they encourage long-run saving. Second, they exclude investment in "collectibles," a major and unproductive kind of investment that in recent years competed fiercely with investment in productive capacity.

"All Savers" Certificates. An administration-supported initiative by Congress created a tax-exempt savings certificate that can be offered by savings associations, banks, credit unions, and mutual savings banks between September 30, 1981, and January 1, 1983. As everybody has been told in thousands of ads, the one-year certificates carry interest rates equal to 70 percent of the rate on a one-year Treasury bill. Single taxpayers can exclude from taxes a thousand dollars in interest income from these certificates, and couples can exclude twice that much.

Institutions offering the certificates are required to invest three fourths of them in home or farm loans. Because the All Savers certificates have been enacted so far for two years only, most of the funds are not suitable for long-term investments and are expected to go mainly to the short end of the market, such as second mortgages and other shorter-term instruments.

From a capital formation viewpoint, All Savers certificates are likely to generate little new saving. The reason is that despite the certificates' title, they are advantageous only to persons in relatively high tax brackets, roughly 32 percent or higher. As a rule, people in higher tax brackets already have substantial savings, and will tend to shift their funds from other savings accounts to these certificates.

From the viewpoint of reindustrialization, All Savers certificates are even less desirable. The thesis of reindustrialization is that *we not only need more capital, but we need to channel it toward certain broad uses*—semi-target it, specifically, to the infrastructure and capital goods sectors. The number one competitor to this investment in recent decades has been investment in residential housing. As we noted earlier, the proportion of income invested in residential housing has, for the past few decades, been double what it was in the 1870s, at the height of the first industrialization of America. This was not because "natural" market forces played up this high-cost consumer item, but because various tax benefits, not available to other investments, made housing the preferred tax shelter. Indeed, according to one report, 22 percent of the home purchases in 1979 were made by single persons, many of whom bought family-sized houses for investment reasons.[6] Of course, tax consideration also played a role in the considerations of other home buyers, especially those deciding to buy second homes or larger homes than they would have bought otherwise.

A decade of reindustrialization would need to channel funds away from housing (even if, for social reasons, one would increase funds available for low-income housing) because houses do not add to productive capacity; rather, they compete with investment in it.

All Savers certificates were not initiated by an economist's concept of how to redevelop America or set it on the road to economic recovery, but by a lobby anxious to bail out the savings and loan associations, which had invested heavily in housing and were stuck with long-term, low-return mortgages. There were many much less costly ways to bail out these associations, if that was desired. And bailing industries out is contrary to economic reconstruction, which depends in part on allowing inefficient corporations to fail. The Reagan administration, lacking a clear conception of reindustrialization and faced with a lobbying blitz in Congress for the All Savers Act, did not resist. This could be corrected by not extending the life of the All Savers Act when the legislation comes up for renewal. At a minimum, restrictions on the investment of the funds generated should be removed.

"Leasing." Rules were liberalized to allow many more transactions to be characterized as "leasing." Under the new rules, a company showing little or no profit, and thus unable to use its full depreciation allowances and tax credits, can in effect sell those tax benefits to another company. To do this, it arranges to "sell" some of its equipment (or other assets) to another company, and then to lease it back; it retains title to the equipment, but the buyer, now the "lessor," is treated by both companies as if it were the owner. The lessee gains an immediate infusion of cash; the lessor acquires the tax benefits. Alan Greenspan, an advisor to Reagan, has called this new tax provi-

sion "sort of the equivalent of food stamps for undernourished corporations," providing for subsidies to sectors of the economy that the private market wouldn't support.[7]

From a reindustrialization viewpoint this is a highly undesirable measure. The main beneficiaries of the changed leasing rules are weak corporations, corporations that have had little or no profit—or even only losses—often for years in a row; otherwise they could have used the tax benefits themselves. A corporation may be weak for many reasons, including some that are its own fault and some that result from external factors over which it has no control. But if the economy is to adjust to changes in technology and world markets, indeed to the cumulative effect of all changes, corporations that do not adapt, whatever the reason, must be allowed to reduce their size, even go out of business (with some exceptions for genuine national security reasons or in cases of temporary setbacks, such as "dumping"). Humanitarian and social considerations suggest that workers laid off be helped to find new jobs, and that investors be compensated if their loss was due not to their bad judgment but, say, to a change in government policy. Neither requires shoring up failing corporations, which in most cases just delays the adaptation of the economy, and reduces its ability to innovate.

In fact, the new leasing rules smack of industrial policy, since among the prime beneficiaries are two failing industries, autos and steel. (Ford was reported to be selling IBM $100 million to $200 million worth of investment tax credits and depreciation deductions.)[8] Both industries might well have to reduce capacity. U.S. needs for domestic auto and steel production seem to have declined permanently; and national security needs could be met so long as production of certain specialty steels is not endangered and so long as 40 to 60 percent of capacity for all-purpose steel is maintained.

The tax revenues lost through these changes in the leasing rules were estimated to run to $27 billion. Clearly, the sooner this change of leasing regulations is voided, the better for reindustrialization.

Accelerated Depreciation

Conceived as a massive stimulus to new investment, the overhaul of existing depreciation regulations represents the largest business tax cut since the end of World War II. It scraps previous rules, which allowed companies to write off an investment over the "useful life" of the asset, a period that could be twenty years or more. Instead, investments in 1981 or later can be written off over one of four periods, depending on the kind of asset involved: three years for cars, light trucks, equipment for research and development, and equipment that has a useful life of four years or less; five years for virtually all other industrial equipment. This represents a dramatic shortening of writeoff periods for much heavy equipment. For example, previously the normal writeoff period was thirteen years for oil refineries, ten years for pulp and paper manufacturing plants, twelve years for steel mills. Computers (formerly eight years) and aerospace equipment (also eight years) benefit less. Real estate and public utility property can now be written off in ten or fifteen years.

This plan, initiated through a bipartisan effort directed by Senator Lloyd Bentsen (D-Texas) during his tenure as chairman of the Joint Economic Committee, and embraced by both the Carter and the Reagan administrations, constitutes an excellent example of a semi-targeted, reindustrialization approach. It does not seek to continue differentiating among some *three hundred* different kinds of machinery and equipment, each—in the past—calculated to have a different "useful life," but deals with four broad categories. Furthermore, by substantially shortening the "useful life" assumed for most categories, it allows business to write off the expenses involved much more rapidly; that is, to recapture much sooner, via lower taxes, whatever part of the expenditures involved can be recaptured in that way. The net effect is expected to be substantially increased cash flow to corporations and a sizable incentive to replace obsolescent and wornout equipment and machinery, thus making the nation's industry more innovative, or to replace equipment and machinery that are energy-inefficient, thus increasing conservation and reducing inflationary costs.

When I discuss this bill with various groups across the country, I am often asked by the more liberal-minded members of the audience why machinery that makes, say, cosmetics, should be grouped together with oil drills, or autos with main frame computers. My response is that to screen more closely, an approach compatible with industrial policy, would create a bureaucratic and regulatory nightmare and would be highly wasteful in other ways, since those in charge would frequently err in what they encouraged or discouraged. It seems best to set wide supportive contexts, as the tax law does, and let the market do the rest.

Research and Development

In the 1981 tax bill, to spur growth in innovation, corporations are given a 25 percent tax credit for research and experimentation costs, to the extent that current or future expenditures exceed previous investments in the field. The base period for calculating this amount is the average expenditure over the three previous years. In addition, corporations giving new scientific equipment to colleges and universities can in many cases claim a higher tax deduction than would have been allowed under prior law.

We have seen the cardinal role played by innovations in the first industrialization of America, innovations based on strong domestic R&D as well as the imported fruits of R&D in other countries. During the era of underdevelopment in the United States, especially in the 1970s, R&D was shown by several indicators to have weakened both in scope and in application. The new tax credit is a way to provide incentives for the private sector to increase its R&D expenditures.

It is semi-targeted in that it rewards those corporations that increase their expenditures but does not prefer one line of research over another. It contrasts sharply, for instance, with the suggestion to commit $20 billion of federal funds to fusion research, based on a 1980 congressional decision that this specific research project deserves funds over numerous others. Indeed, in the past most public funds for R&D were allocated on the basis of project-by-project reviews. The Reagan approach in this instance favors a more semi-targeted approach, compatible with reindustrialization.

Nevertheless, there is little disagreement among those who study the American R&D sector that the 1981 Economic Recovery Tax Act did much less for R&D than for capital formation. Typically, a General Electric executive said, "It biases the system in the right way, but I don't expect it to have a major stimulative effect."[9] The benefits of the tax credit are estimated to amount to $3.35 billion, or about 1 to 2 percent of what industry is expected to spend on research over the next five years.[10]

It is unclear whether additional semi-targeted tax incentives are the best way to encourage more R&D. The main difficulty in going further in this direction is that while the "R" part of R&D is covered by the new incentives, the "D" part is where the main expenditures are made. They often amount to two-thirds or more of the total R&D expenditures. However, including "Development" in special tax incentives raises the problem that it is very difficult to separate development activities from regular production activities. It is therefore feared that special incentives for development will constitute little more than an open invitation to large-scale tax abuse.

Another suggestion has been made that the government provide capital to certain high-technology industries. This would allow, for instance, the development of the next generation of computers, an area in which the United States is believed to face a concentrated attempt by Japanese firms, backed by hundreds of millions in government money, to push American computer makers out of the market.[11] A similar Japanese thrust is reported in the new field of biotechnology.[12] This bit of industrial policy is rejected by most American business representatives, including those in the industries that would benefit from it, on the same grounds on which industrial policy is typically rejected in the United States: That it would constitute additional government intervention in the marketplace when less is what is needed; that the government would be favoring some corporations over others, and not necessarily the most innovative ones; and that all beneficiaries of its support would be subject to the vicissitudes of future changes in the political climate.

Attention necessarily turns to nonfinancial factors that encourage R&D. Deregulation is widely favored. While few would remove all restrictions, a faster regulatory approval track, and a less costly one, is widely held to be beneficial, especially for the approval of drugs. This constitutes a compromise between those who are concerned with safety and efficacy and those who are anxious to keep drug R&D in the United States (rather than in overseas research centers, thus contributing to their growth), and, above all, to keep American drug-making profitable and competitive. A faster track presumably would allow the needed testing without stretching it over many years. The search is also on for less costly ways of conducting the needed tests.

Suggestions also abound for changes in the institutional framework.[13] Patent policies are said to be important to R&D, since the "ability to control a new technology as property determines in large measure whether new technology development will be undertaken at all"[14]—and it is patent policy that makes a developed technology a controllable property.

Another approach to the institutional framework of R&D, which is beginning to make its first breakthroughs, is university–corporate collaboration. Until recently, universities and corporations regarded each other with considerable suspicion. Universities feared that any close involvement with corporate research would undermine their commitment to basic research, threaten their academic freedom, and entangle them in "crass commercialism." Corporations often viewed universities as loaded with impractical professors and liberal-to-left ideas, hostile to the corporations and their capitalist world. It is not that collaboration did not take place here and there, but it was—and still is—the exception to the rule, often accompanied by considerable trepidation and breast-beating on both sides.

One major recent effort to bring the two worlds closer together was made by the National Commission on Research. It spoke warmly of the benefits for both sides if they could find ways of getting together. For universities: A "market connection" that can improve university researchers' understanding of innovation, development, and marketing, and thus stimulate new research opportunities; "access to additional or complementary technical and physical resources made available by industry"; "longer-term and consistent additional funding for research." For industry: "Specialized equipment with large capital costs not justifiable in an industrial budget"; "expansion . . . in some additional areas of research" beyond an industry's immediate needs, without the expense of developing its own experimental program.[15]

If the Commission's report provided a source of new legitimation, the slower increases in federal research funds for universities generate economic pressure for collaboration. A major attempt to implement these notions came in 1981 from a private businessman, Edwin C. Whitehead, who put up $127 million, a pretty penny, for MIT, a prestigious institution and therefore trendsetting, to open a biomedical research institute. It is not clear to what extent the findings of the institute will be open to all, as the findings of basic research are supposed to be, and to what extent they will be the property of the Whitehead Institute, or will help enrich Revlon, of which Whitehead is a major shareholder and which is moving into the biomedical field. One thing is clear: MIT allowed a major intrusion into the traditional prerogative of a university to appoint its staff according to its own criteria of academic excellence; most of the senior researchers at the Whitehead Institute have been assured professorial status at MIT.[16] (Professor Jonathan King of MIT decried the "commercialization" of university research.)[17] The arrangement might ultimately be modified, but for now it sets a major precedent for universities and corporations if they are to work closely in the age of reindustrialization, in which applied research is of more immediate, urgent priority than basic research.

In a somewhat different approach to the problem, Brookhaven National Laboratory evolved a "participating research team" with IBM, Bell Laboratories, Exxon, and Xerox. Here the private corporations paid for the construction of an experimental station at the university-like Brookhaven, in exchange for the right to share in the research field.

Finally, attention must be paid to the human, motivational element. As I see it, U.S. R&D efforts, applied yield must be increased. American research efforts are highly "basic" in their orientation, *i.e.*, oriented toward science as an end in itself, rather than toward direct utility or service. There is a widely held notion that basic research leads to applications that lead to technological solutions. Hence, the more basic research, sooner or later the more solutions. The following statement from the 1979 final report of the Advisory Committee on Industrial Innovation is typical:

> The importance of basic research to the quality of innovation is extremely important. Without a flow of new basic research, ideas are not present to be explored for commercial application.[18]

Actually, study upon study has shown that each of these areas has its own autonomous development and core of knowledge, and each contributes to the others. Thus, Edison was a technologist, not a scientist, and discovered much through trial and error, not through work derived from scientific principles. And the discovery of technological items such as the telescope, microscope, and IBM card did as much for basic knowledge in astronomy, biology, and the social sciences as for the relevant applied fields.

In the world of research, the matter of prestige cuts as deeply as profit does in the business world. (A scientist will work twenty-five years hoping to be invited to join the Royal Academy or win a Nobel Prize.) Many of the best investigative minds are committed to *basic* research (in universities, or even in government agencies such as the NIH research complex in Bethesda, Maryland, whose annual basic research budget is nearly $2 billion).[19]

Here, rewards and promotion go to those who carry out studies that have no necessary applications and who *publish* results in scientific journals rather than communicate them to citizens or policymakers who might apply them. At present there is considerable stigma, as well as economic penalty, attached to both the "popularizers" of findings and to those who conduct applied research. This is reflected in the survey finding that while only 1 percent of 2,051 scientists doing basic research expressed a desire to engage in applied research, 55 percent of 379 applied scientists wished to work in basic research.[20] Moreover, a grant to study an applied problem will often be "bootlegged" to turn it into basic research.[21] The Law Enforcement Assistance Administration reported at a meeting called by the General Accounting Office in 1973 that, even using a variety of evaluation methods, it has been hard pressed to identify any results from research monies given on a "hands-off" basis to a number of selected universities.[22]

Opponents of a tilt toward applied research—proposed to correct for the present tilt toward basic research—suggest that such guidance interferes with the freedom of science. However, with about 70 percent of basic research publicly funded (and much of the rest funded by industry), very little R&D is really "free." It is committees and agencies that decide what to budget this year for biology and physiology, or whatever, and which topics and research proposals to fund. They could just as easily support a bit more applied work.

The Reagan administration has been rather unaware of this issue. Indeed, by one of those flukes of history, for unrelated reasons, it has been promoting basic research over applied work.[23] This came about through the administration's belief that applied work should be done in the private sector, while basic research is inherently unprofitable and so may deserve some public support. Hence, the administration has been cutting the budgets for applied work more than those for basic research. (That applied research is more costly also favors basic research in a period when the federal budget is being scrutinized line by line to find items to cut.) However, the net result may be quite different from what was intended. The private sector has picked up only a fraction of the applied work the federal government has cut, with the probable result (figures are not yet in) that the American R&D sector will continue to favor basic research over applied.

All this is not an "attack" on basic research, as it probably will be described by some of the high priests of the scientific status quo. Of course, basic research should continue to be funded. However, more funds for applied and developmental work, and above all, recognition of its original contributions and societal merits, would increase the *near term* yield of American R&D as a whole.

HUMAN CAPITAL

While the Reagan administration did go a long way in providing semi-targeted incentives for capital formation, most of them quite suitable to reindustrialization (especially those with the big price tags), it did much less for R&D, and it did even less, systematically, for other elements of reindustrialization. Regarding human capital, no schemes were advanced or even developed to allow workers to participate in productivity gains. This is an essential element if workers are to become more motivated to contribute to progress, and if the American industrial system is to shift gradually from reliance on cost of living allowances to a productivity-based reward system, more compatible with reindustrialization.

Representatives of the administration may say that it did take a giant step in motivating people of all backgrounds—investors and executives, workers and entrepreneurs—when it engineered as its lead item (in terms of public attention) the personal income tax cut of 25 percent over three years. However, because of rising Social Security taxes and the movement of people into higher brackets during these same years due to inflation, the personal income tax is expected actually to decline by a net of only 3 percent, which for most people will amount to a rather small dollar amount.

Moreover, from a reindustrialization viewpoint, the fact that the personal income tax is non-targeted means that much of the previously taxed monies left in individual hands will flow to consumption rather than to savings and investment. Supply-side economists suggest, and have some data to show, that concentrating the tax-cut dollar at higher income levels concentrates it where people save and invest most. (It is estimated that in 1982 roughly 35 percent of all these lost revenues will go to taxpayers whose annual income is fifty thousand dollars or higher, and only 16 percent to those whose income is twenty thousand dollars or less.)[24] It remains to be seen whether individuals, even in these brackets, will save and invest much of the tax revenues released to them in a relatively high-inflation environment.

Little was done to motivate workers beyond these general, non-targeted approaches. Possibly not much more can be done by the government. Precisely because we deal here with the human element—with values, sentiments, perceptions, and motivations—the government is a particularly unsuited agent, certainly for close and detailed intervention as distinct from broad-gauged economic incentives. Much more must come from the private sector, where until recently there has been precious little movement in this direction. Three ideas illustrate the kind of thinking and experimentation that is needed: Scanlon plans, ESOP, and Quality of Worklife.

All three are basically cross-commitment ideas. They seek to satisfy the workers, but not at the cost of production and efficiency; on the contrary, they are to enhance production as well. The following examples are not intended to do justice to the programs themselves but to illustrate an approach.

Scanlon plans provide company-wide incentive systems based on two elements: work force suggestions for cost-saving and other ways to enhance productivity, evaluated by labor-management teams; and a bonus system based on measurements of gains in productivity and a formula for sharing 75 percent of the gains among the workers. Although the first Scanlon plan was introduced in 1945, the extent to which such plans have been used is not clearly known; according to a 1967 estimate, they had been tried by about five hundred American corporations, mainly small ones.[25]

Several case studies show that if the organizational climate is supportive, the Scanlon plan can produce substantial gains, but there is no conclusive confirmation of the value of the plan. Nor has it been successfully introduced in large corporations, where the relationship between corporate success and individual efforts and attitudes is much more tenuous and less visible than in small companies.

Much more widely used are *profit-sharing plans* in which part of employees' wages is paid in stock in the company they work for, or in cash bonuses dependent on its success, or held until some future date. There were an estimated 250,000 such plans in the United States in the seventies. One plan alone, established by Sears, Roebuck in 1916, had $3 billion in assets by 1973.[26]

The difficulties with these plans are similar to those of Scanlon plans—the relationship of individual efforts to results is far from clear. Unlike Scanlon plans, these plans establish no specific channel to seek workers' suggestions and evaluate and implement them. Also, the total amounts of compensation involved are often too small to motivate much. Finally, labor unions tend to oppose these plans because they bring workers closer to the corporation, away from the union.

For twenty-five years Louis Kelso has been advocating another version of this idea, which captured the support of Senator Russell Long and which has been tried by several corporations. Economists consider Kelso a crank, according to *Forbes*, which hurried to add that this might be the best thing going for him.[27] Without going into the odd arguments Kelso advances for his program or subscribing to the analysis that underlies it, one can readily outline the idea itself. The plan, called the *Employee Stock Ownership Plan* (*ESOP*), calls for corporations to raise the credit they need to expand production by issuing stock to their workers; that is, part of the workers' wages goes to pay for the credit, and in exchange they get to own part of the corporation, collect dividends, and benefit from appreciation of the stock. Presumably, owner-workers would care more about their corporation and their work than nonowning workers.

More recently, especially following the widespread notion that Japan has found a more effective way to motivate the labor force than the United States, there has been great interest and very substantial experimentation in major American corporations, including General Motors, Honeywell, and numerous others, in *Quality of Worklife* (QWL) programs or "circles." As is often the case in such developments, until the dust settles, until the hoopla dies, it is hard to tell how much is fad and how much is lasting improvement in organizational structure.

According to Paul Greenberg and Edward Glaser, who are among the leading students of the field, QWL requires "the existence of a real and ever-present opportunity for individuals or task groups at any level in the organization to influence their working environment."[28] The emphasis should be on "real," as distinct from posturing by those who believe that creating an image of participatory, open management is enough. Also, it serves to separate real QWL from what is advanced by managers who are quite sincere in their intentions but for reasons of personality or ingrained organizational habits find it impossible to let workers participate in some measure in decision-making (which often implies criticism by those lower in rank). As Greenberg and Glaser continue, "real" QWL requires

> a climate and structure that differs from the traditional hierarchical organization. It calls for an open style of management, such that information is shared and challenges or suggestions . . . are genuinely encouraged. It also requires expeditious, respectful and appropriate responses to inputs of those kinds.[29]

When implemented in that way, QWL is said to lead to less labor-management conflict, more effective upward flow of cost-saving and other ideas from the lower in rank, and a higher sense of satisfaction, involvement, and responsibility among workers. All these, in turn, lead, though not necessarily in the very strict way one might hope for, to higher productivity, better quality of products, lower absenteeism, and less turnover.[30]

One of the first and most influential programs of this kind was introduced by Sidney Harman at a plant in Bolivar, Tennessee. The program, started in 1972, involved both opening management to workers' ideas and providing numerous educational opportunities for them. The result is reported to have been a near doubling of output on several production lines.[31] No wonder many came to study Harman's methods and try to emulate them.

In a steel plant in Louisville, Ohio, workers suggested that management improve the organization of orders for stainless steel of differing specifications, and thus reduce the amount of time spent changing rolls. This and related reforms resulted in a 19 percent increase in the production the first year it was tried, with output rising from 18 tons to 21.37 tons per hour.[32]

A Gallup survey of workers found that many of them have been thinking about possible changes in their company that would improve its performance. A remarkable 44 percent say they have thought about it "a lot of the time," and another 18 percent "sometimes." But, as economist William Bowen commented, "It is a pretty safe bet that many of those workers had never been made to feel that their ideas on improving performance would be welcomed and appreciated, let alone rewarded."[33] In the same vein, Michael Maccoby argues, in his book *The Leader,* that the essential requirement for human capital for the eighties is a manager who is more sensitive to the feelings of the new breed of workers.[34] In short, the proper use of human capital, particularly important in an era of redevelopment short on capital, has a long way yet to go.

Public policy has some limited roles here. It can provide a model for such plans by QWL circles in government agencies, call attention to successful efforts in the private sector, and in some situations provide tax benefits, as it does in effect for ESOP plans. However, quite suitably in a new semi-targeted era, much of the actual modification of the work patterns must be done by the corporations themselves and their workers.

More important are the relations between labor and the administration in the public arena itself. The basic question is whether cooperation is sought and achieved or an implicit assumption is made that economic reconstruction can be undertaken without labor's support. The first road leads to consultation with labor leaders, to an American Reindustrialization Board or its equivalent, to policies that reduce the pain of adjustment to technological changes (*e.g.,* support for retraining programs and for enhanced labor mobility from declining areas to rising ones), and so on. The opposite approach assumes that rising market pressures, high unemployment, and decline in public support for labor unions, will suffice for the administration to have its way, whether the workers and their representatives like it or not. The American tradition of adversary relations among the main sectors—business, labor, and government—promotes the second approach. However, in view of the sizable pain a major reindustrialization drive is likely to entail, in a period when "givebacks" are needed to keep up with international competition where once hefty raises were the rule, it seems that a policy of collaboration is called for.

Superficially it is easy to talk about Working Together for a Revitalized America, my recommendation for an election slogan. True, we have already witnessed, during the 1981–82 recessions, management and labor unions reopening contracts and working out givebacks, job security, and—in one case—even labor representation on the corporate board (Douglas A. Fraser on Chrysler's board). Eastern Airlines worked out a "trade" of salary and wage cuts in exchange for profit-sharing, and so on. And there has been a relative absence of prolonged strikes and shutouts.[35] However, for a deeper change to occur, one that will last beyond the recessions, a basic change of orientation is necessary. Management has to come to view workers as persons of equal status, persons one can reason with, learn from, cooperate with, and respect. Workers have to shed a paranoid view of management. Some of this change has taken place; much is yet to be achieved.

OTHER ELEMENTS

The Reagan economic recovery program has so far focused on the elements of capital; it is here that its contribution to reindustrialization is clearest. Other elements—energy, transportation, and financial/legal institutions—are basically viewed as likely to benefit from less government and from across-the-board incentives, without a series of additional semi-targeted steps. Thus, typically, one of the Reagan administration's first steps was complete decontrol of the domestic price of oil. Later, it sought to remove special tax benefits for those who insulate their homes, on the assumption that the high price of energy, expressed in the market, is a quite sufficient motivation to conserve (and also because the budget deficit needed trimming). The idea of abolishing the Department of Energy (while transferring many of its programs to other departments) is largely a symbolic tribute to the notion that no specific policies are needed in the energy area. The 1980–81 oil glut, which stopped the rapid rise of oil prices, further discouraged specific action.

Energy

From a reindustrialization viewpoint, semi-targeted incentives to conserve and to produce energy from alternate sources seem called for. The main reasons are two. One is that between 1973 and 1980 the cost of oil increased much more than prices in general. That means that oil, which used to be a relatively cheap means of production, has become a very costly one. Unless it is used more efficiently, the whole economy will continue to suffer from the need to spend more on energy and hence less on other means of production, from R&D to human capital. Some tax incentives to conserve, some additional investment in energy-related R&D, would help accelerate the "rewiring" of America, increasing its energy efficiency more rapidly. Free-market purists might be willing to grant this sector a temporary dispensation on the ground that it was thrown out of kilter by non-market forces, including foreign governments, and allow that some adjustment assistance might be appropriate.

Second, reindustrialization suffers from a huge wealth transfer caused by the post-1973 increase in the cost of imported oil. To reiterate, the U.S. oil bill for 1980 was $82 billion, while the total value of the American corporations listed on the New York Stock Exchange was about $900 billion.[36] Thus it would take OPEC and company little more than five years to buy up half of these corporations. Of course, the notion of such a purchase is sheerly hypothetical. Congress would pass laws to prohibit it (as it acted recently when foreign control of American banks seemed excessive), and a run on Wall Street by the oil-rich would drive up the price well beyond $900 billion. The point, though, is that they are doing *worse* to us; rather than buying stocks in American corporations, they are transferring our assets overseas and building oil refineries, steel mills, and whatnot in their countries. Hence, calling attention to the size of the wealth drain engineered by OPEC is not a call to lock the gates of the New York Stock Exchange to protect American companies from alien buyers, but a way to highlight the enormity of the "tax" imposed by the oil exporters.

"Tax" is a proper term. The price of imported oil does not reflect production costs, which in the case of Saudi Arabia amounts to but a few percent of the price charged. Like a tax, the price of most imported oil is set by governments, not the marketplace. And, like a tax, it is used as an instrument to transfer wealth from the people (of oil-consuming countries) to a bunch of governments, to be lavished on those they favor.

Various reasons have been advanced that Americans need not worry too much about this mountainous transfer of wealth.

1. Tit-for-Tat Selling. "The more we pay them, the more they buy from us—agricultural products, industrial plants, military hardware. Trade increases. No harm done. What will they do with all these dollars, eat them?" This notion ignores the *real* exchange rate, which reflects how many work-hours we have to put into paying for each item we buy. With the drastic change against us in this exchange rate, reflected in the more rapid increase in oil prices than in the prices of our exports, we have to work ever longer and harder to pay for what we import, raising their standard of living, and lowering ours.

2. Recycling. "Banks can finesse the oil problem by arranging for loans from the oil exporters to us; in this way we can keep paying for the imports." Aside from disregarding the wealth drain issue, this narrow financing/banking view of the solution overlooks a rather troubling detail: Our interest payments on oil exporters' loans will soon exceed what we used to pay for *total* oil imports. Interest on interest is added to our pyramid of debt to oil exporters. The total outflow of dollars has increased to the point that banks find it difficult to continue to recycle such amounts, although the original alarm was exaggerated. And the financial fix creates a very powerful dependency second only to an oil-based one: If the oil-exporting countries ever come calling for their loans—or only, say 25 percent of them . . .

3. Conservation and Development. "If we just get our domestic energy act together, use less imported oil, dig more of our own oil wells, develop alternative sources of energy, and conserve more energy in general, our oil bill and dependency will decline and, soon, disappear." Indeed, the high price of oil is a free-market spur to develop and conserve. However, in seven years of talking increased production and conservation, we *increased* our dependence on imported oil from roughly 35 percent of our oil needs to about 45 percent in 1979. (We did better in 1980–82, largely because of temporarily smaller need due to two recessions.)

Moreover, whatever we gain in reduction of our demand on the world's oil can be quite readily offset by supply cuts. In recent years the U.S. press has been full of "encouraging" accounts of new American drilling spurred by partial deregulation of domestic oil prices. Indeed, 1978 saw a rare increase in U.S. oil production; output increased by about half a million barrels a day from 1977 to 1978. In view of the "aging," deterioration, and exhaustion of many U.S. wells, this is considered quite a record. *However,* Saudi Arabia in the past cut production, in one fell swoop, by a million barrels a day. Assume we really pulled our belts tighter and doubled 1978's achievements; with their own oil fields deteriorating, and their need for additional revenues rather limited, they could cut production by another million barrels a day before you could say "development."

Given the sharply increased price of oil and the enormous wealth drain to oil-exporting countries, it seems desirable both to encourage lower American use of oil and to reduce the wealth transfer immediately by imposing a levy on imported oil (not to be confused with a tax on domestic sales of gasoline). The levy would be absorbed, at least in part, by oil-exporting countries, especially if introduced while there is an oil glut. The billions in revenue generated this way could be dedicated to helping finance American reindustrialization, especially energy-related R&D and the development of alternative energy sources.*

Transportation

The Reagan administration has no specific transportation redevelopment policy. Deregulation is to be applied to railroads but retracted for trucking. Returning publicly run railroads to the private sector—or closing them down—has been suggested, in line with the nontargeted approach. However, if only to make up for decades of neglect, transportation systems need some semi-targeted help, even some infusion of public funds, above and beyond reliance on the private sector alone, to rehabilitate and maintain them and to introduce innovations.

A criterion not often relied upon in the past should be pivotal in the future: the degree to which various transportation systems and mixes are capital-intensive. The reasons are that capital will continue to be scarce, and hence expensive, and that so much is needed for the reindustrialization period. This will be reflected in higher interest rates throughout the eighties than in the preceding decades. As a result, reindustrialization favors less capital-intensive systems—communications (*e.g.* conference calls) over travel, for instance, and buses over rapid transit systems for the movement of people. Which systems are most suited, from this viewpoint, for the movement of goods requires an extensive study, which has yet to be undertaken.

This is not to suggest that the government should involve itself in detailed, industrial policy-like decision-making. But I believe the context created by the polity should favor a market that will promote transportation systems that are less capital-intensive. For the same reason, and via the same mechanisms, transportation systems dealing with freight should take priority over those that transport mainly people, airlines especially.

---

* These lines were written before this idea resurfaced in the 1982 Budget deliberations. The author previously advocated this policy idea. See "Stop That Wealth Drain," *National Journal*, Vol. 13, No. 26 (June 27, 1981), pp. 1181–1182.

Financial/Legal

Changes in financial/legal institutions are already rushing along toward greater adaptation to the new age, first and foremost by deregulation of savings and loans, banks, and other financial institutions. Much more leeway for venture capital and modified antitrust laws are also among the main changes. Some, such as MIT economist Lester Thurow, have called for total repeal of antitrust laws.[37] But this would be one of those instances in which social insensitivity sets in. Preserving the prohibition on price-fixing and concern about excessive concentration of corporate power by intra-industry mergers are justified, if only to keep the market working. At the same time, several elements of the antitrust laws could be modified. These include the notions that the important issue is what share of the national market a company controls rather than what share of the national and international market; and that corporations should not collaborate even in research and development of safety devices and pollution-abatement equipment or in exports.

Specialists in venture capital tend to agree that the reduction of the capital gains tax was the most important step for this sector, already turning it around from a parched area to a richly watered one. Some even suggest that since the second reduction in capital gains tax in 1981, a shortage of investment opportunities for venture capital has replaced the previous shortage of venture capital. Numerous specific legal changes to make it easier to start and sustain small businesses, which is where most venture capital is placed, have also been undertaken as a sort of a semi-targeted benefit to the most innovative (and the most labor-intensive) sector of the economy. Other plans are afoot to make it easier for new and small companies to sell stocks privately.

In the area of financial/legal institutions, the initiative that most needs to be undertaken is the one both policymakers and the public seem quite unprepared to tackle: the need to channel credit to productive purposes, away from consumer goods, for the duration of the reindustrialization period. Allocation of credit is generally considered an anathema, an intervention of the grossest kind in the marketplace. Little understood or even noted is that the government intervenes heavily in credit allocation all the time, although these interventions are based on spot decisions rather than on national policy. For years, to the tune of many scores of billions of dollars, government has provided low-cost credit to residential housing (low-income housing, FHA), to college students, and—via tax-exempt bonds—to schools, sewer systems, hospital construction, and municipal governments, all dedicated largely or wholly to consumer goods or services. Low-cost credit has also been made available for industrial development and new sources of energy, but only recently, and in much smaller amounts in comparison. The basic reason is that since a national credit policy (outlining which sectors to favor) is considered "unthinkable," each decision is made independently, by an agency working with "its" congressional committees and constituencies. Thus, HUD, in developing low-income housing policy, getting authorization, and so on, deals with the Senate Subcommittee on Housing and Urban Affairs and with the House Subcommittee on Housing and Community Development. The Department of Education, in dealing with student loans, with the House Subcommittee on Education, Arts, and Humanities and the Senate Subcommittee on Post-Secondary Education.

OMB has moved in recent years to form an overview of these government-provided credits, but even it was unable to establish their full scope. There are so many different ways and channels for the government to subsidize credit that it is difficult to know where government support, often provided through several layers of intermediaries, stops. By one estimate, in FY 1980 the net funds involved totaled $105 billion, roughly 23 percent of the total credit in the American economy.[38] OMB estimated that in 1980 hidden subsidies generated $24 billion worth of incentives, much of it in forms that make reindustrialization more difficult (by drawing capital to other uses) rather than enhancing it.[39] Aside from charting these credits, OMB has focused its efforts almost completely on cutting back the total amount of government borrowing (to free credit for private use) rather than on making sense of the implied priorities as tools of semi-targeted signals.[40]

Felix Rohatyn, New York City investment banker and Chairman of the Municipal Assistance Corporation, has suggested a revival of the RFC for these purposes. The Reconstruction Finance Corporation was introduced by Herbert Hoover in 1932. It invested some $40.6 billion in supporting private industries over twenty-one years of depression and two world wars. The renewed RFC would purchase the stocks of industries in need of support, and thus allow them to gain capital when the private markets are closed to the industries because they are considered too risky. It would also issue loans at favorable rates to developers of the infrastructure, including local governments.

There is no doubt in my mind that some channels of credit to productive uses are needed. We channel it anyhow; only currently the direction reflects largely the priority of the Golden Age of Consumption rather than reindustrialization. There remain important subsidiary questions as to the scope of the confusion and the degree to which the decisions involved are going to be industry- or even corporation-specific, which would push an RFC toward industrial policy; or—I would recommend—keep the support broad in scope, sector-wide, and letting the market render the micro-decisions.

IN SUMMARY

The 1981 Economic Recovery Tax Act, combined with the policies of less government, indicated a clear choice—at the critical policy junction. It sought to return America to a pathway of high economic growth. In this effort, first priority had been accorded to capital formation, through a wide range of semi-targeted tax incentives, and a second place to promoting R&D. The other elements of reindustrialization in larger measure have been left to benefit from the general climate and from reduction of the government; that is, from nontargeted measures.

Within the sizable tax incentive package, (estimated at $750 billion) and a notable departure from past policies, the changes in IRAs and Keoghs are particularly suitable to reindustrialization, because they encourage longer-run investment and exclude investment in nonproductive "collectibles." Even more clearly semi-targeted are the accelerated depreciation and R&D incentives. Particularly unsuitable are All Savers certificates, which generate little net new saving at great losses to the U.S. Treasury, and which channel funds toward residential housing, an already bloated consumer good. Similarly, the changed rules on leasing provide major benefits to unprofitable industries, a misguided touch of industrial policy. Much more must be done to secure a well-prepared and motivated labor force, to form energy and transportation policies, and to spur innovation.

The main difficulties are not those internal to the approach; those can be corrected readily by not extending the All Savers, eliminating the leasing rules, and a few other such modifications. The main difficulties lie in the combination of massive tax incentives with other approaches aimed at other policy targets, especially the Thatcherist, monetarist tight-money-supply policy of the Federal Reserve, and the high defense outlays. The first aim of the tight-money-supply approach is to reduce inflation, not to spur economic growth. Moreover, the tight monetary policy seeks to get its way by engineering an economic slowdown, if not a prolonged recession, while other elements of the Reagan economic program, especially the supply-side tax cut for individuals, seek to cure inflation by stimulating higher production.[41]

The clash between monetary policy and fiscal policy in 1981–82 resulted in very high "real" interest rates, which made investment so costly it was widely discouraged, and which more than offset the gain due to beneficial tax incentives. Brookings economist Barry Bosworth calculated that high interest rates offset 90 percent of the tax break for "short-lived assets" (equipment); for longer-lasting machinery and buildings, which were treated somewhat less generously in the 1981 tax bill, the interest rates more than offset the tax breaks.[42] The monumental deficits that resulted from a very steep increase in defense spending, very large tax cuts, and comparatively smaller cuts in government expenditures other than defense, caused the Reagan administration to replace one kind of big government by another, one ready to absorb, most of all, personal savings to finance those deficits, leaving little to finance the work of the private sector, let alone reindustrialization.[43]

The issue runs much deeper than a technical dissonance between monetary and fiscal policies. At issue is our inability to advance several economic goals simultaneously, and the need to choose which one to favor. Political leadership, in both the Carter and the Reagan administrations, has tended to deny the need for a choice and to promise progress on all fronts simultaneously, or at least in close succession. However, recent experience suggests that such multiple achievements may be elusive, indeed that in the present environment the simultaneous pursuit of partially incompatible economic goals may itself cause major economic difficulties.

Implicit in the various specific policies advanced are choices. The restrictive monetary policy of the Federal Reserve in effect puts fighting inflation first, even if the Fed hopes that a less inflationary world will later be best for economic growth. The supply-siders are fundamentally concerned with growth, even if they say it is the best way to fight inflation. Neither is as concerned with full employment as the press releases say, though higher growth is more compatible with high employment than is restrictive monetary policy. In this setting of priorities among economic goals, reindustrialization sides with those that stress economic growth.

High defense spending, for reasons discussed above, seems essential, even though one may disagree about specific items of expenditure, and especially oppose the rapid pace of the buildup. And, as necessary as defense spending is, from a narrow economic perspective it adds little to goods and services people can buy and much to government expenditures—that is, it is highly inflationary.

The main point of all this is that the very considerable start toward reindustrialization may be derailed not so much because of major intrinsic shortcomings in the approach, but because of the combination of this policy with others that are based either on incompatible assumptions or on other priorities.

Last but not least, the policies reviewed so far deal largely with economic factors. A full commitment to reindustrialization, though, entails changes in other factors, on the human, educational, community level, in which the role and potential of public policy are much more limited.

CHAPTER FOURTEEN

Societal Reconstruction

Economic policies are the easiest part of the reindustrialization drive; wise persons can formulate them, and corporate leaders, bankers, managers, and labor leaders can put them into effect. I am not underestimating the limitations of the scientific disciplines involved, the black holes in the needed data, the difficulties of evolving consensus among experts, between Congress and the Federal Reserve Board, and so on. Nevertheless, economic policy is relatively "malleable," subject to engineering.

However, for reindustrialization to take place, for the appropriate policies to be successfully implemented, there must be parallel changes in American power relations, institutions, and mentality. Otherwise the needed economic policies will not be propelled forward by sufficient commitment. Compared to economic policies, these noneconomic developments are much less subject to public policy, more determined by ongoing societal processes that no one can control. Fortunately, these processes have been moving most Americans to a stage at which, after decades of retreat and ambivalence, they seem ready to be mobilized for reaffirmation in general, and for support of reindustrialization in particular.

If we follow the pendulum notion that the societal focus shifts back and forth between instrumental needs (such as production) and social priorities (such as concern with social justice), by 1980 a swing toward economic priorities, technology, and administrative efficiency was "overdue." A swing toward reconstruction of community of the kind outlined earlier, which strengthens the ability to commit and to act and generates energies that can be dedicated to economic redevelopment, has begun. Progress on this front has been quite uneven. Changes in mentality, shoring up the legitimation of rationality, have advanced faster than the reconstruction of key institutions, especially the schools and the family. The power base supportive of reindustrialization has evolved even more rapidly, and therein lies a major potential danger.

POWER: WILL THE VICTORS BE SINGLE-MINDED?

The Return of the Pro-Industrial Groups

The pro-industrial groups, taken aback by the rising tide of social groups and for a time relatively weak and inactive, by 1982 were on their way to re-establishing their capacity to act individually, and even in coalition.[1]

During the last years of the seventies, and as the eighties began, the various business groups became much more active politically. There was a rapid increase in the number and power of business-based political action committees, often referred to as PACs. In 1975 there were only eighty-nine corporate PACs; by 1979 they numbered eight hundred.[2] In 1980, business PACs gave $35 million to congressional candidates, nearly three times what labor gave. A few years back, in 1976, labor outspent business, by $8.2 million to $7.1 million.[3]

PACs started to flourish after Congress, in the mid-seventies, limited the contributions individuals can make to political candidates, while federal laws were interpreted to mean that corporations could pool the contributions of their employees and, on their behalf, spend the money on political action. The decision-makers of most corporate PACs, those who decide where the funds are to flow, are typically management-level officials. In addition to corporations, industrial and trade associations formed their own PACs; among the largest are the Automobile and Truck Dealers Election Action Committee, the Realtors Political Action Committee, and the Transportation Political Education League.[4]

As business leaders have become less reluctant and more sophisticated in political action, they have regained impressive power. As it was summed up in the *Wall Street Journal:*

Generally, these days top corporate managers aren't dumb about politics any more. Big business leaders such as Irving Shapiro of Du Pont, Reginald Jones of General Electric and Clifton Garvin of Exxon understand and play power politics, both domestically and internationally, as well as anyone. They have welded the Business Roundtable, representing the nation's top corporations, into one of the most powerful lobbying forces in Washington. If anyone doubts their clout, take another look at the tax bill Congress just passed, which includes more tax breaks for business than anyone would have thought imaginable just a couple of years ago.[5]

An additional comment, as to what business groups can do in Washington with the increased war chests, must be read slowly to savor fully the delicate way it is put. It testifies both to the renewed power of business in Washington (in which even the Democrats were for the first time in memory fighting in 1981 for a tax bill that would give business more benefits than individuals) and to what businessmen do not do "wholesale," but only on the retail side:

It is likely that top managers of giant corporations are too honest and too smart to try wholesale bribery of U.S. politicians. They don't have to. The inherent political power of the mega-corporations, bolstered by legal campaign contributions via their PACs, gives them enormous and still growing clout.[6]

Almost as significant for the power base as the increased mobilization of single corporations and industrial groups has been coalition-building. The *National Journal* reported in 1980 that "business groups have put coalitions together in virtually every successful major lobbying effort they have made in the past three years," including efforts to roll back and cut into labor law reform, the consumer protection agency, and FTC legislation.[7]

One of the problems faced by any group in the field of political action is that it must cope not only with the opposition of groups that have conflicting interests, but also with the resistance of other groups that represent the same general interests but have divergent interpretations of the situation and different ideas about what is to be done. Thus, for instance, the history of the labor unions tells not only of confrontations with business groups, but also of prolonged struggles within the labor movement due to differences such as those between the CIO and the AFL, as to whether mass-production industries should be organized along industrial or craft lines, and how much effort should be channeled into political versus industrial action. Similarly, the black community faced not only white conservative opposition but also conflicts among the NAACP, CORE, and the Urban League. In the case of the business community, often seen by critics as a monolithic "Wall Street," rivalry among various industries, and among various industial action groups, has often weakened each of them, and all of them together.

A case in point: During the 1976 Carter election campaign, the business community pushed for the removal of double taxation on dividends, which are taxed once as corporate earnings and again after they are paid out to investors. When Carter won and his staff started to work on the 1977 tax bill, they faced two facts: First, removing double taxation of dividends would be rather costly; it was estimated that the revenues lost to the U.S. Treasury would run as high as $17 billion. Second, several major industries showed little interest in the suggested tax change. Thus, AT&T was said to be much more concerned than the semiconductor industry, which rarely paid any dividends. The item was dropped.

The lesson was not lost on the rising pro-industrial groups. In 1980 the various industrial groups agreed informally, under the leadership of the Business Roundtable, to go for accelerated depreciation, which would eventually yield the industries an estimated $142.8 billion over five years.[8] Some industries had little to gain from the bill, because they use rather few machines (such as the insurance industry) or were particularly interested in other items (such as the semiconductor industry, which was more interested in tax credits for R&D). However, it was agreed that even those industries would line up to support accelerated depreciation in 1980, and that in future tax years "their turn would come" and their demands would be supported by all involved. Indeed, various other tax measures, such as those favoring R&D and the savings and loan associations, were added to the 1981 tax bill only after accelerated depreciation was safely locked in.

This major instance and some others of successful coalition-building (*e.g.*, in favor of reducing taxes on capital gains, and generally in support of the 1981 Reagan economic package), do not suggest that differences of interest and perspective have vanished from the business community or that various member groups will no longer collide. But they do suggest that a greater capacity to act in unison has been achieved than existed for much of the preceding two decades.

In 1980, under the heading "The Business Lobby Discovers That in Unity There Is Strength," the *National Journal* commented:

> Business lobbyists are cooperating more closely and trying to avoid overlapping or conflicting positions. . . . Until 1978, business was very much on the defensive as it resisted proposals backed by liberals and labor leaders. Now it is clearly seizing the offensive and setting its own agenda.[9]

The president of the U.S. Chamber of Commerce, Richard L. Lesher, was given credit for having sought a wider coalition, working with such groups as the National Association of Manufacturers and the Business Roundtable.[10] In addition, various business lobbyists coordinate their efforts in a special tax policy group called, after the hotel where they met, the "Carlton group."[11]

We have already seen that as business groups gained strength, the groups that could oppose them had largely weakened. Liberals, consumer groups, and labor unions had lost in membership, contributions, and the support of the public at large.[12] The environmental groups had probably weakened less than the others. And the social groups' ability to act in unison, as a coalition, had become particularly low.

The net result of the increase in the power of one set of groups and the decline in that of the opposing groups was a fairly sharp shift in the power balance in favor of the groups supporting economic over social priorities in general, key reindustrialization policies—and their own special interests. About the only thing that might be said to make the change less surprising, and to put it in truer historical perspective, is to recall that while the pro-industrial groups were relatively weak during the golden age of consumption and social priorities, they were never weak in an absolute sense, but only relatively less strong than before. Having lost only part of their strength, they recovered rather speedily.

The danger in the rapid resurgence of the pro-industrial groups is that as they enter the eighties, they may be carried away by their rediscovered power and try to turn the social clocks back to the nineteenth century. Instead of being content to be the most powerful coalition, able to sustain the societal core project, the top priority of economic growth, and to hold at bay other claimants to this status, they may try to dominate to the point that all other considerations are swept aside, all other groups and needs neglected, in a combination of zeal with a touch of revenge. Such domination would entail little interest in searching for and working out strategies of cross-commitment, which allow the same resources to be used for both industrial and social advancement, or acknowledging the legitimacy of service to other needs.

Domination is, on the power side, the parallel of narrow, focused rationality: It furthers social insensitivity. Thus, it is one thing to question the extent to which a weakened economy, in its reconstruction drive, can afford to satisfy ever-greater environmental demands, and quite another to see in all questions raised by the public about the safety of nuclear plants, for instance, an undue intrusion into good business judgment. It is one thing to oppose the excessive regulatory zeal of OSHA and the Consumer Product Safety Commission, and quite another to label the drive for worker or consumer protection a mad quest for a "risk-free society." It is one thing to oppose featherbedding and increases in wages and, especially, in fringe benefits that are not justified by increases in productivity, and quite another to go union-busting.

True, social movements and political actions never have the precision of gold scales; some overreaction is inherent in political action by all camps. Nevertheless, uninhibited attempts to push for economic priorities, will run into the fact that other societal elements have not changed direction nearly so sharply as the power base. That is, legitimation of economic priorities, based on the rational mentality, and reconstruction of societal institutions are not nearly as tilted toward economic growth as is the power base. Moreover, the distribution of power itself is not one-sided enough to sustain a socially insensitive policy.

Aside from being historically out of touch and out of step, such narrowly focused reindustrialization is undesirable because it would intensify the swing of the sociological pendulum, while what is called for is moderating it. Societies, we have seen, have a multiplicity of needs, instrumental and expressive, productive and social. Economic needs were neglected in recent decades, and in this sense a return to an economic *priority* is called for, even overdue. But single-minded preoccupation with production needs (and related ones of economic growth, technology, and administrative efficiency), combined with prolonged neglect of all other needs, will lead to a violent swing in the opposite direction. It is not accidental, for instance, that Secretary of the Interior James Watt, who acted more extremely on behalf of pro-production needs and groups than the White House or the heads of other agencies, "succeeded" in mobilizing the environmental groups much more effectively than, say, Commerce did in mobilizing its natural opposition, the consumer groups. Across the board, the almost total disregard by the Reagan administration for black, labor, and other social needs has had a similar Watt-effect. As of 1982, social groups report a growing flow of contributions and renewal of membership interest. And a growing segment of the public sees the Reagan administration as "unfair" and tilted toward the rich.

The same issue extends outside the government arena to the self-perception and action of business groups in the marketplace and in society. Indeed, the traditional argument has been revived that these most powerful groups in the American society *should not* concern themselves with any business other than business.

According to this view of business responsibility, business goals and behavior are—and ought to be—primarily motivated by profit and guided by criteria of economic efficiency and growth in production of goods and services; this by itself will serve the community:

> Profits are kept to reasonable or appropriate levels by market competition, which leads the firm pursuing its own self-interest to an end that is no part of its conscious intention: enhancement of the public welfare. It need not recognize any responsibility to the public to accomplish this result.[13]

The catchline used to be: "what's good for General Motors is good for America." More recently it has become "The business of business is business."

According to Milton Friedman, a hands-down favorite intellectual of the business community,

> There is one and only one social responsibility of business—to use its resources and engage in activities designed to increase its profits as long as it stays within the rules of the game, which is to say, engages in free and open competition, without deception or fraud.[14]

Asked to comment on the social responsibilities of the business corporation, Friedman replied,

> Most of the talk has been utter hogwash. In the first place, the only entities who can have responsibilities are individuals; a business cannot have responsibilities. So, the question is, do *corporate executives*, provided they stay within the law, have responsibilities in their business activities other than to make as much money for their stockholders as possible? And my answer to that is, no, they do not. . . . The great virtue of the private enterprise system is precisely that by maximizing corporate profits, corporate executives contribute far more to the social welfare than they do by spending stockholders' money on what they as individuals regard as worthwhile activity.[15]

Peter Drucker, a widely followed authority on business management, although he would qualify this traditional position, recognizes a core of validity in it. In his view, to state

> that business should stick to its business, that is, to the economic sphere, is not a denial of responsibility. It is indeed the only consistent position in a free society. It can be argued with great force that any other position . . . can only mean that business will take over power, authority, and decision-making in areas outside of the economic sphere, in areas which are or should be reserved to government or to the individual or to other institutions.[16]

The position Friedman, to an extent Drucker, and many in the business community rally against is that of "social responsibility." "The once flamboyant robber barons are gone," observes Yale professor Charles E. Lindblom, yet corporate leaders still have great power and privilege.

> We do not control their decisions on who will find jobs and who will not, on the shape of city and countryside, on the quality of air we breathe, on the powerful productive technologies—from assembly line to nuclear energy—that both shape and risk our lives.[17]

In the late fifties, sixties, and early seventies, critics demanded that in making these far-reaching decisions, business be more "socially responsible" and work for a cleaner, safer, more just world, not merely a richer one. Dr. Howard Schomer, an official of the United Church Board of World Ministries, states as the purpose of business "to provide *quality* products at *just* prices with the conditions of their *humane* production and an *equitable* distribution of earnings between management, labor, shareholder, and the community."[18] The list of specifics business has been expected to work for is almost endless. It encompasses providing employment for the handicapped, inner-city youth, and ex-cons; cleaning up the environment; supporting the arts; withdrawing investment from South Africa until it ends apartheid; stopping trade with the U.S.S.R. until it lets its Jews go.

In the terms of the present discourse neither position is tenable: neither that of unbounded social responsibility nor that of corporate disregard of shared needs, mutuality, and civility. Social responsibility, carried to the advanced level many of its champions call for, would not allow the society's production units to discharge their first duty, responsibility if you wish, to produce the resources society requires. While it is true that few social acts would alone have such a depleting effect, in accumulation they would render a "responsible" corporation unable to compete with others, if not at home then overseas, and ultimately leave it without resources to carry out its business. Thus, a corporation that would not sell to or buy from regimes whose human rights policies we disapprove would have to give up the lion's share of the world's trade. If, further, it refused to conduct its business in states that have not ratified the ERA, with farms and businesses that are not unionized, and so on and so forth, it would barely need to open its doors.

Equally untenable is the corporate parallel of the ego-centered mentality, which takes the position that all the corporation need worry about is its own goals. A corporation looking out only for itself will not do well in the longer run and will damage the societal fabric to boot. The basic reason is that of license and legitimation. Corporations are based on a socially granted charter, in effect a license. It allows them to conduct business in a highly unusual manner, unknown before the modern era, that of limited liability. This arrangement, which is as important to a modern free economy as the wheel to transportation, allows a large amount of capital to be amassed, as it must be for large-scale production, from thousands, if not millions, of individuals. This is possible only if the individual investor's risk is limited to the amount of capital he puts forward to buy stock. Otherwise, with unlimited liability, facing the danger that if the business goes into bankruptcy all his worldly goods may be attached, the investor would have to be much more thoroughly informed and involved in the corporations he chooses to invest in. This, of course, most investors could not do, hence they would invest in "collectibles" (such as gold coins, stamps, china) or small nearby businesses, but not in stocks and bonds of the sizable corporations a modern economy requires.

However, it is this same limited liability that enables a corporation to ignore the danger of marketing an unsafe product, say, tricycles with a tendency to tumble backward, or mattresses not treated with flame retardant. If all goes well, the corporation will be richer, its executives will receive high bonuses, and the stockholders will be richly rewarded; if calamity strikes, no substantial harm will come to investors.

If limited liability is to be maintained, and if it is not to be accompanied by regulations aimed at forcing the corporation to be sensitive to the world of others and the commonweal, as Ralph Nader demands,[19] a measure of mutuality and of civility are required on the side of the corporation. Otherwise, efforts will swell again soon to cut into the license by various restrictive regulations and other public "interventions." The situation is the same for all who command a special privilege granted by society, marked by a license: policemen, for example, have a right to shoot as long as they do not shoot too many innocent bystanders. Otherwise, demand rises first for more regulation and supervision within the police department; if this does not work, for civilian review boards, and ultimately, for disarming the police. When physicians frequently perform unnecessary or poor surgery or otherwise violate the trust implied in their license, they face a swarm of malpractice suits. And while their insurance protects them, soon the insurance rates rise to prohibitive levels.

In short, all licenses are issued with an implicit understanding that the special privileges they accord will be accompanied by some self-restraint and a measure of social sensitivity. Indeed, there is little doubt that the drive in the last two decades to impose ever more regulations on business corporations was propelled in part by various groups, often cheered on by the public at large, which tried to make business more socially sensitive. While excessive use and abuse of this social tool, along with a major political change in the last few years, have helped build support for deregulation, unbounded pursuit of production goals and profit would soon lead to new demands to curb the social license for doing business.

Beyond license is the more encompassing legitimation. No institution can ignore the need for acceptance and approval of its business—and its way of doing business—by the members of society. General disapproval generates much more damage than partial withdrawal of license. In effect, all aspects of performance are deeply affected. Institutions that are highly legitimate find it easy to recruit people, especially people of a high level of talent and motivation; they can reward them with esteem, though not necessarily high pay, and can command volunteers and cooperation. Institutions with low or negative legitimation have great trouble recruiting, must pay dearly for what they get, and find it difficult to win cooperation. Thus, in peacetime the army is often considered a place for people who cannot find another job; it recruits poorly and must pay relatively well (if not in salary, in fringe benefits). In a war considered legitimate, the army can draw many volunteers or willing draftees, gain ready cooperation from various other groups (*e.g.*, labor unions), and so on. On the other hand, massage parlors are considered by most Americans to be engaged in an illegitimate business under any circumstances; they are drummed out of many a neighborhood and often must offer high pay to attract employees—or keep them under duress to keep them at all—and continuously bribe local authorities to keep their doors open.

Historically, business—including finance, commerce, and manufacturing—was often considered an activity of dubious value. It was often delegated to minorities, such as Jews, Armenians, Indians (in Africa), or Chinese (in South Asia). Those engaged in trade, banking, and other aspects of business were ready marks for persecution, discrimination, and revocation of privileges and rights.

While historically, business was much more legitimate in the United States, when it came to be viewed as excessively exploitive, ruthless, and harmful to society, as in the era of robber barons, laws were introduced to curb it. Early in the 1890s, antitrust laws came into being. The appeal to government to act increased as public confidence in business and the business elites suffered during the Depression of the 1930s.

In short, to protect the corporate license and legitimacy, what is needed is a measure of sensitivity to others and to commonweal needs—without losing sight of the primary purpose. While they should not make others' business their prime task, as Peter Drucker puts it,

> Business and the other institutions of our society of organizations cannot be pure, however desirable that may be. Their own self-interest alone forces them to be concerned with society and community and to be prepared to shoulder responsibility beyond their own main areas of task and responsibility. . . . No pluralist society such as ours has become, has ever worked unless its key institutions take responsibility for the common good.[20]

Many of the calls for business to be "socially responsible" focus on what Drucker calls "social problems," what an institution can do *for* society. Drucker makes a helpful distinction between an institution's responsibility for social problems, which he considers questionable, and its responsibility for "social impacts," what it does *to* society, which he considers quite compelling: "Managements of all institutions are responsible for their by-products, that is, the impacts of their legitimate activities on people and on the physical and social environment."[21] These, he says, include the effects of developing technology and the effects of "social and economic innovations and developments,"[22] whether intended or not.

A business should indeed accept responsibility for its social impacts, for the harm its activities might do to other groups (workers, consumers, neighbors) and to society in general (*e.g.*, depletion of scarce and non-renewable resources). If the same basic considerations are used by all corporations in the same line of work, at least within the national market, this enhanced level of mutuality will not put any one corporation at a competitive disadvantage.

National policies, such as those concerning international trade negotiations and import limitations, would have to deal with foreign competitors which might seek to take advantage of a higher level of American corporate social sensitivity. This is far from being a shocking new idea; imported autos are held to the same safety standards and pollution-control levels as American cars, and if American corporations cannot market in the United States drugs that have not been proven safe and effective, foreign corporations cannot either.

There are other ways to deal with social impacts without building on the government. Through an industry or trade association, businesses could agree to a small surcharge on the prices of all materials (even if imported) of a certain kind, and the association could use the funds generated for corrective purposes. A surcharge on chemical raw materials, for instance, could be used to pay for the cleanup of hazardous chemical dumps;* on alcohol, to treat alcoholics, and so on.

Still another way for corporations to enhance their mutuality and civility without regulation, and without untenable costs, is for business groups and the community to work out socially sensitive policies. For example, when all retailers in a community agree to close on Sunday or Saturday, no one will suffer. (True, there are always *some* losses—for example, some people shop only on Sunday, and they may shop instead at garage-sales or unauthorized vendors—but these are not sufficient to seriously undermine the corporations' ability to set socially useful self-limitations.)

---

* In contrast, "Superfund," the trust fund established by Congress in 1980 to finance cleaning up hazardous chemical dumps and accidental spills, and to meet claims for resulting damage to natural resources, was set up to receive roughly 15 percent of its funds from general revenues; the rest was to come from a tax on oil and chemical companies. The fund is administered by the IRS; its resources become available for use by the Environmental Protection Agency through congressional appropriation.

A good example comes from West Germany, where major employers have for a long time trained not just their own workers but others as well. Ford, for example, has a three-year apprentice program at its Cologne plant; some graduates go to work for Ford, but they are not required to do so, and many take jobs with other employers. Helmart Weltzel, Ford's director of training in West Germany, agreed that in the short run, Ford's profits would rise if such training programs were eliminated. However, he added, "we probably would lose our image as a good employer, because part of this image . . . is being a good trainer."[23] In West Germany, Weltzel said, "All bigger companies do their training because they feel that the labor market for skilled people is something like a huge entity where everybody takes out what he needs and everybody brings in his share of trained people."[24]

Business representatives often say they cannot work together like this because of possible violation of antitrust laws, but there seems to be no record of any antitrust action because of such activity; if need be, antitrust laws could be modified to allow explicitly for such collaboration.

Most important, as occasions arise when some additional profit can be squeezed out by ignoring social needs—by taking shortcuts in testing the safety of products, for example, or stinting worker protection, or dumping waste by the roadside at night—businesses should forgo this profit for the sake of the society, as well as to ensure the longer-run opportunity to conduct business in a free society.

While, within the social domain, first attention should clearly go to moderating and compensating for the undesirable side effects of doing business (which cannot be eliminated completely, at least not at tolerable costs to the economy), the second priority should go to making social contributions, above and beyond production. Thus, businesses have long found that encouraging their executives to be involved in community work, from the United Way to the local hospital board, from the school to the opera, is both good in itself and pays off in greater legitimation. The same holds for financial contributions by corporations to colleges, public television, the Urban League, and others.

These principles, which might be referred to as corporate citizenship, fly in the face of the notion put forward by some pro-business writers that since the corporation is not a person, social demands should not be imposed on it. I have already quoted Milton Friedman's statement that "the only entities who can have responsibilities are individuals; a business cannot have responsibilities." Peter Drucker builds a criticism of recent discussions of "business ethics" around this point, which he calls crucial:

> There is only one code of ethics, that of individual behavior, for prince and pauper, for rich and poor, for the mighty and the meek alike. . . . And this fundamental axiom "business ethics" denies. . . . For it asserts that acts that are not immoral or illegal if done by ordinary folk become immoral or illegal if done by "business."[25]

True, corporations are clearly different from persons, and individuals who are employed by corporations are expected to carry out their civil duties like other private citizens. Nevertheless, the corporation itself has a civil-social status, legal rights and privileges; they should be balanced by some duties and by a sense of obligation to the commonweal.

The basic orientation of the corporation is also important. A posture of "my needs are all I have to worry about," however clever the slogans that camouflage it—what's good for G.M. is good for America—will sooner or later generate a societal reaction. Societies can no more thrive on corporate "ego"-centered behavior than on individuals' egotism, and they have objective needs other than production that cannot be slighted even if, for a reconstruction period, those needs must be given a lower priority.

The points made concerning business ethics hold just as much for other power groups as for corporations. When labor unions have shown contempt for the public or have been grossly insensitive to needs other than their members' interests, they have faced a similar loss of public acceptance (although in the United States, they never had quite the legitimacy of business to begin with). Thus, in 1981, the air traffic controllers advanced demands the public considered excessive, such as working thirty-two hours a week and a ten-thousand-dollar raise in base pay, and violated their oath not to strike, and acted in a high-handed manner. At one point during the second round of negotiations between PATCO and the government, following the union's rejection of a contract its representatives had previously accepted, the union gave the government only three days' notice of a new strike deadline. When Transportation Secretary Lewis protested that it was "unfair and unreasonable"[26] to try to settle contract differences totaling over $500 million in three days and asked for a week's postponement of the strike deadline, union members refused any delay. Soon they found the majority of the public lining up behind the drive to fire them all and strip their union of the right to represent them. Moreover, their actions weakened not only their own status, but the legitimacy of labor unions in general, at least those of public employees.

Similarly, unscrupulous acts by the Teamsters and the excesses of some municipal unions, such as long strikes by teachers and strikes by firemen and policemen, contributed to the general decline of the legitimacy of labor unions in the United States over recent years. Other groups, from churches to universities, have likewise found that they cannot act without sensitivity to the public, and to values other than their own dearest ones, and still preserve their status and their freedom to act.

Even so, business groups are particularly vulnerable to the risks of exclusive preoccupation with their own needs and goals. Their gain in power is the most recent, and they command more power than other groups. Hence, in the near future they will be most tempted to endanger their own social license and legitimation—and the societal balance.

The Reagan administration stumbled (some may add "and fell") over the same issue. It was propelled both by concern for the country and its economy and by a desire to please constituencies and interest groups close to it, the various business interests. It started by promising not to cut into a social "safety net," which was said to protect the truly needy; but increasingly it slashed into the very programs it had defined as part of this network. Moreover, it provided huge new benefits to unproductive corporations—such as those made possible by new "leasing" rules—and concessions to special-interest groups. For example, at the same time it was promoting deregulation in matters concerning the protection of consumers, workers, and the environment, it was impeding further deregulation of trucking, already under way—in response to pressure from the Teamsters, which had supported Reagan's election.[27] Opinion polls show a rapid change in the public's feelings on the matter. By September 1981 a majority (52 percent) felt that Reagan "cared" more about upper-income people (compared to only 29 percent in April).[28]

What it all comes down to is that reconstruction of community and a period of reindustrialization seem likely to unfold in the next years. It is much less clear whether the sharp zigzagging of the past will be overcome—whether an excessive and insensitive tilt toward high production and its corollaries will be promoted, only to be followed by a new social reaction and attempts to commit America to a radically different core project; or whether the clearly needed and probably forthcoming pro-production tilt will be moderated this time by greater social sensitivity, making for steadier, more balanced progress over the longer run. It is not that in the latter case America may not again face, after a decade or so of reindustrialization, increased concern with other priorities. However, with moderation now, the swings of the pendulum might be shortened, the social and economic costs of wild swings avoided, and less disruptive shifts back and forth between societal priorities achieved.

INSTITUTIONAL RECONSTRUCTION

Education

The main problem of educational institutions, as far as reindustrialization is concerned, is not the decline in their specific contribution to industrial strength but their general weakness, whose dimensions and nature we have already discussed. Our rough estimate is that half the schools are underpreparing their graduates psychically to function as self-propelling, self-guiding persons. If this estimate is reasonably accurate, these schools are serving most purposes poorly, not merely labor force needs; they graduate not only poor workers, but also poor soldiers and poor citizens.

It is true, though, that this psychic underpreparation, with its corollary of underpreparation in basic skills, is particularly damaging for a modern economy, which makes particularly high demands for self-discipline, deferred gratification, ability to cope with routine. The first contribution reindustrialization seeks from schools is thus the same as the one societal reconstruction calls for: Heal thyself; transform the school into a set of experiences that help young persons move from dependency to self-guidance, control of impulse, and ability to deal with others and with authority.

The argument has been advanced in recent years that major changes in work technology will enable work to be carried out with a lesser degree of structure and will provide more opportunity for work relations that are collaborative rather than hierarchical. This is said to be the case because much more routine work can now be done by machines, freeing the labor force to do more creative work, and because combinations of computers and communication links allow people to work at home or nearby, that is, allow work to be much more decentralized.

There is a considerable measure of truth in this notion, but it is often vastly overstated. Thus, while there is definitely a trend to turn over more routine work to machines, there is also a very considerable amount of routine work yet to be done—coal mining, for instance.

Post-industrial enthusiasts write about a historical shift from work on farms to work in industries (from the "primary" to the "secondary" sectors of the economy, à la Colin and Clark), now followed by a shift from industries to services—and within services to the knowledge industries. But I cannot stress enough that these are shifts of emphasis, not wholesale. American agriculture is still a very important sector. Steel and auto industries may be on the decline, but defense and *manufacturing* of computers are on the rise. And there is even a return to the primary sector, to which mining belongs. In short, it is much more accurate to think about a multi-track society than about a mono-track one, despite the fact that some tracks will carry more than they did in the recent past. And while more people use computers (or terminals) at home for their work, in the foreseeable future most work will still require division of labor, which in turn requires coordination, which makes for hierarchical work relations. There may be somewhat fewer levels of hierarchy in the future, and coordination may be more often indirect either in style or in setup (even built into computer programs set by those higher in rank), but hierarchies at work are not about to vanish.

"Post-modern" industries will be able to work effectively, even benefit, by employing persons who are somewhat less able to relate to authority figures and rules than earlier industrial work required. But not all industries will become "post-modern" in structure over the next ten years, and even post-modern industries will still require a fairly high level of ability to work within a context; they will not be able to work with poorly formed persons. It follows that the inadequacies of the schools still must be corrected.

Beyond the proper psychic preparation, schools might best focus on providing basic cognitive skills, not specific industrial training. If on top of the proper psychic preparation, schools teach youngsters mathematics, reading, and writing, it is not necessary for them to teach what's called in the trade "job-specific" skills, such as keypunching, front-end alignment, or lathe operation, let alone prepare students for specific jobs such as tool- and die-maker or auto mechanic.

The opposition to schools' getting too deeply involved in teaching specific skills is based on several grounds. First, most schools are overloaded as it is, and when they take over duties that can readily be discharged by employers, they become even less able to attend to their own duties, which nobody else is likely to take over. Second, the need for specific skills changes rapidly, and hence youngsters are better off learning generic, widely applicable skills, such as blueprint reading, using a computer, and preparing a resume.

This general position must be moderated for the last two years of school, if graduation at age eighteen is to be continued. In those two years a new mixture of study and work, or "in" and "out," should provide preparation for specific jobs, either in the place of work or in combined work/study programs, not necessarily in the school proper. The same holds with much greater power for junior colleges. Their rich variety of job training programs, from secretarial to accounting, is quite appropriate for reindustrialization. It is only regrettable that the prestige structure tends to downgrade these career education programs (often referred to as vocational) compared with academic ones.

The criticism might be made that I view schools as preparatory to the industrial world, geared to its needs rather than some other set of values, say, humanist. This is not the case; schools must first and foremost graduate individuals who can function on their own while relating constructively to one another (mutuality) and to their community (civility). Such individuals, properly "put together" from a psychosocial viewpoint, will have the most important characteristics workplaces require. Moreover, I recognize that schools need to educate for other values than work, such as culture and citizenship. It is true that for the age of reindustrialization it is necessary that the schools increase their contribution to the world of work and reduce their other roles. But education for work is not their first priority; their first priority is to turn out more graduates who are self-disciplined human beings, a prerequisite of all society, not merely of industry.

The Family

There is next to nothing the family should be expected to do for reindustrialization. It is not a suitable target for public economic policy. At the same time, reindustrialization would be richly rewarded if the nuclear family were rejuvenated for its own sake. A stronger family would be more effective in character formation, which might serve rationality as well as civility and mutuality. And a stronger family would provide a sounder structure for tension management, which in turn could benefit a high-rationality, high-tension industrial society. To reiterate: This is *not* to suggest that the family should be restored in order to increase industrial efficiency; however, if it is restored for other reasons—of which there are plenty—reindustrialization would be an additional, unintended beneficiary.

MENTALITY

Projecting on Super-Papa

An important sign that the American people seek a change of direction and a higher level of commitment—and a troubling indication that their initial approach may be misfocused—is the swelling demand for "strong" leadership.[29] It is clearest in public attitudes toward previous presidents. (The incumbent president's stature as a leader is always contested, no matter who he is, especially among various partisan groups. For example, the black community has been almost unanimous in its disappointment with Reagan, even when large segments of the public ranked him high.)

The overwhelming majority of the American people have been greatly disappointed in the leadership qualities of all the recent presidents, especially since the age of retreat set in, a point explored previously.[30] Carter was thought to be unclear where he was headed and unable to communicate and inspire; he was said to be lost between lofty principles (such as his commitment to the family, which did not translate into a clear conception or policy the public could relate to) and knee-deep involvement in details (which obscured general patterns if there were any). Ford was believed to be not of presidential caliber, a congressman who made it into the White House by an historical fluke, unable to grasp the job, lacking in the mental powers, not to mention the inspirational qualities, required to lead a people. The majority considered Nixon wicked, vindictive, and petty, an abuser of presidential power, not a leader.

Earlier post-war presidents fared better, but not much. Though in retrospect Johnson was viewed as a president who could get things done, at least get things out of Congress, he was seen more as a clever manipulator and arm-twister than as a man who commanded a vision and could inspire the American people to follow him. After all, he got Americans so deeply mired in the war in Vietnam that he lost their support to the extent that he would not even try for reelection. Kennedy was viewed as inspirational but unable to follow through on his ideas. Eisenhower was seen as a sometime president who delegated most of his duties, a kind of chief of the White House staff, not a leader of the American people.

What all this reflects, above and beyond whatever shortcomings the various presidents did or did not have, is an avoidance syndrome found in many nations. Its essence is that people avoid facing the true sources of national problems, especially if those sources are close to home or lie at least in part in the people's own attitudes and limitations. They instead project on the president both the hope for solutions and the blame if they do not work out. Viewing the president as a super-papa allows citizens to go about their private pursuits, seeking to enrich self or be preoccupied with friends and family, and letting the president—the personification of government—take care of national needs, of the commonweal.

In the eyes of the many afflicted by the avoidance syndrome, if the president attends to all these matters, the American people can follow their ego-centered ways. And if he does not, he is to blame, not the rest of us; we can then burn him at the stake of public criticism and derision and look for the next one to dismount from a white horse on the steps of the White House and "clean up the mess." As a result, as one president after another fails to measure up, our sense of disillusionment and retreat grows, as well as the lack of realism in our expectations of the *next* one. Soon we cheer assertive gestures and "tough stands," even if they have little problem-solving content. We seem to say, if we can't get a true leader let's have one who looks like one, talks like one, and acts like the super-papa we have so long waited for.

A second version of this take-me-to-my-leader syndrome, of the super-papa complex, is somewhat less damaging and closer to what is actually called for. This version calls for the president to tell us what is to be done and *make us* do what is necessary. It is as if we realize, in one part of us, that some belt-tightening is required, some increase in self-discipline and commitment is needed, but we would rather be told, made, to take our medicine than lead the way ourselves or meet the president partway.

No president can live up to either version of our unreasonable expectations; we have to do a good part of the reconstruction ourselves. The reasons become clearer if we look at the roles of the president as the master of public policy and as a national galvanizer.

In the first capacity, the president and his staff generate numerous items of public policy, from deregulation to annual budgets, from nominating Supreme Court Justices to Clean Air acts. All these require congressional action. Congress, in turn, by Constitutional and political reality, is not merely subject to whatever pressures the president applies, but is also the butt of the pressures of interest groups and responsive to various constituencies, which simply means all of us. Suppose the president proposed that all farm subsidies be canceled to reduce the budget deficits and to help fight inflation. He would face the farm lobby, often backed by the very groups that would benefit from the president's proposal, the Congressional delegations from urban centers. The farm lobby tells them that if they don't help it stave off the presidential "onslaught," the farm lobby won't support various bills dear to the urban delegations, such as bailouts for New York City, mass transit systems for scores of other cities, and so on). The public at large would be quickly lost in the intricacies of the farm bill (which is set up not as open subsidy but channels billions into farmers' pockets via indirect ways) and swayed by arguments that the farmers will cut next year's production, driving up the price of food, if they don't get support this year. Thus the president's proposal would be left without backing; soon he would not even try to move in such a direction.

True, a president can get some things out of Congress on his own, so to speak, using the prestige and power of his office. But here too there are costs to the uninvolved public, from keeping military bases not where they are efficient or needed but in the districts of members of Congress whose votes are particularly sought, to high tax concessions to some favorite lobby, whether shoes, steel, banking or whatnot.

If we all became more involved in the public arena, through political parties and public interest groups, we could hold special-interest groups at bay and back the president and those members of Congress supportive of needed reforms. Without greater public involvement, the president as master of public policy is often ineffectual or made to act in ways that make him a wheeler and dealer in the public interest, not a leader.

The same holds for the president as national galvanizer, the one who should tell the people what to do, arousing them to take the right positions and action. Here again the mistake lies in dissociating leadership from followership. A leader can be ahead of his flock by only so much or they will not follow him. Imagine for a moment that President Reagan had a midnight conversion and rose tomorrow morning to preach to the American people that the inner journey was more important than material possessions, that they should all give up their wealth to poorer nations, and spend their days in fasting and contemplation. While the president might strike some responsive chords in millions of Americans who favor a simpler life and seek to opt out of the "rat race" of competition and mass consumption, the overwhelming majority would not follow him in this direction whatever he said, however eloquently he put it, however often he repeated it.

To generalize the point, a leader can lead only within the confines of what the followers value and are willing to accept. The president in 1981 could move to reduce regulations, cut government expenditures, and so forth, because the majority of the public strongly believed in these steps as measures of virtue. In contrast, when President Kennedy spoke of the *merits* of unbalanced budgets (many Keynesian economists in his day believed that deficits in years of slow economic growth were necessary if not welcome), he moved outside the public's framework of acceptance and generated such a nationwide torrent of editorial criticism that he never returned to the subject in public. Similarly, most Americans believe in Social Security to the point that when presidential candidate Barry Goldwater attacked it, and when President Reagan tried in 1981 to modify it drastically, each found that this was a direction in which he could not lead.

Franklin Roosevelt, in personality, was certainly as much a leader as Americans have known in the last two generations, a fact acknowledged even by those who did not agree with his policies (who, on the contrary, often complained about the excessive power of his personality). But in a year of speechmaking he could not lead the Americans to join with Britain in the war against Nazi Germany; it took Pearl Harbor to get America involved.

Much strain is generated in the body-society when the public's perceptions and values confine the president to policies that are no longer suitable or adequate. He cannot singlehandedly set, or even in a big way change, this confining context. He must be met at least partway by changes within the public. This is the present situation, as I see it. Retreat from community and from rationality must be replaced by recommitment, a considerable change of the public's framework. How this might happen deserves some detailed attention.

The Role of Intellectual and Moral Leadership

New ideas and directions, as well as reaffirmation of old ones, or spiritual renewal, do not as a rule start in political posts, with elected officials, or in White House conclaves. They are typically initiated by leaders in other realms, especially intellectual and moral. Such ideas are first found at the edges of universities and churches, in think tanks and foundations, in Bohemian quarters (such as the Village in New York), in religious movements. Thus, student leaders played a key role in initiating scores of social movements, including the civil rights movement, the counterculture, and the movement against the war in Vietnam. The war against poverty existed in Michael Harrington's book *The Other America* long before President Kennedy spoke about it and President Johnson advanced it. And without Martin Luther King, Jr., and scores of other such leaders, the public framework supportive of civil rights legislation would not have existed for President Johnson to work in.

More recently, the work of neo-conservative intellectuals such as Irving Kristol, Nathan Glazer, Daniel Bell, Pat Moynihan, and James Q. Wilson, and, farther to the right, the Hoover Institution, the Heritage Foundation, and others, has developed the intellectual context for the conservative revival.

The Many Factors of the Public's Backdrop

Ultimately, though, intellectual and moral leaders too must work within the confines of what the public at large is willing to accept.

There are at any time scores upon scores of conflicting intellectual and moral claimants; they each have arguments in favor of their position, and believe in its validity. What makes one of the scores of books published each month an epoch setter, a book that either refocuses the existing public framework or—even rarer—extends or changes it, is not the book itself but its interaction with changing public predispositions. If one looks at these books (or the authors) they are often very difficult to tell apart from the scores of other aspirants of intellectual and moral leadership who remain just that, aspirants. Thus Michael Harrington's book about poverty, *The Other America*, is not particularly well written or documented, and Betty Friedan's book *The Feminine Mystique* is not the first on the subject, nor is she a stronger personality than many other active women before her.

The difference is that the epoch-setting books, "little magazines," and personalities rose when the public was ready to meet them part of the way, when it was "ripe," sociologically speaking. It is not that these books or persons added nothing; they focused, articulated, enlarged, enriched, and gave content to an evolving public orientation. But they could not have made it if the public had not been moving in that general direction, on its own.

What accounts for the public's direction and what is the process through which it moves? Most people who ask that question wish, understandably, to find relatively simple answers, to find an x factor that if introduced could ready the public. The sociological fact, though, is that the public, that great mass of all of us, does not move in response to one central influence. Many factors play their roles in combination, which is precisely why no one person or force can command the direction.

Economic factors play a role. Thus, the fact that inflation destroyed many people's assets, pension funds, savings put aside to send children to college, is a factor in the current willingness to consider recommitment to a more self-disciplined, less indulgent, less consumerist public and private life.

International events play a role. The Soviet invasion of Afghanistan rekindled fears of Soviet expansionism, which had been receding; the retreat from Vietnam raised new doubts about America's capacity to project its power overseas, as did Iran's holding not only American diplomats but also U.S. foreign policy hostage for fourteen months.

Demographic trends are another factor. Currently the American population is aging and moving away from youth-oriented values to a growing preoccupation with the needs of older people. Changes in the family, migration to the Sunbelt, and many other factors all play a role.

The net result is a complex, changing background, which can hardly be understood in full, and certainly cannot be controlled, by any leader of any kind, or a combination of several. Not only working singly, but also affecting one another, these factors set the changing backdrop against which public predispositions evolve.

The Multi-Billion-Hour Megalogue

While many background factors affect the public mind, it is made up via only one process—many billions of hours of megalogue in families, among friends, on the way to bowling, tennis, or golf, during coffee breaks at the office, and so on. I could say "dialogue," but coining "megalogue" flags the sheer magnitude of this process, which encompasses not only occasional conversations but repeated exchanges, in many different groups, by millions of people across the country. These millions who make up the public are like the molecules of the society: Their megalogue is akin to heatgenerating processes that melt down old positions and fashion new ones. The background factors predispose the probable direction of the process, but they do not dictate the outcome; the public can and does cohere around positions that are not compatible with reality, either to change its position later—or to change reality. Intellectual and moral leadership feed into the megalogue, but they are unable to determine the results. They help focus options and arguments, but the megalogue is the ultimate arbiter and shaping process.

The process of the public's "making up its mind"—above all, "changing its mind"—typically takes several years, to the dismay of those who believe they have the "right" answer and wish to hurry the public in the "right" direction. Even after so long a time, there are minorities that are not won over, but often a fair measure of consensus arises, on which the political leadership can then build and advance. Thus it took several years, while the public daily experienced on color TV the death and lack of success in Vietnam, and was bombarded by hawks and doves with prescriptions for what was to be done—and subjected them to megalogue—before the majority supported cutting out. Similarly, it took the socioeconomic experience of a majority of women in the labor force, the rise of college education for women, the debate between feminists and their opponents—and a megalogue—for the majority of the public to favor equal legal, economic, and social rights for women.

Most relevant to our discussion: During the decades of abundant affluence, a majority of the public was enamored with visions of a quality-of-life society and increasingly involved with ego above other and commonweal; but during the seventies a majority began a megalogue on the virtues of reinstating economic growth as a prime societal value, and of reconstructing societal institutions (especially schools, and to a lesser extent the family) to restore their capacity to act—in particular to act in favor of the rationality nexus and economic growth.

It is this change of perspective by a majority of the public—still uneven in terms of the sectors it embraces, and the intensity of the commitment it commands—that reindustrialization requires. Given this context, political leadership can work out the rest.

Rationality Reinstated, But . . .

What are the specific context-setting predispositions Americans must continue to evolve if their political leadership is to be able to usher in a decade of reindustrialization? What predispositions are needed beyond those generic to any well-integrated and functioning society?

A return to a higher level of legitimation of rationality and its corollaries of self-discipline and deferred gratification is in order, reducing the violations of rationality by impulse or by conflicting values, without returning to the narrow rationality of the nineteenth century.

In the area of science and technology, this means lowering the acceptance of the occult, astrology, and other antiscientific explanations of the world and what makes it tick, and returning to greater reliance on, interest in, and commitment to logical-empirical explanations. These grew increasingly suspect during the high days of the counterculture and the general withdrawal from institutions and authority. Thus in treating illness, ancient notions such as meditation, the laying on of hands, and other psychic treatments are quite possibly highly beneficial for numerous psychic disorders and for general stress, as well as for psychosomatic illnesses such as ulcers and asthma. However, to treat cancer, for example—not patients' anxiety and pain, but the disease itself—solely through meditation and reflection is irrational, and a community that does not clearly see such behavior as intellectually irresponsible allows the irrational to penetrate beyond any acceptable bounds.

The majority must get involved in restoring rationality to its proper status. Those who realize that many attacks on fluoridation of water are based on the intrusion of bigotry into a well-established empirical-logical realm (that fluoridation of water is highly useful to fight tooth decay) must stand up to those who oppose it on irrational grounds. Likewise, the teaching of creationism in school science courses should be actively opposed. One can question how urgent and important it is to introduce the metric system in the United States and how this would best be achieved. But to let people block it because they feel that the traditional measurements are "natural" (the foot "comes" from the body) or sacred is to legitimate the absurd.[31]

There is no need to eye technology once again as an unmixed blessing, ignoring its side effects or the fact that its damage can, in some situations, exceed its benefits. There is clearly a need to assess adverse effects and contain them. But this will only rarely lead to canceling a technology. Thus, for example, one should increase the safety of nuclear reactors and remove them from population centers, not ban all nuclear plants and rely more on coal. Coal may well be less safe if one considers the lives lost mining it and the undesirable environmental side effects of reliance on it. Similarly, solar energy has many virtues, but raising it to the level of an ideology makes it nonrational.

In the area of administration, the well-placed concern with excessive bureaucratization, reflected in unbounded regulatory appetites and avalanches of paperwork, should not lead to blanket endorsement of simplistic notions that small is beautiful. Sometimes it is, but often large-scale organization is the only rational way to achieve economic and security goals.

In the economic area itself, possibly the single most important step is to tie reward more closely to effort. The best way to secure sufficient effort, foresight, saving, and toil is for people to see fewer instances of people who act "irrationally," who do not provide for their future or loved ones, but who nevertheless obtain quite similar rewards as those who labor long and hard. Automatic promotions may be socially comforting, but they are not economically sound. Those who cannot compete because of the continued effects of past discrimination should be helped to catch up, so that they can hold their own, but declaring them winners without a race will not serve their self-esteem, nor will it find public support, especially when the economy is tight.

As with every return to a previous mentality, there is a danger of overreacting rather than benefiting from the lessons of the past. This would occur if the return to a higher degree of rationality, reducing the scope and frequency of intrusion of other values into the logical-empirical selection of means, caused a return to a narrowly based rationality, one that recognizes few or no needs other than the logic of the instruments involved. Thus, to retreat from the position that social values should determine the allocation of rewards, whether choice jobs, promotions, or income, to a position that bases rewards on relevant effort, is not to favor the opposite extreme, a position that disregards social considerations. Taking steps to ensure that all social groupings have access to higher education, and to remedial programs if necessary, is not a violation of rationality but its extension, because it increases the pool of talent that is available. Talented people are born in all social groups; if some are prevented from acquiring the needed preparation for work, their talents are wasted. Similarly, allowing bias against older persons to keep them from being hired not only imposes social costs and psychic damage, but often also deprives industry of an important source of reliable, experienced labor.

Aside from such cross-commitment situations, which advance the goals of production, technological progress, and administrative efficiency simultaneously with social goals, if the proper combinations are sought and implemented, there is room for mitigating rationality where relatively small limitations on rationality yield significant gains on other dimensions. For instance, a limited levy on chemicals to pay for the removal of toxic dumps, which the chemical industry left all over the land before their danger was clearly perceived, could buy much social good at relatively low economic cost.

Similarly, it mitigates rationality to grant minority or women employees some seniority points as soon as they are hired, to make up for past discrimination and to prevent their being at the bottom of the ladder, the first to be fired in any slump. In contrast, it violates rationality to hire by racial and sexual quotas, especially to insist on proportionality at all ranks and in all divisions (as distinct from across the place of employment). Hence, to move from quota hiring to according some seniority points to disadvantged groups would mean considerable gain for rationality in labor force allocation, without making it the only criterion.

In short, the need to make more room for rational selection of means, to restore the legitimacy of the rationality nexus, does not require ignoring other goals or removing mitigating limits on rational decisions. At the same time, these additional considerations should not deflect commitments from the main need, from a reindustrialization perspective: to restore the legitimacy and power of rationality to a higher status, both in the public mentality and in institutions. Only as this is successfully accomplished does one need to guard against overreacting to its recent decline by overextending its status and reach.

The agenda the preceding discussion charts is not a list of tasks for a strong leader, the responsibility of corporations, a job that can or should be undertaken by the government, or a matter that can be left to God and nature. It is clearly an endeavor, indeed a set of endeavors feeding into and building on one another, that we all must undertake. Without critical self-examination, renewal, and commitment by individuals, there is little hope for psychic rebuilding, for institutional reconstruction, for finding the energy to countervail interest groups and to provide for the commonweal and for the future.

Notes

CHAPTER 1

1. John F. Stacks, "It's Rightward On," *Time*, June 1, 1981, p. 12.
2. See Christopher Lasch, *The Culture of Narcissism: American Life in an Age of Diminishing Expectations* (New York: Norton, 1978), and Tom Wolfe, "The Me Decade and the Third Great Awakening," in *Mauve Gloves & Madmen, Clutter & Vine, and Other Stories, Sketches and Essays* (New York: Farrar, Straus and Giroux, 1976), pp. 126–67.
3. CBS News/*New York Times* poll, March 1980.
4. "The Reagan Resolve: One More Time," *Wall Street Journal*, September 28, 1981.
5. Private communication. See also "Supply-Side Tax Cuts Could Be a Mirage," *Business Week*, December 28, 1981, p. 15.
6. Peter Behr, "Bill Slashes Business Taxation, Allows Swapping of Deductions," *Washington Post*, August, 2, 1981.
7. For a fine treatment of the earlier Whigs, see G. H. Guttridge, *English Whiggism and the American Revolution* (Berkeley: University of California Press, 1942).
8. *Ibid.*, p. 5.
9. *Ibid.*
10. Milton Friedman, *Capitalism and Freedom* (Chicago: University of Chicago Press, 1962, 1982), p. 23.
11. Irving Kristol, *Two Cheers for Capitalism* (New York: Basic Books, 1978), p. 268.
12. John Davenport, "An Unrepentant Old Whig," *Fortune*, March 1960, p. 134.
13. "If Inequality Is Inevitable, What Can Be Done About It?" *New York Times*, January 3, 1982.

14. *Ibid.*

15. Robert Nozick, *Anarchy, State, and Utopia* (New York: Basic Books, 1974), pp. *ix*, 4.

16. 1980 Platform of the Libertarian Party, adopted in convention, September 1979.

17. Quoting Henry Heuser, President of Henry Vogt Machine Company, *Vital Speeches,* September 15, 1979, p. 732.

18. "In Praise of the Brown Bag," *Time,* August 16, 1976, p. 20.

19. "Another Uproar over the Freedom to Choose," *Nation's Business,* May 1976, pp. 9–10.

20. Aaron Wildavsky, "No Risk Is the Highest Risk of All," *American Scientist,* vol. 67 (January/February 1979), p. 34.

21. Gary S. Becker, *The Economic Approach to Human Behavior* (Chicago: University of Chicago Press, 1976).

22. Unsigned book note, *Ethics,* January 1978, p. 185.

23. Becker, *op. cit.,* p. 233.

24. See, for example, George C. Homans, *Social Behavior: Its Elementary Forms,* revised ed. (New York: Harcourt, Brace, Jovanovich, 1961, 1974), and Peter M. Blau, *Exchange and Power in Social Life* (New York: Wiley, 1964).

25. Blau, *ibid.,* pp. 26–27 and *passim.*

26. Guttridge, *op. cit.,* p. 1.

27. *Ibid.*

28. Samuel P. Huntington, *The Soldier and the State* (Cambridge: Harvard University Press, Belknap Press, 1957).

29. *Ibid.,* p. 465.

30. *Ibid.*

31. Samuel P. Huntington, "The Democratic Distemper," *The Public Interest,* no. 41 (Fall 1975), pp. 35–36. See also Ernest Van den Haag, "Economics Is Not Enough—Notes on the Anticapitalist Spirit," *The Public Interest,* Fall 1976, pp. 109–22.

32. Samuel P. Huntington, *American Politics: The Promise of Disharmony* (Cambridge: Harvard University Press, Belknap Press, 1981).

33. *Ibid.,* p. 219.

34. Leo Strauss, *Liberalism: Ancient and Modern* (New York: Basic Books, 1968), pp. 222–23.

35. Leo Strauss, "The Liberalism of Classical Political Philosophy," *Review of Metaphysics,* vol. 12 (March 1959), p. 439.

36. Robert A. Nisbet, *The Quest for Community* (New York: Oxford University Press, 1953; reissued in 1962 under the title *Community and Power*).

37. John Dewey, *Individualism Old and New* (New York: Minton, Balch, 1930), pp. 81–82.

38. Nisbet, *op. cit.*, p. 94.

39. *Ibid.*, p. 95.

40. Robert A. Nisbet, *Twilight of Authority* (New York: Oxford University Press, 1975), p. 269.

41. *Ibid.*, p. 238.

42. *Ibid.*, pp. 238–39.

43. *Ibid.*, p. 239.

44. See, for example, Reinhold Niebuhr, "Coercion, Self-Interest, and Love," in Kenneth E. Boulding, *The Organizational Revolution: A Study in the Ethics of Economic Organization* (New York: Harper & Bros., 1953), pp. 228–44.

45. See, for instance, J. L. Talmon, *The Origin of Totalitarian Democracy* (New York: Praeger, 1952); and Michael Walzer, "The Community," *New Republic*, March 31, 1982, pp. 11–17.

46. *International Encyclopedia of the Social Sciences* (New York: Macmillan, 1968), p. 567.

47. See A. James Reichley, *Conservatives in an Age of Change, The Nixon and Ford Administrations* (Washington, DC: Brookings Institution, 1981), especially chapters 8 and 9.

48. Much more needs to be said on this subject and volumes have been written. Few, in recent memory, have provided a more encompassing and penetrating account than Christopher Jencks, in "The Social Basis of Unselfishness," and Joseph Featherstone, in "John Dewey and David Riesman: From the Lost Individual to the Lonely Crowd." Both essays are included in Herbert J. Gans, Nathan Glazer, Joseph R. Gusfield, and Christopher Jencks, eds., *On the Making of Americans: Essays in honor of David Riesman* (Philadelphia: University of Pennsylvania Press, 1979).

49. Kristol, *op. cit.*, p. 253.

CHAPTER 2: RENEWED AMERICANS

1. John W. Gardner, *Self-Renewal: The Individual and the Innovative Society*, revised ed. (New York: Norton, 1981), p. 94. See also Gardner, *Morale* (New York: Norton, 1978).

2. Robert N. Bellah, "Cultural Vision and the Human Future," *Teachers College Record*, vol. 82 (Spring 1981), p. 500.

3. Bernard Berelson and Gary A. Steiner, *Human Behavior: An Inventory of Scientific Findings* (New York: Harcourt, Brace & World, 1964), p. 252.

4. Maurice Small, "On Some Psychical Relations of Society and Solitude," *Pedagogical Seminary*, 1900, vol. VII, no. 1, pp. 13–69, quoted in Paul Halmos, *Solitude and Privacy* (London: Routledge and Kegan Paul, 1952), p. 2.

5. Halmos, *ibid.*, pp. 2–3.

6. Eugene Kinkead, *In Every War But One* (New York: Norton, 1959), p. 161.

7. *Ibid.*, p. 160.

8. *Ibid.*, p. 162.

9. *Ibid.*, pp. 165–66.

10. *Ibid.*, pp. 165, 168.

11. *Ibid.*, p. 168.

12. Knud J. Helsing, Moyses Szklo, and George W. Comstock, "Factors Associated with Mortality after Widowhood," *American Journal of Public Health*, vol. 71 (August 1981), pp. 802–809.

13. See, for example, Richard E. Byrd, *Alone* (New York: G. P. Putnam's Sons, 1938).

14. Bruce H. Frisch, "Solitude: Who Can Take It and Who Can't," *Science Digest*, March 1964, p. 14.

15. Mortimer H. Appley and Richard Trumbull, eds., *Psychological Stress: Issues in Research* (New York: Appleton-Century-Crofts, 1967), p. 78.

16. "Mobility," *Society*, January/February 1977, p. 9. See also Robert Kanigel, "Stay-Put Americans," *Human Behavior*, May 1979.

17. Claude S. Fischer, *Networks and Places: Social Relations in the Urban Setting*, (New York: Macmillan, Free Press, 1977), p. 178.

18. U.S. Bureau of the Census, *Geographical Mobility: March 1975 to March 1976*, Current Population Reports: Population Characteristics, Series P-20, No. 305, January 1977.

19. U.S. Bureau of Labor Statistics, *Monthly Labor Review*, October 1963, p. 1145, and December 1979, p. 48. This trend, which reversed that for the period 1951–63, reflects at least in part the growing proportion of young workers, whose job tenure is much shorter than that of older Americans.

20. Vance Packard, *A Nation of Strangers* (New York: David McKay 1972), pp. 6–7.

21. *Ibid.*, p. 7.

22. Kanigel, *op. cit.*, p. 54.

23. Packard, *op. cit.*, p. 176.

24. Suzanne Gordon, *Lonely in America* (New York: Simon and Schuster, 1975), p. 18.

25. Packard, *op. cit.*, p. 5.

26. *Ibid.*, p. 270.

27. U.S. Bureau of the Census, *Statistical Abstract of the United States: 1980*, Washington, DC, 1980, table 76.

28. "The Age of Indifference," *Psychology Today*, August 1980, pp. 71–72.

29. Psychologist James J. Lynch has devoted several scientific articles and

a semi-popular book to spelling out the consequences of loneliness. See his *The Broken Heart* (New York: Basic Books, 1977).

30. Larry Van Dyne, "All by Myself," *Washingtonian*, December 1981, pp. 140–46.

31. Daniel Yankelovich, *New Rules: Searching for Self-Fulfillment in a World Turned Upside Down*, (New York: Random House, 1981), p. 91.

32. *Ibid.*, Chapters 5 and 7.

33. *Ibid.*, p. 82.

34. Joseph Veroff, Elizabeth Douvan, and Richard A. Kulka, *The Inner American: A Self-Portrait from 1957 to 1976* (New York: Basic Books, 1981), pp. 17–25.

35. *Ibid.*, p. 116.

36. *Ibid.*, p. 115–20. See also Angus Campbell, *The Sense of Well-Being in America: Recent Patterns and Trends* (New York: McGraw-Hill, 1981).

37. *Soundings from DDB*, no. 9 (December 1981), Doyle Dane Bernbach, Inc., New York, 1981, pp. 1–2.

38. Bob Secter, "Peace Corps: a New Breed of Volunteer," *Los Angeles Times*, February 13, 1982.

39. Yankelovich, *op. cit.*, pp. 44–45.

40. *Ibid.*, p. 235.

41. Willard Gaylin, *Caring* (New York: Knopf, 1976), p. 12.

42. For discussion and references see Chapter 3, pp. 62–63.

43. Mildred Newman and Bernard Berkowitz, *How to Be Your Own Best Friend* (New York: Random House, 1971), p. 7.

44. *Ibid.*, p. 32.

45. Quoted in Maurice Friedman, "Aiming at the Self: The Paradox of Encounter and the Human Potential Movement," *Journal of Humanistic Psychology*, vol. 16, no. 2 (Spring 1976), p. 26.

46. Peter Marin, "The New Narcissism," *Harper's*, October 1975, p. 47.

47. Yankelovich, *op. cit.*, p. 242.

48. Bellah, *op. cit.*, p. 500.

49. Donald Heinz, "The Consuming Self," *America*, June 4, 1977, p. 499.

50. Walter Tubbs, "Beyond Perls," *Journal of Humanistic Psychology*, vol. 12, no. 2 (1972), p. 5.

51. Friedman, *op. cit.*, pp. 7–8.

52. *Ibid.*, pp. 12–13.

53. Interview with Mary Marcus, "The Artificial Boundary between Self and Family," *Psychology Today*, January 1977, p. 66.

54. "Families on the Couch," *Newsweek*, May 15, 1978, p. 80.

55. David Krech, Richard S. Crutchfield, and Norman Livson, *Elements of Psychology*, 3rd ed. (New York: Knopf, 1974), p. 591.

56. Barbara Hanrahan, in Stephanie Dowrick and Sibyl Grundberg, eds., *Why Children?* (New York: Harcourt Brace Jovanovich, 1980), p. 53.

57. Betty Rollin, "Motherhood: Who Needs It?" *Look,* September 22, 1970, p. 17.

58. Gail Scott, "Singles: The Mothers' Case for Non-Custody," *Washington Post,* May 6, 1981.

59. Lillian B. Rubin, *Women of a Certain Age: The Midlife Search for Self* (New York: Harper & Row, Harper Colophon Books, 1979).

60. *Ibid.,* pp. 1–2.

61. Betty Friedan, *The Second Stage* (New York: Simon and Schuster, Summit Books, 1981).

62. Paul Zweig, *The Heresy of Self-Love: A Study of Subversive Individualism* (Princeton, NJ: Princeton University Press, 1968; paperback edition, 1980).

63. Peter L. Berger, "New Attack on the Legitimacy of Business," *Harvard Business Review,* vol. 59 (September–October 1981), p. 82.

64. Marin, *op. cit.,* pp. 45, 48.

65. Parker J. Palmer, "A Place Called Community," *Christian Century,* March 16, 1977, p. 253.

66. *Ibid.*

67. John Howard, "The Individual in Society: A Commitment to Discipline and Compassion," *Vital Speeches,* July 15, 1966, p. 595.

CHAPTER 3: CIVILITY: IN THE SERVICE
OF SHARED CONCERNS

1. Garrett Hardin, "The Tragedy of the Commons," *Science,* vol. 162 (December 13, 1968), p. 1244.

2. *Ibid.,* p. 1245.

3. Thomas C. Schelling, *Micromotives and Macrobehavior* (New York: Norton, 1978), p. 111.

4. "A Conversation with Richard Sennett: You Cannot Ever Make People Enjoy Being Ruled," *U.S. News & World Report,* April 27, 1981, p. 79.

5. *Webster's Third New International Dictionary,* unabridged.

6. "The British Riots," *Washington Post,* July 13, 1981.

7. David S. Broder, "Summers of Change," *Washington Post,* July 22, 1981.

8. Adam Smith, *The Wealth of Nations* (New York: Modern Library, 1937), p. 423.

9. Milton and Rose Friedman, *Free to Choose: A Personal Statement* (New York: Harcourt Brace Jovanovich, 1980), pp. 13–14.

10. Robert E. Lane, "Personal Freedom in a Market Society," *Society,* March/April 1981, p. 63.

11. See Marshall B. Clinard, *Sociology of Deviant Behavior,* 4th ed. (New York: Holt, Rinehart & Winston, 1979).

12. *The Professional Thief: By a Professional Thief,* annotated and interpreted by Edwin H. Sutherland (Chicago: University of Chicago Press, 1937), p. 205.

13. *Ibid.*

14. *The Gallup Poll: Public Opinion 1972–1977,* Volume Two, 1976–1977 (Wilmington, DE: Scholarly Resources, 1978), p. 683.

15. *The Gallup Poll: Public Opinion 1935–1971,* Volume Three, 1959–1971. (New York: Random House, 1972), p. 1935, and *The Gallup Poll: Public Opinion 1972–1977, op. cit.,* pp. 48, 230, 531, 532.

16. Carnegie Council on Policy Studies in Higher Education, *Fair Practices in Higher Education* (San Francisco: Jossey-Bass, 1979), pp. 12–13.

17. U.S. Bureau of the Census, *Statistical Abstract of the United States: 1980,* Washington, DC, 1980, table 319.

18. Fred Barbash, "IRS Chief Says Tax System Under 'Strain,'" *Washington Post,* August 9, 1981.

19. "Income Taxes: New Crackdown by IRS?" *U.S. News & World Report,* April 19, 1982, p. 43; and U.S. Internal Revenue Service, "Taxpayer Compliance Measurement Program, Phase III (Individual Returns)," table 1, January 1981.

20. Irwin Ross, "Why the Underground Economy Is Booming," *Fortune,* October 9, 1978, p. 94.

21. *Ibid.,* p. 98.

22. David Iwamoto, with Beatrice C. Lee, "Student Behavior in the Secondary Schools," National Education Association, *Research Report R 12,* 1965.

23. U.S. Department of Defense, Report to the Senate Armed Services Committee, *The Reserve Officers Training Corps., 1980,* pp. 3, 7.

24. "The Talk of the Town," *New Yorker,* April 5, 1976, p. 27.

25. "Guns," *60 Minutes,* CBS News, September 25, 1977, transcript, p. 19.

26. Communication with an aide to Rep. Collins, August 11, 1981. The bill, introduced in March 1981, is H.R. 2389.

27. "Taxpayers' Rights," *The MacNeil/Lehrer Report,* WNET/Thirteen, April 14, 1981, transcript, pp. 1–2.

28. Fred I. Greenstein and Sidney Tarrow, "Political Orientations of Children: The Use of a Semi-Projective Technique in Three Nations," *Sage Professional Papers in Comparative Politics,* vol. 1 (Beverly Hills, CA: Sage Publications, 1970), pp. 480, 522.

29. *The Gallup Poll: Public Opinion 1972–1977, op. cit.,* p. 128.

30. Thomas B. Edsall, "Congress Votes Itself a Break on Taxes, Audit Protection," *Washington Post,* December 17, 1981.

31. See Chapter 9, pp. 227–228.

32. Daniel Bell, "The Revolution of Rising Entitlements," *Fortune,* April 1975, p. 100.

33. Carl V. Patton, "The Politics of Social Security," in Michael J. Boskin, ed., *The Crisis in Social Security: Problems and Prospects* (San Francisco: Institute for Contemporary Studies, 1977), pp. 151–52.

34. Martha Derthick, *Policymaking for Social Security* (Washington, DC: Brookings Institution, 1979), p. 280.

35. Steven V. Roberts, "An Angry Young Congressman Criticizes Special Interest Groups," *New York Times,* January 11, 1981.

36. Joseph A. Califano, Jr., *Governing America: An Insider's Report from the White House and the Cabinet* (New York: Simon and Schuster, 1981), pp. 450–51.

37. "Closing the Historic Party Identification Gap," *National Journal,* June 13, 1981, p. 1081.

38. *Statistical Abstract: 1980, op. cit.,* table 853. Data for 1980 are unofficial.

39. *Ibid.,* calculated from tables 825, 851.

40. Everett Carll Ladd, "How to Tame the Special-Interest Groups," *Fortune,* October 20, 1980, pp. 66–67.

41. *Ibid.,* p. 67.

42. Walter Dean Burnham, "Party Systems and the Political Process," in William Nisbet Chambers and Walter Dean Burnham, eds., *The American Party Systems,* 2nd ed. (New York: Oxford University Press, 1975), p. 305.

43. Rowland Evans and Robert Novak, *The Reagan Revolution: A Blueprint for the Next Four Years* (New York: E. P. Dutton, 1981).

44. William Greider, "The Education of David Stockman," *Atlantic Monthly,* December 1981, p. 46.

45. U.S. Congress, House Committee on Ways and Means, *Tax Incentive Act of 1981: Report on H.R. 4242,* 97th Congress, 1st session, Report no. 97–201, July 24, 1981, p. 20.

46. "Key Provisions of the New Tax Law . . . More Than Just Investment Incentives," *National Journal,* August 8, 1981, p. 1409.

47. Communication with staff members of the Joint Committee on Taxation; see also Robert W. Merry, "AT&T Could Get $14 Billion in Tax Breaks from Obscure Change in Write-Off Rules," *Wall Street Journal,* October 7, 1981.

48. Calculated from information made available by staff members of the Joint Committee on Taxation, in conjunction with data in Joint Committee on Taxation, *General Explanation of the Economic Recovery Tax Act of 1981 (H.R. 4242, 97th Congress; Public Law 97–34),* December 29, 1981, especially Table V-3, pp. 382–91.

49. *The Gallup Opinion Index,* Report no. 174, January 1980, p. 28.

50. *The Gallup Poll: Public Opinion 1972–1977, op. cit.,* pp. 506–7.

51. "Poll Finds Public Supports Variety of Moves in Fight on Inflation," *New York Times,* November 8, 1979.

52. "The Politics of Sugar: Powerful Rivals Clash over Sugar Price Supports," *New York Times,* January 16, 1979.

53. Ward Sinclair, "Hill's Humming over Sugar Producers' Push for Price Supports," *Washington Post,* June 27, 1981.

54. "The Politics of Sugar: Conflicting Interests over Sugar Create Unwanted U.S. Surpluses," *New York Times,* January 14, 1979.

55. *Ibid.*

56. Seth S. King, "Reagan, in Bid for Budget Votes, Reported to Yield on Sugar Prices," *New York Times,* June 27, 1981.

57. Richard L. Hudson, "Big Cost Churns Up Opposition to Dairy Supports," *Wall Street Journal,* October 16, 1980.

58. Ann Crittenden, "Federal Support for Dairy Prices Criticized Anew," *New York Times,* February 16, 1981; and Ward Sinclair, "Dairy Gusher Causing Budget to Curdle," *Washington Post,* March 7, 1982.

59. Robert W. Crandall, "Steel Imports: Dumping or Competition?" *Regulation,* July/August 1980, p. 23.

60. John W. Gardner, Speech delivered at Brown University, March 17, 1980, unpublished. Quoted by permission.

61. *Ibid.*

62. "Reviving the Political Parties," *In Common,* Fall 1979, pp. 19–22.

63. *Statistical Abstract: 1980, op. cit.,* table 441.

64. U.S. Senate, Committee on Governmental Affairs, Hearings before the Permanent Subcommittee on Investigations, "Fraud, Abuse, Waste, and Mismanagement in the Department of Health, Education, and Welfare," 95th Congress, 2nd session, July 20, 1978, p. 15.

65. Joseph Bensman and Robert Lilienfeld, *Between Public and Private: The Lost Boundaries of the Self* (New York: Macmillan, Free Press, 1979), p. *vii.*

66. Harrison Schmitt, Letter, *Science,* vol. 211, January 16, 1981, p. 226.

67. "A Diminished Thrust for Innovation," *Business Week,* June 30, 1980, p. 61.

68. Schelling, *op. cit.,* p. 213.

69. Peter F. Drucker, *Management: Tasks, Responsibilities, Practices* (New York: Harper & Row, 1974), p. 334.

70. *The Gallup Poll: Public Opinion 1972–1977, op. cit.,* p. 370.

71. *Public Opinion,* September/October 1978, p. 34.

72. *Newsweek,* December 15, 1975, p. 44.

73. Everett Carll Ladd, Jr., "What the Voters Really Want," *Fortune,* December 18, 1978, p. 41.

74. "What Price Regulation?" *Newsweek,* March 19, 1979, p. 79.

CHAPTER 4: THE TRIPLE ROLE OF INSTITUTIONS

1. Seymour Martin Lipset, *Political Man* (Garden City, NY: Doubleday, 1960; Anchor edition, 1963), pp. 337–38. For a recent report in line with Lipset's observation, see Robert Lindsey, "Campus Radicals of 60's Are Reshaping Style of Local Government on Coast," *New York Times*, March 14, 1982.

2. See Chapter 6.

3. Frank E. Armbruster, *The Forgotten Americans: A Survey of Values, Beliefs, and Concerns of the Majority* (New Rochelle, NY: Arlington House, 1972), p. 41.

4. *Ibid.*, pp. 42–43.

5. Seymour Martin Lipset and William Schneider, "Organized Labor and the Public: A Troubled Union," *Public Opinion*, August/September 1981, p. 52; Barry Sussman, "Americans Favor Labor Unions, But Hold Leaders in Disrepute," *Washington Post*, February 7, 1982.

6. "Unions on the Run," *U.S. News & World Report*, September 14, 1981, p. 61.

7. "Opinion Roundup," *Public Opinion*, October/November 1979, p. 30.

8. *Ibid.*, See Amitai Etzioni and Thomas A. DiPrete, "The Decline in Confidence in America: The Prime Factor, a Research Note," *Journal of Applied Behavioral Science*, vol. 15 (October-November-December 1979), p. 522.

9. Louis Harris, "Alienation among Americans Has Increased Steadily over the Years," *ABC News–Harris Survey*, vol. II, no. 67 (June 2, 1980).

10. Peter L. Berger and Richard John Neuhaus, *To Empower People: The Role of Mediating Structures in Public Policy* (Washington, DC: American Enterprise Institute, 1977), p. 11.

11. Parker J. Palmer, "A Place Called Community," *Christian Century*, March 16, 1977, p. 253.

12. *Ibid.*

13. Cornelius Ryan and Kathryn Morgan Ryan, *A Private Battle* (New York: Simon and Schuster, 1979).

14. *Ibid.*, p. 67.

15. *Ibid.*, p. 84.

16. *Ibid.*, p. 88.

17. Martha Weinman Lear, *Heartsounds* (New York: Simon and Schuster, 1979).

CHAPTER 5: THE ESSENTIAL FAMILY: EDUCATION FOR MUTUALITY AND CIVILITY

1. Speech to the Economic Development Subcommittee, House Committee on Public Works and Transportation, November 18, 1981.

2. Ron Alexander, "Single Parents Meet to Share a Continuing Quest for Stability," *New York Times,* June 20, 1981.

3. Betty Friedan, "Feminism Takes a New Turn," *New York Times Magazine,* November 18, 1979.

4. Sar A. Levitan, "The U.S. Family," *New York Times,* July 27, 1981. See also Levitan and Richard S. Belous, *What's Happening to the American Family?* (Baltimore: Johns Hopkins University Press, 1981), especially pp. 4–16.

5. "How Marriages Can Last," *Newsweek,* July 13, 1981, p. 73.

6. U.S. Bureau of the Census, *Population Estimates and Projections,* Current Population Reports, series P–25, no. 607, August 1975, p. 12.

7. U.S. Bureau of the Census, *Statistical Abstract of the United States: 1980,* Washington, DC, 1980, table 62.

8. U.S. Bureau of the Census, *Households and Families by Type,* March 1977, calculated from table 5.

9. *Statistical Abstract: 1980, op. cit.,* calculated from table 123.

10. "Opinion Roundup," *Public Opinion,* December/January 1980, p. 32.

11. Lynn Shahan, *Living Alone & Liking It* (Beverly Hills, CA: Stratford Press, 1981).

12. Advertisement, *Washington Post,* August 23, 1981.

13. U.S. Bureau of the Census, *Historical Statistics of the United States: Colonial Times to 1970,* Washington, DC, 1975, series B 126–27. The figure is particularly low due to high infant mortality.

14. *Statistical Abstract: 1980, op. cit.,* table 108.

15. Leslie Aldridge Westoff, "Second-Time Winners," *New York Times Magazine,* August 10, 1975, pp. 10–15. See also Westoff, *The Second Time Around: Remarriage in America* (New York: Viking, 1977).

16. Westoff, "Second-Time Winners," *op. cit.,* p. 11.

17. *Ibid.,* p. 13. See U.S. Bureau of the Census, "Number, Timing, and Duration of Marriages and Divorces in the United States: June 1975," *Current Population Reports,* series P–20, no. 297, 1976, p. 7. Glick's projections are based on 1970 data. More recent projections, although not comparable because of differences in methodology, show a smaller difference between the divorce rates for first marriages and for remarriages, but they too indicate a higher rate for remarriages. These projections suggest that among those aged 25–35 in 1975, about 40 percent of remarriages will end in divorce, compared to about 33 percent of first marriages. For detailed data and comparison of methodologies, see the report cited above, pp. 4–7. On this point see also Andrew Hacker, "Farewell to the Family?" *New York Review of Books,* March 8, 1982, p. 37.

18. George E. Vaillant, *Adaptation to Life* (Boston: Little, Brown, 1977), p. 322.

19. Lawrence A. Kurdek, "An Integrative Perspective on Children's Divorce

Adjustment," *American Psychologist,* vol. 36 (August 1981), pp. 856–66.

20. James M. Herzog, "On Father Hunger," in John Ross, Alan Gerwit, and Stanley Cath, eds., *Father and Child: Development in Clinical Perspective* (Boston: Little, Brown, 1982), pp. 163–74.

21. "One-Parent Families and Their Children: The School's Most Significant Minority," National Association of Elementary School Principals Staff Report, *Principal,* vol. 60 (September 1980), pp. 33–34.

22. Jessie S. Bernard, *Remarriage: A Study of Marriage* (New York: Dryden Press, 1956), ch. 12.

23. This point is highlighted by Andrew J. Cherlin, *Marriage Divorce Remarriage* (Cambridge: Harvard University Press, 1981).

24. Robert F. Bales, "The Equilibrium Problem in Small Groups," in Talcott Parsons, Robert F. Bales, and Edward A. Shils, eds., *Working Papers in the Theory of Action* (Glencoe, IL: Free Press, 1953), pp. 111–61; and Robert F. Bales and Philip E. Slater, "Role Differentiation in Small Decision-Making Groups," in Talcott Parsons and Robert F. Bales, *Family, Socialization and Interaction Process* (Glencoe, IL: Free Press, 1955) pp. 259–306.

25. Morris Zelditch, Jr., "Role Differentiation in the Nuclear Family," in Parsons and Bales, *op. cit.,* pp. 307–51.

26. Quoted from an interview in Rosemary Dinnage, "Understanding Loss: The Bowlby Canon," *Psychology Today,* May 1980, p. 60.

27. U.S. Bureau of the Census, *Statistical Abstract of the United States: 1975,* Washington, DC, 1975, table 565.

28. *Statistical Abstract: 1980, op. cit.,* table 671.

29. "Women Mix Jobs, Maternity," *Washington Post,* June 2, 1981.

30. *Statistical Abstract: 1980, op. cit.,* calculated from table 75.

31. "The Children of Divorce," *Newsweek,* February 11, 1980, p. 59.

32. *Statistical Abstract: 1980, op. cit.,* table 95.

33. *Ibid.,* table 75.

34. *Ibid.,* calculated from table 672.

35. "When School Kids Come Home to an Empty House—," *U.S. News & World Report,* September 14, 1981, p. 42.

36. *Families at Work: Strengths and Strains,* The General Mills American Family Report 1980–81 (Minneapolis: General Mills, Inc., 1981), p. 28.

37. Bales, "The Equilibrium Problem in Small Groups," *op. cit.* See also Edgar F. Borgatta, Arthur Couch, and Robert F. Bales, "Some Findings Relevant to the Great Man Theory of Leadership," *American Sociological Review,* vol. 19 (1954), pp. 755–59.

38. "Opinion Roundup," *Public Opinion,* December/January 1980, p. 27. See also Connie de Boer, "The Polls: Marriage—A Decaying Institution?" *Public Opinion Quarterly,* vol. 45 (1981), p. 272.

39. Michael Novak, "The Family out of Favor," *Harper's,* April 1976, p. 39.

40. "How Marriages Can Last," *op. cit.*

41. Nena O'Neill and George O'Neill, *Open Marriage, A New Life Style for Couples* (New York: M. Evans and Co., 1972), p. 54.

42. *Ibid.,* pp. 54–55.

43. *Ibid.,* p. 55.

44. Peter J. Stein, "Singlehood: An Alternative to Marriage," *Family Coordinator,* vol. 24 (October 1975), p. 489.

45. Genie Chipps, "Liberated Love: Unmarried, Committed, & Free," *Harper's Bazaar,* May 1977, p. 120.

46. *Ibid.,* p. 121.

47. Herbert A. Otto, "The New Marriage: Marriage as a Framework for Developing Personal Potential," in Herbert A. Otto, ed., *The Family in Search of a Future: Alternate Models for Moderns* (New York: Appleton-Century-Crofts, 1970), p. 116.

48. Nick Stinnett and Craig Wayne Birdsong, *The Family and Alternate Life Styles* (Chicago: Nelson-Hall, 1978), p. 89.

49. Don Sloan and Lillian Africano, "Marriage: The Traditional Alternative," *Harper's Bazaar,* May 1977, p. 24.

50. Chipps, *op. cit.,* p. 120.

51. *Ibid.*

52. Amitai Etzioni, "The Husband's Rights in Abortion," *Trial,* vol. 12 (November 1976), pp. 56–58.

53. For a discussion and a list of many other suggestions, see White House Conference on Families, *Listening to America's Families: Action for the Eighties, A Report to the President, Congress and Families of the Nation,* 1980. The suggestions are best examined in the context of the warning raised by Gilbert Y. Steiner in *The Futility of Family Policy* (Washington, DC: Brookings Institution, 1981).

54. For a report of one such effort by the Catholic church see Andree Brooks, "Catholic Courses for Lasting Marriages," *New York Times,* September 21, 1981.

55. See Talcott Parsons, *The Structure of Social Action* (Glencoe, IL: Free Press, 1949).

CHAPTER 6: SCHOOLS: EDUCATIONAL EXPERIENCES FIRST

1. George N. Gallup, "The 12th Annual Gallup Poll of the Public's Attitudes Toward the Public Schools," *Phi Delta Kappan,* September 1980, p. 35.

2. U.S. Department of Health, Education and Welfare, National Institute of Education, *Violent Schools—Safe Schools: The Safe School Study Report to the Congress,* Executive Summary, Washington, DC, 1977, p. 5.

3. U.S. Department of Health, Education and Welfare, National Institute of Education, National Assessment of Educational Progress, *Three National Assessments of Reading: Changes in Performance, 1970–80,* summary no. 11-R-35.

4. Rudolf Flesch, *Why Johnny Can't Read—and What You Can Do About It* (New York: Harper, 1955); "Johnny Can't Count—The Dangers for U.S.," *U.S. News & World Report,* February 15, 1982, p. 45; "Today's High-School Diploma Is Fraudulent," *U.S. News & World Report,* September 7, 1981, p. 53.

5. Flesch, *op. cit.,* and *Why Johnny Still Can't Read: A New Look at the Scandal of Our Schools* (New York: Harper & Row, 1981).

6. Carol Krucoff, "Education: Pushing Kids to Success or Stress?" *Washington Post,* November 24, 1981.

7. For some data and additional discussion, see Part II, Chapter 11.

8. See Dennis Wrong, "The Over-socialized Conception of Man in Modern Sociology," *American Sociological Review,* vol. 26 (1961), pp. 183–93.

9. Kenneth D. Benne, *A Conception of Authority* (New York: Russell and Russell, 1944; reissued 1971).

10. James O'Toole, *Work, Learning and the American Future* (San Francisco: Jossey-Bass, 1977), pp. 117–18.

11. "School's Fourth 'R' is 'Responsibility,'" *New York Times,* June 22, 1981.

12. *Ibid.*

13. Robert Benjamin, *Making Schools Work: A Reporter's Journey Through Some of America's Most Remarkable Classrooms* (New York: Continuum, 1981).

14. Joe Nathan and Herbert Kohl, "Public Alternative Schools and the Future of Democracy," *Phi Delta Kappan,* June 1981, p. 733.

15. Lester C. Thurow, "Vocational Education as a Strategy for Eliminating Poverty," in *The Planning Papers for the Vocational Education Study,* Vocational Education Study Publication No. 1, National Institute of Education, April 1979, p. 327.

16. *Three National Assessments of Reading, op. cit.* See also Gene I. Maeroff, "Reading Skills: New Problems," *New York Times,* April 30, 1981.

17. James S. Coleman, Thomas Hoffer, and Sally Kilgore, *Public and Private Schools* (Chicago: National Opinion Research Center, 1981). See also Coleman, Kilgore, and Hoffer, "Public and Private Schools," *Society,* vol. 19 (January/February 1982), pp. 4–9.

18. Edward B. Fiske, "School Study Said to Fail to Emphasize Main Point," *New York Times,* April 26, 1981.

19. Coleman *et al.*, *Public and Private Schools*, *op. cit.*, p. *xx*.

20. Michael Rutter, Barbara Maughan, Peter Mortimore, Janet Ouston, with Alan Smith, *Fifteen Thousand Hours* (Cambridge, MA: Harvard University Press, 1979).

21. Amitai Etzioni, *A Comparative Analysis of Complex Organizations* (Glencoe, IL: Free Press, 1961).

22. Michael Medved and David Wallechinsky, *What Really Happened to the Class of '65?* (New York: Random House, 1976).

23. Hans G. Furth, *Piaget for Teachers* (Englewood Cliffs, NJ: Prentice-Hall, 1970), p. 146.

24. D. W. McNally, *Piaget, Education and Teaching* (Lewes, England: New Educational Press, 1974), p. 96.

25. Arnold Gesell and Frances L. Ilg, with Janet Learned and Louise B. Ames, *Infant and Child in the Culture of Today: The Guidance of Development in Home and Nursery School* (New York: Harper, 1943), p. 4.

26. *Ibid.*, p. 41.

27. *Ibid.*, p. 57.

28. John Holt, *The Underachieving School* (New York: Dell, 1970), pp. 3–4.

29. John Holt, *Freedom and Beyond* (New York: Dutton, 1972), p. 2.

30. John Holt, *What Do I Do Monday?* (New York: Dutton, 1970), pp. 70–71.

31. Charles E. Silberman, *Crisis in the Classroom: The Remaking of American Education* (New York: Random House, 1970).

32. *Ibid.*, p. 122.

33. Willard Waller, *The Sociology of Teaching* (New York: John Wiley & Sons Science Editions, 1965), quoted in Silberman, *op. cit.*, p. 123.

34. Philip W. Jackson, *Life in Classrooms* (New York: Holt, Rinehart & Winston, 1968), quoted in Silberman, *op. cit.*, p. 123.

35. Silberman, *op. cit.*, p. 137.

36. See. R. L. Thorndike, "Marks and Marking Systems," in *Encyclopedia of Educational Research* (New York: Macmillan, 1969); and J. R. Warren, *College Grading Practices: An Overview* (Washington, DC: Educational Resources Information Center, 1971).

37. David Thornton Moore, "Discovering the Pedagogy of Experience," *Harvard Educational Review*, vol. 51 (May 1981), pp. 287, 288.

38. Ivan Illich, *Deschooling Society* (New York: Harper & Row, 1971).

39. Moore, *op. cit.*, p. 289.

40. Elliott Jaques, *The Changing Culture of a Factory* (London: Tavistock Publications, 1951).

41. Gene Maeroff, *Don't Blame the Kids: The Trouble with America's Public Schools* (New York: McGraw-Hill, 1981).

42. Roland S. Barth, "Discipline: If You Do That Again, _____,"
Phi Delta Kappan, vol. 61 (February 1980), p. 398.

43. *U.S. Department of Education News,* August 21, 1981, p. 1.

44. Fred L. Pincus, "The False Promises of Community Colleges: Class Conflict and Vocational Education," *Harvard Educational Review,* vol. 50 (August 1980), p. 332.

45. See Carnegie Commission on Higher Education, *Priorities for Action: Final Report* and *College Graduates and Jobs* (New York: McGraw-Hill, 1973). See also Richard Freeman, *The Overeducated American* (New York: Academic Press, 1976).

46. "Preschool Works for Low-Income Children, Researchers Find in Analyzing 12 Studies," *Phi Delta Kappan,* vol. 61 (February 1980), p. 378. The full report of the study, *Lasting Effects After Preschool,* is available from ERIC/ECE, College of Education, University of Illinois.

47. See, for instance, Christopher Jencks, *Who Gets Ahead? The Determinants of Economic Success in America* (New York: Basic Books, 1979), p. 97. Note that in assessing the effect of noncognitive or personality traits, Jencks and his colleagues found, rather than one key trait, a number of traits that each make a small difference and that in accumulation are important. However, as I see it, several of these traits are but elements of self-organization.

48. National Commission on Youth, *The Transition of Youth to Adulthood: A Bridge Too Long. A Report to Educators, Sociologists, Legislators, and Youth Policymaking Bodies* (Boulder, CO: Westview Press, 1980).

49. Carnegie Council on Policy Studies in Higher Education, *Giving Youth a Better Chance: Options for Education, Work, and Service* (San Francisco: Jossey-Bass, 1979). See also Torsten Husén, *The School in Question: A Comparative Study of the School and Its Future in Western Societies* (New York: Oxford University Press, 1979).

50. Cited by Sheila Cole, "Send Our Children to Work?" *Psychology Today,* July 1980, pp. 44–68. See also Cole, *Working Kids on Working* (New York: Lothrop, Lee and Shepard, 1980).

51. Dan Morgan, "Out of the Classrooms, into the Communities," *Washington Post,* July 5, 1981.

52. See Charles C. Moskos, "Making the All-Volunteer Force Work: A National Service Approach," *Foreign Affairs,* vol. 60 (Fall 1981), pp. 17–34.

53. U.S. Bureau of the Census, *Statistical Abstract of the United States: 1980,* Washington, DC, 1980, calculated from table 658.

CHAPTER 7: REGIONALISM AND NATION-REBUILDING

1. For a discussion of the decline of patriotism, see Robert Nisbet, *Twilight of Authority* (New York: Oxford, 1975), pp. 69ff.

2. Michael J. McManus, ". . . In the Face of Dire Economic Necessity," *Empire State Report*, vol. 2, no. 9 (1976), p. 345.

3. U.S. Bureau of the Census, *Statistical Abstract of the United States: 1980*, Washington, DC, 1980, table 573.

4. *Ibid.*, table 13.

5. *Ibid.*, table 10.

6. McManus, *op. cit.*, p. 343.

7. *Regional Diversity: Growth in the U.S. 1960–1990*, Joint Center for Urban Studies, Massachusetts Institute of Technology and Harvard University, 1981. For a political-historical perspective on the difference between present-day and earlier regional diversities, see Daniel Patrick Moynihan, *Counting Our Blessings: Reflections on the Future of America* (Boston: Little, Brown, 1980), pp. 216–34.

8. Malcolm S. Forbes, Jr., "We're Supposed to Be One Country," *Forbes*, September 18, 1978, p. 35.

9. James Coates, "A New Civil War Looms over State Taxes on Natural Resources," *Washington Post*, August 19, 1981.

10. Horace Sutton, "Sunbelt vs. Frostbelt: A Second Civil War?" *Saturday Review*, April 15, 1978, p. 35.

11. See, for example, *National Journal*, June 26, 1976, p. 878.

12. Jill Schuker, "The Energy Concerns of New England," in Edward J. Mitchell, ed., *Energy: Regional Goals and the National Interest* (Washington, DC: American Enterprise Institute, 1976), p. 13.

13. McManus, *op. cit.*, p. 344.

14. Coates, *op. cit.*

15. McManus, *op. cit.*, p. 344.

16. Coates, *op. cit.*

17. Alfred R. Light, "Drawing the Wagons into a Circle: Sectionalism and Energy Politics," *Publius*, vol. 8, no. 1 (1978), p. 35.

18. Coates, *op. cit.*

19. *Ibid.*

20. "Now Energy Is What Counts in the War between States," *Business Week*, October 26, 1981, p. 170.

21. *Ibid.*

22. *Statistical Abstract: 1980, op. cit.*, calculated from table 1445, using regional definitions from table 13.

23. *State of the Region*, Northeast-Midwest Congressional Coalition, quoted in *Nation's Business*, November 1980, p. 88.

24. Joel Garreau, *The Nine Nations of North America* (Boston: Houghton-Mifflin, 1981).

25. For additional discussion see Amitai Etzioni, *Political Unification: A Comparative Study of Leaders and Forces* (New York: Holt, Rinehart and Winston, 1965).

26. "Opinion Roundup," *Public Opinion* June/July 1981, p. 28.

27. Private communication from Alec Gallup.

28. George H. Gallup, *The Gallup Poll: Public Opinion 1935–1971*, vol. 3 (New York: Random House, 1972), p. 2292.

29. See above, pp. 96 ff.

30. Everett Carll Ladd, Jr., "205 and Going Strong," *Public Opinion*, June/July 1981, p. 8.

31. *Ibid.*

32. "Opinion Roundup," *Public Opinion*, January/February 1979, p. 21.

33. "Opinion Roundup," *Public Opinion*, June/July 1981, p. 36.

34. See, for example, B. Drummond Ayres, Jr., "President and the Cities," *New York Times*, December 3, 1981; and Richard A. Snelling, interviewed by Ayres, "The 'New Federalism' Looks Good—From Washington," *New York Times*, December 6, 1981.

35. *Statistical Abstract: 1980, op. cit.,* table 519.

36. Nathan Glazer, "Federalism and Ethnicity: The Experience of the United States," *Publius*, vol. 7, no. 4 (1977), pp. 71–87.

CHAPTER 8: THE SEVEN ELEMENTS OF INDUSTRIALIZATION: AN HISTORICAL FLASHBACK

1. Albert O. Hirschman, *The Strategy of Economic Development* (New Haven, CT: Yale University Press, 1958), p. 83.

2. Victor S. Clark, *History of Manufactures in the United States*, vol. 1, 1607–1860 (Washington, DC: Carnegie Institution, 1929), pp. 448–50.

3. Quoted in Edward C. Kirkland, *A History of American Economic Life*, 4th ed. (New York: Appleton-Century-Crofts, 1969), p. 228.

4. Thomas C. Cochran, *Frontiers of Change: Early Industrialism in America* (New York: Oxford University Press, 1981).

5. U.S. Bureau of the Census, *Historical Statistics of the United States: Colonial Times to 1970* (Washington, DC, 1975), series D 167, 170, 174 (labor force and employment), F 239, 241 (value added).

6. Kirkland, *op. cit.,* p. 227. On the "late" dating, see Walter Nugent, *Structures of American Social History* (Bloomington: Indiana University Press, 1981), pp. 87 *ff.*

7. General Motors, *The 3,000-Mile Assembly Line*, 1980.

8. Caroline E. MacGill, *History of Transportation in the United States before 1860* (Washington, DC: Carnegie Institution of Washington, 1917), pp. 85–86. For a more recent discussion of the importance of transportation to industrialization, see Cochran, *op. cit.*

9. Richard K. Vedder, *The American Economy in Historical Perspective* (Belmont, CA: Wadsworth Publishing Company, 1976), pp. 145–50.

10. *Ibid.,* pp. 150, 160.

11. U.S. Bureau of the Census, *Historical Statistics of the United States, Colonial Times to 1957* (Washington DC, 1960), series Q 1–11. According to the Interstate Commerce Commission, reliable earlier data are not available on freight traffic by type of transportation.

12. *Historical Statistics to 1970, op. cit.*, series M 93.

13. *Ibid.*, series P 68, 69.

14. *Ibid.*, series S 44.

15. See Edward F. Denison, *Accounting for United States Economic Growth, 1929–1969* (Washington, DC: Brookings Institution, 1974); John W. Kendrick, "Survey of the Factors Contributing to the Decline in U.S. Productivity Growth," in *The Decline in Productivity Growth*, Federal Reserve Bank of Boston, Conference Series No. 22, June 1980.

16. Denison, *op. cit.*, p. 128.

17. *Historical Statistics to 1970, op. cit.*, series W 99.

18. Gustav Ranis, "Economic Growth: Theory," *International Encyclopedia of the Social Sciences* (New York: Macmillan, 1968), p. 415.

19. Jonathan Hughes, *Industrialization and Economic History: Theses and Conjectures* (New York: McGraw-Hill, 1970), p. 111.

20. For a good review of the literature on this subject, see Stuart W. Bruchey, *The Roots of American Economic Growth, 1607–1861* (New York: Harper & Row, 1968).

21. For background information on this period, see Morton Keller, *Affairs of State: Public Life in Late Nineteenth Century America* (Cambridge MA: Harvard University Press, Belknap Press, 1977), pp. 162–96, 409–38; and Daniel J. Boorstin, *The Americans: The Democratic Experience* (New York: Random House, 1973).

22. Mark Sullivan, *Our Times: 1900–1925*, vol. II of *America Finding Herself* (New York: Charles Scribner's Sons, 1971), p. 325.

23. *Historical Statistics to 1970, op. cit.*, series A 7.

24. *Ibid.*, series C 89, 90.

25. Albert Fishlow, "Levels of Nineteenth-Century American Investment in Education," *Journal of Economic History*, vol. 26 (December 1966), p. 418.

26. *Ibid.*, p. 430.

27. *Historical Statistics to 1970, op. cit.*, series H 419, 599.

28. Kirkland, *op. cit.*, p. 300.

29. *Historical Statistics to 1970, op. cit.*, series P 265.

30. *Ibid.*, series P 353.

31. *Ibid.*, series P 17.

32. *Ibid.*, series D 685.

33. Neil Grant, *The Industrial Revolution* (New York: Franklin Watts, 1973), p. 64.

34. Harry N. Scheiber, Harold G. Vatter, and Harold Underwood Faulkner, *American Economic History*, 9th ed. (New York: Harper & Row, 1976), p. 221.

35. Sumner H. Slichter, *Economic Growth in the United States: Its History, Problems and Prospects* (Baton Rouge: Louisiana State University Press, 1961), pp. 59–62.

36. Grant, *op. cit.*, p. 64.

37. *Historical Statistics to 1970, op. cit.*, series P 13.

38. *Ibid.*, series D 685, F 4.

39. John Kenneth Galbraith, *A Life in Our Times* (Boston: Houghton-Mifflin, 1981), pp. 171–72.

40. Calculated from data in *Historical Statistics to 1970, op. cit.*, series P 13 (1950–1970), and in U.S. Bureau of the Census, *Statistical Abstract of the United States: 1980* (Washington, DC, 1980), table 1436 (1971–75).

41. *Economic Report of the President*, transmitted to the Congress January 1980 (Washington, DC, 1980), table B-2.

42. U.S. Bureau of the Census, *Statistical Abstract of the United States: 1978* (Washington DC, 1978), table 714.

43. *Economic Report of the President, op. cit.*, table B-25.

44. *Ibid.*, table B-22.

45. U.S. Bureau of the Census, *Social Indicators: 1976* (Washington, DC, December 1977), table 3/6.

46. Fred C. Allvine and Fred A. Tarpley, Jr., *The New State of the Economy* (Cambridge, MA: Winthrop Publishers, 1977), p. 3.

47. *Statistical Abstract: 1978, op. cit.*, table 987.

48. *Ibid.*, table 771.

49. For 1960, Ben J. Wattenberg, *The Real America: A Surprising Examination of the State of the Union* (Garden City, NY: Doubleday, 1974), p. 93; for 1970, *Statistical Abstract: 1978, op. cit.*, table 1096.

50. Calculated from *Historical Statistics to 1970, op. cit.*, series H 595–97.

51. Calculated from *Statistical Abstract: 1978, op. cit.*, table 143, using indices of medical care prices from table 141 (1975), and from *Historical Statistics to 1970, op. cit.*, series B 262 (1950).

52. *Statistical Abstract: 1980, op. cit.*, table 106.

53. "Our Endless Pursuit of Happiness," *U.S. News & World Report*, August 10, 1981, p. 62.

54. Calculated from *Statistical Abstract: 1978, op. cit.*, table 400 (1975), and *Historical Statistics to 1970, op. cit.*, series H 878 (1950), using consumer price index from *Statistical Abstract: 1978*, table 792.

55. *Social Indicators: 1976, op. cit.*, table 10/4.

56. U.S. Bureau of the Census, *Statistical Abstract of the United States: 1975* (Washington, DC, 1975), calculated from table 359.

57. *Social Indicators: 1976, op. cit.,* table 10/10.

58. *Statistical Abstract: 1978, op. cit.,* table 393.

59. *Historical Statistics to 1970, op. cit.,* series H 871 (1950); *Statistical Abstract: 1978, op. cit.,* table 401 (1975).

60. *Social Indicators: 1976, op. cit.,* table 10/14 (1955); *Statistical Abstract: 1978, op. cit.,* table 408 (1975).

61. *Statistical Abstract: 1978, op. cit.,* table 518.

62. *Ibid.,* table 515.

63. *Ibid.,* table 518.

64. *Ibid.,* calculated from table 518, using consumer price index from table 792.

65. *Economic Report of the President* (1980) *op. cit.,* calculated from tables B-20, B-70.

66. *Economic Report of the President* (1980) *op. cit.,* table B-20.

67. *Statistical Abstract: 1980, op. cit.,* table 1114.

68. For additional background, see James T. Patterson, *America's Struggle Against Poverty* (Cambridge, MA: Harvard University Press, 1982).

69. *Statistical Abstract: 1978, op. cit.,* tables 734, 735.

70. *Ibid.,* table 756.

71. *Historical Statistics, to 1970, op. cit.,* series G 17.

72. *Statistical Abstract: 1978, op. cit.,* table 754.

73. *Ibid.,* table 734.

74. *Social Indicators: 1976, op. cit.,* table 9/1.

75. *Statistical Abstract: 1978, op. cit.,* table 756.

CHAPTER 9: THE SEVEN ELEMENTS OF INDUSTRIALIZATION REVISITED

1. U.S. Bureau of the Census, *Statistical Abstract of the United States: 1980* (Washington, DC, 1980), table 727.

2. *Ibid.,* table 745.

3. *Economic Report of the President,* transmitted to the Congress January 1980 (Washington, DC, 1980), p. 85.

4. *Ibid.*

5. *Productivity Perspectives,* revised (Houston: American Productivity Center, 1980), p. 9.

6. John W. Kendrick, *Productivity Trends in the United States* (Princeton: Princeton University Press, 1961).

7. *Productivity Perspectives, op. cit.,* p. 9.

8. *Statistical Abstract: 1980, op. cit.,* table 794.

9. *Ibid.,* table 430.

10. For 1950, U.S. Bureau of the Census, *Historical Statistics of the United States: Colonial Times to 1970* (Washington, DC, 1975), series X 138; for 1979, *Statistical Abstract: 1980, op. cit.*, table 863. "Credit market instruments" was used as the measure of consumer debt on the advice of the Flow of Funds Department, Federal Reserve Board. There is a slight difference in the method of computation between the 1979 figure and the 1950 figure.

11. U.S. Department of Transportation, *A Prospectus for Change in the Freight Railroad Industry* (Washington, DC, October 1978), p. 15.

12. Dan Glickman, "America's Railroads Are a Disgrace," *Washington Star*, May 2, 1980.

13. *A Prospectus for Change, op. cit.*, p. 25.

14. *Ibid.*, p. 35.

15. *Ibid.*, p. 29.

16. *Ibid.*, p. 25.

17. *Ibid.*, pp. 11–12.

18. Thomas K. Dyer, Inc., for the Federal Railroad Administration, *United States Class 1 Railroads Fixed Plant Equipment Requirements* (Lexington, MA, October 1977), as quoted in *A Prospectus for Change, op. cit.*, pp. 65, 68.

19. *Statistical Abstract: 1980, op. cit.*, tables 1114, 1109.

20. U.S. Department of Transportation, Federal Highway Administration, *The Status of the Nation's Highways: Conditions and Performance* (Washington, DC, January 1981), p. 16.

21. "93 Million Holes in the Road for Angry Drivers," *U.S. News & World Report*, March 19, 1979, p. 78.

22. Rochelle L. Stanfield, "Hard Times for the Highway Trust Fund May Mean Trouble for Highway Repair," *National Journal*, August 16, 1980, p. 1364.

23. U.S. Senate, Annual Report of the Secretary of Transportation, "Highway Bridge Replacement and Rehabilitation Program," 96th Congress, 2nd Session, 1980, Senate Doc. 96–54, p. 5.

24. *Ibid.*, pp. 206–207. The figure for bridges outside the federally aided system was based on an inventory that was only 48 percent complete. For additional data, see U.S. General Accounting Office, Report by the Comptroller General, "Better Targeting of Federal Funds Needed to Eliminate Unsafe Bridges," August 11, 1981.

25. Phil McCombs, "Empty Fleet Waits at Norfolk for Suddenly Precious Cargo," *Washington Post*, October 13, 1980.

26. Christopher Madison, "Money for Deeper U.S. Coal Ports—Needed or Just More Pork Barrel?" *National Journal*, February 7, 1981, p. 225.

27. McCombs, *op. cit.*

28. Pat Choate and Susan Walter, *America in Ruins: Beyond the Public Works Pork Barrel* (Washington, DC: Council of State Planning Agencies, 1981), p. *xi.*

29. For 1950, *Historical Statistics to 1970, op. cit.,* series F 130, 135–36; for 1979, *Statistical Abstract: 1980, op. cit.,* table 731.

30. For 1950, *Historical Statistics to 1970, op. cit.,* series V 326–27, 331; for 1979, *Statistical Abstract: 1980, op. cit.,* table 940.

31. Charles L. Jackson, "What Will New Technology Bring?" in Roger Sherman, ed., *Perspectives on Postal Service Issues* (Washington, DC: American Enterprise Institute, 1980), p. 120.

32. *Ibid.*

33. Bengt-Arne Vedin, *New Media Survey: A Decision-Maker's Guide to the Communications Explosion* (London: Nord Media, 1978), p. 16.

34. James Martin, *The Wired Society* (Englewood Cliffs, NJ: Prentice-Hall, 1978), p. 139.

35. David Leeson, President, California Microwave, "Satellite Systems," a paper presented at a seminar, "Telecommunications Trends and Directions," sponsored by the Electronics Industry Association in 1979, p. 64. Leeson cites a cost of $1 million per year per transponder, which contains eight hundred voice channels.

36. Gerald W. Brock, *The Telecommunications Industry: The Dynamics of Market Structure* (Cambridge, MA: Harvard University Press, 1981), p. 258.

37. Leeson, *op. cit.,* p. 64.

38. *The Mass Media: Aspen Institute Guide to Communications Industry Trends* (New York: Praeger, 1978), p. 372.

39. For 1952, *Historical Statistics to 1970, op. cit.,* series R 16; for 1979, *Statistical Abstract: 1980, op. cit.,* table 986.

40. *Historical Statistics to 1970, op. cit.,* series R 188.

41. *Statistical Abstract: 1980, op. cit.,* table 981.

42. *Ibid.,* table 977.

43. American Petroleum Institute, *Basic Petroleum Data Book: Petroleum Industry Statistics,* vol. II, no. 1 (January 1982), section VI, tables 10, 11a.

44. See *Statistical Abstract: 1980, op. cit.,* table 725. The implicit price deflator for GNP is used here as the measure of overall price increases; it was 100.0 in 1972 and 165.5 in 1979. The increase in the price of oil is the major factor in rising energy costs, but the cost of energy from all sources has also risen more than other production costs, although the difference is not as great. The producer price index for energy multiplied three and a half times between 1972 and 1979, while for all industrial commodities it doubled. (*Ibid.,* table 797.)

45. Felix G. Rohatyn, "What We Should Do," *Washington Post,* January 30, 1980.

46. Eric Pace, "Delta Plans $7 Billion for Planes," *New York Times,* February 12, 1981.

47. Iver Peterson, "Redesign of American Cars a Boon to Midwest Industry," *New York Times,* March 3, 1980. Although these estimates have since been scaled down, due to the high cost of capital and other considerations, they are still very high and continue to illustrate the point.

48. *Economic Report of the President* (1980), *op. cit.,* p. 115.

49. Federal Energy Administration, *Project Independence, Blueprint,* Final Task Force Report—Finance (Washington, DC, November 1974), table B-1.

50. *Statistical Abstract: 1980, op. cit.,* table 1062.

51. Private communication from John Logsdon, Director, Graduate Program in Science, Technology, and Public Policy, George Washington University, Washington, DC.

52. Robert J. Samuelson, "Don't Forget the Future," *National Journal,* August 2, 1980, p. 1283.

53. National Science Foundation, National Science Board, *Science Indicators—1978* (Washington, DC, 1979), p. 5.

54. Samuelson, *op. cit.,* p. 1283.

55. "Innovation: Has America Lost Its Edge?" *Newsweek,* June 4, 1979, p. 58.

56. *Ibid.,* p. 62.

57. National Science Foundation, National Science Board, *Science Indicators—1976* (Washington, DC, 1977), appendix table 4–18.

58. *Ibid.,* table 4–31.

59. U.S. Department of Commerce, *Advisory Committee on Industrial Innovation: Final Report* (Washington, DC, September 1979), p. 260.

60. Richard Neustadt, *Regulatory Reform: The President's Program,* White House Domestic Policy Staff Report, November 21, 1979.

61. U.S. Executive Office of the President, Office of Management and Budget, *Improving Government Regulations: A Progress Report* (Washington, DC, September 1979), part I, p. 4.

62. U.S. Executive Office of the President, Office of Management and Budget, *Paperwork and Red Tape: New Perspectives, New Directions* (Washington, DC, October 1978), appendix table A. Estimates of the amount of paperwork vary considerably. The General Accounting Office, for instance, estimated in 1978 that the business burden of federal reporting requirements was 169 million hours. (U.S. General Accounting Office, Report by the Comptroller General of the United States, *Federal Paperwork: Its Impact on American Businesses,* November 17, 1978, appendix I.)

63. U.S. Commission on Federal Paperwork, *Final Summary Report* (Washington, DC, 1977), p. 5. A very different estimate is that of the General Accounting Office in 1978 that federal reporting requirements could cost businesses over $1 billion annually. (*Federal Paperwork: Its Impact on American Businesses, op. cit.,* appendix I.)

64. Arthur Andersen & Co., *Cost of Government Regulation Study for the Business Roundtable: Executive Summary* (Chicago, March 1979), p. 14.

65. Timothy B. Clark, "The Costs and Benefits of Regulation—Who Knows How Great They Really Are?" *National Journal,* December 1, 1979, p. 2024. For details see Murray L. Weidenbaum and Robert DeFina, *The Cost of Federal Regulation of Economic Activity* (Washington, DC: American Enterprise Institute, 1978), pp. 2–3. See also Weidenbaum, "The High Cost of Government Regulation," *Challenge,* November–December 1979, pp. 32–39.

66. Clark, *op. cit.,* p. 2024.

67. Arthur Andersen & Co., *op. cit.,* p. 20.

68. Clark, *op. cit.,* p. 2025.

69. *Ibid.*

70. "Antitrust Grows Unpopular," *Business Week,* January 12, 1981, p. 92.

71. Lester C. Thurow, "Let's Abolish the Antitrust Laws," *New York Times,* October 19, 1980.

72. *Ibid.*

73. *Ibid.*

74. *Statistical Abstract: 1980, op. cit.,* table 657, and *Historical Statistics to 1970. op. cit.,* series D 29–41.

75. *Statistical Abstract: 1980, op. cit.,* calculated from tables 696, 698.

76. Angus Campbell, Philip E. Converse, and Willard L. Rodgers, *The Quality of American Life: Perceptions, Evaluations, and Satisfactions* (New York: Russell Sage Foundation, 1976), p. 291.

77. Edward F. Denison, *Accounting for Slower Economic Growth: The United States in the 1970s* (Washington, DC: Brookings Institution, 1979), p. 35.

78. *Ibid.,* p. 134.

79. *Ibid.,* quoting his own *The Sources of Economic Growth in the United States and the Alternatives before Us* (New York: Committee for Economic Development, 1962), p. 166.

80. Denison, *Accounting for Slower Economic Growth, op. cit.,* p. 135.

81. *Ibid.,* quoting his own *Why Growth Rates Differ: Postwar Experience in Nine Western Countries* (Washington, DC: Brookings Institution, 1967), pp. 112–14.

82. "Opinion Roundup: Working in America," *Public Opinion*, August–September 1981, p. 25.

83. Florence Skelly, "How to Manage New Values vs. Old Values: Performance Is the Key," *Bell Telephone Magazine*, vol. 59, ed. 3 (1980), p. 17.

84. Daniel Yankelovich, "The New Psychological Contracts at Work," *Psychology Today*, May 1978, p. 49.

85. *Ibid.*, p. 50. A very similar position is advanced in a recent book by James O'Toole, *Making America Work: Productivity and Responsibility* (New York: Continuum, 1981).

86. Hisashi Owada, Japanese Foreign Ministry, quoted by Hobart Rowen, "Yankee Ingenuity Come Home," *Washington Post*, November 1, 1979.

87. Masayoshi Kanabayashi, "Honda's Accord," *Wall Street Journal*, October 2, 1981.

88. "Leaning on a Shovel," *Economist*, vol. 261 (December 18, 1976), p. 98.

89. "Skipping Work," *Human Behavior*, September 1970, p. 60; Daniel R. Ilgen and John H. Hollenback, "The Role of Job Satisfaction in Absence Behavior," *Organizational Behavior and Human Performance*, vol. 19 (1977), p. 159.

90. "A $40 Billion Crime Wave Swamps American Business," *U.S. News & World Report*, February 21, 1977, p. 47.

91. William M. Carley, "Nuts & Bolts Issue: Closing of a Ford Plant Reflects Rising Worry of Car Makers: Quality," *Wall Street Journal*, June 16, 1980.

92. *Ibid.*

93. *Ibid.*

94. *Ibid.*

95. "Ways Employers Can Help Drinkers, Drug Addicts," *U.S. News & World Report*, August 27, 1979, p. 61.

96. Robert H. Hayes and William J. Abernathy, "Managing Our Way to Economic Decline," *Harvard Business Review*, vol. 58 (July–August 1980), p. 68.

97. *Ibid.*, p. 70.

98. *Ibid.*, p. 68.

99. *Ibid.*, p. 70.

100. *Ibid.*, p. 72.

101. David T. Kearns, "Let's Take Risks Again," *Newsweek*, May 5, 1980, p. 13.

102. Economics Department, McGraw-Hill Publications, *How Modern Is American Industry? A Progress Report* (New York, November 27, 1978), p. 7.

103. *Ibid.*, p. 1.

104. U.S. Congress, Joint Economic Committee, *The 1980 Joint Economic Report*, 96th Congress, 2nd Session, Senate Report no. 96–618 (February 28, 1980), p. 70.

105. Michael J. Boskin, "U.S. Economy at the Crossroads," in Michael J. Boskin, ed., *The Economy in the 1980s: A Program for Growth and Stability* (San Francisco: Institute for Contemporary Studies, 1980), p. 14.

106. *The 1980 Joint Economic Report, op. cit.*, p. 70.

107. U.S. Congress, Joint Economic Committee, *The 1979 Joint Economic Report*, 96th Congress, 1st Session, Report no. 96–44 (March 22, 1979), pp. 59–60.

108. Fletcher L. Byrom, Chairman, Koppers Company, Inc., and Chairman of the Board of Trustees, Committee for Economic Development, "Towards an Industrial Strategy for the United States," statement before Subcommittee on the City, Committee on Banking, Finance and Urban Affairs, U.S. House of Representatives, September 16, 1980. Machine copied release, p. 5.

109. *Ibid.*, p. 6.

110. Robert M. Dunn, Jr., *Economic Growth Among Industrialized Countries: Why the United States Lags* (Washington, DC: National Planning Association, 1980), p. 29.

CHAPTER 10: THE RATIONAL MENTALITY AND ITS CHALLENGES

1. For additional discussion see Amitai Etzioni, *Modern Organizations* (Englewood Cliffs, NJ: Prentice Hall, 1964).

2. See Meyer Friedman and Ray H. Rosenman, *Type A Behavior and Your Heart* (New York: Alfred A. Knopf, 1974).

3. Seymour Martin Lipset, *The First New Nation: The United States in Historical and Comparative Perspective* (New York: Basic Books, 1963), p. 57.

4. Joseph A. Schumpeter, *Capitalism, Socialism, and Democracy,* 3rd ed. (New York: Harper & Bros., 1950), pp. 131–34.

5. John Kenneth Galbraith, *The Affluent Society* (Boston: Houghton-Mifflin, 1958).

6. David Riesman, "The Nylon War," *Common Cause*, vol. 4, no. 6 (1951), pp. 379–85; and "Abundance for What?" in *Problems of United States Economic Development*, vol. 1 (New York: Committee for Economic Development, 1958).

7. Donald O. Parsons and Douglas R. Munro, "Intergenerational Transfers in Social Security," in Michael J. Boskin, ed., *The Crisis in Social Security: Problems and Prospects* (San Francisco: Institute for Contemporary Studies, 1977), p. 75.

8. *Ibid.*, p. 78.

9. Lipset, *op. cit.*, Chapter 3.

10. Herbert J. Gans, *More Equality* (New York: Random House, Pantheon, 1973), p. *xi.*

11. *Ibid.*, pp. 64–65.

12. For a recent account, see William Ryan, *Equality* (New York: Random House, Pantheon, 1981).

13. "Maximizing Employment Potential," unpublished draft report, prepared by Miriam Jacobson of JWK International Corporation, Annandale, VA, 1980, p. 23.

14. Liz Roman Gallese, "The Price of Progress: Universities Fear They Will Be Hurt Financially by Federal Regulations to Help the Handicapped," *Wall Street Journal*, October 21, 1977.

15. *A Survey of Special Education Costs in Local School Districts* (Washington, DC: National School Board Association, June 1979), p. 13.

16. E. Clarke Ross, "UCPA [United Cerebral Palsy Associations] Affiliates Report Implementation Experiences with P.L. 94–142: The 'Education for All Handicapped Act,'" *Analysis*, vol. 7, no. 5 (June 1978), in U.S. House Committee on Education and Labor, Subcommittee on Elementary, Secondary, and Vocational Education jointly with Subcommittee on Select Education, *Oversight Hearing on Education of Handicapped Children* (March 27, 1979), p. 93. 96th Congress, 1st Session.

17. "Special Education and Training Employment Services: A Policy Analysis," draft policy paper prepared for the Office of the Assistant Secretary for Planning and Evaluation, U.S. Department of Health and Human Services, by JWK International Corporation, Annandale, VA, June 25, 1980, p. 42.

18. *Ibid.*, pp. 40–46.

19. Sar A. Levitan and Robert Taggart, "Employment Problems of Disabled Persons," *Monthly Labor Review*, March 1977, p. 3.

20. "Mainstreaming: What's It All About?" *Today's Education*, March/ April 1976, p. 18.

21. The Harris Poll, April 1977, in "Quality Preferred to Quantity," *Current Opinion*, July 1977.

22. The Harris Survey, February 1976, in *Current Opinion*, June 1976.

23. *The Cambridge Report*, 15 (Cambridge, MA: Cambridge Reports, second quarter 1978), Executive Summary, p. *v.*

24. U.S. Department of Labor and U.S. Department of Health, Education and Welfare, *Employment and Training Report of the President*, 1979.

25. "Social Science and the Citizen," *Society*, vol. 15 (January/February 1978), p. 6.

CHAPTER 11: THE PRO-INDUSTRIAL COALITION AND INSTITUTIONS

1. Seymour Martin Lipset, *The First New Nation: The United States in Historical and Comparative Perspective* (New York: Basic Books, 1963), p. 59. See also Morton Keller, *Affairs of State: Public Life in Late Nineteenth Century America* (Cambridge, MA: Belknap Press, 1977); and Robert H. Wiebe, *The Search for Order, 1877–1920* (New York: Hill and Wang, 1967).

2. Washington Irving, "The Creole Village," in *Wolfert's Roost and Other Papers*, revised edition (Philadelphia: Lippincott, 1870).

3. William Dean Howells, *A Traveler from Altruria* (New York: Harper & Bros., 1894).

4. Robert S. Lynd and Helen M. Lynd, *Middletown: A Study in Contemporary American Culture* (New York: Harcourt, Brace, 1929), p. 48.

5. Robert S. Lynd and Helen M. Lynd, *Middletown in Transition: A Study in Cultural Conflicts* (New York: Harcourt, Brace, 1937), p. 99.

6. *Ibid.*, pp. 74–101.

7. For a full discussion of the implications of the Civil War, see Keller, *op. cit.*

8. U.S. Bureau of Census, *Historical Statistics of the United States: Colonial Times to 1970* (Washington, DC, 1975), series D 75, 77.

9. *Ibid.*, series D 156.

10. Richard K. Vedder, *The American Economy in Historical Perspective* (Belmont, CA: Wadsworth Publishing Company, 1976), pp. 477–78.

11. H. Gregg Lewis, *Unionism and Relative Wages in the United States* (Chicago: University of Chicago Press, 1963).

12. U.S. Department of Labor, Bureau of Labor Statistics, *Selected Earnings and Demographic Characteristics of Union Members, 1970*, report no. 417 (October 1972), p. 2.

13. U.S. Bureau of the Census, *Statistical Abstract of the United States: 1980*, (Washington, DC, 1980), table 712.

14. Vedder, *op. cit.*, p. 470.

15. Edward S. Herman, *Corporate Control, Corporate Power* (Cambridge: at the University Press, 1981), pp. 243–44.

16. See Chapter 7.

17. Norman C. Miller, "The Political Danger of New Mega-Corporations," *Wall Street Journal*, August 20, 1981.

18. For a comprehensive treatment of the history of American education, see the work of Lawrence A. Cremin: *The Transformation of the School: Progressivism in American Education, 1876–1957* (New York: Knopf, 1961); *American Education: The Colonial Experience* (New York: Harper & Row, 1970); *American Education: The National Experience, 1783–1876* (New York: Harper & Row, 1980).

19. *Historical Statistics to 1970, op. cit.,* series A 57, 69.

20. *Ibid.,* series H 520.

21. *Ibid.,* series H 433.

22. *Ibid.,* series H 522.

23. Calvin Grieder and Stephen Romine, *American Education: An Introduction to the Teaching Profession* (New York: Ronald Press, 1965), p. 184.

24. *Ibid.,* p. 198.

25. Carnegie Commission on Higher Education, *New Students and New Places* (New York: McGraw-Hill, 1971), p. 127.

26. For a useful discussion of the relationship between business values and education in America see Thomas C. Cochran, *Business in American Life: A History* (New York: McGraw-Hill, 1972).

27. *Historical Statistics to 1970, op. cit.,* series H 707.

28. Daniel J. Boorstin, *The Americans: The Democratic Experience* (New York: Random House, 1973), p. 480.

29. See Chapter 9, pp. 231–237, discussion of human capital.

30. U.S. Bureau of the Census, *Statistical Abstract of the United States: 1978,* (Washington, DC, 1978), table 211.

31. For a succinct discussion of recent research see Carl N. Degler, *At Odds: Women and the Family in America from the Revolution to the Present Age* (New York: Oxford, 1980), pp. 5–6.

32. See Chapter 13, pp. 328–333, on human capital.

CHAPTER 12: JUNCTION AMERICA

1. See Bernard D. Nossiter, *Britain: A Future That Works* (Boston: Houghton, Mifflin, 1978). See also Geoffrey Smith and Nelson W. Polsby, *British Government and Its Discontents* (New York: Basic Books, 1980).

2. See above, pp. 96–97.

3. See above, pp. 259–60.

4. For justification, see Amitai Etzioni, "Choose We Must," in Carl A. Bramlette, Jr., and Michael N. Mescon, eds., *The Individual and the Future of Organizations,* vol. 9, 1978–79, Franklin Foundation Lecture Series (Atlanta: Georgia State University, 1980), pp. 25–40.

5. Office of Management and Budget, "Mid-Season Review of the 1982 Budget," July 15, 1981, p. 68.

6. Nestor E. Terleckyj, *Improvements in the Quality of Life: Estimates of Possibilities in the United States, 1974–1983* (Washington, DC: National Planning Association, 1975), pp. 51–52.

7. Angus Campbell, Philip E. Converse, and Willard L. Rodgers, *The Quality of American Life: Perceptions, Evaluations, and Satisfactions* (New York: Russell Sage Foundation, 1976), p. 26.

8. "We'd Have Problems," *Newsweek*, July 14, 1980, p. 35. For a comprehensive report, see U.S. Senate Committee on Armed Services, *Achieving America's Goals: National Service or the All-Volunteer Armed Force?* 95th Congress, 1st Session, February 1977.

9. Speech by Stephen Joel Trachtenberg, president, University of Hartford, cited by Albert Shanker, "U.S. Defense Needs Strong Schools," *New York Times*, July 5, 1981.

10. See Jacques S. Gansler, *The Defense Industry* (Cambridge, MA: MIT Press, 1980); Eliot Marshall, "William Perry and the Weapons Gamble," *Science*, vol. 211 (February 13, 1981), pp. 681–83; U.S. House Committee on Armed Services, *The Ailing Defense Industrial Base: Unready for Crisis*, Report of the Defense Industrial Base Panel, 96th Congress 2nd Session, December 31, 1980.

11. I advanced this position before it grew in popularity in *The Hard Way to Peace: A New Strategy* (New York: Collier, 1962), and *Winning without War* (Garden City, NY: Doubleday, 1964).

12. Some interesting and relevant observations are to be found in James Fallows, *National Defense* (New York: Random House, 1981).

13. For an overview see Timothy B. Clark, "Everybody Wants More for Defense—But Is There Room in the Budget?" *National Journal*, May 17, 1980, pp. 800–805.

14. Roger Starr and James Carlson, "Pollution and Poverty: The Strategy of Cross Commitment," *The Public Interest*, no. 10 (Winter 1968), p. 130.

15. Talcott Parsons, Robert F. Bales, and Edward A. Shils, *Working Papers in the Theory of Action* (Glencoe, IL: Free Press, 1953), pp. 163–269, especially pp. 163–72.

16. Samuel Rezneck, "The Rise and Early Development of Industrial Consciousness in the United States, 1760–1830," *Journal of Economic and Business History*, vol. 4 (1932), p. 788.

CHAPTER 13: REINDUSTRIALIZATION POLICIES

1. Sheldon S. Wolin, "The People's Two Bodies," *Democracy*, January 1981, p. 23.

2. Ezra F. Vogel, *Japan As Number One: Lessons for America* (New York: Harper Colophon Books, 1979). A similar National Investment Authority is also favored by Robert Lekachman, *Greed Is Not Enough: Reaganomics* (New York: Pantheon, 1982).

3. "The U.S. Needs an Industrial Policy," interview with Frank A. Weil, *Fortune*, March 24, 1980, p. 150.

4. See Gar Alperovitz and Jeff Faux, "Conservative Chic: Reindustrialization," *Social Policy*, November/December 1980, pp. 6–9; Ronald E. Müller, *Revitalizing America: Politics for Prosperity* (New York: Simon &

Schuster, 1980), especially p. 278f.; Ira C. Magaziner and Robert B. Reich, *Minding America's Business: The Decline and Rise of the American Economy* (New York: Harcourt Brace Jovanovich, 1982). See also Richard Bolling and John Bowles, *America's Competitive Edge* (New York: McGraw-Hill, 1982), especially Chapters 8 and 9.

5. This point was made by Paul W. McCracken, "A United States 'Industrial Policy,'" *Wall Street Journal*, January 12, 1981.

6. Anthony Downs, "Too Much Capital for Housing?" *Brookings Bulletin*, vol. 17 (Summer 1980), p. 3.

7. Quoted by William H. Jones, "Well-Off Firms Wooing Money Losers to Acquire Their Surplus Tax Benefits," *Washington Post*, September 26, 1981.

8. Barnaby J. Feder, "Ford to Sell Tax Credits to I.B.M.," *New York Times*, November 6, 1981.

9. Arthur Bueche, senior vice president for corporate technology, General Electric Company, quoted by Barnaby J. Feder, "The Research Aid in New Tax Law," *New York Times*, September 29, 1981. Edwin Mansfield provides a particularly well-balanced and encompassing account of suggestions for more extensive tax policies in his "Tax Policy and Innovation," *Science*, vol. 215 (March 12, 1982), pp. 1365–71.

10. Feder, "The Research Aid in New Tax Law," *op. cit.*

11. Philip H. Abelson, editorial, "America's Vanishing Lead in Electronics," *Science*, vol. 210 (December 5, 1980); and Gina Bari Kolata, "Who Will Build the Next Supercomputer?" *Science*, vol. 211 (January 16, 1981), p. 268.

12. Masayoshi Kanabayashi and Hal Lancaster, "Japan's Aggressive Move in Biotechnology Worries U.S. Firms Fearful of Losing Lead," *Wall Street Journal*, October 9, 1981.

13. For a recent report by a person close to the Reagan administration, see Simon Ramo, *America's Technology Slip* (New York: Wiley, 1980), especially Chapter 17.

14. Research and Policy Committee of the Committee for Economic Development, *Stimulating Technological Progress* (New York: Committee for Economic Development, 1980), p. 52.

15. National Commission on Research, *Industry and the Universities: Developing Cooperative Research Relationships in the National Interest*, 1980, p. 15.

16. "MIT Agonizes over Links with Research Unit," *Science*, vol. 214 (October 23, 1981), pp. 416–17.

17. Quoted in Kim McDonald, " 'Commercialization' of University Science Is Decried," *Chronicle of Higher Education*, January 13, 1982, p. 9. For a recent collection of fine essays on this "new" issue, see John C. Hoy and

Melvin H. Bernstein, eds., *Business and Academia* (Hanover, NH: University Press of New England, 1981).

18. U.S. Department of Commerce, *Advisory Committee on Industrial Innovation: Final Report,* September 1979, p. 13.

19. See, for example, Bernice T. Eiduson, *Scientists: Their Psychological World* (New York: Basic Books, 1962); and Anne Roe, *The Making of a Scientist* (New York: Dodd, Mead, 1953).

20. Howard M. Vollmer, "Basic and Applied Research," in Saad Z. Nagi and Ronald G. Corwin, eds., *The Social Contexts of Research* (New York: Wiley, 1972), p. 71.

21. Stephen Parks Strickland, *Politics, Science and Dread Disease* (Cambridge, MA: Harvard University Press, 1972). On "bootlegging," see also Howard M. Vollmer, *Adaptations of Scientists and Organizations* (Palo Alto, CA: Pacific Books, 1974), Chapter 10.

22. *Evaluation of Law Enforcement Assistance Administration Programs: A Conference Summary* (Washington, DC: National Academy of Public Administration and the U.S. General Accounting Office, February 22–23, 1973), p. 9. Quoted in Stuart Adams, "Evaluative Research in Corrections: Status and Prospects," *Federal Probation,* vol. 38 (1974), p. 18.

23. See Tom Alexander, "The Right Remedy for R&D Lag," *Fortune,* January 25, 1982, p. 66.

24. U.S. Joint Committee on Taxation, *General Explanation of the Economic Recovery Tax Act of 1981 (H.R. 4242, 97th Congress; Public Law 97–34),* staff report, December 29, 1981, calculated from table IV-1.

25. Karl Frieden, *Workplace Democracy and Productivity* (Washington, DC: National Center for Economic Alternatives, 1980), p. 27.

26. *Ibid.,* p. 79.

27. Allan Sloan, "An Idea Whose Time Has Come?" *Forbes,* July 20, 1981.

28. Paul D. Greenberg and Edward M. Glaser, *Some Issues in Joint Union-Management Quality of Worklife Improvement Efforts* (Kalamazoo, MI: W. E. Upjohn Institute for Employment Research, 1980), p. 3.

29. *Ibid.* For much additional background and analysis, see John F. Witte, *Democracy, Authority, and Alienation in Work: Workers' Participation in an American Corporation* (Chicago: University of Chicago Press, 1980).

30. Greenberg and Glaser, *op. cit.,* p. 8.

31. *The Bolivar Project of Joint Management-Union Determination of Change According to Principles of Security, Equity, Individuation and Democracy: Final Technical Report,* National Commission on Productivity (with the W. E. Upjohn Institute for Employment Research), February 1974. See also *Business Week,* May 11, 1981, p. 90.

32. "Steel Seeks Higher Output via Workplace Reform," *Business Week,* August 18, 1980, p. 102.

33. William Bowen, "How to Regain Our Competitive Edge," *Fortune*, March 9, 1981, p. 84.

34. Michael Maccoby, *The Leader* (New York: Simon and Schuster, 1981).

35. See A. H. Raskin, "The Cooperative Economy," *New York Times*, February 14, 1982.

36. Felix G. Rohatyn, "What We Should Do," *Washington Post*, January 30, 1980.

37. Lester C. Thurow, "Let's Abolish the Antitrust Laws," *New York Times*, October 19, 1980.

38. Herman B. Leonard and Elizabeth H. Rhyne, "Federal Credit and the 'Shadow Budget,'" *The Public Interest*, no. 65, (Fall 1981), pp. 43, 47.

39. Robert J. Samuelson, "Administration Slips and Stumbles in Efforts to Cut Off-Budget Spending," *National Journal*, June 13, 1981, p. 1067.

40. Lester C. Thurow has argued repeatedly and consistently for the need to channel credit to productive sectors of the economy, both in his book *The Zero-Sum Society* (New York: Basic Books, 1980), and in numerous articles. See, for instance, his "How to Rescue a Drowning Economy," *New York Review of Books*, April 1, 1982, p. 3.

41. See Alan Wolfe, *America's Impasse* (New York: Pantheon, 1981) on the pivotal role of economic growth.

42. Quoted in Caroline Atkinson, "Interest Rates, Recession Muffle Investment Boom," *Washington Post*, February 14, 1982.

43. This point was summarized by Harvard economist Benjamin M. Friedman in his op-ed article "Look Past Inflation," *New York Times*, March 12, 1982. Related points have been made on several occasions by Rudy Penner of the American Enterprise Institute and by Albert T. Sommers of the Conference Board.

CHAPTER 14: SOCIETAL RECONSTRUCTION

1. See Chapter 11, pp. 265–272.

2. Interview with Fred Wertheimer, "Pro and Con: Keep Business Cash Out of Politics?" *U.S. News & World Report*, April 30, 1979, p. 53.

3. Norman C. Miller, "The Political Danger of New Mega-Corporations," *Wall Street Journal*, August 20, 1981.

4. Richard E. Cohen, "Congressional Democrats Beware—Here Come the Corporate PACs," *National Journal*, August 9, 1980, p. 1307.

5. Miller, *op. cit.*

6. *Ibid.*

7. James W. Singer, "Behind the New Aggressiveness," *National Journal*, August 16, 1980, p. 1367.

8. "Key Provisions of the New Tax Law . . . More Than Just Investment

Incentives," *National Journal,* August 8, 1981, p. 1409. (Estimates are for 1982–86.)

9. Richard E. Cohen, "The Business Lobby Discovers That in Unity There Is Strength," *National Journal,* June 28, 1980, p. 1050.

10. *Ibid.,* p. 1051.

11. *Ibid.,* p. 1054.

12. See above, p. 96.

13. James W. McKie, "Changing Views," in James W. McKie, ed., *Social Responsibility and the Business Predicament* (Washington, DC: Brookings Institution, 1974), pp. 18–19.

14. Milton Friedman, *Capitalism and Freedom* (Chicago: University of Chicago Press, 1962, 1982), p. 133.

15. "Milton Friedman Responds: A Business and Society Review Interview," *Business and Society Review,* Spring 1972, pp. 6–7.

16. Peter F. Drucker, *Management: Tasks, Responsibilities, Practices* (New York: Harper & Row, 1974), p. 348.

17. Charles E. Lindblom, "The Business of America Is Still Business," *New York Times,* January 4, 1978.

18. Dr. Howard Schomer, quoted by Charlotte Saikowski in "Does Capitalism Conflict with Morality?," *Christian Science Monitor,* April 19, 1976.

19. Ralph Nader, Mark Green, and Joel Seligman, *Taming the Giant Corporation* (New York: W. W. Norton and Co., Inc., 1976).

20. Drucker, *op. cit.,* p. 349.

21. *Ibid.,* p. 312.

22. *Ibid.,* p. 333.

23. NBC White Paper, "America Works When America Works," produced by NBC, June 1981, p. 52 of transcript.

24. *Ibid.,* pp. 49–50.

25. Peter F. Drucker, "Ethical Chic," *Forbes,* September 14, 1981, pp. 160–61.

26. Richard Witkin, "Air Control Strike Deadline Is Set for Monday as Talks Are Renewed," *New York Times,* August 1, 1981.

27. "The Wrong Way with Trucks," *New York Times,* December 1, 1981.

28. *Washington Post*/ABC News Poll, reported by Barry Sussman in "Budget Cuts Too Severe, Public Says," *Washington Post,* September 23, 1981.

29. For a recent examination of the limitations on the President's power, see Godfrey Hodgson, *All Things to All Men: The False Promise of the Modern American Presidency* (New York: Simon and Schuster, 1980).

30. See Chapter 7, pp. 171–173.

31. See Calvin Trillin, "Anti-Metrics," *New Yorker,* August 31, 1981, pp. 82–85.

Permissions

Milton Friedman, *Capitalism and Freedom,* The University of Chicago Press. • Edwin H. Sutherland, *The Professional Thief,* © 1937 by The University of Chicago. All rights reserved. Published November 1937. Fifth Impression 1956. Composed and printed by The University of Chicago Press, Chicago, Ill., U.S.A. • G. H. Guttridge, *English Whiggism and the American Revolution,* (Berkeley: University of California Press, 1942). • Vance Packard, *A Nation of Strangers,* (New York: David McKay, 1972). • Peter J. Stein, "Singlehood: An Alternative to Marriage," *The Family Coordinator,* Vol. 24, (October 1975). Copyrighted 1975 by the National Council on Family Relations. Reprinted by permission. • Genie Chipps, "Liberated Love: Unmarried, Committed & Free." Copyright © 1977 The Hearst Corporation. Courtesy of *Harper's Bazaar.* • Don Sloan and Lillian Africano, "Marriage: The Traditional Alternative." Copyright © 1977 The Hearst Corporation. Courtesy of *Harper's Bazaar.* • From the September 22, 1970, issue of *Look* magazine; © 1970 by Cowles Broadcasting, Inc. • Robert Nozick, "If Inequality Is Inevitable, What Can Be Done about It?" © 1982 by The New York Times Company. Reprinted by permission.

Steven V. Roberts, "An Angry Young Congressman Criticizes Special Interest Groups. © 1981 by The New York Times Company. Reprinted by permission. • Lester C. Thurow, "Let's Abolish the Antitrust Laws." © 1980 by The New York Times Company. Reprinted by permission. • Charles E. Lindblom, "The Business of America Is Still Business." © 1978 by The New York Times Company. Reprinted by permission. • Leo Strauss, "The Liberalism of Classical Political Philosophy," *Review of Metaphysics,* Vol. 12, (March 1959). • Robert Nisbet, *Twilight of Authority,* Oxford University Press. • Eugene Kinkead, *In Every War but One,* (New York: W. W. Norton & Company, Inc., 1959). • Charles E. Silberman, *Crisis in the Classroom: The Remaking of American Education,* © 1970, Random House, Inc., Alfred A. Knopf, Inc. • Daniel J. Boorstin, *The Americans: The Democratic Experience,* © 1973, Random House, Inc., Alfred A. Knopf, Inc. • Daniel Yankelovich, *New Rules: Searching for Self-fulfillment in a World Turned Upside Down,* © 1981, Random House, Inc., Alfred A. Knopf, Inc. • Herbert Gans, *More Equality,* © 1974, Random House, Inc., Alfred A. Knopf, Inc.

From *Why Children?* by Stephanie Dorwick and Sibyl Grundberg. Reprinted by permission of Harcourt Brace Jovanovich, Inc. • John Howard, "The Individual in Society: A Commitment to Discipline and Compassion," *Vital Speeches,* City News Publishing Co., July 15,

Index